PUTTING
FAMILIES
◦FIRST◦

PUTTING
FAMILIES
▫FIRST▫

America's
Family Support Movement
and the Challenge of
Change

Sharon L. Kagan and Bernice Weissbourd
Editors

Jossey-Bass Publishers • San Francisco

HV
699
P88
1994

Substantial discounts on bulk quantities of Jossey-Bass books are available to corporations, professional associations, and other organizations. For details and discount information, contact the special sales department at Jossey-Bass Inc., Publishers. (415) 433-1740; Fax (415) 433-0499.

For international orders, please contact your local Paramount Publishing International office.

Manufactured in the United States of America. Nearly all Jossey-Bass books and jackets are printed on recycled paper that contains at least 50 percent recycled waste, including 10 percent postconsumer waste. Many of our materials are also printed with vegetable-based ink; during the printing process these inks emit fewer volatile organic compounds (VOCs) than petroleum-based inks. VOCs contribute to the formation of smog.

Library of Congress Cataloging-in-Publication Data

Putting families first : America's family support movement and the challenge of change / Sharon L. Kagan, Bernice Weissbourd, editors. — 1st ed.
    p.   cm. — (A joint publication in the Jossey-Bass social and behavioral science series and the Jossey-Bass educational series)
    Includes bibliographical references and indexes.
    ISBN 1-55542-667-0
    1. Family social work — United States. 2. Family policy — United States. I. Kagan, Sharon L. II. Weissbourd, Bernice. III. Series: Jossey-Bass social and behavioral science series. IV. Series: Jossey-Bass education series.
HV699.P88 1994
362.82'0973 — dc20   94-9713
                                                      CIP

FIRST EDITION
HB Printing   10 9 8 7 6 5 4 3 2 1   *Code 9464*

☐ **Contents** ☐

□ Foreword □

Over the years, the concept of family support has undergone considerable growth and change, from an interventionist philosophy rooted in the early days of the Head Start program to a full-scale national movement. This transformation has itself evolved from fundamental changes in the composition and needs of American families. With the continuing rise in single-parent families, teen parenting, and the number of mothers who work outside the home, family support services have become increasingly critical to parents engaged in the important task of raising their children. Family support programs provide emotional, informational, and instrumental assistance to young and older families, particularly to families isolated by poverty, joblessness, poor health, or other factors. Unlike many of the programs that arose in the 1960s and 1970s, however, present-day family support programs typically are available to people in all segments of society, rather than being focused on people in particular social or economic categories. In short, these programs offer many of the social supports that were once provided by a network of stable, extended families within a community.

The appearance of this volume marks an important stage in the life history of the family support movement. Philosophically grounded in the ecological approach of Bronfenbrenner (1979), the family support movement recognizes both the importance of parents as socializers of their children and the interconnectedness of family life with the social and cultural institutions in which families are embedded. In the years since the publication of *America's Family Support Programs* (Kagan, Powell, Weissbourd, & Zigler, 1987), those aspects of social disintegration that initially gave rise to the family support movement have only intensified. Thus the watchword of the movement must be *prevention*. Despite increases in poverty, substance abuse, poor health care, child abuse, and the concomitant emotional and physical damage these social ills can cause, the many successes of existing family support programs give us hope for the future. We can take what we have learned over the past decades and apply this knowledge to assisting families before irreparable harm occurs.

In its focus on prevention, family support as a movement has been closely linked with early childhood intervention as a method of overcoming the deleterious effects of an impoverished environment. Both movements evolved in a historical period characterized by theoretical and political controversy. Although early childhood intervention was initially championed by politically liberal policy makers, programs like Head Start are now widely endorsed by more conservative elements of the political spectrum. The theoretical debate, turning on the question of whether early childhood programs have actually shown long-term benefits, has also approached resolution (Zigler, 1990). Given the publication of the Cornell Consortium data (Darlington, Royce, Snipper, Murray, & Lazar, 1980), as well as the findings of the High/Scope group (Berrueta-Clement, Schweinhart, Barnett, Epstein, & Weikart, 1984) and of the Department of Health and Human Services (Copple, Cline, & Smith, 1987), the scientific controversy regarding the efficacy of early childhood intervention has been put to rest.

In spite of these compelling research findings, an ideological debate continues as some members of the political right protest what they appear to view as the intrusion of interventionist programs into family life. Unfortunately — and ironically, since the *idea* of family support generally enjoys the favor of liberal and conservative citizens alike — some protests have also been extended to the family support *movement*. For example, one bill making its way through the Illinois state legislature would prohibit the home-visiting component of the Parents as Teachers (PAT) program from being offered to parents in that state. Such legislative action reveals a disturbing misunderstanding of the completely voluntary nature of family support programs. Families are not forced to participate in such programs or to admit program staff into their homes. Services are offered to parents, and those who wish to utilize particular services may do so. Every family has different needs as it progresses through its own life cycle. At one time, a family may not need any assistance; at another, the same family may experience difficulties and ask for help. What family support programs do is make that help available.

Contrary to the thinking of those who advocate a hands-off family policy, childhood interventions that include a large amount of parental involvement are the most efficacious for children and families and have the most far-reaching, long-term benefits for all family members (Seitz, 1990; Provence & Naylor, 1983). Such programs are properly characterized as employing a family support model. By viewing the entire family as the unit of treatment, the proponents of parental involvement recognize the necessity of adopting a "whole child" approach, one that seeks long-term benefits for the child by improving the daily conditions of life for the family, which remains the most influential agent in a child's development.

The persuasiveness of a family support model is most easily seen when we look to the most comprehensive and continuous form of intervention we know, one that is found in nature: the good, secure family (Zigler & Seitz, 1982). The goal of family support is to render services that assist families in becoming as strong and secure as possible. Thus it is puzzling that some adherents to far-right politics consider family support services potentially destructive of family life. In fact, the availability of services like child care, health care, and parent education is what makes a semblance of secure family life possible for many families, and especially for high-risk children and their parents. As a society, we must disabuse ourselves of the notion that people — particularly very young, impoverished, and socially isolated people — spring into being fully formed as healthy, wise, patient, and developmentally aware parents simply because they have given birth to a child. For many a person who has grown to maturity in a single-child home, the very first infant with whom he or she has significant contact is his or her own child. Good parents are not born. They are made — through intensive and varied contact with young children, and through the counsel of other and more experienced parents, doctors, and knowledge-able members of the community. Where learning opportunities and forms of assistance have not been available to parents, family support programs must step into the breach.

Family support has been shown to reduce family stress, foster a sense of community, and help prevent such stress-related forms of family dysfunction as drug and alcohol use and child abuse. Heather Weiss and I have already noted the accumulat-ing body of research on relationships among stress, support, and family well-being (Zigler & Weiss, 1985). The methodology for investigating the precise nature of these connections is still under-going refinement, but the social support research holds out the promise of also being able to indicate causal relationships be-tween family support and reduction of social stress.

Parental involvement and family support have been central to the success of our country's largest interventionist project: Head Start, which was grounded in the belief that parents who were encouraged to become active participants in their children's early education would enjoy greater self-determination, as well as a heightened sense of competence and satisfaction in parenting (for detailed discussions, see Zigler & Valentine, 1979; Zigler & Muenchow, 1992).

One of the earliest precursors of the family support move-ment was part of Head Start. This was the short-lived Child and Family Resource Program, committed to the idea that the way to help the child is to help the family (Nauta & Travers, 1982). In this program, an array of interventions was made avail-able to children and families, beginning at the child's birth and extending to age eight. Rather than attempting to force a fam-ily into a single mold by offering only one set of services, this program recognized the individuality of families and gave each family the opportunity to select those services it found helpful. In addition to providing regular home visits, the program en-deavored to connect families with local social and health ser-vices and offered center-based activities for parents and chil-dren. In this program were found many of the elements that characterize the family support movement as we know it today (Kagan, Powell, Weissbourd, & Zigler, 1987; for historical background on family support, see Weissbourd, 1987). Two of the program's components, family assessment and service integration, have since been made part of regional and federal efforts at training and technical assistance.

Another exemplar of the family support philosophy is the aforementioned Parents as Teachers (PAT) program. Based in Missouri, the PAT program was initiated in 1981 to demonstrate that a partnership between home and school that began in the preschool years could greatly enhance a young child's readiness for formal schooling. Since its founding, PAT has expanded to forty-two states. Unlike some previous interventions, the PAT program has been offered to parents of all socioeconomic backgrounds since its inception. Concentrating on first-time parents, who are usually the most interested in this form of support, PAT begins its services with the third trimester of pregnancy and continues them until the child reaches the age of three. The program's prenatal information and guidance help the family prepare for parenthood. Monthly visits in the home or in a PAT center help each family design an individual program. PAT provides information about what parents can expect as their child develops, as well as guidance in fostering their baby's linguistic, cognitive, social, and motor-skill development. The program also provides screening of the child's visual, auditory, and educational development, to discover potential sources of difficulty and refer the family to appropriate resources if problems are detected. In addition, monthly group sessions allow parents to discuss common concerns.

The results of the PAT program have been impressive. Children in the program have shown more advanced intellectual and language development and have exhibited more aspects of positive social development than have children in a comparison group. Their parents have been shown to be more knowledgeable about child-rearing practices and child development, and they have had more positive perceptions of local schools. Moreover, children threatened by risk factors have been more likely to have these risks identified and their causes remedied;

more than half of observed risk factors were corrected or improved by the end of the program's first three years (Pfannenstiel, Lambson, & Yarnell, 1991). Legislation later expanded the project throughout the state of Missouri, where it continues to operate successfully.

Versions of the PAT model have been assimilated into other programs offering a variety of family support services, notably the School of the 21st Century, a program available to all families in a community. Based on our knowledge that the most effective programs for strengthening families are those that offer a broad range of services, the School of the 21st Century was designed to incorporate these features into one comprehensive program (Zigler, Finn-Stevenson, & Linkins, 1992; Zigler & Lang, 1991). This model places the neighborhood school at the center of a network of services for child care and family support. The home-school nexus is forged early, with a high degree of home-to-school continuity and parental involvement. In addition, high-quality affordable child care is offered to parents, to be used as individual family requirements dictate. This program, with individual community variations, is now operating successfully to support families in many regions of the country.

The evolution of projects like these illustrates how the knowledge base of the family support movement has been built up over the years, and how this interdisciplinary body of wisdom has been shared across programs. Although some political factions would have us believe otherwise, the goal of parental empowerment and the consideration of parental choice have not diminished over time. If anything, these principles of the family support movement have grown ever stronger as workers in the field of family support have become more focused on presenting parents from diverse backgrounds with genuine life options for themselves and their children. This is the essence of parental freedom and choice.

The family support movement has come a long way from the early days, when biased scholars unflinchingly advanced the theory that families in poverty suffered from so-called cultural deprivation, a concept that made it necessary for us to direct our interventions toward making all families more closely reflect the values and behavior of the mainstream middle-class socio-economic culture. We know now that such attempts at homogenization are neither desirable nor possible, but it is still important for us to avoid hubris in the wake of the many programmatic successes that the last decade has brought to proponents of family support. In many circumstances, even the most comprehensive program cannot alter the ecology of the larger environment enough to make a significant difference for great numbers of families. Even unlimited counseling, early childhood education, and home visits cannot compensate for the absence of jobs, which in turn can provide reasonable income, affordable and safe housing, adequate health care, and access to an integrated neighborhood where children encounter positive role models (Zigler & Muenchow, 1992). To effect these fundamental changes, we have to change the basic features of society itself.

A glance at the chapter headings of this timely volume indicates the impressive and rapid strides made by the family support movement. As the demographics and needs of our society have changed, the family support field has managed both to grow and to alter itself to fit its changing service population. Family support no longer resembles a patchwork effort in which only families meeting specific narrow criteria can be served. Family support is taking on the appearance of a stronger and more supple safety net that sustains a family through many of the changes and events it is likely to undergo in its life cycle. Programs extend from school to the workplace, from prisons to houses of worship, from national to local initiatives. In this era of service integration, family support projects may succeed in creating, through the pooling of knowledge and ideas, what may one day become an effective yet sensitive system for assisting all families on a wide scale.

Sharon L. Kagan and Bernice Weissbourd deserve our admiration for producing this book, which chronicles the extension of the family support movement into new and critical social arenas. One of the strengths of this volume is its insightful examination of family support as it moves from a programmatic to a systemic approach. The movement is clearly a vital one—adapting to different environments, meeting culturally diverse needs, being mindful of its mistakes, and staying concerned about the quality and appropriateness of the assistance it renders. This is an exciting historical moment for family support, and I am grateful to the editors and authors of this volume for their contributions to our understanding.

June 1994   Edward Zigler
                                             Sterling Professor of Psychology
                                             Yale University
                                             New Haven, Connecticut

References

Berrueta-Clement, J., Schweinhart, L., Barnett, W., Epstein, A., & Weikert, D. (1984). *Changed lives: The effects of the Perry Preschool Program on youths through age 19.* Monographs of the High/Scope Educational Research Foundation, No. 8. Ypsilanti, MI: High/Scope Press.

Bronfenbrenner, U. (1979). *The ecology of human development: Experiments by nature and design.* Cambridge, MA: Harvard University Press.

Copple, C. E., Cline, M. G., & Smith, A. N. (1987). *Path to the future: Long-term effects of Head Start in the Philadelphia school district.* Washington, DC: U.S. Department of Health and Human Services.

Darlington, R. B., Royce, J. M., Snipper, A. S., Murray, H. W., & Lazar, I. (1980). Preschool programs and later competence of children from low income families. *Science, 208,* 202–204.

Kagan, S. L., Powell, D. R., Weissbourd, B., & Zigler, E. F. (Eds.). (1987). *America's family support programs: Perspectives and prospects.* New Haven, CT: Yale University Press.

Nauta, M., & Travers, J. (1982). *The effects of a social program: Executive summary of CFRP's infant-toddler component.* Cambridge, MA: Abt Associates.

Pfannenstiel, J., Lambson, T., & Yarnell, V. (1991). *Second wave study of the Parents as Teachers program: Final report.* St. Louis, MO: Research and Training Associates.

Provence, S., & Naylor, A. (1983). *Working with disadvantaged parents and children: Scientific issues and practice.* New Haven, CT: Yale University Press.

Seitz, V. (1990). Intervention programs for impoverished children: A comparison of eduational and family support models. *Annals of Child Development, 7,* 73–103.

Weissbourd, B. (1987). A brief history of family support programs. In S. L. Kagan, D. R. Powell, B. Weissbourd, & E. F. Zigler (Eds.), *America's family support programs: Perspectives and prospects.* (pp. 38–56). New Haven, CT: Yale University Press.

Zigler, E. F. (1990). Foreword. In S. J. Meisels & J. P. Shonkoff (Eds.), *Handbook of early childhood intervention* (pp. ix–xiv). New York: Cambridge University Press.

Zigler, E. F., Finn-Stevenson, M., & Linkins, K. (1992). Meeting the needs of children and families with Schools of the 21st Century. *Yale Law & Policy Review, 10*(1), 69–81.

Zigler, E. F., & Lang, M. (1991). *Child care choices: Balancing the needs of children, families, and society.* New York: Free Press.

Zigler, E. F., & Muenchow, S. (1992). *Head Start: The inside story of America's most successful educational experiment.* New York: Basic Books.

Zigler, E. F., & Seitz, V. (1982). Social policy and intelligence. In R. Sternberg (Ed.), *Handbook of human intelligence* (pp. 586–641). New York: Cambridge University Press.

Zigler, E. F., & Valentine, J. (Eds.). (1979). *Project Head Start: A legacy of the War on Poverty.* New York: Free Press.

Zigler, E. F., & Weiss, H. (1985). Family support systems: An ecological approach to child development. In N. Rappaport (Ed.), *Children, youth and families: The action-research relationship* (pp. 166–205). New York: Cambridge University Press.

To our families and to
Urie Bronfenbrenner and Edward Zigler,
whose vision and wisdom
guided the development of
America's family support movement

□ **Preface** □

The call to strengthen the family can be heard from widely divergent sectors. The corporate, foundation, and banking worlds join forces with the human services and education communities in recognizing that families are responsible for their children's development, and that no family can function alone. Such widespread support reflects a context that has changed.

But that is not the only change: family support itself has been altered dramatically. It is no longer seen solely as a series of programs dotting the national landscape, but rather as the cornerstone of systemic and institutional reform. It is taking root in new terrain as diverse as prisons, hospitals, and local libraries. The extent to which the philosophy of family support has permeated the social fabric is evident in the use of such phrases as *family-centered services, family-focused communities,* and a *family-friendly nation.* The emphasis has shifted from what is provided to how it is provided, and for whom.

As family support has grown in public recognition, it has also matured in its own domains. Academics and professionals work with practitioners to define the characteristics and qualities of family resource and support, to enunciate guidelines for best practices in program delivery, and to evaluate program effectiveness. A body of literature exploring the many aspects of family support exists and is constantly expanding. The federally funded National Clearinghouse for Family Support Programs is situated within the Family Resource Coalition, a recognized national organizational resource for the family support field.

The rapid pace of change, both inside and outside the realm of family support, has created the need for a single book to chronicle these changes, making them accessible to policy makers, practitioners, and those recently introduced to family support. Our goal was to produce a volume that would explore the changes and analyze them in terms of the context and content of the family resource movement as it exists today. In this volume, we seek to raise the issues that change inevitably makes relevant and, in doing so, to challenge the thinking of the field regarding second-decade strategies. Our intention was to present diverse and unique perspectives that would stimulate interest and encourage further pursuit of knowledge, and we hope that the book will serve as a catalyst to the development of a fresh new agenda.

Clearly, however, we had to set boundaries on goals as ambitious as these. Some issues have had to be dealt with less completely than others, and none has been covered in its entirety. To our regret, space limitations prohibited us from including all the exciting developments in the field. Therefore, we chose to focus on those changes that appear to have the greatest impact, and to discuss the major challenges that the future of the family support movement will bring.

Our authors are among those well-known scholar-practitioners whose thinking represents the cutting edge of the integration of theory and practice, and who themselves are charting new directions in policy development. Each contributor speaks in his or her own voice, and not always in terms with which we agree; more important to us is that the volume reflect current thought and present those issues with which the field must grapple.

Overview of the Contents

The book opens with a section on the sociocultural context of family resource and support. In the chapter by Bronfenbrenner and Neville, the authors detail the fragmented structure of families in America and its implications for children, indicating that these conditions cry out for family-supportive policies in this country, which do not exist. This lack is particularly evident by comparison with international standards. Examining American sociocultural roots, the authors suggest that a value system glorifying individualism is what underlies our neglect. The values of volunteerism, which foster community action, and of economic competitiveness, which depend on families' well-being, could form the basis of a family support agenda.

In the following chapter, Weissbourd discusses the evolution of family support principles and the effects of their implementation on national policy. As systems and institutions change to be more responsive to families, they also influence national awareness of the concept that families require and deserve support. Both chapters in Part One show that a family-supportive nation could be built on a value system derived from our best national ideals and tempered by new understanding of the relationship between families and society.

The fact that family support can no longer be defined in terms of isolated programs is the explicit focus of Part Two, whose six chapters address the forms that family support is taking as it moves into mainstream institutions. Chapters on schools, social services, the workplace, and prisons indicate the extent to which institutions are expanding their services to families and/or reorienting their approaches to be responsive to family concerns. Although these chapters deal with issues related to infusing family support into established systems, the fact that family support has long been lodged in some institutions is sharply brought to our attention in Chapter Seven. Taken together, the chapters in this part give a perspective on the vast scope of changes occurring as family support principles are embraced by established systems and, concurrently, as the family support movement recognizes the role of those institutions that traditionally have been supports for families and anchors for communities.

Discussing schools, Bowman (Chapter Three) points out that success in school depends on complicated sets of conditions and variables, and so family support efforts must reflect the family's, the children's, and the community's context and prior experiences. In so doing, family support will take a variety of forms; but, whatever the form, the crucial underlying premise must be continuity between home and school.

Healthy families also depend on a complex set of factors, and Zuckerman and Brazelton (Chapter Four) stress that a truly preventive health care system starts with meeting the basic needs of families: good nutrition, housing, safety, and supportive communities. The authors project a community-based health care program that provides a two-generational approach to health care (that is, for parents and children), serves as a resource for information on children's development, and thereby enables parents to respond more appropriately to their children's behavior.

In Chapter Five, Massinga extends this ecological approach to systemic change. Writing of policy initiatives, she describes the central role that policies play in determining the potential effectiveness of the child welfare system. Underlying our child welfare services, she points out, is a value system that dictates whether we will ultimately encourage the development of all of America's families and children or selectively encourage some while expecting others to fend for themselves.

The increasing number of mothers in the work force means that businesses must recognize the family responsibilities of their employees. Galinsky, in Chapter Six, indicates that workplace supports for family life constitute a win-win situation: employees experience less stress, while companies benefit from employees' increased loyalty and reduced absenteeism.

Caldwell, Greene, and Billingsley, in Chapter Seven, remind us that understanding the role of the church, especially in African American communities, is essential to an understanding of the community. This arena is given too little attention by many family support proponents; the chapter alerts us to the formal and informal social networks that already exist in a community.

In Chapter Eight, Adalist-Estrin takes up the plight of children whose lives are suddenly disrupted when a parent is incarcerated. The family support movement has not yet recognized involvement in the justice system as an issue important to children and families, nor has it made sufficient inroads into the mental health and substance-abuse treatment systems with which the criminal justice system is closely linked. Nevertheless, there are a few significant family support initiatives in prisons.

These models suggest that, even in restrictive settings, providing opportunities for inmates to be responsible for their families is an empowering process, which contributes to inmates' overall functioning as parents.

In Part Three, we turn to the programmatic challenges that must be addressed if family support is to nourish both its roots and its new branches. In four chapters, areas fundamental to program development are considered, and it becomes apparent that a growing body of knowledge is available to inform program decisions. The discussion in each of these areas reveals how family support is functioning in ever-widening spheres. Staffing issues must include staffing in programs across the life span, considering the needs of the elderly as well as those of parents and children. Funding strategies will require reconsideration as federal funding becomes available. The principle of cultural responsiveness assumes far greater importance as the demographics of our country shift and the population becomes increasingly multiethnic and multiracial. Throughout Part Three, cautions as well as future directions are extrapolated from past lessons.

The complexity of staffing issues is compounded by the fact that, since family support personnel tend to be givers and helpers, it is all too easy for them to neglect their own needs for support. Stott and Musick, in Chapter Nine, discuss the essential role of supervision as a support to staff of varied backgrounds. The authors especially emphasize the crucial role of supervision in ensuring opportunities for self-reflection and personal growth. They are concerned because paraprofessionals, whose lives may resemble those of the families with which they work, often find it difficult to lead these families into more positive ways of functioning. The discussion suggests that paraprofessional staff, like all other staff, must be carefully selected. Once on board, they must receive the intensive and tailored supervision necessary for ensuring that all appropriate goals are met.

The theme of supporting the worker is carried on by Gottlieb and Gignac (Chapter Ten). The worker in this case is a relative who assumes caregiving responsibility for an elderly family member. The authors caution that the caregiver requires not only personal support but also a responsive formal support system for the elderly person, as necessary, so that the caregiver is neither coerced into the caregiving role nor precluded from assuming it.

Issues arising from programmatic changes in family support are never more apparent than when they mirror issues of major importance to society at large. As the subject of cultural diversity moves again to the foreground in America, Garcia challenges us, in Chapter Eleven, to think of culture as individual-centered, and to reject the notion of homogeneity within cultural groups. Garcia's challenge requires us to revise the traditional focus of social services, and it creates an opportunity for the family support movement to provide leadership based on recent knowledge of best practices with diverse groups.

Since family support is not yet part of the social fabric, funding has been a continual problem, becoming even more challenging as programs have expanded. Linking funding to programs' development, and not just to their survival, as Carter suggests in Chapter Twelve, offers an approach that changes the question of who will pay into the question of how funds will be spent. Attention to the profound implications of funding strategies could ensure a more solid base for planning as new resources become available, and as innovative ways of combining old funding sources are explored.

Focusing on policy change, the four chapters in Part Four deal with federalist perspectives on family support, explicating how communities, cities, states, and the nation as a whole are and should be continuing to operate as family support moves into the mainstream. Some authors describe actual accomplishments. Others predict future strategies. All of them reveal potential implications for policy making.

Discussing family support and community development, Garbarino and Kostelny (Chapter Thirteen) give particular attention to high-risk neighborhoods, questioning the capacity of family support to reach and address the needs of the neediest families without cooperation from other institutions. They suggest that family resource efforts in these communities must be linked with more sweeping reforms throughout the community's institutions, since high social disintegration in communities tends to be reflected in the disorganization and ineffectiveness of both informal service networks and formal service agencies.

Implementation of family support on a citywide level and across socioeconomic groupings is discussed in Chapter Fourteen by Mayor Norman Rice of Seattle, who describes urban family support strategies, specifically highlighting the exemplary efforts of the City of Seattle. Since cities are closely involved with the policies and services (such as public health, safety, and recreation) that affect the family's quality of life, they can play a leading role in stimulating partnerships among local businesses, school boards, and service providers. In so doing, cities engage in processes similar to those of communities and must deal with the issues of high-risk neighborhoods and inadequately functioning service systems.

On the level of the state, Bruner (Chapter Fifteen) tackles the problems associated with instituting family support approaches across services that are still fragmented. Bruner addresses the critical issues that are involved when program change means systems change. He suggests that bringing family support up to scale will test its potential for helping families and its ability to shape the service system's approach to serving families.

Farrow, in Chapter Sixteen, urges the infusion of family support premises and principles into a wide range of federal programs and funding sources. This, he says, would be preferable to allowing family support to become yet another categorical program. Farrow proposes that federal funding for family resource initiatives be structured in a way that promotes state, local, and parental ownership of the initiatives. By emphasizing the creative role that the federal government should play in maintaining the infrastructure necessary for strengthening state and local family resource initiatives, Farrow challenges the field to develop the capacity to inform and validate its own efforts.

Together, the challenges posed in each of the first sixteen chapters represent a determination not to let the acceptance of family support by a continually wider audience detract from attention to ensuring its quality, enhancing its knowledge base, and strengthening its infrastructure. To that end, Part Five is devoted to discussing quality, training, and evaluation efforts from the perspective of the family support movement.

In Chapter Seventeen, Kagan reminds us that quality has always been a concern of practitioners, but only in recent years has the field itself created a demand for defining quality and its constituent best practices. Kagan presents guidelines for the field to ponder as it grapples with reaching a definition of quality, and she couples them with a discussion of potential implementation strategies.

Norton, in Chapter Eighteen, further emphasizes the development of the field in her discussion of training for family support personnel. She posits a common core of knowledge based on the principles of family support as a construct for training. Norton envisions the education of family support workers as a training as comprehensive as that of other professions, to be accomplished through classes, observation, and supervised experiences and to be acknowledged, as in other professions, by credentials or certification.

Chapter Nineteen, by Powell, draws out a theme that reverberates throughout this volume and is critically important for the widespread legitimation and advancement of the family support movement. Powell presents a comprehensive summary of existing evaluation studies; but, most important, he suggests possible solutions to a major problem in evaluation, uniformly expressed by the other authors: the lack of suitable measures for addressing the essence of family support at the multiple levels of the individual, the family, and the community.

In Chapter Twenty, the editors conclude with an analysis of family support as it faces and shapes its future. We postulate that family support is a new normative system with a durable structure and an environment supportive of its development. The phrase "an environment supportive of family support" epitomizes this volume's themes. Family support is not just a program, nor is it only an approach. As family support moves toward making communities and systems work for families, it is shaping the policies of our nation. If the big picture does not change, any progress made with families in programs and systems inevitably will be undermined.

Today, family support is defined as programs with discernible characteristics, as principles that guide relationships between services and families, and as the expression of common values derived from our founding fathers' vision of democracy — respect for human dignity, responsible citizenship, and concern for the welfare of others. Our hope is that every policy and institution that touches children and their families will function in ways that undergird and promote family health. In its broadest sense, the family resource agenda is an agenda for social justice.

Acknowledgments

No volume would be complete without the assistance of numerous individuals. We are indebted to Luba Lynch and the A. L. Mailman Family Foundation, whose support made this and many other significant advances in family support possible. Without their confidence, inspiration, and encouragement, this book would have remained an unrealized dream.

The solid and steady staff support we received facilitated each step of the process. We especially thank Peter Neville, who took pains with every aspect of the preparation of this volume. His keen intellect, patience, and willingness to do each and every job associated with researching, writing, and editing were invaluable. We appreciate Carol Hanson's and Eliza Pritchard's research and writing assistance, as well as the spirit of cooperation in which they did whatever we asked. Finally, we thank Darlene Logan-Francellno, who is able to keep things running smoothly, make reminders ever so gently, and never lose sight of the details that bring it all together.

June 1994   Sharon L. Kagan
                                                    New Haven, Connecticut

                                                    Bernice Weissbourd
                                                    Chicago, Illinois

☐ The Editors ☐

SHARON L. KAGAN, senior associate at Yale University's Bush Center in Child Development and Social Policy, is recognized nationally and internationally for her work related to the care and education of young children and their families. A frequent consultant to the White House, Congress, the National Governors' Association, the U.S. Departments of Health and Human Services, and numerous national foundations, corporations, and professional associations, Kagan plays a leadership role in the early childhood field. She is chairperson of the Family Resource Coalition's board of directors, chairperson of the National Education Goals Panel Readiness Technical Committee, a former governing board member of the National Association for the Education of Young Children, a recipient of an honorary doctoral degree from Wheelock College, and a member of over thirty international and national commissions, panels, advisory groups, and editorial boards.

As a researcher, writer, and policy analyst, Kagan focuses in her scholarship on improving schools and other institutions that serve young children. In over one hundred publications, she has investigated such issues as organizational change and school reform, the role of the private sector in delivering child care and early education, the role of parents in their children's education, strategies for collaboration, the facilitation of home-school transitions for children and families, and the readiness of children and schools for learning.

BERNICE WEISSBOURD is an early childhood educator, well known as an initiator and leader of the family support movement. In 1976 she founded Family Focus, a not-for-profit organization providing comprehensive programs for families in diverse communities, with a focus on prospective parents and parents with children from birth to three. In 1981 she created the Family Resource Coalition, a national organization serving as a resource on family support to practitioners, theoreticians, researchers, policy makers, and the media. In 1989, with T. Berry Brazelton and Susan DeConcini, she founded Parent Action, an advocacy organization for parents across the country to speak out on policies affecting their families.

Weissbourd is a contributing editor to *Parents* magazine and has authored and edited numerous publications on family support policies and practices. She is past president of the American Orthopsychiatric Association, a congressional appointee to the National Commission on Children, and former vice-president of the National Association for the Education of Young Children. She is a lecturer at the School of Social Service Administration, University of Chicago.

□ The Contributors □

ANN ADALIST-ESTRIN is founder and director of the Parent Resource Center, in Wyncote, Pennsylvania, and director of Incarcerated Parents and Their Children Consulting Services. She is a practicing child and family therapist, lecturer, trainer, and consultant to a wide variety of agencies serving children and families and to criminal justice programs in the United States and Canada. She received her B.A. degree (1981) in early childhood education from Temple University and her M.S. degree (1987) in counseling psychology from Villanova University. She serves on the board of the Family Resource Coalition and on the steering committee of the Family & Corrections Network.

ANDREW BILLINGSLEY is professor and chair in the Department of Family Studies at the University of Maryland, College Park. He is the author of numerous articles and books, including *Black Families in White America* (1968), *Children of the Storm* (1974), and *Climbing Jacob's Ladder: The Enduring Legacy of African American Families* (1993). He holds degrees in social work and sociology and formerly taught at Morgan State University, Howard University, and the University of California, Berkeley.

BARBARA T. BOWMAN is vice-president for academic programs at Erikson Institute, affiliated with Loyola University of Chicago. She attended Sarah Lawrence College (B.A.) and the University of Chicago (M.A.). Currently, in addition to her administration role, she teaches graduate courses in the history and philosophy of early childhood education, administration, and early childhood curriculum. She has also taught in universities in Iran and China. She is a frequent consultant to Head

Start, public schools, and day-care programs. A past president of the National Association for the Education of Young Children, Bowman is active in a number of professional organizations and a member of the advisory board of the Black Child Development Institute. She is also a member of the boards of the Great Books Foundation, the Family Resource Coalition, and High/Scope Educational Foundation. She has served on numerous municipal, state, and national committees and at present is a member of advisory committees for the Illinois State Board of Education on Early Childhood Education, the National Board for Professional Standards Early Childhood Panel, the Chicago Community Trust Community Initiatives Program, and the Teachers College Press Early Childhood Series. She speaks and writes frequently on issues related to children and families. She also directs projects in the Chicago public schools to establish appropriate assessment strategies and parent-support programs.

T. BERRY BRAZELTON is clinical professor of pediatrics (emeritus) at Harvard Medical School and founder of the Child Development Unit at Children's Hospital, Boston. He is also past president of the Society for Research in Child Development and of the Zero-to-Three National Center for Clinical Infant Programs. In 1989 he was appointed by Congress to the National Commission on Children. He has published more than 180 scientific papers and has written numerous books on pediatrics and child development. His most recent book is *Touchpoints: Your Child's Emotional and Behavioral Development, The Essential Reference* (1992). He also writes a weekly column syndicated by the *New York Times* and is a regular contributor to *Family Circle Magazine*.

URIE BRONFENBRENNER is Jacob Gould Schurman Professor Emeritus of Human Development and Family Studies and of Psychology at Cornell University. In 1993 the American Psychological Society awarded him the James McKeen Cattell Award for Distinguished Scientific Contributions. One of the founders of Head Start, he has been honored by the Society for Research in Child Development for his outstanding contributions to science and social policy. His book *The Ecology of Human Development: Experiments by Nature and Design* (1979) received the 1981 Anisfield-Wolf Award in Race Relations.

CHARLES BRUNER is director of the Child and Family Policy Center, a nonprofit center in Des Moines, Iowa, designed to "better link research and policy on issues vital to children and families." He heads the technical assistance resource network of the National Center for Service Integration and served twelve years as a state legislator in the Iowa General Assembly. He received his B.A. degree (1970) from Macalester College and his M.A. (1972) and Ph.D. (1978) degrees from Stanford University, all in political science. He is the author of several books on state policy, including *Improving Children's Welfare* (1990), *Thinking Collaboratively* (1991), and *Making Welfare Work* (1992).

CLEOPATRA HOWARD CALDWELL is a research investigator with the African American Mental Health Research Center, Research Center for Group Dynamics, Institute for Social Research, University of Michigan. She has published journal articles in the areas of help-seeking behaviors and informal social support among African Americans and on the black church as a social service institution, as well as on race-related socialization and academic achievement among African American youth. Her current research focuses on intergenerational family influences on early childbearing and on self-efficacy, exercise, and sexual behaviors of African American adolescent females. She received her Ph.D. (1986) in social psychology from the University of Michigan.

JUDY LANGFORD CARTER is executive director of the Family Resource Coalition, a national organization of more than two thousand family resource programs and practitioners who work with them. She was formerly executive director of the Ounce of Prevention Fund, an $11 million public-private partnership that designs, monitors, and provides technical assistance, training, and evaluation for more than forty community-based, innovative family and children's projects in Illinois. She has been a contributing editor of *Redbook* magazine and served as honorary chair of the President's Advisory Committee for Women. She is the founder of the AIDS Foundation of Chicago and is a Leadership Greater Chicago Fellow. She is currently on the board of directors of the Women's Legal Defense Fund, World Centre San Francisco, and Business and Professional People for the Public Interest. She is a graduate of the University of Georgia and holds a master's degree in early childhood education from Georgia State University.

FRANK FARROW is director of children's services policy at the Center for the Study of Social Policy, Washington, D.C. He was formerly executive director of the Social Services Administration in Maryland's Department of Human Resources and has directed innovative family service programs at the local level. He received his B.A. degree (1969) from Yale University and his M.A. degree (1971) in social welfare policy from the University of Chicago.

ELLEN GALINSKY, one of the founders of the field of work and family life, is co-president of Families and Work Institute, a New York-based, nonprofit center for policy research on issues of the changing work force and changing family life. She has conducted numerous groundbreaking studies and is a national and international spokesperson. Galinksy is author and coauthor of thirteen books and more than seventy articles including *The Changing Workforce: Highlights of the National Study, The Corporate Reference Guide to Work-Family Programs, Beyond the Parental Leave Debate, Education Before School: Investing in Quality Child Care, The Six Stages of Parenthood,* and *The Preschool Years.* She has been heard extensively on television and radio and in lecture, appearing on such television shows as *The Today Show* and *The MacNeil/ Lehrer News Hour.* In 1988 she was selected one of the one hundred outstanding women in America by *Ladies Home Journal.* A native of West Virginia, Galinsky holds degrees from Vassar College and Bank Street College of Education. She is a past president of the National Association for the Education of Young Children.

JAMES GARBARINO is director of the Family Life Development Center and professor of Human Development and Family
Studies at Cornell University. From 1985 to 1994 he was president of the Erikson Institute for Advanced Study in Child Development. He received his Ph.D. (1973) in human development
and family studies from Cornell University. He received the
American Psychological Association's (APA's) 1989 award for
Distinguished Professional Contributions to Public Service. In
1994, he received the Nicholas Hobbs Award from APA's Division 37 (Child, Youth, and Family Services) and the Dale
Richmond Award from the American Academy of Pediatrics,
Section on Developmental and Behavioral Pediatrics. Among
the fifteen books he has authored or edited are *Children in Danger*
(1992), *Children and Families in the Social Environment* (1992), *What
Children Can Tell Us* (1989), *The Psychologically Battered Child* (1986),
Growing Up in a Socially Toxic Environment: Childhood in the 1990s
(in press), and for children, *Let's Talk About Living in a World
With Violence* (1993).

EUGENE E. GARCIA is director of the Office of Bilingual Education and Minority Languages Affairs in the U.S. Office of
Education. He is on leave from the University of California,
Santa Cruz, where he is professor of education and psychology. His research and scholarly interests include bilingualism,
education of diverse populations, and early childhood education.

MONIQUE A. M. GIGNAC holds a postdoctoral fellowship in
the Gerontology Research Centre at the University of Guelph,
Canada. She received her B.Sc. degree (1985) in psychology
from the University of Toronto and her M.A. (1988) and Ph.D.
(1991) degrees in social psychology from the University of
Waterloo.

BENJAMIN H. GOTTLIEB is professor of psychology in the
Department of Psychology at the University of Guelph, Canada.
He received his B.A. (1968), M.S.W. (1970), and Ph.D. (1973)
degrees in psychology and social work from the University of
Michigan. His current research centers on coping with chronic

stress, a subject that he is investigating among people who are caring for a relative with dementia and among employees who must balance job and family responsibilities. He is the editor of two volumes and the author of a third, *Social Support Strategies: Guidelines for Mental Health Practice.*

ANGELA DUNGEE GREENE is a Ph.D. candidate in sociology at Howard University. She has collaborated on several journal articles, technical reports, and professional presentations pertaining to various social, economic, and health-related issues for African American families. Her research interests include sociodemographic predictors of low birthweight, infant mortality, and other adverse outcomes; predictors of paternal involvement; paternal involvement as a predictor of delinquency and risk-taking behavior among adolescents; and social institutions as sources of family support and service delivery.

KATHLEEN KOSTELNY is a research associate at the Erikson Institute for Advanced Study in Child Development. She has conducted research on children who live in dangerous environments, including Cambodia, Nicaragua, Mozambique, Northern Ireland, the Israeli occupied territories, and inner-city Chicago. She is coauthor of *Children in Danger: Coping with the Consequences of Community Violence* (1992) and *No Place to Be a Child: Growing Up in a War Zone* (1991). She received her Ph.D. (1993) in child development from Erikson Institute/Loyola University.

RUTH W. MASSINGA is chief executive of The Casey Family Program in Seattle, having begun her tenure in this position in April 1989. From 1983 to 1989 she served as secretary of the Maryland Department of Human Resources. She is past president of the American Public Welfare Association and since 1989 has been a member of the National Commission on Children and of the board of the Family Resource Coalition. She was appointed to the American Humane Association board in 1990. She also is a member of the committee on the urban underclass of the Social Science Research Council, the board of advisors at the National Center on Child Poverty, and the board of visitors at the School of Family Resources and Consumer

Sciences, University of Wisconsin. Massinga received her B.S. degree from Southern University and her M.S. degree in social services from Boston University.

JUDITH S. MUSICK was the first director of the Ounce of Prevention Fund and currently serves as the vice-chair of its board. She is a visiting faculty member at the Erikson Institute for Advanced Study in Child Development. She is the author of the forthcoming *Infant Development: From Theory to Practice* and of *Young, Poor, and Pregnant: The Psychology of Adolescent Motherhood.* She has spent the last ten years developing and studying preventive intervention programs for families and children and was the recipient of a multiyear grant from the Rockefeller Foundation to synthesize and write about this work. She received her B.A. degree (1972) in psychology from Mundelein College and her Ph.D. degree (1976) in child development and educational psychology from Northwestern University.

PETER R. NEVILLE is currently a program assistant at Victim Services Agency in New York City. Previously, he served as a research assistant at the Bush Center in Child Development and Social Policy at Yale University. He has worked and written on issues of education, job training, and family education for Head Start families. He received his B.A. in psychology from Wesleyan University.

DOLORES G. NORTON is a professor in the School of Social Service Administration at the University of Chicago, where she also directs a longitudinal study of inner-city African American children from birth through grade five. She received her M.S.S. (1960) and her Ph.D. (1969) degrees from the Graduate School of Social Work and Social Research, Bryn Mawr College. She teaches in the area of early human development and the ecological environment, and is the chair of the family support specialization program.

DOUGLAS R. POWELL is professor and head of the Department of Child Development and Family Studies at Purdue Uni-

versity. He has conducted major evaluations of parent education and support programs with a variety of populations. He
is the editor of *Early Childhood Research Quarterly* and the author
of numerous publications on early childhood programs, family
support, and program evaluation. He received his Ph.D. from
Northwestern University.

NORMAN B. RICE was reelected in 1993 to a second term
as mayor of Seattle and is recognized nationally as a leader on
urban education issues. As mayor, he has spearheaded Seattle's
efforts to invest in the health and social needs of children, build
a stronger partnership between schools and the larger community, and increase academic achievement. He has also cochaired
the National League of Cities Task Force on Children and Education and chaired the U.S. Conference of Mayors' Committee
on Youth, Families, and Education.

FRANCES STOTT is a professor of child development and
dean of academic programs at the Erikson Institute in Chicago
and a clinical psychologist in private practice. She received her
B.A. degree (1963) in education from the University of Chicago,
her M.A. degree (1974) in educational psychology from the
University of Chicago, and her Ph.D. degree (1980) in educational psychology and child development from Northwestern
University. She is the coauthor (with James Garbarino and the
faculty of the Erikson Institute) of *What Children Can Tell Us*.
Her research interests include the study of children who are at
risk for psychological problems, with a special focus on the children of psychiatrically ill mothers.

BARRY ZUCKERMAN is professor and chairman of pediatrics
at Boston University School of Medicine and Boston City Hospital. He has over twenty years' experience as a pediatrician working with children and their families in inner-city Boston. He
has developed innovative programs for high-risk children by
linking different child and family specialists in pediatric primary-
care settings. He conducts research on and has published over
one hundred scientific articles about the impact of biological and

social factors on the health and development of children. He is a member of the National Commission on Children and the Carnegie Commission on Young Children and is a past chairman of the section on developmental and behavioral pediatrics of the American Academy of Pediatrics. He is also a board member of the National Center for Clinical Infant Programs, as well as a member of numerous editorial boards and state and national organizations.

Putting Families First

☐ **Part One** ☐

FAMILY SUPPORT
IN A CHANGING CONTEXT

====== □ 1 □ ======

America's Children
and Families

An International Perspective

Urie Bronfenbrenner
Peter R. Neville

Compared with other developed nations, the United States reluctantly finds itself at or near the top of the list on multiple indicators of family fragmentation and instability. Plagued by high levels of divorce, single parenthood, environmental stress, teenage pregnancy, and poverty, American families are all too often forced to operate under conditions that inhibit their ability to provide the nurturing environments necessary for children's healthy growth and development. Close examination of the current circumstances of American families, from the perspective of a bioecological model of development (Bronfenbrenner, 1979; 1986), helps delineate the specific barriers that such sociocontextual conditions pose for American children and their families. Further, it provides a clear rationale for the provision of family support and assistance in overcoming these barriers and suggests guidelines for developing family-supportive practices and policies.

Given the current condition of families in our nation, the

Material for this chapter was drawn in part from Bronfenbrenner, 1989 and 1992a. For a more extensive account of relevant research see Bronfenbrenner, 1979, 1986, 1990, 1992b, 1993, in press, and Bronfenbrenner and Ceci, 1993.

need for family support is clear and urgent. Indeed, we seem to be developing a good sense of many of the characteristics of an appropriate and sufficient family support system, as will be described throughout this volume. However, this urgency and this clarity have not yet been reflected on a widespread basis in our society's policies and day-to-day operations. To the contrary, the United States demonstrates disturbing shortcomings and insufficiencies in its family support capacity by comparison with other modern nations. It is the purpose of this chapter to revisit the current need and capacity for family support in the United States by comparison with other countries, to draw out the implications of these conditions for the well-being of children and their families, and to suggest potential strategies, rooted in the American sociocultural context, for enacting broad-based improvements in our nation's responsiveness to family needs.

The Changing Family

Results from international studies of family structure reveal that families in the United States stand apart from those in other developed countries, demonstrating an extraordinary degree of structural fragmentation and often operating under overwhelming conditions of stress, even across socioeconomic levels. For example, in 1990, the U.S. Bureau of the Census published its first international comparison of the status of families and children (Hobbs & Lippman, 1990), which stated:

> *Children in the U.S. are the most likely to live with only one parent.* The proportion of U.S. children living in single-parent families grew 2.5 times between 1960 and 1986. Nearly 1 in 4 now lives with only one parent. More children, by far, both in number and percent, live in single-parent families in the United States than in other countries compared. The percentage has also increased substantially since 1960 in every country studied, but the gap between the United States and other developed countries has widened. [p. 7; emphasis in original]

Disappointingly, in support of the above statements the report cites specific percentages for only five countries.[1] Some basis for a more extended comparison, however, is provided by available data on divorce rates for a large number of modern nations.[2] In this comparison as well, the United States ranks highest, with a divorce rate that for a quarter of a century has also been the highest in the world (see Figure 1.1).

Figure 1.1. Divorce Rates in Ten Developed Countries.

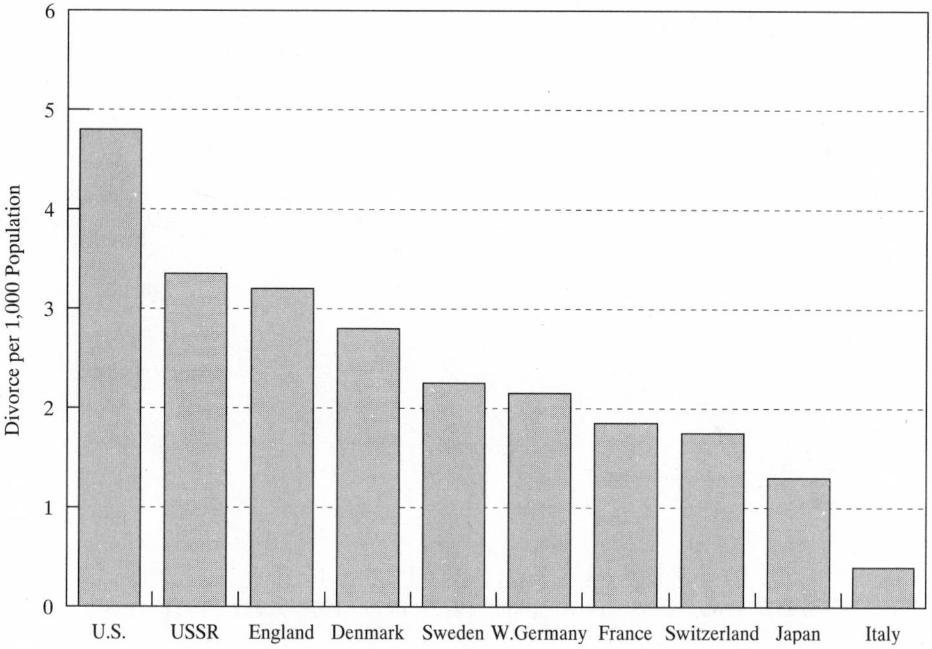

Source: Adapted from United Nations, 1990.

Given our interest in the context of time as well as of place, it is also instructive to examine the course of this trend in the United States, as compared with divorce rates for six other developed nations. The data depicted in Figure 1.2 reveal that, in general, a marked increase in divorce rates began in the second half of the 1960s, with the United States showing by far

Figure 1.2. Divorce Across the Decades in Seven Developed Societies.

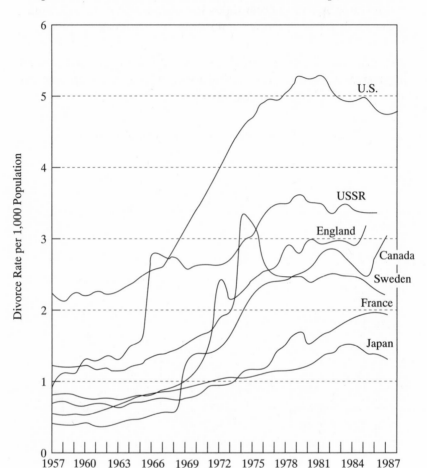

Source: Adapted from United Nations, 1957–1990.

the steepest rise. The trend reached its maximum at the end of the 1970s and has since shown a slight downward trend.

There are, of course, other forms of single parenthood besides divorce, most notably unmarried motherhood and separated couples with children. No comparable statistics exist to permit any assessing of the relative frequency of these phenomena across countries, but the information is available for the United States.[3] It is summarized in Figure 1.3, with specific

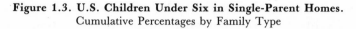

Figure 1.3. U.S. Children Under Six in Single-Parent Homes.
Cumulative Percentages by Family Type

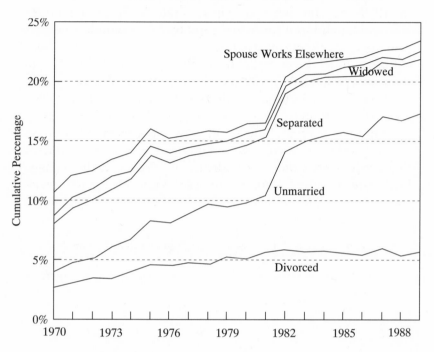

reference to children under six years of age.[4] The graph indicates that, although the relative frequency of young children
living with a divorced parent leveled off in the 1980s, the proportion born to unmarried mothers grew during the same period.
It is primarily this phenomenon that results in the continuing
increase in the percentage of children living in single-parent families in the United States. That figure is now 23 percent for children under six, and a full 25 percent for all children under
eighteen.

An important addition to this comparison would be the
labor-force participation in each land of single parents with
young children. Unfortunately, comparable data on an international basis are available only for maternal labor-force participation in eight countries (Sorrentino, 1990). The rates are
for all single mothers with children under three and range from
a high of 81 percent for Denmark to a low of 23 percent for

the United Kingdom, with the United States ranking fifth at
45 percent.[5] One should bear in mind, however, that during
the 1980s the labor-force participation rate of American mothers
with young children increased rapidly. For example, the percentage of mothers (married or single) in the labor force with
children under three rose, from about one-third in 1975 to
slightly over one-half in 1988 (U.S. Department of Labor, 1990,
table 56). The rates for all mothers with children under six were
proportionally higher, rising during the same period from 39
percent to 56 percent. This trend may be expected to continue.

Another characteristic of American families and children
that distinguishes them from their counterparts is the teenage
birth rate. Figure 1.4 shows comparative levels for ten developed nations. The contrast revealed in Figure 1.4 has its roots

Figure 1.4. Rates of Teenage Birth in Ten Developed Countries.

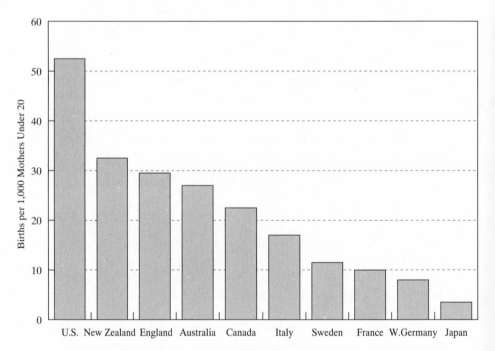

Source: Adapted from United Nations, 1990.

in corresponding differences in adolescent birth rates; see Figure 1.5, which displays results from a comparative study of adolescent pregnancy published by the United Nations Department of International Economic and Social Affairs (1988). Although the set of West European nations included in the figure differs somewhat from the set included in Figure 1.4, the findings reveal a similar pattern.

Apart from these indicators of fragmentation and instability in family structure, the United States also takes the lead, among developed nations (followed closely by Australia), with respect to poverty. The findings depicted in Figure 1.6 are highlighted in a recently published U.S. Bureau of the Census international comparison of the status of children and families in developing societies (Hobbs & Lippman, 1990) and are based

Figure 1.5. Teenage Pregnancy in Selected Developed Countries.

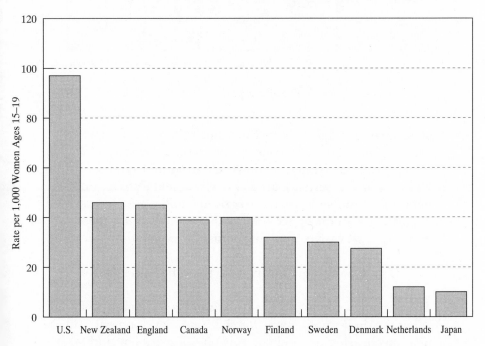

Source: Adapted from United Nations, 1988.

Figure 1.6. Poverty Among Children in Eight Developed Societies.

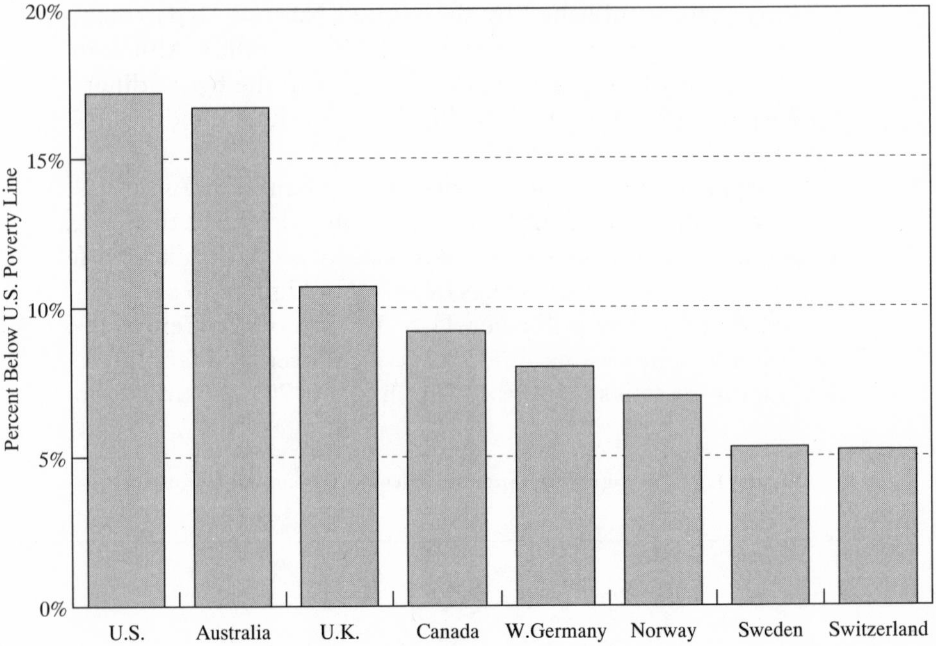

Source: Adapted from Smeeding, Torrey, & Rein, 1988.

on an analysis carried out by Smeeding, Torrey, & Rein (1988).[6] Once again, the data are consistent with the general trend among economically developed nations: children and families in the United States experience greater environmental stress. Further, many of the problems facing American families are not restricted to particular ethnic or economic subgroups. Rather, these conditions are pervasive, applying across the population spectrum.

The Changing Family and the Changing Child

These changes taking place in American family life are profound. What are their implications for children's development? Investigations bearing precisely on this question are few and far between. What is available, however, is a growing body of research evidence that sheds light on the conditions and processes that foster the development of competence and character in the young. In this section, we summarize these findings in the form of five propositions. We also examine the changes that have been occurring in American family life in light of these propositions, to arrive at an estimate of the effect of the observed social changes on the well-being and development of today's children and tomorrow's adults.[7]

Proposition 1

In order to develop — intellectually, socially, and morally — a child requires participation in progressively more complex reciprocal activity, on a regular basis over an extended period in the child's life, with one or more persons with whom the child develops a strong, mutual, irrational, emotional attachment and who are committed to the child's well-being and development, preferably for life.

Although this proposition has the merit of being fairly compact, it is also complex. Therefore, we will examine its key elements one by one.

What is meant by "progressively more complex reciprocal activity"? Perhaps an analogy will help. It is what happens in a Ping-Pong game between two players. As the game gets going and the partners become familiar with each other, each adapts to the other's style. The game starts to move faster, and the shots in both directions tend to become more complicated as each player in effect challenges the other. This process evolves with increasing complexity in two ways: the same game becomes more complicated, and new moves are added by both parties as familiarity and skill increase.

Crucial to the establishment and maintenance of this progressive trajectory is ready responsiveness by a familiar adult to the young child's initiatives, as well as the adult's introduction of activity-engaging objects and experiences appropriate to the youngster's evolving capacities. In the absence of such responsiveness and presentation of opportunities, the child's general psychological development is hindered, particularly if the child has been exposed to biological, economic, or social stress.

A second key element of proposition 1 stipulates that to be developmentally effective, joint activity must occur "on a regular basis over an extended period in the child's life." In the process of informal mutual education, neither the young child nor the adult caregiver can learn much from the other if they get together only now and then for short periods, with frequent interruptions.

The final clause of proposition 1 imposes a further requirement: the adult must be someone "with whom the child develops a strong, mutual, irrational, emotional attachment and who [is] committed to the child's well-being and development, preferably for life." This means that the adult regards the particular child as somehow special — it is the illusion that comes with love. The illusion flows in both directions. For the child, the adult is also someone special — someone to whom the child turns most readily when experiencing both trouble and joy, and whose comings and goings are central to the child's experience and well-being.

What is the relevance of this mutual emotional relationship for establishing "progressively more complex reciprocal activity" between child and adult? Research evidence indicates that such reciprocal interaction promotes high levels of motivation, attentiveness, sensitivity, and persistence on the part of both participants, and that these qualities are more apt to arise and be sustained in relationships characterized by strong, mutual, emotional attachment. Moreover, once such a strong mutual attachment is established, it tends to endure, thus enhancing the likelihood of a continuing pattern of reciprocal interactions at successively more complex levels throughout the child's life.

Proposition 2

The establishment of patterns of progressive interpersonal interaction under conditions of strong mutual attachment enhances the young child's responsiveness to other features of the immediate physical, social, and — in due course — symbolic environment that invite exploration, manipulation, elaboration, and imagination. In turn, such activities also accelerate the child's psychological growth.

Moving beyond the child-adult relationship, this proposition encompasses children's interaction with other elements in their environment. Specifically, the youngster's active orientation toward the physical and symbolic environment may be mediated by prior and persistent patterns of interpersonal interaction in the context of a strong, enduring emotional relationship with one or more adults, usually including the child's parents. These ongoing experiences may serve as a potent, liberating, and energizing force, not only in relation to the physical environment but also in relation to the social world. They may enable the child to relate to persons beyond the immediate family, including peers as well as adults, and to involve them effectively in meeting his or her own developmental needs. More broadly, the child's newly acquired abilities make it possible for her or him to benefit from experiences in other settings and, most notably, to learn in school.

But the effects of this process work in both directions. As other people and elements are drawn into the child's environment, such involvement and activity in turn may further enhance the commitment and effectiveness of parents (see Lamb & Malkin, 1986). Indeed, the establishment of close relationships with specific adults, on the one hand, and interaction with other adults, peers, objects, and symbols, on the other, may be independent yet mutually reinforcing processes, with both simultaneously contributing to the child's development.

The research evidence indicates further that when the elements stipulated in the first two propositions are provided on a continuing basis, the positive effects on the child's development are indeed substantial. Accordingly, a society that seeks the well-being and development of its children is well advised to provide them with the kinds of environments and experiences specified in the first two propositions.

But there is a catch: research findings also reveal that the processes of interaction between child and environment that foster development, as described in propositions 1 and 2, operate efficiently only if certain conditions exist in the broader environment where these proximal processes take place. The remaining three propositions deal with the nature of these enabling and disabling circumstances.

Proposition 3

The establishment and maintenance of patterns of progressively more complex interaction and emotional attachment between caregiver and child depend in substantial degree on the availability and involvement of another adult or a third party — spouse, relative, neighbor, or formal service provider — who assists, encourages, spells, gives status to, and expresses admiration and affection for the person caring for and engaging in joint activity with the child.

Proposition 3 focuses on the impact of many of the family issues raised by the international comparison on developmental processes already described, and thus it begins to reveal implications for children and families in the United States, by comparison with those in other modern societies. Further, it suggests the need for support systems to enable families to provide nurturing environments and develop the relationships necessary for healthy child development.

Some of the evidence for this proposition comes from studies of the rapid rise in the proportion of single-parent households, in developed and developing nations alike. Results indicate that, especially in a context of comparatively low support for families in the United States, as documented later in this discussion, children growing up in single-parent households are at greater risk for a variety of behavioral and educational problems, including extremes of hyperactivity or withdrawal, inattentiveness in the classroom, difficulty in deferring gratification, impaired academic achievement, misbehavior at school, absenteeism, dropping out, involvement in socially alienated peer groups, and especially the so-called teenage syndrome of behaviors that tend to cluster together — smoking, drinking, early and frequent sexual experience, a cynical attitude toward school and work, adolescent pregnancy, and, in the more extreme cases, drug use, vandalism, violence, other criminal acts, and suicide. Most of these effects are much more pronounced for boys than for girls. More intensive investigations of these phenomena have identified a common predisposing factor for the emergence of such problems — namely, a history of impaired parent-child interaction and relationships, beginning in early childhood.

In addition to the effect of family structure, two other types of environmental context pose developmental risks, with associated outcomes very similar to (though often greater in degree than) those for single parenthood. The first and most destructive of these is poverty. Because many single-parent families are also poor, parents and their children are in double jeopardy. But research in developed and developing countries reveals that even when two parents are present, processes of parent-child interaction and environmentally oriented child activity are more difficult to initiate and sustain in households living under stressful economic and social conditions. By comparison with families living under more favorable circumstances, much more parental effort and perseverance are required to achieve the same effect, particularly when (as is often the case) the mother is the only parent or even the only adult in the home. These difficulties often increase by the time children are of preschool age or older and are exposed to impoverished and disruptive settings outside the home.

But good developmental processes are now threatened not only in poor and single-parent families; during the 1970s and 1980s, other highly vulnerable contexts have evolved that cut across the domains of class, family structure, and culture. Recent studies revealed a second major disruptive factor in the lives of families and children: the increasing instability, inconsistency, and hectic character of daily family life. The following commentary on the American scene is evocative of this pervasive trend:

> In a world in which both parents usually have to work, often at a considerable distance from home, every family member, through the waking hours from morning till night, is "on the run." The need to coordinate conflicting demands of job and child care, often involving varied arrangements that shift from day to day, can produce a situation in which everyone has to be transported several times a day in different directions, usually at the same time — a state of affairs that prompted a foreign colleague to comment: "It seems to me that in your country,

most children are being brought up in moving vehicles." (Bronfenbrenner, 1989, p. 13)

Many other factors also contribute to the disruption of
daily family life. These include jobs that require one or the other
parent to be away for extended periods; frequent changes in
employment, and the associated moves for the whole family,
or moves that leave part of the family behind, waiting until the
school term ends or adequate housing can be found; and the
increasing rates of divorce, remarriage, and redivorce. In this
regard, the most recent evidence suggests that the disruptive
effects of remarriage on children may be even greater than those
of divorce (Hetherington & Clingenpeel, 1992).

Nevertheless, not all families living under these conditions exhibit disturbed relationships and suffer from their disruptive effects on development. Systematic studies of the exceptions have identified what may be described as a general
"immunizing" factor. For example, children of a single mother
are less likely to experience developmental problems when the
mother receives practical help and emotional support from other
adults living in the home or from nearby relatives, friends, or
neighbors, from members of religious groups, and, when possible, from staff members of family support and child-care programs (Cochran, Larner, Riley, Gunnarsson, & Henderson,
1990; Hetherington & Clingenpeel, 1992). With respect to
poverty and environmental stress, research also indicates the
potential for such support systems to assist families in surmount-
ing these barriers and providing children with positive environments for development (Bronfenbrenner, 1987; Kagan, Powell,
Weissbourd, & Zigler, 1987; Weissbourd & Kagan, 1989).

What are the implications of proposition 3 for the United
States? To put the matter succinctly, the conditions in which
American children all too often live may stand in direct opposi-
tion to those that foster healthy development. Such conditions,
frequently extending across economic classes, can make it difficult to establish and sustain relationships and to provide the opportunities and activities necessary for fostering successful development. For this reason, evidence of the immunizing effect

of family support suggests that we turn our attention to the types of support and services that may best help minimize the disruptive effects of family stress.

Proposition 4

The effective functioning of child-rearing processes in the family and in other settings requires establishing ongoing patterns of exchange of information, two-way communication, mutual accommodation, and mutual trust between the principal settings in which children and their parents live their lives. In contemporary societies, these settings are the home, child-care programs, the school, and the parents' place of work.

With their foundation already weakened, American families must also cope with the competing demands of settings that may include schedules, policies, and philosophies in substantial conflict with one another. Proposition 4 has particular relevance to the parents' workplaces. Research shows that a major source of stress and disarray for families and children is job stress — conflict between the needs of families and the demands of employers (Crouter & McHale, 1993; Eckenrode & Gore, 1990; Kamerman & Hayes, 1982). At the same time, experience in our own and other societies points to policies and practices that reduce work-family stress. Among them are flexible work schedules, as well as the availability of part-time jobs (for men as well as for women) without loss of job benefits and opportunities for advancement. Another accommodation would be the establishment, in each work organization, of a family resources office or specialist. This office or specialist would serve as an advocate in relation to family-work issues, maintain a file of nontechnical publications and resource materials related to child development and parenthood, provide referrals to family services available in the community, and serve as a catalyst and resource for cost-effective workplace policies and practices that could reduce unnecessary stress resulting from the conflicting demands of work and family life, with due regard to the primary need of the work setting to fulfill its productive and service responsibilities. What is the quid pro quo? Research indicates that such measures increase attendance, improve employee morale and loyalty, and reduce turnover without causing decreases in productivity (Families and Work Institute, 1993).

Proposition 5

The effective functioning of child-rearing processes in the family and other settings requires public policies and practices in support of child-rearing activities on the part of parents, caregivers, teachers and other professionals, relatives, friends, neighbors, co-workers, communities and major economic, social, and political institutions.

As proposition 5 implies, a longer-range approach is to include family support strategies in broad policies and practices throughout society. Such policies and practices would be characterized by the guiding principle that the family is the primary and most efficient and effective instrument for promoting child development. Further, they should be guided by the following general principle:

> The need is to create formal systems of challenge and support that generate and strengthen informal systems of challenge and support, that in turn reduce the need for the formal systems (Bronfenbrenner & Weiss, 1983, p. 405).

In sum, the goal of society should be to provide families with the support — including places, time, stability, status, recognition, beliefs, customs, and actions — that will enable them to establish the relationships and the environment necessary for healthy child development.

Family Support in the United States: A Comparative View

The approach described by these five propositions is ecological; that is, it lays out the dependence of successful child development on multiple contextual conditions. Many of these conditions are weak or lacking in American families today.

To what degree does the United States provide the support that such conditions require? How much have our social policies and institutional practices been infused with the family-supportive guidelines alluded to in propositions 4 and 5? how supportive of families are our schools, social services, and workplaces?

Unfortunately, the answers are not terribly encouraging. The extent of this nation's unique position among other modern nations is well reflected in the following passages from a recent comparative assessment of social policies and practices in Europe and in the United States:

> Almost all European countries — including Belgium, Denmark, France, Italy, and West Germany — provide free (or low-fee) and optional, public or privately financed preschool or child care programs for children about age 3 (or younger) to school age. . . . All the countries mentioned thus far, and many others including Japan, but not the United States, provide health insurance or health services for children and their families. All have somewhat comparable social insurance systems. . . . The U.S. unemployment insurance system compares unfavorably in both replacement rates and duration, thus adding poverty and low-income problems affecting families with children.

> In contrast to the United States, almost all industrial countries provide a public, universal child benefit — a child or family allowance — either as a direct cash benefit or a refundable tax credit, based on the presence and number of children in a family. Typically, such allowances are equal to about 5 percent to 10 percent of average gross wages for each child. . . .

> A growing trend among European countries is the provision of a guaranteed minimum child support payment. This benefit is advanced to the custodial or caretaking parent by a government agency when child support payments owed by the absent

> parent are not paid, paid irregularly, or too low. . . .
> Austria, Denmark, France, Israel, the Netherlands,
> Norway, Sweden, and West Germany are among
> the countries with such a policy. (Kamerman &
> Kahn, 1988, pp. 354–355, 363–364)

The same pattern reappears in comparisons of child care in the United States: "While the demand for child care spaces exceeds the supply for one or more age groups of children in most countries surveyed, Canada ranks with the United States and the United Kingdom in the bottom third of the countries studied with respect to coverage" (Cooke, 1986, p. 271).

In the absence of a coherent national policy or a federal level of support for families, small-scale family support programs, both public and private, have proliferated throughout the United States. They are effective, but their valiant efforts are limited by the lack of broader policies and programs on the national level. Recently, however, these localized efforts are meeting with increasing interest and activity. In addition, following the long-established lead of numerous developed and developing nations, in 1993 the United States enacted family-leave legislation, providing for up to twelve weeks of unpaid leave for childbirth, adoption, or serious family illness. The legislation is groundbreaking for the United States, but it still comes up short, in many ways, when compared with the policies of European nations, most of which provide paid maternity leave (ranging from 80 percent to 100 percent of regular wages[8]) of longer duration (up to thirty-four weeks in Scandinavian countries; see Towson, 1985). It remains to be seen what the actual impact of the legislation will be on children in the United States, and whether it signals a sea change in American family policy, but the attention to family-support issues that this legislation indicates certainly represents a step in the right direction. Furthermore, new national initiatives have been proposed in the areas of health care and welfare reform.

A Sociocultural Basis for Improved Family Support

Recent policy proposals and the promise of future change are providing new grounds for believing that national action based on family-support principles may at last be possible. To be effective over the long haul, however, such change must be predicated on an examination of how we got to where we are today. Specifically, we must examine the values, embedded in our culture, that have permitted our insufficient system to come into being and coexist with far more advanced family-support systems in other countries. Only with such knowledge can we begin to create a plan for broad, systemic improvement, building on different values, which do exist in our culture but now need to be reinvoked.

Roots of the Current Policy Context

Why is such comparatively low priority accorded to children and families in the United States? Kamerman and Kahn (1988) have evaluated possible explanations and rejected most of them. For example, after comparing demographic data on the family in Western European countries, they reach the following conclusion:

> In short, there is nothing unique in any of these statistics or in the family situation of children in the United States — the number of earners in families, the level of employment, the level of earnings or even family structure — that by *itself* would explain fully the distinctly poorer U.S. economic situation for children, even though we do not rule out several elements as a part of the picture. . . .
>
> Another explanation is U.S. federalism. Most of the European countries discussed here have unitary governments (and are smaller). But federalism cannot be an adequate explanation for our policy toward children. . . . Our own social insurance system is national and uniform, as is our own welfare system for the aged, blind, and disabled, and food stamps. The U.S. readiness to federalize major programs for the elderly but not for children is part of the question, not the answer. (Kamerman and Kahn, 1988, pp. 354, 273; emphasis in original)

Why "not for children"? A key to the riddle is found in the account of a remarkable early observer of the American scene, Count Alexis de Tocqueville (1835/1961). After visiting the United States in the 1830s, he identified the emphasis on individualism as the hallmark of American society. As many scholars have noted since then, this orientation continues to permeate American life and social institutions. Kamerman and Kahn (1988, p. 375) describe how the link between individualism and belief in the hegemony of the family has caused family issues to be viewed as beyond the purview of public influence and responsibility: "American society has found symbols and values different from social solidarity and family policy around which to construct its unity. As others have noted, this country has chosen individualism as a central value. It has sustained its complex multicultural and multireligious diversity, and avoided value confrontations by separating church from state and keeping national government out of the family, unless it can define a particular family as dangerous or endangered."

Foundations of Future Reform

Past lack of commitment to family-supportive policies may be traceable to ingrained sociocultural values. Likewise, however, we may be able to draw on other, equally established values on which increased action in behalf of families could be based. In short, the success of any future change must rest on values that are consistent with who we are as a society and who we wish to be. In light of recent indications that family support is moving to the fore of our national agenda, it is even more critical that our actions be based firmly in our sociocultural identity, in order to ensure their long-range success.

But what might such values be? Once again, Alexis de Tocqueville (1835/1961) provides us with a clue. In his perceptive view, individualism was but the first of two orientations distinguishing the newly established American social order. The second was a propensity — as he perceived it, almost a passion — for voluntarism, especially in the form of grass-roots initiative and cooperation. The national propensity for localized, individual, and community initiative is activated by the provision of opportunity, encouragement, guiding structure, and ongoing support for voluntarism. Such an orientation, when public policy serves to facilitate and guide, rather than narrowly mandate, is effective. Head Start is a prime example. Not only parents and relatives but also members of local communities were encouraged to take an active role in the implementation and direction of that program, and they did so on a fairly large scale (Zigler & Muenchow, 1992; Zigler & Styfco, 1993; Zigler & Valentine, 1979). This is probably one of the principal reasons for the demonstrated effectiveness of this program and for its initial and continuing widespread acceptance across the diverse social and political strata of American society. The success of Head Start has strong policy implications for future improvements in family support. It seems that in many cases the will to change is present, but the capacity and structure to do so are not.

An additional salient American value has come to play an increasingly prominent role across many segments of society in recent years: the emphasis on economic success and its rewards in power and material possessions. Paradoxically, this growing orientation is what has been generating new concern for the state of the nation's families. The emerging interest in child and family policy springs from growing apprehension on the part of the nation's business leaders with respect to two rapidly escalating economic problems: the quality and dependability of the available work force in an age of increasing domestic and international competition, and the increasingly enormous cost of providing for (or, alternatively and more frequently, neglecting) the growing population of so-called uneducables and unemployables.

In addition to being firmly rooted in the American sociocultural context, these and other foundational values for increased attention to family needs show particular promise in light of recent developments in this country. We are becoming more aware of the conditions in which families live. At the same time, their need for support is increasing. Modest advances in policy and practice are becoming more frequent and extensive.

As we learn from the examples of other developed nations, and as our understanding of the characteristics of effective family support services becomes clearer, it becomes even more important to base societal commitment to families on deeply ingrained cultural values and traditions, so as to ensure long-term change. The stage is being set. Exactly how the drama of change unfolds remains to be seen.

Notes

1. These countries are Canada, Norway, Sweden, England, and the United States.
2. The figures are average rates per 1,000 population. Although they include divorces between couples without children, a comparison of trends with data from countries in which separate rates for families with children are published reveals very similar patterns.
3. The data are drawn from successive reports on marital status and living arrangements, published annually by the U.S. Bureau of the Census in the *Current Population Reports,* Series P-20.
4. The labels for the successive bands in Figure 1.3 are self-explanatory, with the possible exception of "Spouse Works Elsewhere," which refers to the situation wherein a parent lives away from home because of job requirements (for example, because of a military assignment). The graph shows the percentage of children living with a single parent, whether mother or father. Those residing with the mother are in the majority, of course, but the proportion of all children under six having the father as a single parent grew steadily, from 0.6 percent in the early 1970s to 2.4 percent in the late 1980s.
5. The figures for all mothers with children under six in the countries named are about 10 percentage points higher. Other countries included were Canada, West Germany, France, Italy, and Sweden.
6. The poverty rate was computed as the percentage of children living in families "with adjusted incomes below the

official U.S. Government three-person poverty line con-
verted into other currencies using OECD purchasing power
parities" (Smeeding, Torrey, & Rein, 1988, p. 96).
7. Research on which the propositions are based is summarized and cited in Bronfenbrenner, 1986, 1992b, and 1993.
8. Specific figures should be viewed with caution, since (except in the United States) they have been changing rapidly
in recent years, usually increasing.

References

Bronfenbrenner, U. (1979). *The ecology of human development: Experiments by nature and design.* Cambridge, MA: Harvard University Press.

Bronfenbrenner, U. (1986). Ecology of the family as a context for
human development. *Developmental Psychology, 22*(6), 723–742.

Bronfenbrenner, U. (1987). Family support: The quiet revolution. In S. L. Kagan, D. R. Powell, B. Weissbourd, & E. F.
Zigler (Eds.), *America's family support programs: Perspectives and
prospects* (pp. xi–xvii). New Haven, CT: Yale University Press.

Bronfenbrenner, U. (1989). *Who cares for children?* Bilingual publication No. 188. Paris: UNESCO.

Bronfenbrenner, U. (1990). Discovering what families do. In
D. Blankenhorn, S. Bayme, & J. B. Elshtain (Eds.), *Rebuilding
the nest: A new commitment to the American family* (pp. 27–38).
Milwaukee, WI: Family Service America.

Bronfenbrenner, U. (1992a). Child care in the Anglo-Saxon
mode. In M. E. Lamb, K. Sternberg, C. P. Hwang, & A. G.
Broberg (Eds.), *Child care in context: Cross-cultural perspectives*
(pp. 281–291). Hillsdale, NJ: Erlbaum.

Bronfenbrenner, U. (1992b). Ecological systems theory. In R.
Vasta (Ed.), *Six theories of child development: Revised formulations
and current issues* (pp. 187–250). London and Philadelphia: Jes-
sica Kingsley Publishers.

Bronfenbrenner, U. (1993). The ecology of cognitive development: Research models and fugitive findings. In R. H. Woz-
niak & K. Fischer (Eds.), *Scientific environments* (pp. 3–44).
Hillsdale, NJ: Erlbaum.

Bronfenbrenner, U. (in press). Ecological models of human development. In T. Husen and T. N. Postlethwaite (Eds.), *International encyclopedia of education*. Elmsford, NY: Pergamon Press.

Bronfenbrenner, U., & Ceci, S. J. (1994). Nature-nurture reconceptualized in developmental perspective. *Psychological Review, 101.*

Bronfenbrenner, U., & Weiss, H. B. (1983). Beyond policies without people: An ecological perspective on child and family policy. In E. F. Zigler, S. L. Kagan, & E. Klugman (Eds.), *Children, families, and government* (pp. 393–414). New York: Cambridge University Press.

Cochran, M., Larner, M. Riley, D., Gunnarsson, L., & Henderson, C., Jr. (1990). *Extending families: The social networks of parents and their children*. New York: Cambridge University Press.

Cooke, K. (1986). *Report of the task force on child care*. Ottawa, Canada: Ministry for the Status of Women.

Crouter, A. C., & McHale, S. M. (1993). The long arm of the job: Influences of parental work on child rearing. In T. Luster & L. Okagaki (Eds.), *Parenting: An ecological perspective* (pp. 179–202). Hillsdale, NJ: Erlbaum.

Eckenrode, J., & Gore, S. (1990). *Stress between family and work*. New York: Plenum.

Families and Work Institute. (1993). *An evaluation of Johnson and Johnson's work-family initiative*. New York: Author.

Hetherington, E. M., & Clingenpeel, W. G. (1992). Coping with marital transitions. *Monographs of the Society for Research in Child Development, 57*(2-3, Serial No. 227).

Hobbs, F., & Lippman, L. (1990). *Children's well-being: An international comparison*. Washington, DC: U.S. Bureau of the Census.

Kagan, S. L., Powell, D. R., Weissbourd, B., & Zigler, E. F. (Eds.). (1987). *America's family support programs: Perspectives and prospects*. New Haven, CT: Yale University Press.

Kamerman, S. B., & Hayes, C. D. (Eds.). (1982). *Families that work: Children in a changing world*. Washington, DC: National Academy Press.

Kamerman, S. B., & Kahn, A. J. (1988). Social policy and children in the United States and Europe. In J. L. Palmer, T. Smeeding, & B. B. Torrey (Eds.), *The vulnerable* (pp. 351–380). Washington, DC: Urban Institute Press.

Lamb, M., & Malkin, J. (1986). Development of social expectations in distress-relief sequences: A longitudinal study. *International Journal of Child Behavioral Development, 9,* 235–249.

Smeeding, T., Torrey, B. B., & Rein, M. (1988). Patterns of income and poverty: The economic status of children and the elderly in eight countries. In J. L. Palmer, T. Smeeding, & B. B. Torrey (Eds.), *The vulnerable* (pp. 89–119). Washington, DC: Urban Institute Press.

Sorrentino, C. (1990). The changing family in international perspective. *Monthly Labor Review, 113,* 41–58.

Tocqueville, A. de. (1961). *Democracy in America.* New York: Schocken Books. (Original work published 1835)

Towson, M. (1985). *Paid parental leave policies: An international comparison.* Ottawa, Canada: Task Force on Child Care.

United Nations. (1957–1990). *Demographic yearbook.* New York: Author.

United Nations. Department of International Economic and Social Affairs. (1988). *Adolescent reproductive behavior.* New York: Author.

U.S. Department of Labor, Bureau of Labor Statistics. (1990). *Handbook of labor statistics.* Washington, DC: U.S. Government Printing Office.

Weissbourd, B., & Kagan, S. L. (1989). Family support programs: Catalysts for change. *American Journal of Orthopsychiatry, 59*(1), 20–31.

Zigler, E. F., & Muenchow, S. (1992). *Head Start: The inside story of America's most successful educational experiment.* New York: Basic Books.

Zigler, E. F., & Styfco, S. J. (Eds.). (1993). *Head Start and beyond: A national plan for extended childhood intervention.* New Haven, CT: Yale University Press.

Zigler, E. F., & Valentine, J. (Eds.). (1979). *Project Head Start: A legacy of the War on Poverty.* New York: Free Press.

$$=== \quad \square \ 2 \ \square \quad ===$$

The Evolution of
the Family Resource Movement

Bernice Weissbourd

The twenty-year history of family resource and support reflects the character of family support itself. Flexible and responsive, it is constantly and deliberately evolving in new dimensions and in greater depth. Initially signifying a multitude of diverse programs based on a defined set of assumptions, today these assumptions undergird new orientations, implemented in a vast array of services and policies focused on children and families.

The purpose of this chapter is to give a brief overview of the origins of family support and its growth since the first programs appeared, in the middle 1970s. It will describe the status of family support today in its multilevel forms and discuss its influence on state and national policies, as well as the expansion and refinement of its principles. The chapter will conclude with questions and issues that emerge out of the experience of the past.

Past As Prologue

The richness of the variation in composition and focus of family resource and support programs today may be attributed to its roots. The parent-education movement of the early twentieth

28

century contributed to family support an appreciation for the role that scientific knowledge can play in creating a better understanding of child development and of the usefulness of making that information available to parents.

The practices of self-help, which originated in postindustrial England and later created such organizations as Alcoholics Anonymous, the American Association for Retarded Children, and the United Cerebral Palsy Foundation had a significant impact as well. Based on the simple but important concept that supportive connections established among people with common issues and concerns enhance an individual's coping abilities and facilitate a sense of empowerment, the self-help philosophy is reflected in the family support program's emphasis on fostering peer support.

The emphasis that is placed in family resource and support programs on advocating for families in the context of the communities in which they live originated in the Settlement House Movement of the early 1900s. Settlement houses were described at the time as an "experimental effort to aid in the solution of the social and industrial problems which are engendered by the modern conditions of life" (Addams, 1910/1972, p. 125). This description is surprisingly applicable to contemporary family resource and support programs, in which a primary focus lies in creating a spirit of community and in becoming the axis around which community-based advocacy efforts may revolve.

The spirit of the 1960s and the social service initiatives that came out of that time were influential in fostering the climate in which these separate strands of thinking came together and ultimately spawned the first family resource and support programs (Zigler & Freedman, 1987). For many, the grand-scale antipoverty programs instituted by the Kennedy and Johnson administrations had offered hope for the reclamation of vast numbers of American children who were being lost to poverty, ill health, and educational failure.

A number of program designs of that period, including Head Start and Legal Aid, made a significant impact and may be credited with contributing to progress made in the ongoing struggle to combat the dire effects of poverty (Edelman & Radin, 1991). Although greatly improved from the pre-1960s era, however, services for families had, for the most part, retained a deficit-oriented, narrow approach. Except for the highly successful Head Start program, with its well-developed parent-involvement component (Zigler & Freedman), services still tended to treat rather than prevent illness and difficulties. They continued to serve individual members of families, disregarding the role played by the family as a unit, and they rarely addressed the impact that the community has on family functioning. Largely categorical in their approach, service providers had little or no contact with one another, even when individuals or families had established ongoing relationships with several institutions. The system was a maze of isolated programs, both too complex to administer effectively and too simple in conception. There seemed to be a program for each narrowly defined need (Weissbourd, 1991).

The family resource and support programs that emerged across the country during the 1970s responded to lessons learned from Head Start, as well as to concerns about the failure of other systems to adequately reach and serve children and families. They were fueled by new realities. Primary among these was burgeoning knowledge about the competencies of infants, coupled with research findings indicating the significance of the years from birth to age three. Head Start, like most other programs for young children at that time, opened its doors to three- and four-year-olds. Few services existed for children under three years of age, despite strong evidence of the positive effects of early intervention from such early childhood efforts as the Syracuse University Family Development Research Project, the Perry Preschool Program, and the Yale University Child Study Center (Schorr & Schorr, 1988). It became increasingly clear that it was possible to stem the tide of dysfunction by moving from a remedial, crisis-oriented approach to a prevention mode.

Concurrent with these findings was the emergence of an ecological theory of human development. First enunciated by Bronfenbrenner, the theory views the interrelationship between child, family, community, and the larger society as the point of departure for understanding human development. In this context, the significance of cultural, racial, and socioeconomic characteristics of the community, as well as the policies of the nation, are factors to be included in considering the determinants of family functioning (Bronfenbrenner, 1979).

Equally influential in spawning a new type of program were the urgent needs that surfaced as by-products of demographic change (mothers joining the work force in numbers not seen since World War II, skyrocketing rates of divorce, growing numbers of children in poverty, and an increase in the incidence of teenage pregnancy). The suddenness of the changes inspired an ongoing dialogue about the resilience of the American family, abounding with questions about whether it would survive its own transformation.

The family resource and support programs that resulted were an innovation in services with roots in the past, designed to meet new social conditions and implement new understandings of child and family development. As such, they were a unique product of their environment. The first programs were small and operated on minimal budgets. They appeared in all types of communities, from rural to suburban to urban, in settings as varied as storefronts, churches, and people's homes. The families who became involved were just as likely to be middle-class or white families as to be poor or minority-group families. The sources of funding for programs ranged just as broadly, although the original programs were funded from private and corporate foundations, rather than from public sources (Weissbourd, 1987). In response to new information about the significance of the years from birth to age three, and in response to the fact that very few programs were available for that population, the majority of the early programs targeted that age group.

The interest in and rapid proliferation of programs had not been predicted by the pioneers in family resource and support, who throughout the country were shaping programs to fit their own communities. The manner in which the concepts of family resource and support were embraced in the broader arenas was an indication of the determination of professionals, parents, and policy makers to find relevant and effective ways to deal with the continuing crisis in families and the parallel erosion of supportive communities. The early literature on family support has documented the strength of the perceived need, the enthusiasm over emerging family support programs, and the energy invested in program development (Center for the Study of Social Policy, 1990).

Some of the original programs were more focused on parent education, others on home visiting or support groups. Still others preferred the flexibility of a drop-in model. Typically, the demands of the families that were served encouraged expansion of whichever program design was operative, causing it to become more comprehensive and to offer a broader range of activities and resources.

By the early 1980s, the family resource and support concept had become widespread enough to warrant a conference, called by Family Focus in 1981. Over 300 attendees gathered in Evanston, Illinois, to share information and perspectives on the work they were doing. At the close of the conference, attendees voted to establish the Family Resource Coalition (FRC), a membership organization that remains today at the core of national networking and advocacy efforts for family resource and support. FRC houses the National Resource Center for Family Support Programs (NRC/FSP), which makes up-to-date information about family support available to policy makers, program providers, researchers, academicians, and the media.

Within approximately ten years of the time when the first programs were conceived, family resource and support began to set the tone for the changes in services, systems, and policies that are taking place today. Then as now, a transformation in approach was articulated through principles that, although variously defined, are founded on basic assumptions:

- The most effective approach to families emanates from a perspective of health and well-being.
- The capacity of parents to raise their children effectively is influenced by their own development.
- Child-rearing techniques and values are influenced by cultural and community values and mores.

- Social support networks are essential to family well-being.
- Information about child development enhances parents' capacity to respond appropriately to their children.
- Families that receive support become empowered to advocate on their own behalf.

In every instance, the family resource and support perspective underscores the importance of the fact that a child's sense of self is inextricably tied to that of his or her parent and that the quality of the parent's life is affected by the resources and environment of the community in which the family lives.

The confusion often engendered by what is now called a *movement* results from an essential requirement for family support: that it be driven not only by the needs but also by the desires and wishes of the families involved. If parents are regarded as resources in this way, programs will inevitably vary and defy neat, clean categories. Confusion dissipates once it is understood that it is considered a strength to incorporate, rather than ignore, the variability that naturally occurs in families and communities.

Viewing change in programs and systems not as an end but as a process through which support is given to families also allows us to see the continually emerging and inventive characteristics that constitute the mosaic of family support. The process is dynamic, always changing to fit new conditions and circumstances, the principles lay the foundation, and the goal remains constant: to empower the family as its own unit, so that it can support and enable the growth and development of its children (Kagan & Shelley, 1987).

The State of the Art Today

Statistics show that during the last decade, the quality of life of the American family has continued to erode. Two million children have joined the ranks of the American poor (National Commission on Children [NCC], 1991); the proportion of children living in single-parent families has soared to over 25 percent (NCC, 1991); and the number of reported cases of child abuse and neglect has increased by 300 percent (Family Resource

Coalition, n.d.[b]). Accounts from staff members throughout the social services indicate that ever-increasing numbers of families find themselves unable to cope without support and assistance. Meeting the needs of these families has become increasingly difficult, and particularly so now that continual budget retrenchment causes the resources that would normally go to families to be overburdened and in short supply. The response of social service administrators and practitioners, as well as policy makers at the state and federal levels, has been to explore new solutions.

Because family resource and support programs and principles represent a promising approach, states across the nation, beginning in the middle 1980s, gravitated toward them. As a result, state officials, many of whom merely a decade ago would not have been able to define the term *family support,* became staunch advocates of the family resource and support movement (Farrow, 1991).

Family resource and support initiatives at the state level rely strongly on the use of collaboration as a tool to increase the capability of the social service network. According to Bruner, collaboration is "a process to reach goals that cannot be achieved acting singly" (1991, p. 6). Focusing their efforts on creating a more collaborative and thereby comprehensive system of services for families, a number of states have established government-sponsored organizations to serve as vehicles through which information among service providers can be readily exchanged, joint planning can be accomplished, and responsibility for the delivery of services can be shared.

New York state has been a pioneer in this area, having legislated the establishment of the New York State Council on Children and Families in 1977. Its members, including commissioners and the directors of all of the major state-level human services agencies, work toward increasing collaboration and reducing fragmentation throughout the statewide social service system. The states of New Mexico and Colorado followed suit by establishing, respectively, the Children's Continuum task force, in 1989, and the Commission on Families and Children, in 1990.

Similar initiatives now exist at the city level as well. Kids-Place was jointly founded in 1983 by the City of Seattle, the Junior League of Seattle, and the YMCA. Now being replicated in several other urban areas, its intent is to make urban communities more suitable environments for children.

It is estimated that at the state and local level, there are from forty to seventy-five other major collaborative initiatives under way and hundreds of smaller ones, all of which are utilizing family resource and support concepts to integrate the diverse available services and respond to needs more adequately (Ooms, 1992).

There has been an increase in the number of programs implemented at the state level that target specific populations. The Kentucky Education Reform Act, passed in 1990, established family resource and support centers in elementary schools and youth service centers in middle and high schools that serve low-income students (Family Resource Coalition, n.d.[a]). In Maryland, the needs of adolescent parents are addressed through Family Support Centers, a network of thirteen programs administered by Friends of the Family to provide resources and support to families with young children. Hawaii's highly acclaimed Healthy Start program assists families across the state in finding access to screening and assessment for infants and young children, primary health care, parental support resources, and parent education.

Funding initiatives at both the state level and the local level, the Child and Adolescent Service System Program (CASSP), administered by the National Center for Mental Health Services under the auspices of the federal Substance Abuse and Mental Health Services Administration, utilizes a community-based family support approach in providing multiagency services for children and adolescents who have severe emotional disturbances.

At the federal level, family resource and support principles have been instrumental in the process of reconfiguring many of the projects administered through the Department of Health and Human Services. That influence is most evident in the Runaway and Homeless Youth program, Head Start's Parent and Child Centers and Family Service Centers, the Comprehensive Child Development Program, and Healthy Start. The family resource and support orientation has also shaped the Office of Community Services' Homeless Families Support Services Demonstration Program, which was recently funded at a level that will allow twenty-five to thirty grants to be administered, an allocation totaling $5.5 million.

Representing a landmark in the family resource and support movement, in 1990 the first federal legislation was enacted to support state networks of family resource and support programs in local communities. To date, $4.91 million accompanies the legislation. The next piece of legislation was a major thrust forward. Part of the Clinton administration's 1993 budget agreement allots $879 million over five years to fund a capped entitlement for family preservation and family support services. It will allow states to operate programs on both ends of the continuum: crisis care for families at risk, and preventive care for all families.

Many private foundations are supporting the efforts of family resource and support programs by funding research as well as local and statewide initiatives. The recent Pew Charitable Trusts' Children's Initiative serves as an example. In 1992, grants were distributed to Florida, Georgia, Kentucky, Rhode Island, and Minnesota: "The overarching goal of the initiative is to ensure that children reach school age healthy, safe and prepared to learn, and that they are given the opportunity to complete their school years as free as possible from barriers to learning and healthy development" (Leiderman, Reveal, Rosewater, Stephens, and Wolf, 1991, p. ii).

This proliferation of programs and services suggests a potential gap in capacity to implement them effectively. There is concern that too few people are trained to function in the nonprescriptive, flexible, community-responsive settings necessary for program success. Awareness of this problem has led to the initiation of multiple training programs aimed at workers in state systems serving children and families, as well as at staff in local programs. In addition, preservice training courses are increasingly being introduced into the curricula of schools that prepare professionals to work in the social services. Pioneers in this area include the School of Social Service Administration at the University of Chicago; Nova University's Center for the Advancement of Education, in Florida; and the Department of Child Development and Family Studies at Purdue University. Another important indication of the professionalization of the family resource and support field is the launching of the Family Resource Coalition's Best Practices Project. Funded by the A. L. Mailman Family Foundation, this project will generate a blueprint for professional standardization by providing a definitive statement to be used as the basis for establishing universal standards of quality for program operation and practitioner training.

The constructs of family resource and support constitute a fundamental change in the traditional belief system, reflecting a change from assuming that the role of government is to be a resource for families in crisis to recognizing the responsibility of our society to promote the well-being of all families. The extent to which such values have been adopted across the political spectrum is exemplified throughout the bipartisan report of the National Commission on Children, which recommends "that federal, state, and local governments, in partnership with private community organizations, develop and expand community-based family support programs to provide parents with the knowledge, skills, and support they need to raise their children" (1991, p. 277).

Evolution of the Principles

As previously stated, family resource and support principles were initially formulated as a basis for program development, and they served as the binding force for a wide diversity of program forms. Today these principles delineate an approach to families that has become basic to the effort in many states to reconstitute service systems. At the national level, family resource and support principles are the tenets that underlie the mandate to integrate a component for family support into other service initiatives.

Programs continue to evolve in form and content, and principles continue to evolve in meaning. Their evolution reflects experiences in program development, as well as lessons learned from relationships with parents and with the communities in which they live. The following are a few examples that delineate an ongoing process in which the principles assume greater meaning.

From Personal to Public Advocacy

From the start, there was recognition of the role that state and national policies played in enhancing or hindering a family's capacity to function well, but programs generally considered the policy-making arena to be outside their jurisdiction. In keeping with this point of view, organizational boundaries defined the roles of programs. For example, staff members would assist a family in finding housing but would not consider it their role to initiate efforts to improve housing conditions in the overall community.

The situations repeatedly confronting staff, in which their efforts to support participants were thwarted either by bureaucratic barriers in the human service system or by substandard living conditions in communities, motivated the rethinking of their roles. Program providers have become active in their local communities, to make the systems more responsive to and respectful of participants' needs. Offices such as the Problem Resolution Office within KidsPEPP, in Chicago, were established to function as a link between program providers and system agents.

As providers have become involved on a broader scale, influencing both policies and service systems at the state and national levels, there has been a merging of the boundaries between programs and policies. Programs alone cannot remedy all the ills of our society (Zigler & Freedman, 1987), but personal advocacy — assisting individual families in getting their needs met — is no longer the sole advocacy function. The recognized interrelatedness of programs and policies motivates activity in the public policy arena.

As staff members assume advocacy roles in relation to communities and to other service providers, parents become more actively involved as well. At the legislative level, it is commonly mandated that parents participate in the decision-making process in programs related to children and families. At the community level, parents have organized through such groups as Head Start Parent Association, Parent Action, and the national PTA, which has recently become more policy-oriented, to ensure that they will have a voice in policies that affect their children. Since family resource and support programs represent an ecological approach, the movement toward policy advocacy can be seen as a natural development. The full strength of public advocacy on the part of providers and parents has yet to unfold.

From Community Linking to Community Building

With principles enunciating the vital role that the community plays in influencing the quality of life of its families, a major priority for family resource pioneers was to establish linkages between themselves and other resources that were available for families. Being *community-linked* meant that community members who represented every aspect of community life were invited to participate, often as advisory-board members or representatives on steering committees, as staff members, or as program volunteers. It also meant that, in a reciprocal manner, members of the family resource program team became involved in neighborhood task forces, agency and school boards, and family-related local events. It was through this web of relationships that programs were able to make effective referrals and keep abreast of community issues that might affect families.

In the early days, such relationships appeared to serve programs well. As family resource programs and ideas found acceptance, however, staff members increasingly recognized that, in addition to their linkage role, they could play a leadership role in developing a collaborative effort based on a mission to make the entire community work for its families. By utilizing the alliances already established with family-serving institutions and parents, providers have created new resources or upgraded established ones.

In this process of building the community, family resource and support programs, besides acting as initiators of a collaborative system of services and resources for families, have often functioned as the baseline — the point of entry for a tier of preventive services, including early intervention programs and programs for families in crisis. In either case, the intent was to extend well beyond the initial goal of establishing linkages and to work instead to build a comprehensive community of support for parents.

This vastly expanded approach has its roots in the Saul Alinsky–style community organizing of the 1960s, which was built on the premises that the potential for power and leadership already exists in poor and disenfranchised communities, and that the process of securing a more equitable distribution of resources must include efforts to mobilize those strengths (Alinsky, 1969). Although the approaches and lessons learned during that period do inform the community building that takes place today, the goals differ. Today's efforts constitute a process by which institutions, agencies, and leaders, together with families, rally around the goal of improving the lives of families and children by encouraging the community to function in a family-supportive way. Given that family resource and support is based on the premise of universality, this approach to community building applies to the manner in which services and resources should be organized and rendered in every community, regardless of its racial, ethnic, or socioeconomic composition. The assumptions of prevention, cultural responsiveness, and comprehensiveness in family resource and support underlie all efforts at community building, and family resource and support personnel have become key players in that process.

Redefining Empowerment

Closely connected with the acceptance of family support principles in the larger domain of systems and policies is the expanded concept of empowerment. Starting from an understanding that parents become empowered through a program environment in which they are esteemed and involved, we define the term *empowerment* today in a broad context, as "an intentional, ongoing process centered in the local community, involving mutual respect, critical reflection, caring, and group participation, through which people lacking an equal share of valued resources gain greater access to and control over those resources" (The Cornell Empowerment Group, cited in Cochran, 1990, p. 53). This definition may seem particularly related to disenfranchised populations, but it applies to all people, since all are "disadvantaged by the way that society is currently structured" (p. 54). The full measure of empowerment, as now defined, is not only the extent to which people are enabled to feel competent and to advocate on their own behalf but also the power that people can wield to facilitate change in their communities and in the nation.

From Prevention to Promotion

The prevention orientation of the original programs, while it enabled them to gain ready acceptance within the traditional social services, also has tended to perpetuate an image of family resource and support as a deficit model. The current emphasis is on the promotion of *family well-being,* and on the necessity of moving from a prevention model to a promotion model. Dunst, Trivette, and Thompson (1990) define the latter as "the enhancement and optimization of positive functioning" (p. 30). This change in perspective creates the requirement for a similar change in understanding the role of society in relation to families. That role is based on two premises: that assisting families prevents problems and is cost-effective, and that promoting the well-being of families is an inherent responsibility of a democracy.

Moving from prevention to promotion highlights one further evolution that has occurred in relation to the principles of family resource and support. In a period when many sectors in our society are decrying the loss of values and the decline in moral behavior, the family resource and support movement has assumed the dimensions of a value system. Its commitment to caring for others, and to building strong and vibrant communities that provide a healthy environment for children and families, resonates with these concerns. It is not accidental that the African proverb "It takes a whole village to raise a child" has been embraced by children's advocates nationwide. The proverb, which so eloquently expresses the responsibility of society to care for all its children, directly contradicts the focus on individualism that remains so prevalent in our country. In the present state of anxiety over lack of commitment and lack of common values, the concept is embraced by conservatives and liberals alike, and it serves as a common ground for the reform of systems and institutions to better serve children and families.

Putting Principles into Practice: Some Issues

This evolution, in which the application of family support principles has been broadened, is indicative of expanding directions, but it does not imply accomplished ends. Rather, it is evident that, in growth processes, emerging problems require attention. One such problem is associated with implementing the principle of creating community-based programs, which by definition have broad agendas. How prepared are the staff members of community-based programs to deal with multiproblem families? How can family resource programs work in collaboration with more intensive services, without becoming labeled as therapy programs? How can centers that serve communities with a wide range of economic backgrounds help families find common ground?

Another issue, continually identified and discussed, is related to the principle of working with parents as partners. Putting this principle into practice has unearthed barriers that are a result of the biases that professionals hold toward parents, and vice versa (Powell, 1989). It will be important to learn how to discuss biases with staff and parents alike, and to talk about program practices that can be developed to dissolve those biases.

Still another problem is that parents are sometimes placed in decision-making roles for which they are unprepared and inexperienced, and so the parents are already programmed for defeat. It may be essential for programs to incorporate leadership training, to ensure that parents will be equipped to handle their new roles. A related concern is the fact that most staff members have had no training or experience in developing partnerships with parents. The delicate balance — between being both a partner and a source of information and advice — is difficult to maintain.

There are great complexities inherent in efforts to change the status quo. Implementing change is difficult; the more pervasive its goal, the more complex its process. To serve families better, agencies are urged to become less bureaucratic and more participatory, to move from being problem-oriented to being strength-oriented, and to begin addressing the needs of the entire family instead of treating singular concerns. To make progress in this direction, we must overcome several barriers. Staff people need to give up their resistance to changing old patterns of functioning. Administrators must learn to rely on inclusiveness rather than exclusiveness as a mode of management. Moreover, there are ever-present biases that militate, individually and collectively, against our having confidence that most people, given the opportunity, can draw on competencies that will serve them well.

Even a brief overview of two decades of the family resource and support movement will reveal its rapid movement from an isolated, local orientation to a national orientation. Such widespread acceptance cannot be taken at face value, however. Family resource and support, although considerably more familiar than it used to be, is still the new kid on the block, dealing with the problems that arise from entrenched ways of thinking. Moreover, as a nascent movement, family resource and support requires further analysis and conceptualization.

Proponents of family support are faced with persistent pressure from policy makers to validate their commitment. Those who seek more data to inform their decisions are making specific demands. Primary among these is that family support define itself. Family resource and support principles have been defined over the years (Dunst, Trivette, & Thompson, 1990; Pooley & Littell, 1986; Weiss & Halpern, 1991; Weissbourd, 1990); the fact that any confusion persists indicates that the communication is still unclear. Is family support a program with specific characteristics? Is it a set of principles applicable to all social service delivery systems? Is it an approach? Or is it all of the above? The fact that the term *family resource and support* covers such a broad area accounts for some of the difficulty of providing a simple definition. But the definition does need refinement, not only for the purpose of explaining the field to others but also (and just as important) for the purpose of fostering a better understanding and a wider consensus on the part of those involved in family resource and support.

Decision makers are also asking family support to prove its effectiveness. There is a steadily growing number of evaluations of family resource and support programs, but nagging questions remain. They are primarily related to whether appropriate measures have been devised for evaluating programs as flexible and comprehensive as these are. How do we know that family resource and support programs make a difference? Our ability to answer this repeated and urgent question may be a decisive factor in their broad acceptance. Our society does not assume that support for families is a given. Definitive proof of these programs' value is now essential to their growth.

The past and the present alike clearly show us that family support will continue to evolve. To date, its essential characteristics have been maintained. The evolving nature of family support defies imagination yet alerts proponents to the fact that new issues and problems will inevitably arise. It engenders excitement while cautioning us against promising too much. Program dimensions will be altered as demographics change, as communities either develop or deteriorate, and as public policies define a structural framework for family support. States now serving as laboratories for developing family-supportive systems are positioning themselves to become models for other states that are seeking new directions in providing services to families. Each state's plans will necessarily develop according to the state's particular structure, priorities, and strengths.

The evolution of family support on the national scale may depend less on the characteristics of flexibility and responsiveness than on willingness to embrace the concepts of prevention and society's responsibility for promoting the health of all children and families. Such a shift in national thinking may depend on the extent to which our field's effectiveness has been measured, or on the extent to which the budgetary value of preventive services has been determined. Ideally, this shift should reflect the understanding that all families both need and deserve support.

Advocacy for family-supportive approaches throughout service delivery systems and national policies represents the recognition that reciprocal relationships among programs, systems, and policies parallel the ecological approach to children, families, communities, and society. Acknowledging such reciprocal relationships sets the framework for evaluation and for the implementation of change. If we can judge from the past, there is every reason to believe that family support premises and principles will continue to inform new directions in program and policies at every level, from building strong communities to setting national priorities.

References

Addams, J. (1972). *The spirit of youth and the city streets.* Urbana: University of Illinois Press. (Original work published 1910)

Alinsky, S. (1969). *Reveille for radicals.* New York: Vintage Books.

Bronfenbrenner, U. (1979). *The ecology of human development: Experiments by nature and design.* Cambridge, MA: Harvard University Press.

Bruner, C. (1991). *Thinking collaboratively: Ten questions and answers to help policy makers improve children's services.* Washington, DC: Education and Human Services Consortium.

Center for the Study of Social Policy. (1990, April). *Helping families grow strong: New directions in public policy.* Paper presented at the Colloquium on Public Policy and Family Support of the Family Resource Coalition, Chicago.

Cochran, M. (1990). Personal social networks as a focus of support. In D. G. Unger & D. R. Powell (Eds.), *Families as nurturing systems: Support across the life span* (pp. 45–68). New York: Haworth Press.

Dunst, C. J., Trivette, C. M., & Thompson, R. B. (1990).
New directions for family resource and support programs.
In D. G. Unger & D. R. Powell (Eds.), *Families as nurturing
systems: Support across the life span* (pp. 19–44). New York:
Haworth Press.

Edelman, P. B., & Radin, B. A. (1991). *Serving children and families effectively: How the past can help chart the future.* Washington, DC: Education and Human Services Consortium.

Family Resource Coalition. (n.d.[a]). *Creating new schools.* Chicago: Author.

Family Resource Coalition. (n.d.[b]). *Family support programs and
the prevention of child abuse.* Fact sheet. Chicago: Author.

Farrow, F. (1991). The view from the states: Family resource
programs and state policy. *Family Resource Coalition Report,
10*(1), pp. 12, 13.

Kagan, S. L., & Shelley, A. (1987). The promise and problems of family support programs. In S. L. Kagan, D. R.
Powell, B. Weissbourd, and E. F. Zigler (Eds.), *America's family support programs: Perspectives and prospects* (pp. 3–18). New
Haven, CT: Yale University Press.

Leiderman, S., Reveal, E., Rosewater, A., Stephens, S., &
Wolf, W. (1991, November). *The children's initiative: Making
systems work.* Bala Cynwyd, PA: Center for Assessment and
Policy Development.

National Commission on Children. (1991). *Beyond rhetoric: A new
American agenda for children and families.* Washington, DC: U.S.
Government Printing Office.

Ooms, T. (1992). *Coordination, collaboration, integration: Strategies
for serving families more effectively: Part 2. State and local initiatives.*
Family Impact Seminar with Consortium on Family Organizations.

Pooley, L., & Littell, J. (1986). *Family resource program builder:
Blueprints for designing and operating programs for parents.* Chicago:
Family Resource Coalition.

Powell, D. R. (1989). *Families and early childhood programs.* Washington, DC: National Association for the Education of Young
Children.

Schorr, L. B., & Schorr, D. (1988). *Within our reach: Breaking
the cycle of disadvantage.* New York: Doubleday.

Weiss, H., & Halpern, R. (1991). *Community-based family support and education programs: Something old or something new?* New York: National Center for Children in Poverty, Columbia University.

Weissbourd, B. (1987). A brief history of family support programs. In S. L. Kagan, D. R. Powell, B. Weissbourd, & E. F. Zigler (Eds.), *America's family support programs: Perspectives and prospects* (pp. 38–56). New Haven, CT: Yale University Press.

Weissbourd, B. (1990). Family resource and support programs: Changes and challenges in human services. In D. G. Unger & D. R. Powell (Eds.), *Families as nurturing systems: Support across the life span* (pp. 69–89). New York: Haworth Press.

Weissbourd, R. (1991). *Making the system work for poor children.* Cambridge, MA: John F. Kennedy School of Government, Malcolm Wiener Center for Social Policy, Harvard University.

Zigler, E. F., & Freedman, J. (1987). Head Start: A pioneer of family support. In S. L. Kagan, D. R. Powell, B. Weissbourd, & E. F. Zigler (Eds.), *America's family support programs: Perspectives and prospects* (pp. 57–78). New Haven, CT: Yale University Press.

□ Part Two □

INSTITUTIONAL CHANGE AND FAMILY SUPPORT

□ 3 □

Home and School

The Unresolved Relationship

Barbara T. Bowman

Ever since *A Nation At Risk* (National Commission on Excellence, 1983) called attention to the crisis in American education, an intensive national debate about what is wrong with schools has preoccupied politicians, parents, and educators. While some researchers have noted that the so-called crisis was not caused by deterioration of public education—which has held its own and improved the outcomes for many children (Cawelti, 1993; Zill & Rogers, 1988)—few Americans believe that schools are functioning as effectively as they must to meet future social and economic challenges. The effort to improve education has moved in two directions. One has focused on the internal functioning of schools—teacher certification, teachers' working conditions and autonomy, principals' management, curricula, teaching methods, and assessment practices. The other has seen the problem as tied to the relationship between home and school. Followers of the second direction see a need to reform home and school relationships in order to improve children's achievement.

The connection between parents and schools has deep roots in American education, and the perception of shared responsibility is reflected in community control of funding and school policy. But the joint venture often has been uneasy as

51

each party has struggled to define, in its own terms, the other's responsibilities. The issue, depending on which side asks the question, is either "How can schools get families to support their values and practices?" or "How can families get schools to be responsive to their needs and aspirations?" Today, restructuring the relationship between schools and families is high on many lists of "things to do" to fix schools. Increasing numbers of Americans have revised the question so that it asks what the whole community needs to do for families to ensure children's healthy development and school success.

Family Support Programs

One of the more powerful models for defining the family-school relationship is *family support*. More a movement than a program, it has been described as "different in character, orientation, and mission from other school/family programs" (Kagan, Powell, Weissbourd, & Zigler, 1987, p. 177). Weissbourd (1990) defined *family support* as a set of principles (rather than a list of activities) that includes the following:

- Promoting family health and well-being
- Inspiring parental confidence and competence
- Responding to family cultural preferences and values
- Providing concrete help for real-life problems
- Giving information tailored to parental needs
- Empowering relationships between individuals and between families and helping institutions
- Encouraging voluntary participation by parents

Central to the mission of family support is its stance as a prevention strategy whose purpose is to optimize the development of children in all domains of their lives. The goal is building healthy families that will raise healthy children, rather than using resources to repair damage once it has occurred — a more expensive and less successful strategy (National Resource Center for Family Support Programs, n.d.).

In the family support movement, families are viewed as

the dominant support for children's development. Partnerships between families and helping agencies — including schools — must acknowledge families' primacy. Family support is based on the premise that effective parents must have their needs met for work, for a rewarding and supporting social life, and for a healthy self-image. It is assumed that if social, economic, mental, or physical stress is too great, parents are distracted from their task of monitoring and assisting their children, which compromises the children's development and education. Families cannot provide the necessary support for their children when their basic socioeconomic and social-emotional needs are unmet (Clark, 1983, p. 209). Circumstances that stress children and families are well known; poverty, poor quality of housing and health care, substance abuse, child abuse, and foster-home placement are among the most important factors. Family support programs help families play their roles by providing whatever services are needed. In some instances, help may consist of providing health, social, and employment services so that parents have the time, energy, and means for parenting. In other instances, help may mean providing information and social activities and encouraging involvement and decision making. Ease of access and coordination among services are important aspects of such programs.

Gaining the cooperation and collaboration of parents is not primarily a function of the activities provided. The family support movement emphasizes that learning is supported through social relationships with emotionally significant people. Program effects are mediated by people, and relationships between program personnel and parents are critical. Social ties are probably the most important predictors of whether a parent program works (Stevens, 1985).

Family support is considered important for all parents — rich or poor, well educated and not, teenagers or middle-aged. The type of support that parents need varies. The Parents as Teachers program, connected to the Missouri public schools, lists among its purposes giving parents increased knowledge of child development and age-appropriate child-rearing practices, enhanced observation skills, and awareness of conditions that affect optimal development (Treffeisen, n.d., p. 11). Activities may involve informal social contacts, life-skills training, information classes, support groups, parent-child groups, family activities, employment training, professional help with mental and physical health problems, informal time with staff members and other parents, information and referral services, crisis intervention or family counseling, and such auxiliary support services as clothing exchanges, emergency food, and transportation.

One of the major principles of family support is cooperative planning. Programs must understand the nature of problems as conceived by the parents before designing services and allocating personnel. Comer (1980) cautions programs against committing "personnel and psychological resources before the nature of the problem is adequately understood" (p. 67), contending that preplanned programs inflexibly imposed on families are likely to encounter resistance from participants. In the family support movement, parents are to be pivotal in defining problems and in designing and implementing services.

Family Support and School Achievement

Although the family support movement has been adamant that all families need support services, parents from low-income groups are often targets for interventions because of the developmental and achievement-related challenges to their children. America's poor, living in cities in the North, rural areas of the South and the Southwest, and reservations throughout the United States, are disproportionately children of color — African American, Hispanic, Native American, and Asian. The poorer school performance of these children is well established, although explanations for their underachievement are controversial and contentious. It is generally agreed, however, that the role of parents (or primary caregivers) is crucial. As in all families, parents are the prime (if not the sole) mediators of children's affective and cognitive development, helping them regulate their behavior and emotions, motivating them to learn, and buffering stress for them (Clark, 1983). Thus parents are frequently at the heart of the services designed to improve the achievement of poor children.

Four themes dominate interpretations of class and caste differences in academic achievement:

1. Characteristics inherent in the child impede learning.
2. Family child-rearing techniques and values conflict with those of the school and interfere with children's acquisition of school-valued knowledge and skills.
3. Discriminatory administrative and teaching practices and inequitable resource allocations place poor and minority children at a disadvantage.
4. School practices and policies, embedded in larger social contexts, have different effects on individuals and groups, depending on their place in the society.

Controversies regarding these themes, having sparked many of the education policy and practice debates of the last fifteen years, deserve attention.

The first theme assumes that there is something amiss in the children themselves to account for their poor academic performance. Genetic inequality in intelligence among groups is one proposal (Jensen, 1969). Most geneticists, however, reject this theory as inconsistent with what is known about inheritance and group differences (Lewontin, 1992). Nevertheless, the belief in genetic inferiority continues to guide the thinking of many Americans about poor and minority children. Low self-esteem in minority children is also postulated as causal because of its positive correlation with school performance. Self-esteem, however, is a poorly defined concept and is evidently responsive to social context. For instance, Spencer (1985) found that young African American children (often cited as lacking in self-esteem) were highly self-valuing within their own families and communities. This suggests that self-esteem is context-specific and not a generic quality in the children themselves. Nonetheless, many school programs are designed to raise self-esteem and often encourage parents to use praise as positive reinforcement, on the assumption that if children feel better about themselves, they will perform better in school.

The second theme explains achievement by focusing on

the life-style of poor and minority groups. Low socioeconomic status correlates with high levels of community violence, unemployment, underemployment, family dissolution, and cultural and personal devaluation. Poor parents are viewed as especially in need of support programs because they have fewer material resources on which to draw and are often exposed to "tremendous psychic overload" (Clark, 1983). Therefore, they are less able to buffer their children's negative experiences or endorse those that lead to school success. Life-style characteristics associated with children's school readiness and success include parental aspirations and expectation for achievement, parental strategies for controlling children's behavior, maternal teaching style (affective and contingent), linguistic orientation, beliefs about the causes of children's success and failure in school, children's home environment (as measured by the HOME scale), and family stress and poverty (Becher, 1986; Powell, 1991). Other family factors implicated in children's school performance include such characteristics as divorce, adolescent and out-of-wedlock child rearing, and maternal employment. These factors have not proved very robust, however, since African American youth, who have had the highest increase in the incidence of such factors in their lives over the past twenty years, have improved their school performance in the same time period (Zill & Rogers, 1988). Nor is poverty alone a consistent predictor of underachievement in school. Clark (1983) investigated low-income African American families whose children were satisfactory achievers and found some poor families were well able to buffer the effects of poverty on their children. Mordkowitz and Ginsburg (1987) describe poor Asian immigrant families whose children were quite successful in school, even though the families did not provide the same types of support typical of middle-class American families. This study suggests that the convergence of family and school values may be more important than the extent of family resources or the specific activities that families engage in with their children. Nevertheless, Kamerman's (1988) comparison between the United States and those European countries that provide family support allocations, free maternal and child health care, job protection, and high-quality day care suggests that early economic supports result in healthier children and greater school success. Family resources, values, structure, and activities all have been found to be related to school achievement, but how these factors may operate to impede children's school achievement is not clear.

The third theme focuses on within-school factors to explain the underachievement of children from low-income and minority families. This research supports the belief that the cure for at-risk children's academic problems lies in how schools are managed. Studies of schools in which poor and minority children were successful indicated that effective schools had strong leadership, well-focused curricula, high expectations for children's achievement, and shared cultural values and practices between school personnel and families. But Chubb and Moe (1990) challenge the view that the quality of the school explains the underachievement of poor and minority children. They point out that when poor children and children of color attend schools similar to those serving white middle-class children, they still achieve less (Zill & Rogers, 1988). This observation has led to two different conclusions: one, that the quality of the school is relatively less important than family life in determining academic achievement (Jencks, 1972), a conclusion that diminishes the importance of instruction in educational performance; and, two, that the culture which children learn at home and in their communities inhibits their ability to learn in school, a conclusion that gives rise to theories of cultural poverty, said to warp children and prevent them from learning normally in school.

The fourth theme proposes more complex models for explaining differences in scholastic performance among children. Schlossman (1978) describes a shift from "naive environmentalism" to a more complex view in which the "whole child," the family, and the community are interwoven in complex patterns. Questioning narrow explanations based on family inadequacies, he contends that such research rests on the incorrect proposition that parents are solely responsible for determining their children's futures. According to a more ecological view, the child, the family, and the school are embedded in relationships within the broader society and derive their meaning from these social and political contexts. Ogbu (1992), for instance, suggests that children's academic performance must be understood against the backdrop of racism in America. He writes that groups denied access to mainstream society (such as African Americans, Native Americans, Puerto Ricans, and Native Hawaiians) may engage in behavior that is oppositional to mainstream institutional values and practices, as a way of defining and defending themselves. To be a school achiever is to identify with the hostile majority and to deny the tie to one's own group. Thus the poorer school performance of children of color may be an identity statement and may not be related to learning ability or to specific characteristics of families or schools.

As is apparent, there is little agreement about the reasons for the poorer achievement of children from low economic circumstances and from particular minorities. Two conclusions can be drawn, however: first, children at risk for failure in school are not an undifferentiated group whose members' individual performance is attributable to all the same causes, since poor and minority children do not do well in school for a variety of different reasons; and, second, the same programs will not successfully address all the various reasons why different children fail in school.

Family Support and Public Schools

Although family support is a mix of activities, four of its major components have roots in the school: parental education, parental empowerment, parental involvement, and systems collaboration. While these activities are not mutually exclusive, they do all have distinguishable histories that affect how family support is conceived and practiced. What follows is a set of brief descriptions of each of these home-school interaction patterns, with a summary of the research on each one's effectiveness, particularly with poor and minority families.

Parental Education

The idea that parents affect their children's development is certainly not new. The belief in the perfectibility of the child through proper parenting was made explicit in the Bible with the admonition to spare the rod and spoil the child. Similarly, the notion of parents' needing expert help to raise their children correctly is also an ancient one: in the first century A.D., Quintilian wrote in *The Teacher's Work* extensive instructions for fathers about how to evaluate and supervise the education of their sons.

The idea of educating parents for child rearing has enjoyed considerable popularity throughout this century. Responding to the shift in developmental thinking that occurred in the 1920s, a shift whereby early childhood (as opposed to adolescence) was visualized as the ideal time to direct children onto the path of personal and social competence (Schlossman, 1976), schools developed programs specifically to influence child rearing. Early childhood programs led the way in focusing on the synergy between children's and parents' education, an idea that is widely accepted in school-based programs today. Mothers in particular were encouraged to observe and learn about children under the guidance of professional teachers, a move that joined parents' and children's education (Schlossman, 1976).

The essence of the parental education approach is to change parenting practices through the dissemination of "scientific" information. Child-rearing practices embedded in family traditions and responding to life challenges, as perceived by community residents, are replaced by a decontextualized and generalized "child development" perspective. Over the last century, the emphasis of scientifically oriented parental education has shifted its focus several times: from physical health (primarily sanitation and inoculations) to mental health (relationships and emotional well-being) at midcentury, and, as the century ends, to cognitive and social development (school success and social tractability).

In many ways, parental education has been a two-edged sword. With parents' child-rearing practices guided over the past century, morbidity and mortality rates for American children have been sharply reduced, and children's educational potential was improved (National Center for Health Statistics, 1984). Unfortunately, however, parental education programs have also subjected parents to a barrage of inconsistent and frequently incorrect advice, which has been sometimes destructive and often expensive. As each of the human sciences and theories of development enjoyed public interest and acclaim, and as new findings were touted in isolation from other factors affecting children's development, parents were sometimes encouraged to jump from one parenting practice to a diametrically opposing one. Advice to parents has been diverse, often contradictory and faddish, and has covered a variety of problems through a variety of formats: child observation, home visits, workshops, study groups, books and periodicals, organizational activities, and lectures.

Early in this century, schools for poor, immigrant, and ill children incorporated "parent work" into their institutional missions, taking the position that parents must be trained to carry out their parenting responsibilities. Unlike schools serving middle-class parents, these programs assumed that poor and culturally diverse families would not voluntarily change their child-rearing practices. Parents in middle-class schools were considered capable of educating themselves and were therefore offered voluntary opportunities for improving their parenting. Economically poor parents were seen as incompetent and as needing more direction from professionals and other representatives of the social elite. This approach to families reflected two interlocking legacies: a view of social pathology as primarily a family responsibility, and of poor and culturally different families as inept and irresponsible. Schlossman (1976) asserts that this perspective is driven by and interpreted to reflect a "conservative social philosophy, a parochial view of the family's relationship to the larger social, economic, political, and historical forces, and a stereotypical image of woman's social role" (p. 794). Many compensatory school programs for poor children continue to reflect this view by requiring economically disadvantaged parents (particularly mothers) to attend child development and family management lectures and workshops.

Some parental education programs have been effective in improving the cognitive functioning of children, as measured by standardized intelligence tests, performance on language tests, school behavior, and performance on standardized achievement tests (Becher, 1986). Changes in parents attributed to parental education include changes in parents' teaching styles, in their

interactions with their children, and in the provision of a stimulating home environment. For instance, children's reading
scores have been shown to increase when their mothers read
to their children and interact with them around reading (Becher,
1986).

Apparently, all the strategies associated with parental education are not equally compelling. Becher (1986) notes, for example, that home visits, in combination with preschool classes,
are more useful than parental meetings and classes; one-to-one
teacher-parent relationships are more effective than groups; and
highly structured programs and teaching techniques are no better
than the encouragement of general styles of interaction. Evidently, parental education that consists solely or primarily of
information transmission is less effective than programs that
combine information with supportive arrangements (Powell,
1991).

It is difficult to separate the effects of each parental education strategy and to judge the relative importance of the kind
and/or amount of information parents receive against the values
of group membership, identification with the group leader, and
concrete help in areas of need. Evidently, simply giving new
information to families does not significantly alter parenting
practices. As Weiss and Rittenburg (1991) conclude, "Research
suggests that programs which simply provide information about
parenting and child development, without interaction with families and provision of other services and supports, are unlikely
to change parenting practices and lead to enhanced child development" (p. 5).

Nevertheless, many people are enthusiastic supporters of
classes for parents. Social planners are often anxious to find better (cheaper) ways to change educational outcomes for children
than those that require restructuring schools, providing supportive services, and/or changing society. Others may seek to avoid
the blame for children's educational failure by placing the responsibility on the children's parents. Schlossman (1978) accounts
for the popularity of parental education programs by citing the
fact that they displace accountability for children's academic
failure from the "professional educator to the poverty parent"

(p. 790). By telling parents how best to raise their children, the schools (and society) transfer the onus of responsibility to those parents who fail to do as they are told. Telling poor and minority parents how to raise their children continues to be one of the most popular of the home-school patterns, despite the lack of evidence for its effectiveness.

Parental Empowerment

Another component of family support is best described as parental empowerment. According to this view, parents — as advocates for their children — must insist that schools be responsive to them. Two somewhat different positions have developed from this perspective: the parent as monitor, and the parent as sole determiner of educational policies and practices.

The first path, parent as monitor, defines the role of parents as working with the school to determine their children's educational arrangements. Parents are encouraged to oversee their children's schooling, to guarantee that they get the quality of education due them. Ferguson and Mazin (1989), subscribing to this position, write, "Your child's education begins with you. You have the right, obligation, and ability to see that your child gets a good education" (p. 5). The role of the parent as monitor has been institutionalized in special-education legislation, which requires parents to approve services for their special-needs children before the local school's plans can be implemented. A number of national parent organizations, the PTA among them (Cutright, 1989), have been in the forefront of the effort to help parents monitor school services and lobby for change.

Other advocates of parental power assert that the problem with schools cannot be cured by cooperating with them. Chubb and Moe (1990) believe that the failure of schools to adequately educate children is the result of an imbalance of power between parents (who have the best interests of their children at heart) and the bureaucratic school (motivated by its own self-interest). Subscribing to this position, Walberg, Bakalis, Bart, and Baer (1988) contend, "If a mechanism existed whereby parents could choose their child's school, individual schools that were failing to provide a safe and positive learning environment would lose students to those that did. Soon a bottom line would emerge for these schools and they would have to begin listening to parents' suggestions in order to get back their enrollment" (p. 70). According to this view, the professionalization and bureaucratization of public schools have shattered the primacy of parents in the school-home paradigm, and parents must regain their power if schools are to be transformed into effective educational institutions. Citing Coleman, who found that private schools are more effective than public schools in teaching "the typical student," Chubb and Moe (1990) conclude that parental control of resources, through parents' selection of the schools their children attend, will force schools to be responsive in the marketplace as they compete for parental tax dollars. Chubb and Moe envision this change in the parent-school relationship as resulting in improved schools, since "democratic control" (through elected representatives) "normally produces ineffective schools" (p. 227).

Critics of this view believe "choice" solutions favor those who are already educated and powerful, because they are in the best position to make informed choices. Further, choice options that include the use of private schools are criticized as undemocratic, because they would let well-to-do parents use exclusive educational institutions for their children, while poor children would attend less well supported schools.

Closely allied to this position is one put forward by some minority groups (primarily African American, Hispanic, and Native American) who portray schools as institutional perpetrators of society's injustices. They contend that schools duplicate society as they reenact the relationship of powerless minorities to the majority. The power of the school is used to reinforce the role of these groups in society: prejudicial and discriminatory educational policies and practices reproduce the status quo and impede children's learning. Minority children's academic failure is accounted for by the power disparity between their communities and the social mainstream that controls the school. Some advocates recommend that minorities take the power of the schools (and their tax dollars) into their own hands, either by segregating their children in schools that they control or by introducing culturally and linguistically relevant methods and curricula into the schools that their children attend. Some critics of this position brand resegregation as counterproductive in the search for equality. Others voice the concern that emphasis on too many minority concerns and issues diminishes the common culture of the schools.

Parental-power advocates are frequently an interesting alliance of political conservatives and racial minorities, both seeking to segregate schools for their own purposes. As yet, however, there is no convincing evidence that such segregation improves children's academic performance. Nevertheless, race and social class continue to be flash points in power struggles between various school constituencies.

Parental Involvement

Perhaps the most prevalent point of view of the parent-school relationship rests on parental involvement. The underlying rationale for this approach is that children learn best in school when their parents and their schools are in partnership. It is assumed that when parents back up the school's social and educational goals and strategies, and when they encourage their children to feel that school is a safe and desirable environment and that teachers are worthy role models, children will learn better. To involve parents in a home-school partnership, schools encourage parents to participate in school activities, to press the school district's interests with taxpayers and legislators, and to approve of school policies and practices. Becher (1986) points out that parental involvement has affected parents' feelings and behavior with respect to developing more positive attitudes about schools, gathering community support for schools, becoming more involved in community activities, and making increased contact with schools. Parental involvement differs from other strategies in that its primary purpose is to engage parents' support, not to solicit or recognize parents' control, change their child-rearing practices, or enhance families' capabilities.

Communication is the key to parental involvement, and schools use a variety of forms: open houses, parent-teacher conferences, telephoning, writing notes (including sending school lunch menus home), school visits by parents, home visits by school personnel, and parents' signing children's completed homework. Many of the activities designed to bring parents into the school's orbit are so common as to be almost universal. Love, Logue, Trudeau, and Thayer (1992) found that 37 percent of public schools in their sample offered workshops for parents during children's kindergarten year, a number exceeded only by the numbers representing opportunities for parents to volunteer (78 percent of schools) and supervise children's learning at home (56 percent).

Lightfoot (1978) criticizes the involvement approach to parent-school relationships, contending that "Parent-Teacher Association meetings and open house rituals at the beginning of the school year are contrived occasions that symbolically reaffirm the idealized parent-school relationship, but rarely provide the chance for authentic interaction" (p. 28).

Systems Collaboration

The enormous changes in family life over the past generation have rekindled interest in the delivery of social services in and through public schools. Collaborations with public health and social services are not new to schools, particularly during periods of acute social stress, such as during the Depression of the 1930s, when children's health and welfare needs were addressed in many public schools. Today, working mothers, divorce, "ghettoization" and isolation within neighborhoods, and the erosion of volunteer institutions have created crises in many children's lives, which schools have not been able to ignore. Gradually, and often reluctantly, an array of services that had become lodged in other institutions and organizations was shifted to schools, including child care, mental and physical health care, social and psychological services, and employment-related activities. As a consequence, many schools have become deliverers of comprehensive and integrated service initiatives (Kagan, 1991; National Resource Centers for Family Support Programs, n.d.).

Kagan (1991; Kagan, Powell, Weissbourd, & Zigler, 1987) points out that implementing family support programs in public schools is often difficult. First, collaboration between schools and parents, an essential aspect of the family support philosophy, frequently disturbs public school personnel who are unwilling to share power with parents. Second, collaboration between schools and other service delivery systems is difficult. Public education, even less than health and social service systems, has been self-contained and reluctant to make the changes necessary for a collaborative approach to family issues. Consequently, efforts to support families within schools have been slow to take hold. Gradually, however, as schools have recognized the benefits of this new model for home-school relationships, the movement for collaboration has gained momentum, with many states initiating projects to make the school the center of a system for parental and child support.

Theoretical Differences in Family Approaches

Two interactive but subtle theoretical and research perspectives dominate how parental programs are conceived. One perspective, backed by behavioral theories and research, suggests that changes in children's development and behavior can be achieved through changes in parents' behavior. This perspective stresses standardized practices leading to desired outcomes. The other perspective sees child-rearing practices as embedded in ecological social systems (Bronfenbrenner, 1979), with the same behavior not necessarily having the same meaning in different social groupings. From this perspective, the crux of providing family support is to understand and help change the social context in which families raise their children, rather than focusing on the desired behavior itself. These contrasting perspectives influence programs' focus and activities. Behavioral approaches — based on the belief that parents can change their children's school achievement by doing more of the things that parents of successful children do — stress getting parents to behave in approved ways, such as volunteering at school, signing homework, and attending meetings. Those using the more ecological perspective believe that children's school trajectory is changed when their parents become better role models of competence and effectiveness, and so the focus becomes helping parents restructure their personal lives. Proponents of both approaches can point to some degree of success, which suggests that it is necessary to change both what parents *do* and who parents *are* in order for their children to be successful in school.

Yes, but . . .

Can we improve children's school performance through family interventions? Is family support a tool in the struggle for educational parity between rich and poor, between mainstream and minority families? The answers seem to be yes—but with reservations.

No one type of program is effective for all children and families (Weiss, 1989). Moreover, "children are different, families are different, and societies are different" (Clark, 1983, p. 210), and so school-home relationships are complicated. Simplistic paradigms of interaction are fraught with danger because they lead to faddish policies and practices. Therefore, programs should not look to "quick fixes" in implementing family support.

The key to understanding home-school relationships is not to be found either in individuals or in single elements of either the family or school systems, but rather within the social context that defines how the two interact. Family values and practices are related to a variety of factors in people's lives, including income, housing, and values and behavior of parents' social groups. According to Halpern (1990), "Parent support and education programs cannot be expected to alter basic parenting capacities and styles, acquired through a life time of experience in a particular familial and social world, and often continually reinforced in the present. Nor can they alter families' basic life situation" (p. 305).

School personnel, then, must know what children learn outside of school, the family conditions that influence children's acquisition of knowledge and skills, the factors that affect parents' ability to support children's school achievement, the similarities and differences of the educational process between home and school, and how to effect a closer liaison between home and school (Spodek & Saracho, 1990). Building and maintaining positive relationships with families must resonate throughout programs—in the physical environment, in activities, in administrative and policy guidelines, and in programmatic features. But, most important, what is needed is to establish shared responsibility for children's education, a school program in which instruction, discipline, social activities, and relationships in school are coordinated with those in the family, and whereby children and families are provided with opportunities to enhance their self-esteem (Comer, 1980). Positive relationships between children and all the players in the educational venture are essential as both the details and the overarching philosophy are interwoven to create an interpersonal environment for children that is a secure base from which to venture forth, learn, and grow.

Family support requires collaboration and coordination between home and school, and all the issues that affect this relationship must be addressed. Questions of who has the power, which activities are provided for parents, and what instructional practices are used by schools must be viewed against the backdrop of the larger community context in which both home and school are embedded. The behavior of public schools toward parents has not always reflected a concern for family support, and attitudes toward families from low socioeconomic groups and families of color usually have been hostile or neglectful. Changing this orientation, so that services to parents are delivered in an atmosphere of mutual respect and empowerment, will require massive changes in schools' practices. Epstein (1990) suggests that we think of the child, the home, the school, the child's peers, and the community as bidirectional, with "overlapping spheres" of influence. Such a model breaches the wall between parents and school: instead of emphasizing the divisions of labor between them, it combines roles and functions to make "school like families" and "family like schools" (p. 104).

To incorporate this perspective into teacher preparation would require a major rethinking of how teachers are trained. The current emphasis on instructional methods, which assumes that all children learn from similar "best practices," would have to be exchanged for one in which teachers are helped to derive their practices from an understanding of the complex environments of home and school, and of the worlds in which children actually live. Teacher preparation would have to value both knowledge about and the ability to work with parents, just as teacher preparation now values both knowledge about and the ability to work with children. Such changes would be radical, but they might be the best way to ensure schools' success.

The proper relationship between home and school is a political as well as an educational issue. Analysis of parent-school problems, and recommendations for what to do about them, are deeply embedded in political beliefs and social benefit systems. Changing this perspective would require an energized school leadership team that understands the diversity in the community of parents. Leaders would have to educate their constituencies about similarities in family goals and aspirations and develop alternative rather than standardized ways of achieving their objectives.

School competence results from the interaction between children, their various environments, and their families' and communities' previous experience, rather than from a single factor, such as the school, the home, or the child's natural endowments. This slant on performance raises the possibility that children may function well in some environments and not in others, a possibility that raises doubt about the notion that success in school represents some general level of competence in the child (Bowman & Zvetina, 1992), or the idea that success and failure are caused solely by the actions of either parent or school.

Family support is not a quick and easy solution to school achievement. It can only help. And supportive services for families will need to be as diverse as the populations served.

References

Becher, R. (1986). Parent involvement: A review of research and principles of successful practice. In L. Katz (Ed.), *Current topics in early childhood education* (pp. 85–122). Norwood, NJ: Ablex.

Bowman, B., & Zvetina, D. (1992). *Social/emotional readiness.* Paper prepared for the National Goals Panel, Erikson Institute, Chicago.

Bronfenbrenner, U. (1979). *The ecology of human development: Experiments by nature and design.* Cambridge, MA: Harvard University Press.

Cawelti, G. (1993). Conclusion: The search for a system. In G. Cawelti (Ed.), *Challenges and achievements of American education* (pp. 193–202). Alexandria, VA: Association for Supervision and Curriculum Development.

Chubb, J., & Moe, T. (1990). *Politics, markets, and American schools.* Washington, DC: Brookings Institute.

Clark, R. (1983). *Family life and school achievement: Why poor children succeed or fail.* Chicago: University of Chicago Press.

Comer, J. (1980). *School power: Implications of an intervention project.* New York: Free Press.

Cutright, M. (1989). *The national PTA talks to parents.* New York: Doubleday.

Epstein, J. (1990). School and family connections: Theory, research, and implications for integrating sociologies of education and family. In D. Unger & M. Sussman (Eds.), *Families in community settings: Interdisciplinary perspectives* (pp. 96–126). New York: Hawthorn Press.

Ferguson, S., & Mazin, L. (1989). *Parent power.* New York: Clarkson N. Potter.

Halpern, R. (1990). Parent support and education programs. *Children and Youth Services Review, 12,* 285–308.

Jencks, C. (1972). *Inequality.* New York: HarperCollins.

Jensen, A. (1969). How much can we boost IQ and scholastic achievement? *Harvard Educational Review, 69*(1), 1–123.

Kagan, S. L. (1991). *United we stand: Collaboration for child care and early education services.* New York: Teachers College Press.

Kagan, S. L., Powell, D. R., Weissbourd, B., & Zigler, E. F. (Eds.). (1987). *America's family support programs: Perspectives and prospects.* New Haven, CT: Yale University Press.

Kamerman, S. B. (1988, August). *Child care policies and programs: An international overview.* Preprint prepared for Workshop on International Developments in Child Care, Arlie, VA.

Lewontin, R. (1992). *Biology as ideology*. New York: Harper-Collins.

Lightfoot, S. (1978). *Worlds apart: Relationships between families and schools*. New York: Basic Books.

Love, J., Logue, M., Trudeau, J., & Thayer, K. (1992). *Transitions to kindergarten in American schools*. Portsmouth, NH: RMC Research Corporation.

Mordkowitz, E., & Ginsburg, H. (1987). Early academic socialization of successful Asian-American college students. *Quarterly Newsletter of the Laboratory of Comparative Human Cognition, 9*(2), 85–91.

National Center for Health Statistics. (1984). *Health United States*. U.S. Department of Health and Human Services Publication No. 85-1232. Washington, DC: U.S. Government Printing Office.

National Commission on Excellence in Education. (1984). *Nation at risk: The full account*. Portland, OR: U.S.A. Research.

National Resource Center for Family Support Programs. (n.d.). *Family support programs and school-linked services*. Chicago: Family Resource Coalition.

Ogbu, J. (1992). Understanding cultural diversity and learning. *Educational Researcher, 21*, 5–14.

Powell, D. (1991). *Strengthening parental contributions to school readiness*. Washington, DC: U.S. Department of Education, Office of Educational Research and Improvement.

Schlossman, S. (1976). Before Home Start: Notes toward a history of parent education in America, 1897–1929. *Harvard Educational Review, 46*(3), 436–467.

Schlossman, S. (1978). The parent education game: The politics of child psychology in the 1970's. *Teacher College Record, 79*, 789–808.

Spencer, M. (1985). Cultural cognition and social cognition as identity correlates of Black children's personal-social development. In M. Spencer, G. Brookins, & W. Allen (Eds.), *Beginnings: The social and affective development of Black children* (pp. 215–230). Hillsdale, NJ: Erlbaum.

Spodek, B., & Saracho, O. (1990). Preparing early childhood teachers for the twenty-first century. In B. Spodek & O. Saracho

(Eds.), *Early Childhood Teacher Preparation* (pp. 23–44). New York: Teachers College Press.

Stevens, J. (1985). *Parenting skill: Does social support matter?* Presentation to the Society for Research in Child Development, Toronto, Canada.

Treffeisen, S. (n.d.). *Parents as Teachers: Adaptation in child care center.* Report from the University of Missouri–St. Louis Parents as Teachers National Center. St. Louis: Parents as Teachers National Center.

Walberg, H., Bakalis, M., Bast, J., & Baer, S. (1988). *We can rescue our children.* Chicago: Heartland Institute.

Weiss, H. (1989). The challenge of new and widespread interest in early, family-oriented interventions. In R. Egbert (Ed.), *Improving life chances for young children* (pp. 111–130). Lincoln, NE: Center for Curriculum and Instruction.

Weiss, H., & Rittenburg, A. (1991). *OERI Ready-to-Learn Project: Harvard family research project final report on parenting and readiness materials.* Washington, DC: U.S. Department of Education.

Weissbourd, B. (1990). Family resource and support programs: Changes and challenges in human services. In D. G. Unger & D. R. Powell (Eds.), *Families as nurturing systems: Support across the life span* (pp. 69–89). New York: Haworth Press.

Zill, N., & Rogers, C. (1988). Recent trends in the well-being of children in the United States and their implications for public policy. In A. Cherlin (Ed.), *The changing American family* (pp. 31–116). Washington, DC: Urban Institute Press.

□ 4 □

Strategies for a Family-Supportive Child Health Care System

Barry Zuckerman
T. Berry Brazelton

The movement in pediatrics away from a narrow focus on diagnosis and treatment of disease and toward prevention and health promotion is consistent with the goals of family support. Medicine's approach to childbirth offers an excellent historical example of this shift of emphasis (Shonkoff, 1987). During the first half of the twentieth century, as the ability to deal with medical complications improved, physicians became overseers of pregnancy, labor, and delivery. This trend progressed so that by midcentury, childbirth was treated as an illness requiring hospitalization, medication, and the technical expertise of physicians. In the past two decades, parents have regained autonomy and control over childbirth. Preventive measures involving self-help and individual behavioral changes have become an important part of prenatal care. Prevention of childhood problems has moved beyond the traditional problems of physical growth and illness to problems of development and behavior.

This work was supported in part by a grant from the Maternal and Child Health Bureau and the Deland Fellowship in Health Care and Society of the Brigham and Women's Hospital/Harvard University, Boston, Massachusetts. We thank Jeanne McCarthy and Margaret Lavoye for their help in preparing the manuscript.

Programs that involve parents as partners have been the most effective.

Since health is multiply determined, and since health and learning and behavioral problems are interrelated, health services need to be comprehensive, family-centered, and community-based. Structural components of programs need to build on three fundamental premises. First, future strategies need to be based on an understanding of the principles of human development. Second, infants are important to parents, and the best way to reach parents is through their infants. Third, relationships are important: growth and change are more likely to occur in the context of relationships between clinician and parent, parent and child, and clinician and child.

This chapter presents approaches to promoting the optimal health and development of children. The first approach, providing the most basic level of care, requires public policies to ensure that children's basic needs for food, shelter, safety, and access to health care are met. The second approach that needs to be developed is a two-generational strategy reflecting an understanding of the link between parental health and child health and development. The third and most specific approach described here suggests a clinical strategy for developing an alliance with parents and providing needed information. The development of an alliance requires an understanding of parental concerns about children's behavior and development, and sometimes an understanding of cultural, class, or other differences as well.

Ensuring the Basics

There are longstanding precedents for government policies to protect the health of children. In response to a high death rate of children from diarrheal diseases spread by contaminated milk, the government established milk stations to distribute fresh milk. With the addition of other preventive measures to combat infection, such as good sanitation and immunizations, childhood mortality was drastically reduced between 1900 and the present. At a minimum, good health depends on good basic nutrition, a place to live, a safe environment, and access to health care. While many parents can meet these basic needs of their children, others cannot, especially those living in poverty. In 1991, more than 20 percent of children in the United States were living in poverty (National Commission on Children, 1991). Children in poverty experience double jeopardy (Parker, Greer, & Zuckerman, 1988). First, compared with children who are not poor, they suffer higher rates of low birthweight, malnutrition, prematurity, anemia, lead poisoning, prenatal exposure to alcohol, cocaine or other psychoactive substances, and congenital infections. Second, they suffer more serious consequences from these problems than do children of higher socioeconomic status.

Many children suffer from poor nutrition, as reflected in high rates of reported hunger and in hard data on growth. While the Special Supplemental Food Program for Women, Infants and Children (WIC) has a long-established record of medical effectiveness (Rush, 1988; Stockhaver, 1987), only one-half of all eligible families nationally receive nutritional supplementation. During the winter months, 9 percent of children under the age of six seen in one urban hospital were underweight for age and/or height; this finding indicates undernutrition at almost double the expected level (Frank et al., 1991). This rate is higher than in the warmer months, suggesting that families' limited funds may be diverted from paying for food to paying for fuel (Frank et al., 1991). Diversion of limited funds from food to other needs can also be inferred from a report showing a lower incidence of iron deficiency among children whose parents received housing subsidies than among those whose parents did not (Meyers, Rubin, Napoleone, & Nichols, 1993). Aid to Families with Dependent Children (AFDC) housing subsidies reduce by half the amount that families have to spend on rent, in many cases freeing more money to be spent on food. Therefore, it seems likely that full funding of these subsidies would prevent many nutritional problems.

Children who live in poor neighborhoods are more likely to be exposed to toxic levels of lead (Needleman, Schell, Bellinger, Leviton, & Alfred, 1990). Even at levels once thought to be safe, exposure increases sevenfold a child's risk of dropping out of school and sixfold the risk of having a reading disability (Needleman, Schell, Bellinger, Leviton, & Alfred, 1990). Another environmental hazard is seen in the high incidence of childhood asthma, due in part to allergic responses to cockroaches, mites, and rat hairs, especially in lower socioeconomic urban communities (Call, Smith, Morris, Chapman, & Platts-Mills, 1992).

Far too many urban families are living in fear and isolation. Death and injuries from violence have become the number one public health threat in all major cities. The effect on these children of witnessing real (not television) violence is not adequately acknowledged. These experiences can significantly impair health and development (McAlister-Groves, Zuckerman, Marans, & Cohen, 1993). Children who think that their lives are vulnerable and tenuous may fail to take care of themselves. As they get older, these children may seek relief from intolerable fear and anxiety through alcohol or other drug abuse. In one survey, 47 percent of mothers reported that their children had heard gunshots in their neighborhood, and one in ten of these children had witnessed a knifing or shooting before the age of six (Taylor, Zuckerman, Harik, & Groves, in press). Communities that have been the most successful in eliminating crime and violence need to be studied and replicated.

Limited access to prenatal health care impairs the nation's capacity to promote healthy births, despite our technical capacity to treat diseases associated with low birthweight. Thus the infant mortality rate of the United States is higher than in twenty-one other industrialized countries (National Commission on Children, 1991). The present health care system leaves at least 8,000,000 children and 430,000 pregnant women uninsured (National Commission on Children, 1991). Families without health insurance receive less preventive health care (Short & Lefkowitz, 1992). Immunization rates for preschool children have fallen in recent years (National Center for Health Statistics, 1990). In 1990, there were 49 deaths from measles among children under five (Centers for Disease Control, 1992). In addition to not receiving preventive care, families without health insurance may put off taking their children to the doctor because of the cost. When the doctor finally is consulted, the illness may have progressed to a point requiring hospitalization or may have caused more serious consequences than if it had been treated earlier. The effects of poverty and poor access to health care are tragically illustrated by the death of an infant described in the medical literature as due in part to the parents' inability to pay for a basic oral rehydration treatment for diarrhea (Meyers, Siegel, & Vinci, 1991).

Thus federal policies ensuring adequate income, adequate nutrition, safe homes and neighborhoods, and universal access to medical care are essential, and policy recommendations to address these and other basic needs of children have been issued (National Commission on Children, 1991). Examples of specific recommendations include a $1,000 refundable tax credit for all children, enhanced enforcement of court-ordered child support coupled with government-insured benefits for children whose parents do not meet their support obligations, universal health insurance for pregnant women and children, and full funding of the WIC Special Supplemental Food Program for all eligible children.

Two-Generational Approach to Children's Health

One of the best ways of helping children is to help their parents. The relationship between parental health and children's health has received inadequate attention in the past. New research findings show a clear link between selective aspects of parental health and children's health. Furthermore, new and effective treatment of some of these adult health problems has recently become available. These findings suggest a need for a new, two-generational approach to children's health that needs to be integrated with other human services, especially family support services.

Parental Health Behavior

Health behavior — action that affects health — involves exercise; nutrition; stress management; use of cigarettes, alcohol, and other psychoactive substances; and sexual practices. Good health behavior also includes compliance with medication, use of such health services as prenatal care, and regular health checkups. All parental health behavior has at least an indirect effect on children's health, and some profoundly influences children's health and well-being. It is becoming more widely appreciated that preventive interventions to encourage good health behavior must reach women before as well as during and after pregnancy. Thus such community programs as Head Start and programs for child care and family support need to be linked to health systems to ensure women access to these services. The children's health system must better address the health needs of parents.

Planned childbearing is an important health behavior that affects children, since a wanted child is more likely to be a healthy child. Between 1985 and 1988, 12 percent of births to women between fifteen and thirty were unwanted (Forrest & Singh, 1990). Unlike women with wanted pregnancies, those with unwanted pregnancies receive prenatal care later or not at all and are more likely to smoke cigarettes, both of which have harmful effects on the fetus (Pamuk & Mosher, 1988). Unwanted children are more likely to suffer abuse and neglect and to have behavioral problems than their wanted peers (Zurarin, 1987; David, 1986). Unplanned and unwanted births to very young mothers, or to mothers suffering from such adverse conditions as HIV infection or addiction to psychoactive substances, carry even higher risk of childhood morbidity and mortality.

Contraceptive failure or imperfect use of a contraceptive method results in 47 percent of unintended pregnancies in the United States, 1.7 million annually. The remaining 53 percent of unintended pregnancies occur to the 10 percent of the women at risk for unintended pregnancy, who use no contraceptive method at all (Harlap, Koch, & Forrest, 1991). Thus well-informed, consistent use of contraception is an important parental health behavior. Health care providers must continue to address the prevalence of unintended pregnancy among teenagers, but they must also be aware that older women, including those who already have children, give birth to three times as many unplanned children as do teenagers (Ferguson, 1993). New and better contraceptives, such as Norplant and Depo-Provera, provide greater effectiveness in preventing unplanned and unwanted pregnancies (Medical Letter, 1992a). These technologies need to be accessible to women so that they can plan childbirth. Linkages between health and other community programs are critical to achieving this goal.

While the importance of prenatal care to infant outcomes is well known and accepted, women's health before conception has recently received increasing attention. First, recent studies have confirmed initial observations that vitamin supplementation prior to conception, especially with folic acid, prevents birth defects, especially spina bifida (Vitamin Study Research Group, 1991). Women of childbearing age, and especially those who are trying to conceive, should receive vitamin supplementation in order to reduce their likelihood of having a child with a birth defect. Second, counseling regarding safe sex is needed to reduce the likelihood of a woman's contracting HIV or another sexually transmitted disease and transmitting it to her fetus.

Maternal use of excessive alcohol, psychoactive drugs, and cigarettes during pregnancy are important determinants of children's health (Zuckerman & Bresnahan, 1991). The best-known effects of alcohol and drug use during pregnancy are the fetal alcohol syndrome and the neonatal abstinence syndrome. Other adverse effects associated with drug use during pregnancy include prematurity, low birthweight, and increased risk of congenital syphilis, AIDS, or other sexually transmitted diseases, especially in mothers who use intravenous drugs or whose addiction to crack cocaine or other drugs is associated with prostitution (Zuckerman & Bresnahan, 1991). Maternal smoking may account for as much as 20 to 30 percent of cases of low birthweight and for 10 percent of infant mortality (Kleinman, Pierre, Madon, Lang, & Schramm, 1988). Smoking-cessation programs during pregnancy have proved effective in reducing smoking and raising birthweight (Sexton & Herbel, 1984).

Although most studies have focused on the use of these agents during pregnancy, the use of drugs and cigarettes can affect children's health throughout childhood. Passive smoking during the first two years of life increases the risk of colds, ear infections, respiratory problems (especially asthma), sudden infant death syndrome, and behavioral problems (Schoendorf & Kiely, 1992; Weitzman, Gortmaker, Walker, & Sobol, 1990; Chilmouczyk et al., 1993). Nicotine gum (Lam, Sacks, Sze, & Chalmert, 1987) and nicotine patches (Medical Letter, 1992b) are inappropriate for mothers during pregnancy, but they are possible aids to mothers who try to stop smoking after the birth of their child, or for fathers at any point.

Maternal Mental Health

Depression. Depression is a common mental health problem with well-documented adverse effects on children's health (Zuckerman & Beardslee, 1987). Loss of interest or pleasure, emotional emptiness, and a feeling of "flatness" distinguish depression from the normal human experience of sadness. The boundary between normal and abnormal symptoms is sometimes unclear, but when these feelings are intense, persistent, and interfere with everyday living, treatment by a mental health professional is warranted. Major depression occurs in 3 percent of adult men and in 4 to 9 percent of adult women.

Infants born to depressed mothers are at increased risk for low birthweight and irritability at birth (Zuckerman, Bauchner, Parker, & Cabral, 1990) and for sleep problems during infancy (Zuckerman, Stevenson, & Bailey, 1987a). During the preschool years, children of depressed mothers may continue to have sleep problems, and they show increased incidence of other behavioral problems, psychosomatic symptoms, and accidents. Depression, attention-deficit hyperactivity disorder, and other behavioral and learning problems are seen during school age and adolescence (Zuckerman & Beardslee, 1987).

Parental depression can affect children through a variety of mechanisms. The genetic predisposition to depressive disorders has been well established in studies of twins (Nurnberger & Gershon, 1982). Furthermore, the parenting behavior of depressed parents is poor. Depressed mothers have difficulty with emotional regulation, separation, and individualization and are less likely to encourage achievement. Discipline is often inconsistent and induces guilt; promises are often made and then forgotten (Susman et al., 1985). These behaviors may reflect helplessness, self-preoccupation, or decreased memory, which are all characteristics of depression.

Depression can be effectively treated with both medication and psychotherapy. Women who exhibit depressed affect or express hopelessness, lack of energy, and loss of interest need a mental health referral for assessment and treatment. It is important to remember that depressed mothers will be especially vulnerable to feeling guilty and to blaming themselves for everything. Children's health and family support programs can help a depressed mother address the social origins of depressive feelings, including isolation, lack of financial resources, housing dissatisfaction, and marital discord. Access to home visitation services is especially beneficial to infants. Home-visited infants of depressed mothers had higher developmental scores than nonvisited infants of depressed mothers and were more likely to be securely attached at twelve months of age (Lyons-Ruth, Connell, & Grunebaum, 1990). In order to help families with a depressed parent, close collaboration between mental health, child health, and family support programs is needed.

Addiction. Addiction is the compulsive use of a psychoactive substance (or substances), loss of control over that use, and continued use despite adverse consequences. The majority of addicted women have suffered repeated trauma and loss, experiences that give rise to overwhelming feelings of depression, anxiety, low self-esteem, and bouts of panic and rage that often result in self-medication to relieve the painful affect (Brooks, Zuckerman, Bamforth, Cole, & Kaplan-Sanoff, in press). The exhortation "just say no" indicates great naïveté about the causes of addiction and the loss of control inherent in addiction.

Parental addiction has far-reaching adverse consequences beyond pregnancy. Addiction prevents a mother from responding to her infant's needs; her primary focus is on her drug of choice, not on her child. Her life is organized around getting the drug, not around taking her children to health care visits or to educational services.

Alcoholism is the most common parental addiction. Approximately one in six or eight children has an alcholic parent. While the prenatal effects of alcohol abuse (such as fetal alcohol syndrome) are important, the health and developmental implications of parenting by an active alcoholic are equally important. Children of alcoholics are at increased risk for injuries (Bijur, Kurzon, Overpeck, & Scheidt, 1992), including increased risk for motor vehicle fatalities (Margolis, Kotch, & Lacey, 1986). Overall, they have more hospital admissions and longer stays than children whose parents are not alcoholic (Children of Alcoholics Foundation, Inc., 1988). Adolescent children of problem drinkers have higher rates of depression and lower self-esteem and drink more heavily than their peers do (Roosa, Sadles, Beals, & Shant, 1988).

Numerous barriers stand between women, especially mothers, and drug treatment. For example, women often resist entering treatment programs because they must release their children to someone else's care and fear never seeing them again. Despite this reality, only a handful of residential drug-treatment programs accept women with their children. Treatment programs need to be developed that treat parents, especially mothers, in the context of their families.

Developing an Alliance with Families

Parenting is bound to be stressful; historically, the extended family and the community acted as cushions at stressful times. But now the extended family is no longer available as a support system for most young parents, and one of the most serious problems for parents today is the loss of a sense of community. If we wish parents to be successful, we must recreate communities that provide peer-group support for the normal and inevitable crises of parenting.

The Importance of Communities

If modern health care is to emphasize prevention and support, health education systems and community health systems are essential. Because parents are ultimately responsible for their children's health, we must create systems that empower parents to provide adequate preventive health care for their children. Parents must be adequately informed about the importance of the mother's health behavior during pregnancy, about environmental hazards to their children, about the prevention of injury or illness, about diets, and about physical and mental abuse. Each contact between a health care provider and a parent is a chance to reach out and develop a relationship that makes information accessible. But we need to value the goals of all parents as contributing to their children's optimal outcomes. Outreach programs can work effectively even for difficult-to-reach populations if the approach includes parents and respects their capacity to be involved in their children's health care.

Medical people are well trained in diagnosing disease and failure. The next generations of physicians and nurses must also be trained to look for strengths and success, to be sensitive to parents' values (as opposed to the clinician's, in many cases), and to emphasize the value of establishing a partnership that will ultimately benefit the child's physical and mental health.

Cultural and Class Differences

There are special challenges and skills required in working with parents whose culture or social class differs from the provider's. Child-rearing practices differ widely among different groups, but they serve the same important functions in preparing children for life.

Infant and child behavior can be used as a bridge between clinicians and parents from different cultures. Starting with observation, the clinician can ask about the meaning of a behavior to the parents and proceed to explore the parents' attitudes and feelings. When the clinician understands a parent's interpretation of the behavior and the parent's goals, alternative meanings or strategies to meet the parenting goals can be suggested. This is especially important if the parent's child-rearing practice has unintended adverse health or developmental effects on the child. For example, parents who come from areas of extreme poverty, chronic malnutrition, and high infant mortality, such as Southeast Asia, Haiti, or parts of South Central America, put a high value on fattening up their babies because they believe that a fat baby is less likely to die of an infection. At the other extreme are educated parents who, because of a family history of heart disease or overconcern with their own well-being, limit their children's dietary fat to inadequate levels.

Parents' handling of temper tantrums provides an excellent example of how different cultures view the normal expression of frustration during the toddler years (Kohlenberg, Joseph, Prudent, & Richardson, in press). Hispanic families often view tantrums as part of a nervous temperament, but they may worry that tantrums, especially if they are violent and involve head banging, may cause brain damage or a seizure. Because of these worries, the family may give in to whatever the child demands. An African American family would probably view a tantrum as "acting up" that is intended to embarrass the parents or manipulate the situation. Since the tantrum would be seen as a control issue, the response might range from spanking to withholding of treats. A Haitian family might see a tantrum as indicating that a child has not learned good manners and is showing disrespect. Because of the importance to them of respect, Haitian parents may be embarrassed by tantrums, and their response might be to shout at the child or hit the child with hand or belt. Clinical information and recommendations regarding tantrums are best accepted when they are presented in the context of mutual understanding and appreciation of the parents' concerns.

For families living in poverty, the focus on survival issues is exhausting. The television or a school-age sibling may serve as the babysitter while adults try to borrow money for food or solve problems with agencies. In neighborhoods where random shootings are common, obedience and self-reliance may be the most valuable skills for a child to acquire. When families live with such stresses, family survival is a parenting achievement that should be recognized. This is also true in less dangerous situations. For example, when a young mother tells us she is "spoiling" her infant, we have learned that she may in fact be telling us that she is working hard to give her infant more than the minimal care. When she tells us that the father also "spoils" the infant, this may mean that he is involved in caring for the infant. Once the clinician has shown understanding of what the parents face and appreciation of their efforts to care for their infants, the parents are more likely to accept the clinician's recommendations.

Parental drug addiction poses a special problem that may prevent clinicians from reaching parents. Clinicians, nurses, and educators often feel angry with mothers whose behavior is putting their children at risk, but these negative and punitive feelings, while understandable, create barriers to helpful intervention. When a mother senses judgment and criticism, she will not be able to trust the professional and will be less likely to accept help. Recovery is a difficult process, which seldom progresses neatly from one stage to the next. Parenting recommendations made to a mother during recovery, and especially during early recovery, need to be short-term and success-oriented; long-term recommendations may lead to further frustration and failure.

In summary, the quality of the relationship between clinicians and parents and their children is a critical ingredient in parents' ability to promote children's health and development. When the clinician builds a relationship that encompasses the child's adaptation with parents, peers, and teachers, the parents are more likely to request and accept advice and support.

A Strategy for Supporting Parents

Even in the absence of cultural differences, identifying and discussing children's behavior serves as a special opportunity for developing an alliance with parents. Parents struggle to understand their children's behavior and welcome the opportunity to discuss their observations, theories, and concerns. For example, at six months, mouthing and banging are developmentally appropriate ways of learning about objects, but parents' reactions to these behaviors often include annoyance with banging and worries that mouthing is bad and dirty. When the clinician reframes these as normal learning behaviors and praises the child's exploration and curiosity, parents will often be relieved and proud. They will also enjoy joining with the clinician as observers of their child's developing strategies for exploring the world and be open to hearing about behaviors that will be emerging in the coming months.

Developmental spurts commonly create crises for parents and children, which can be turned into an opportunities for promoting children's health and development. Talking with parents about emerging behaviors helps facilitate parent-child adaptation and reduce stresses. These conversations need not be limited to clinicians and their clients. Indeed, sharing of ideas and issues with peer groups can be a particularly effective strategy. Ideally, meetings with a clinician or a peer group should be timed to occur at *touchpoints* — that is, at times when parents need information about the child's next predictable spurt in development — in order to optimize the process of crisis and advancement (Brazelton, 1992). No aspect of development — cognitive, motor or emotional — proceeds in a straight upward line of progress. Each developmental line moves in a series of rapid spurts, followed by periods of leveling off and homeostasis. The rapid spurt creates added stress for the entire family, and the family must participate and contribute to that development.

Just before each developmental change, there is a short and predictable period of disorganization in the baby's behavior. Parents are likely to wonder why the baby is falling apart. They are likely to feel that the baby needs more intervention and structure, at a time when the baby actually needs space and the freedom to regress and reorganize. With an understanding of the reasons for the regression and reorganization, any parent can feel more confident and can support the baby in the necessary behavior. When the next burst of learning occurs, as predicted, the parent will feel that it is his or her achievement as well as the baby's. Each touchpoint, then, becomes an opportunity for success and for sharing information.

Touchpoints may be optimal times for getting the parents and the infant in for health checkups, immunizations, and other benefits, as well as for sharing experiences. Parents will not be likely to miss an opportunity to get the information they need. Compliance could be improved, outreach with transportation could be provided, and emphasis on peer relationships would be maintained at each return visit so that the parents would have formed a community by the time day care is needed. Ideally, day care would be provided in the community center. The touchpoint strategy could empower parents by giving them the information they need to ensure physical checkups, immunizations, and health supervision, and it would supply a mechanism for identifying delays in development so that early intervention could be instituted.

First Touchpoint: Pregnancy. The first touchpoint for parents to meet and form alliances would be pregnancy. A physical checkup for the mother, and prenatal care for the fetus, would be provided. Groups with mutual interests would be formed. Childbirth education and information about health, breastfeeding, and circumcision could become the shared focus of the groups. Fetuses respond behaviorally to auditory and visual stimuli; by the seventh month, these reactions can be demonstrated to the prospective parents. If it could be made available, an ultrasound machine could be used to observe the fetus and its behavior. Attachment to the fetus as a person would begin.

Second Touchpoint: The Neonatal Stage. A health care provider, or a staff member from a family support center, could visit the parents and the baby in the lying-in hospital. The Neonatal Behavioral Assessment Scale could be used to demonstrate the behavioral responses of the newborn and capture the new parents for that baby, as well as for the community: "All of your peers have had their babies, and they all want to compare them with yours. Let's plan to have a reunion when your babies are two to three weeks old. At that time, you can compare your babies. We will provide checkups for you and your baby. Your benefits can be made available. You'll see all of your friends' babies, and you can discuss feeding and sleeping. Mainly, though, we'll discuss the crying at the end of the day that most babies will do when they reach three to twelve weeks of age. It is a kind of crying that drives parents to overreact and do too much to try to stop it. If you can learn what to do, and how to see this as a normal part of each day, you won't be so worried. So be sure you come back at that time."

Third Touchpoint: Weeks Two to Three. Irritable crying at the end of each day will probably occur in over half the babies. This crying serves the purpose of relieving the overload on an immature nervous system at the end of the day. The baby has cycled through various states during the day and has managed the stimuli, but the baby's nervous system has overloaded each time. By the end of the day, he or she must become actively irritable in order to discharge the stored-up overload. After the period of fussy crying, the baby will be reorganized for the next twenty-four hours. If parents can be forewarned about the normality of this phenomenon, they will not add to the baby's overload with too many maneuvers. One or two hours of irritable crying can become four to six hours of colicky crying when parents are too anxious and too active in their attempts to interfere and shut the baby up. By forewarning the parents, we have cut the duration of the crying from three hours to one hour a day, by using a soothing routine of gentle handling, letting the baby fuss for five to ten minutes at a time, and using warm water in a bottle to allow for sucking. When this fussing ends, at twelve weeks, the parents will feel a sense of conquest and will probably return for each subsequent touchpoint. At each one, medical checkups for mother and baby, inoculations, benefits, and participation in the family resource groups will be the format. Brazelton (1992) outlines subsequent touchpoints and goals for prevention.

An Ecological System of Support

If parents can be prepared for predictable problems and can discuss their handling in peer groups with common values, they will feel a sense of success and of community, which may enhance their self-image as competent parents. When work issues develop, and when necessary separations for child care and schooling occur, the community members can support one another in seeking quality care and education. Working as a group, they will be more involved and more powerful in demanding high-quality child care and educational resources.

Health care systems must develop linkages to other support systems to create a whole system based on the ecological principles of human development. If health care clinicians can reach out to young parents at times when they are beginning to make attachments within the family, especially to a new baby, children's health and development can be improved.

References

Bijur, P. E., Kurzon, M., Overpeck, M. D., & Scheidt, P. C. (1992). Parental alcohol use, problem drinking and children's injuries. *Journal of the American Medical Association, 367,* 3166–3172.

Brazelton, T. B. (1992). *Touchpoints.* Reading, MA: Addison-Wesley.

Brooks, C., Zuckerman, B., Bamforth, A., Cole, J., & Kaplan-Sanoff, M. (in press). Clinical issues related to substance abuse–involved mothers and their infants. *Journal of Infant Mental Health.*

Call, R., Smith, T., Morris, E., Chapman, M., & Platts-Mill, T. (1992). Risk factors for asthma in inner-city children. *Journal of Pediatrics, 121,* 862–866.

Centers for Disease Control. (1992). National Health Interview Survey. *Morbidity and Mortality Weekly Report, 4022,* entire issue.

Children of Alcoholics Foundation, Inc. (1988). *Children of alcoholics in the medical system: Hidden problems, hidden costs.* New York: Author.

Chilmouczyk, B., Salmin, L., Megathin, K., Neupux, L., Polomak, G., Knight, G., Pulkkinen, M., Haddow, J. (1993). Association between exposure to environmental tobacco smoke and exacerbations of asthma in children. *New England Journal of Medicine, 328,* 1665–1669.

David, H. P. (1986). Unwanted children: A follow-up from Prague. *Family Planning Perspective, 18,* 143–144.

Ferguson, B. (1993). Increases in unwanted births: Origins and consequences. *American Journal of Public Health, 83,* 1180.

Forrest, J. D., & Singh, S. (1990). The sexual and reproductive behavior of American women. *Family Planning Perspective, 22,* 206–214.

Frank, D., Napoleone, M., Meyers, A., Roos, N., Peterson, K., et al. (1991). *A heat-or-eat effect? Seasonal changes in weight for age in a pediatric emergency room.* Paper presented at the annual meeting of the American Public Health Association, Atlanta.

Harlap, S., Koch, S., and Forrest, J. D. (1991). *Preventing pregnancy, protecting health: A new look at birth control choices in the United States.* New York: Alan Guttmacher Institute.

Kleinman, J. C., Pierre, M. O., Madon, J. H., Lang, G. H., & Schramm, W. F. (1988). The effects of maternal smoking on fetal and infant mortality. *American Journal of Epidemiology, 127,* 274–282.

Kohlenberg, T., Joseph, H., Prudent, N., & Richardson, V. (in press). Culture and the family's response to a child's problem. *Developmental and Behavioral Pediatrics: A Handbook for Primary Care.* Boston: Little, Brown.

Lam, W., Sacks, H., Sze, P., & Chalmert, T. (1987). Meta-analysis of randomised, controlled trials of nicotine chewing gum. *Lancet, ii,* 27–29.

Lyons-Ruth, K., Connell, D. B., & Grunebaum, A. (1990). Infants at social risk: Maternal depression and family support services as mediators of infant development and security of attachment. *Child Development, 61,* 85–98.

McAlister-Groves, B., Zuckerman, B., Marans, S., & Cohen, D. J. (1993). Silent victims: Children who witness violence. *Journal of the American Medical Association, 269,* 262–264.

Margolis, L. H., Kotch, J., & Lacey, J. H. (1986). Children and alcohol-related motor vehicle crashes. *Pediatrics, 77,* 870–872.

Medical Letter, "Choice of Contraceptives," *34,* 111–114, 1992a.

Medical Letter, "Nicotine Patches," *34,* 37–38, 1992b.

Meyers, A., Rubin, D., Napoleone, M., & Nichols, K. (1993). Public housing subsidies may improve poor children's nutrition. *American Journal of Public Health, 83,* 115.

Meyers, A., Siegel, B., & Vinci, R. (1991). Economic barriers to the use of oral rehydration therapy. *Journal of the American Medical Association, 265,* 1724–1725.

National Center for Health Statistics. (1990). *Health United States.* Hyattsville, MD: U.S. Public Health Service.

National Commission on Children. (1991). *Beyond rhetoric: A new American agenda for children and families.* Washington, DC: U.S. Government Printing Office.

Needleman, H., Schell, A., Bellinger, D., Leviton, A., Alfred, E. (1990). The long-term effects of exposure to low doses of lead in childhood. *New England Journal of Medicine, 322,* 83.

Nurnberger, J. L., & Gershon, E. S. (1982). Genetics of affective disorder. In E. S. Paykel (Ed.), *Handbook of Affective Disorders* (pp. 125–145). New York: Guilford Press.

Pamuk, E. R., & Mosher, W. D. (1988). Health aspects of pregnancy and childbirth, United States, 1982. *Vital and Health Statistics,* Series 23, No. 16. Washington, DC: U.S. Government Printing Office.

Parker, S., Greer, S., & Zuckerman, B. (1988). Double jeopardy. *Pediatric Clinics of North America, 35,* 1227–1240.

Roosa, M., Sadles, J., Beals, J., & Shant, J. (1988). Risk status of adolescent children of problem drinking parents. *American Journal of Common Psychology, 16,* 225–239.

Rush, D., et al. (1988). The national WIC evaluation: Evaluation of the Special Supplemental Food Program for Women, Infants, and Children. *American Journal of Clinical Nutrition, 48* (Suppl.), 389–519.

Schoendorf, K. C., & Kiely, J. L. (1992). Relationship of Sudden Infant Death Syndrome to maternal smoking before and after pregnancy. *Pediatrics, 90,* 905–908.

Sexton, M., & Herbel, J. R. (1984). A clinical trial of change in maternal smoking and its effect on birthweight. *Journal of the American Medical Association, 251,* 915–922.

Shonkoff, J. P. (1987). Family beginnings: Infancy and support. In S. L. Kagan, D. R. Powell, B. Weissbourd, & E. F. Zigler (Eds.), *America's Family Support Programs: Perspectives and prospects* (pp. 79–98). New Haven, CT: Yale University Press.

Short, P. F., & Lefkowitz, D. C. (1992). Encouraging preventive services for low-income children: The effect of expanding Medicaid. *Medical Care, 30,* 766–780.

Stockhaver, J. W. (1987). WIC, prenatal participation and its relationship to pregnancy outcome in Missouri: A second look. *American Journal of Public Health, 77,* 813–818.

Susman, E. J., et al. (1985). Child rearing patterns and depressed, abusive and normal mothers. *American Journal of Orthopsychiatry, 55,* 237–249.

Taylor, L., Zuckerman, B., Harik, V., & McAlister-Groves, B. M. (1994). Witnessing violence by children and their mothers. *Journal of Developmental and Behavioral Pediatrics, 15,* 120–123.

Vitamin Study Research Group. (1991). Prevention of Neural-tube defects: Results of the Medical Research Council vitamin study. *Lancet, 338,* 131–137.

Weitzman, M., Gortmaker, S., Walker, D. K., & Sobol, A. (1990). Maternal smoking and childhood asthma. *Pediatrics, 85,* 505–511.

Zuckerman, B., Bauchner, H., Parker, S., & Cabral, H. (1990). Maternal depressive symptoms during pregnancy and newborn irritability. *Journal of Developmental and Behavioral Pediatrics, 11,* 190–194.

Zuckerman, B., & Beardslee, W. (1987). Maternal depression: An issue for pediatricians. *Pediatrics, 79,* 110–117.

Zuckerman, B., & Bresnahan, K. (1991). Developmental and behavioral consequences of prenatal drug and alcohol exposure. *Pediatric Clinics of North America, 83,* 1387–1407.

Zuckerman, B., Stevenson, J., & Bailey, V. (1987a). Sleep problems in early childhood continuities, predictive factors, and behavioral correlates. *Pediatrics, 80,* 664–671.

Zuckerman, B., Stevenson, J., & Bailey, V. (1987b). Stomachaches and headaches in a community sample of preschool children. *Pediatrics, 79,* 677–682.

Zurarin, S. J. (1987). Unplanned pregnancies, family planning problems and child maltreatment. *Family Relations, 36,* 135–139.

Transforming Social Services

Family-Supportive Strategies

Ruth W. Massinga

The beginning of the second decade of the family support movement signaled a push from practitioners and advocates to secure federal legislative endorsement for family support principles, together with sufficient appropriations that could change the programmatic direction of major human services systems in the country. Within fewer than fifteen years from the beginning of the movement, a substantial achievement of both aims was celebrated, and the full promise of large-scale implementation of family support programs lay ahead.

In the bruising budget battles of the summer of 1993, an alliance of elected leaders, child and family advocates, and urban and civil rights champions coalesced behind initiatives proposed by President Clinton and enacted by Congress in the Omnibus Budget Reconciliation Act of 1993, which were designed to provide both attention and money to expand and develop states' capacity to operate family-preservation services to help families at risk or in crisis, as well as to establish broad-based family support services within communities. The new capped entitlement totals $930 million through FY 1998 and specifically calls for all state-level child welfare agencies to develop program and expenditure plans in consultation with private, nonprofit, and community-based organizations with experience in transforming service programs for children and families.

As important as these new resources are for establishment of these community institutions, a new milestone was reached in helping individual working-poor families address income disparities between themselves and lower-middle-income families. Congress added $21 billion over the next five years to the earned-income tax credit, providing families with two or more children, and a full-time worker earning between $8,425 and $11,000, an annual maximum credit of $3,370. This, along with broadened eligibility for federal food stamps and increased services (for example, child care and immunization for low-income children and families), will allow significant numbers of working families to surpass the poverty level for a family of four of $25,000.

The budget bill also includes a number of new mandates for states to establish paternity and expand the medical coverage that children receive from noncustodial parents. The bill does the following:

1. Prohibits insurers from denying enrollment of a child on the grounds that the child was born out of wedlock, was not claimed as a dependent on the parent's federal income tax return, or does not reside with the parent
2. Requires insurers of noncustodial parents to provide information to the custodial parent necessary for the child to obtain medical benefits and permit the custodial parent to submit claims and receive reimbursement
3. Provides for the garnishment of wages if the noncustodial parent fails to reimburse the custodial parent when reimbursement is provided by the insurer
4. Provides for open enrollment of health insurance and child support cases

This combination of expanded opportunities and obligations for individual parents and communities alike is responsive to many recent calls, notably from the National Commission on Children, that the nation develop a comprehensive income security system, as well as a comprehensive community-level approach, to strengthen families (National Commission on Children, 1991). Further, if successfully combined with the $1 billion addition to the Title XX Social Services Block Grant to create empowerment zones and enterprise communities in selected poor and distressed urban and rural areas around the country through combinations of social services funds, employment, and tax incentives, these federal initiatives can go a long way toward creating a universally available system of state and local public social services, not contemplated since the beginnings of the social security system more than fifty years ago.

Having achieved its goal, the family support movement has to face a dilemma — how to address a potential negative reaction from consumers and taxpayers. What hope have we for publicly administered social service systems to rise from decades of public disfavor with recipients, employees, and citizens alike and respond to deserved calls for major system rejuvenation, if not re-creation?

The status of America's public social services system reflects our deep ambivalence about which families we collectively encourage to thrive and which must fend for themselves. In a real sense, system reform can be a slick, technologically supported recasting of triage arrangements, or it can begin with a courageous rethinking of societal institutions and values. We might start with a question: What kind of society do we want to be, and thus have mirrored in our human services institutions? If we value mutual support and shared responsibility between the public sector institutions and all families for solid development of all America's children, the means we undertake to reach those goals should reflect those values and affect all families equally.

But if the meaning of shared responsibility is weighted more toward individual families' shouldering of responsibility for good outcomes for children defined as "at risk," then let us define the consequences of goal achievement and goal failure primarily in terms of those individuals' behaviors, with public institutions playing only a subsidiary role. Our current national rhetoric promotes a both/and rather than an either/or decision path. At best, it sets out confusing goals that are difficult to sort through and reach, both for individual families and for social service institutions. At worst, it paralyzes and defers the collective focus, leaving the field to determined and organized interest groups. While it is important to reform seriously flawed systems, a purely instrumental or technocratic approach to reform will leave the public, the reformers, and the families as unsatisfied as we say we are now. In large measure, defining our value preferences about families is at the heart of the current political debate about the direction the nation must take into the twenty-first century. As Bellah et al. observe (1992), "what the family most needs is a context of relationships and institutions that give it attention, not just money" (p. 262).

The extraordinarily close votes in both houses of Congress that resulted in the budget plan leave the values question squarely on the table. Although the predominant public discussions centered on the degree to which the budget achieved deficit reduction, and on which portion of the public most of the taxes would fall, a major theme of the political debate was a reprise of the discussions begun in 1980, when government support for social programs was reduced. Stockman (1986) has declared that the frontal assault on the American welfare state was based on "sound money [and] lower tax rates," and that "a vast curtailment of federal spending, welfare, and subsidies was the only recipe for sustained economic growth and social progress" (p. 3).

Now, with a new moderate Democratic president elected by a plurality vote, there is recognition that our collective understanding about American families is evolving, among political conservatives and liberals alike, in ways that can help us reach common ground. This new learning leads us to change our expectations of the public institutions that focus on children and family concerns. Zill (1993, pp. 48–50) describes some "troublesome truths for conservatives":

- Federal programs have made a difference in children's lives.
- The U.S. economy has changed in ways that make it hard for young families to "play by the rules" and still do well.
- The connections between family living patterns and chil-

dren's well-being are more complicated than they are usually portrayed as being.
- It costs money to change values and behavior.

He goes on to list some "irksome conclusions for liberals":

- Many problems of today's children do stem from detrimental behavior patterns, either those of parents or those of the young people themselves.
- The growth in single-parent families has not been good for children.
- We do not yet know how to take a child born into multiple-risk family circumstances and transform him or her into a healthy, happy, productive adult.

Given the uncertain cultural and political context within which we appreciate these realities, it is self-evident that social service leaders must proceed to take advantage of the challenges that lie ahead, with exhilaration tinged with humility and caution. The task is no less than that of creating new forums within which people of good will can forge a new model of private and public commitment to reform institutions that meet all of our needs. Bellah et al. (1992) suggest a way to frame the decision-making processes needed to implement new strategies for action:

> Programs of widened citizen participation in actual policy planning and decision making complement another principle we consider crucial in dealing with the scale and complexity of modern society — the principle of "subsidiary." According to this principle, power should devolve on the lowest, most local level at which decisions can be reasonably made, with the function of the larger unit being to support and assist the local body in carrying out its tasks. . . . As we use it here, subsidiary implies that higher-level associations such as the state should never replace what lower-level associations can do effectively, but it also implies their obligation to help

when the lower-level associations lack resources to
do the job alone. (p. 262)

This notion of vastly expanded inclusion is wholly consistent with the history of an ever-widening circle of actors involved in managing organizational effectiveness. Weisbord
(1993) describes a series of ever more complex evolutions and
expectations: first experts solved problems (1900s), and then
everybody solved problems (1940s), and then experts improved
whole systems (1950s), and everybody will soon be improving
whole systems (by the year 2000). Within modern organizations,
including social services systems, this trend is interlaced with
movements to actively engage front-line staff in decision making about the nature of their work, with a goal of improving
that work significantly. Moreover, if one believes that most enterprises use only a part of the potential talent available to them,
broader involvement in tackling and resolving stubborn social
services delivery problems makes eminent sense.

It is fortunate that, over the past decade, institutional
change models in the social service arena have been tested by
the states and localities, in full partnership with national and
community foundations, national child and family support advocacy and development organizations, and hundreds of thousands of families, all of which are engaged in creating a "new"
social service network with changed roles and functions. By examining those experiences, we can begin to predict the future
evolution of social services, cast in a new framework of family
support. Let us begin by looking at child welfare reform efforts.

Child Welfare System Changes

In 1980, Congress enacted the Child Welfare and Adoption Assistance Act to reform the child welfare system and prevent children in the state's protective custody from being "lost" in substitute care. This law was intended to prevent the removal of
children from their homes except when absolutely necessary,
and, through "permanency planning," to return children to their
families or place them in relatives' homes, adoptive homes, or

other permanent living arrangements. Initially, the law succeeded in meeting its major goals. From the late 1970s to 1985,
there were significant decreases in the number of children in
out-of-home care, reductions in the average time children remained in the child welfare system, and increases in the foster-
care turnover rates, suggesting that most children were moving
to permanent situations without delay. More intensive in-home
services for vulnerable children and their families were being
put in place, replicating the successful model of family preservation used by Homebuilders, a private child welfare program
based in Tacoma, Washington. These trends were slowed and
then reversed in the middle 1980s. The growing number of troubled families (because of drug use, inadequate drug-treatment
facilities, and increased violence in homes and communities)
has overwhelmed the child welfare system. More children are
placed outside their homes, largely because of limited alternatives for support and services to strengthen and reunify their
families.

Moreover, until the passage of the Clinton budget bill,
the growing number of children in out-of-home placements—
442,000 as of 1992, according to Tatara (1993)—was the product
of misguided federal and state funding incentives. Federal funding for preventive and family support services was fixed each
year and barely grew in the past decade, while funding for out-
of-home care was supported by an open-ended entitlement that
grew automatically according to need. Under Title IV-E of the
Child Welfare Law, the federal government continues to provide open-ended matching funds to states for out-of-home placement. Funding for Title IV-E federal and state outlays increased
dramatically during the 1980s, in response to the rising number of children placed in alternative care and the growing claims
for state and local administrative responsibilities. Between 1981
and 1991, administrative and program-related expenses increased, from $30 million to $882 million. Administrative expenses include more than just record keeping and reporting,
however. By law, they include referral of troubled families to
child welfare services, preparation for and participation in judicial determinations of child placement, initial development

and continued review of a foster child's case plan to determine
when reunification with the family or adoption is appropriate,
and recruitment and licensing of foster homes and institutions.
The administrative burden of these decision-making processes
has led to significantly more federal outlays for out-of-home
placement than for support services to strengthen families and
prevent removal of children from their homes. Strict legal mandates and low funding levels for alternative preventive services
have resulted in states' placement of children in out-of-home care
rather than in helping troubled families overcome their problems and maintain custody of their children.

With the enactment of the Omnibus Budget Reconciliation Act of 1993, Title IV-B of the Child Welfare and Adoption Assistance Act, which provides funds to states for family
support, prevention, and reunification services, was significantly
increased for the first time in twelve years. With the $1 billion
increase in funds has come a major shift in policy direction,
which arises out of states' experience with family support values
and program direction.

Beginning in earnest in the late 1980s, increasing numbers of states and localities have spent increasingly precious local funds to accelerate family preservation and family support.
Counter to the federal policy direction, these initiatives have
aimed at redirecting the flow of youth from foster care back to
their own families, which were receiving community-based help
in realizing their own potential to raise their children adequately.
Some states have been assisted by grants and by the policy
impetus of several national foundations, notably the Annie E.
Casey Foundation, Edna McConnell Clark Foundation, and
the McKnight Foundation, together with important program
and administrative intermediaries (for example, the Center for
the Study of Social Policy, the Philadelphia-based Center for
Analysis and Policy Development, and multiple evaluative bodies). Together, these public-private partnerships have given life
to the long-term comprehensive child welfare system that was
contemplated but frustrated in the implementation of the Child
Welfare and Adoption Assistance Act.

In 1988, The Annie E. Casey Foundation began a multiyear relationship with the states of Maryland, Connecticut, and North Dakota, focused on reducing out-of-home placements in those states across the major systems (child welfare, mental health, and juvenile justice). More recently, Casey has provided assistance to the states of Tennessee and Kentucky, as well as the District of Columbia, in related efforts to reform child welfare systems. In 1992, the foundation initiated a new round of family foster-care reforms, Family to Family, in which three states will receive funds to transform family foster-care systems into neighborhood-based helping networks. In all these efforts, the foundation is helping to reinforce the goals of state child welfare systems: to strengthen families and communities that want children to remain at home, with good services that permit parents to resolve the multiple stresses that interfere with their provision of adequate child protection. Key to these initiatives is the promotion of family support principles, as well as the establishment of family support centers as a fundamental building block of the "new" child and family services system.

Similarly, the Edna McConnell Clark Foundation has provided long-term support for the establishment and evaluation of family preservation in fourteen states. The Clark effort is increasingly focused on developing strong family preservation across categorical boundaries (mental health, developmental disabilities, and drug treatment). Largely because of the successful dissemination of research findings sponsored by Clark, fourteen states are making services for family preservation available statewide. Of course, that will be multiplied severalfold with the availability of new federal funds for this work.

Understanding that people in trouble are frequently the best diagnosticians of the help that they need, in the fall of 1992 the Hennepin County (Minnesota) Community Service Department initiated Family Options, a demonstration project in which six hundred families at high risk for child maltreatment are provided with a family service account of $3,500 maximum for a twelve-month period. It can be used to pay for services at the agencies of each family's choice. The family and "host" community agency set out a plan of core service, designed to address the factors that place children in danger of maltreatment.

The demonstration seeks to document how family discretion and decision-making authority addresses the following issues:

- Changes in provider response and adjustment to the family's definition of its needs
- Systems-level changes in resource-allocation patterns, as well as changes in service access, provision, and reimbursement
- Cost-effectiveness and financial benefits of enhanced consumer choice, as compared to comparable public and private costs.

The aim of the project is to reduce the rate of child abuse and neglect by at least 15 percent lower than the rate of the comparison group. The project is supported in part by funds from the McKnight Foundation. Early reports are encouraging, as fewer project families are reported for recurrences of suspected child maltreatment.

Almost before these initiatives to improve child welfare outcomes began to thrive and mature, second-, third-, and fourth-generation service reform and integration efforts involving several disciplines (child welfare, health, education, and income support) were burgeoning across the country, some with similar partnerships involving foundations and federal and state government, and some initiated at the state or the local level, but all linked by certain common values and operating assumptions:

- Multidisciplinary efforts are more effective ways to provide services to families.
- Multigenerational bundling of services is a more helpful and effective way to engage stressed families, whose members frequently are unable to comprehend and negotiate a single system.
- Child protection and maternal and child health networks and family support networks are housed in schools or neighborhood centers, facilitating participants' access to multiple services.
- Staff training and job descriptions should place high value on flexible, family-centered work provided in settings and at times convenient for optimum family participation.

- Multiple funding streams, blended to maximize eligibility and comprehensiveness of service, must be put together.
- Merged or collaborative services require new methods of funding, with various funders planning together in order to uncover potentially new uses of federal and state funds, as well as more efficient and creative uses of currently available funds. Fungibility is *in;* single streams of financial support are *out.*

At bottom, the emerging social services paradigm, service integration as contrasted with rigid categorization of service streams, is based on the assumption that government systems, too, can operate from the same principles of mutual obligation, collaboration, and reciprocity of responsibility that families are expected to follow when they seek help from our systems. It is instructive that the public systems most widely perceived to be ineffective in meeting the basic goals of their missions — education, health, and child welfare — are working hard to combine their efforts, especially in addressing the needs of poor children and families. This is occurring in large part because program staffs recognize that the interactive effects of inadequate academic mastery, ill health, poverty, and family dysfunction are toxic for families and neighborhoods. The antidotes must be applied with vigor and, it is believed, in concentrated doses.

Providing services all at once in one place reduces the stresses that families experience in asking for and getting help and improves the possibility that program staff members who can help reduce risks are available when families and their colleagues need them. Evolving school reform initiatives increasingly anticipate linking and even integrating multidisciplinary, family-focused services. Kentucky's Family Resource and Youth Service Centers are the most ambitious of these efforts to date, anticipating resource centers linked to 1,200 schools. Behrman (1992) describes efforts now under way to link and integrate social services to families and children within the orbit of schools.

In the end, these complicated and bold reform initiatives, wherever they are lodged and whatever their primary goals, will succeed less because of the instrumental or structural changes undertaken, critical though they are, than because stakeholders at all levels—line social workers, eligibility workers, teachers, nurses and, most important, engaged citizens—are willing to trust and legitimize one another's motives, perceptions, and interests in discovering new or blended service designs. We all recognize that the creative process will accentuate differences in language, approaches, and strategies, even if the end goals are the same. Anticipating and managing differences is a major key to planning and sorting through effective multiple efforts. For real collaboration to occur, we must buy into a belief, a vision, and a set of values that affirm the creative potential of managing differences, together with "a constructive process for designing creative solutions to complex multi-party problems" (Gray, 1989, pp. 24–25). As Schorr notes (1993, p. 99), "Collaboration solves many problems, but, by itself, will not improve outcomes. It is futile to put together services that are of mediocre quality, that are rendered grudgingly, that are rendered by professionals who do not know how to work collaboratively with families and are unable to respond to the unique characteristics of the community they serve."

The challenge of ensuring that the principles of family support are embedded in the child welfare services reform movement calls for continued reinforcement of the four attributes of successful programs, as described by Schorr (1993):

- Successful programs are comprehensive, intensive, flexible and responsive.
- Successful programs deal with children as part of families, and with families as part of neighborhoods and communities.
- Staff in successful programs have the time, skills, and support to build relationships of trust and respect with children and families.
- Successful programs have a long-term, preventive orientation and continue to evolve over time.

If these elements require relentless attention in child welfare systems, consider the odds of reorienting the public welfare system toward family support.

Income Security System Reform

Sitting in the U.S. Senate gallery and listening to the final debate on the bill that became the Family Support Act of 1988, public welfare commissioners, advocates, and staff members of the National Governors Association, who had championed the bill, believed that a new social contract between the government and welfare recipients, between liberals and conservatives, between states and the federal government, was being ushered in. Families receiving public assistance were to be required to take and maintain steps actively to become economically self-supporting. At the same time, government assumed the obligation to provide the means to assist these families' move from the welfare system, by authorizing up to $1.3 billion in federal matching funds for the new JOBS program by 1995, when 20 percent of nonexempt welfare recipients are to participate in state employment, education, and training services.

Since the new law provided that parents of children three years old and older were required to participate in the JOBS program, open-ended federal matching funds for child care were to be made available, at a rate ranging from 50 to 80 percent federal and state contributions, based on the current Medicaid funding rate for the respective state. Medicaid benefits were to be continued for up to twelve months after the recipient started work, and a beefed-up child support system provided states with incentives directed toward establishing and collecting financial support from the absent parent. All these provisions were built on previous evidence from state experiments, demonstrating that, in combination, a balance between sufficient, easily obtained incentives and fairly determined, consistently applied obligations and responsibilities would make work pay off, both for welfare recipients and for taxpayers.

How have states responded to the challenge of implementing this ambitious reform? Not as aggressively as legislators envisioned: the overarching influence is scarce state dollars. A study of ten states' initial efforts concludes:

> States are making widely varying efforts to fund JOBS. The majority are spending considerably

more on JOBS than on previous welfare employment programs. Oregon plans to spend enough, or
almost enough, to draw down its full allocation of
funds, as does Maryland, while Mississippi and
Tennessee have appropriated very limited additional revenues for JOBS services. Administrators
in half the states reviewed attributed their states'
decisions to limit expenditures to constrained fiscal
conditions. Funding may also have been restricted
for JOBS by the need to comply with mandates of
the Family Support Act . . . . (Hagen & Lurie,
1992, pp. 140–142)

In fact, at the same time as the intended welfare reforms were
due to be implemented in earnest by the states, the recession
of 1989–1992 led to twenty-five straight months of unprecedented
numbers of eligible families applying for food stamps. Starting
in 1989, there was an accelerating growth in average cases of
Aid to Families with Dependent Children of 305,000 per year
(American Public Welfare Association, 1993). Generally slug-
gish job growth and significant layoffs across various economic
sectors in many regions of the country have also led to a shortage
of jobs for public welfare recipients, mandate notwithstanding.
Looking to the future impacts of the laudable income-support
features of the Clinton budget, we must recognize that the expanded provisions are predicated on having a job, no matter
how poorly it may pay.

President Clinton was elected on a promise to "end welfare as we know it." One of the most controversial aspects of
his plan is to hold participation in public welfare programs to
a specific time-limit for the able-bodied, after which the person
gets a job or performs community service. The president articulates a broad feeling within the American public, which at its
most noble argues that it is clearly in the best interests of the
larger society that our national productivity and earnings be
increased by the work of as many citizens as possible. It is not
useful to the nation, or to poor families, that men and women
who could be productive remain out of the work force. Our na-

tional reliance on their work must be unequivocally stated. The obligation of heads of households who could work to do so needs clear affirmation, along with associated consequences that can be fairly and seriously applied.

At the same time, the opportunity structures that support job creation, job training, and support for working families must be extended to these new entrants into the work force, initially with more concentrated community efforts and costs, which will diminish as the new workers grow economically sturdier. Here again, how can the goals of reforms be met in ways that are consistent with the family support principle that promotes programs respectful of families across the developmental continuum of parents and children and sets out to encourage poor families to be active agents in determining how the results that all of us want for them — economic self-sufficiency — can be achieved?

The Manpower Demonstration Research Corporation (MDRC) has undertaken several studies of welfare reform initiatives over the last decade, including studies of two statewide reform efforts, GAIN in California and LEAP in Ohio. In May 1993, MDRC issued reports on the results of those changes that suggest beginning ways to solve the implementation puzzle, keeping family support ideas at the forefront.

GAIN, California's version of JOBS authorized by the 1988 Family Support Act, resulted in increased earnings and reduction in welfare costs in the six counties studied. Overall, single parents' second-year earnings were increased by 24 percent and welfare payments were reduced by 7 percent. In Riverside County, earnings went up by 53 percent and welfare costs were decreased by 17 percent. In a preliminary analysis of Riverside County's distinctive ability to achieve its goals at a rate far exceeding other counties in the experiment, reseachers noted "its particular combination of practices and conditions. Its pervasive employment message and job development efforts, its strong commitment of securing the participation of all mandatory registrants (and having adequate resources to apply this objective), its greater reliance on GAIN's formal enforcement mechanisms (a strategy that, in general, may be associated with greater welfare savings across the six counties), and its more equal use of job search and education and training activities comprised a constellation of practices not found in any other county. And, Riverside's approach may have enjoyed an 'added boost' from its growing economy" (Friedlander, 1993, pp. 136–138).

It would appear that consistent messages, vigorously applied, along with making the means to achieve the goals available to staff and affected families, combine to yield the desired results. Simply put, if people know what is expected of them, and all of the relevant systems reinforce those expectations, they will fulfill their obligations to meet program goals and become more self-reliant.

Support for this conclusion also comes from the report on the Ohio LEAP program, a statewide initiative that uses financial incentives, case management, and support services, all aimed at increasing school attendance by teenage mothers on welfare. Eligible teens who enroll in school and attend regularly receive a $62 bonus in their monthly welfare grants. Those who fail to enroll or attend poorly have their grants reduced by $62. The program goals are the reduction of long-term welfare receipt, to which teen mothers are particularly susceptible, as well as promotion of high school graduation. More than twenty thousand teenagers have participated in the program. Based on comparison of seven thousand teenagers randomly assigned to a program group or a control group of nonparticipants, findings indicate a 10 percent increase in continuous school enrollment during the year participants who stayed in school became eligible for LEAP. There was a 13 percent increase in the rate at which school dropouts returned to school or entered a GED program. Early evidence suggests that LEAP may produce significant increases in high school graduation and GED completion.

One of the interesting features of the LEAP study design is the use of focus groups to get a sense of the attitudes and beliefs of the teenage mothers. Young women who indicated that they had close relationships with staff members said the staff had pushed them to succeed. Positive reinforcement from these staff members seemed critically important to these teenagers and included help with food, clothing, and transportation. Participants who reported little contact with workers appeared less likely to understand the program rules and more likely to be sanctioned for failing to provide proper evidence of good cause for nonattendance at school. The successful participants said that LEAP had caused them to speed up the return to school that they had been planning anyway, helped them to stay in school, and motivated them to take and pass the GED test, in order to avoid sanctions (Bloom, 1993).

Not surprisingly, when staff members take the time to help a family understand goals and deal with the individual developmental needs of the person identified as the primary client, results are more consistently achieved. In turn, worker satisfaction is enhanced and further collaboration between staff and families can be enhanced. This principle is supported by Hagen, Lurie, & Wang (1993) who report that workers want stronger emphasis on the JOBS program within their agencies and are especially interested in staff training to enhance their effectiveness, particularly in terms of access to local education, employment, and training services on behalf of their clients. These findings, and others that stress a customer focus to organizing government services, are being widely studied and applied by public welfare commissioners. Managers are increasingly convinced that when the consumers of the service feel that they are approached in a respectful manner and are part of the planning process, even within a highly proscribed service, they respond in a positive, goal-oriented manner.

Can Public Social Services Support Families?

The vitality and richness of current innovations in social services are likely to produce shifts in the context within which those services are delivered. As we anticipate these shifts, it is less important to describe in detail the social service "programs" that will emerge than to be clear about having a social service system that is built on citizen and consumer participation, is focused on the strengths and skills of the consumers and their communities, and is responsive to the differing cultural and developmental needs of family members. Such a system is more likely to exhibit family support principles in the methods used to craft services and is more likely to be regarded as effective by consumers and taxpayers. Pursuing such strategies for system redesign will permit us to refute those critics who doubt the possibility that public social services can be truly family-supportive. These systems *are* ready to address the opportunities that lie ahead.

It is probably wise for us to encourage the proliferation of new models of service delivery in which we practice blending the new values with new expectations of our social service system. That new system will probably look like a family support center, or a school, or a multidisciplinary home-visiting team. The system will stress the inputs of citizen-planners, who may volunteer to deliver homemaker services one day, be on an evaluation team for a child-care center the next, and give advice as foster-care alumni on yet another day. Most important, we must be bold and wise simultaneously, willing to constantly examine whether our means are adequate to our goals. As we maintain a respectful irreverence for current pioneering efforts, we must experiment and evaluate relentlessly, recognizing that not all the first- or fifth-generation system redesigns will be effective. From the mix of possibilities we will discern several robust archetypes of the new system that will work, for a time.

None of our models fully matches our rhetoric — yet. None is fully responsive to family diversity or inclusive enough of the varieties of citizen system builders. Nevertheless, by insisting on measuring the results of system reform by family support principles, we are more likely to get closer to a satisfactory system.

The transformation of social services that we seek involves high stakes. It is being spun out of systems that enjoy little public confidence and few expectations of real improvement. The hoped-for results are uncertain, and our change processes are also uncertain at best. But the contract between the governed and government for the twenty-first century must assume that American social service institutions will be competent and responsive in aiding the most vulnerable citizens, who are being rightly challenged to become more productive.

References

American Public Welfare Association. (1993). Forecasting AFDC caseloads, with an emphasis on economic factors. *This Week in Washington, 14*(34), 1-2.

Behrman, R. (Ed.). (1992). *Journal for the Future of Children, 2*(1), entire issue.

Bellah, R. N., et al. (1992). *The good society.* New York: Knopf.

Bloom, D. (1993). *LEAP: Interim findings on a welfare initiative to improve school attendance among teenage parents.* New York: Manpower Demonstration Research Corporation.

Friedlander, D. (1993). *GAIN: Two-year impacts in six counties.* New York: Manpower Demonstration Research Corporation.

Gray, B. (1989). *Collaborating: Finding common ground for multiparty problems.* San Francisco: Jossey-Bass.

Hagen, J., & Lurie, I. (1992). *Implementing JOBS: Initial state choices.* Albany: Nelson A. Rockefeller Institute of Government, State University of New York.

Hagen, J., Lurie, I., & Wang, L. (1993) *Implementing JOBS: The perspective of front-line workers.* Albany: Nelson A. Rockefeller Institute of Government, State University of New York.

National Commission on Children. (1991). *Beyond rhetoric: A new American agenda for children and families.* Washington, DC: U.S. Government Printing Office.

Schorr, L. B. (1993). Daring to learn from our successes. *Aspen Institute Quarterly, 5*(1), 99.

Stockman, D. (1986). *The triumph of politics.* New York: Harper-Collins.

Tatara, T. (1993). *Voluntary cooperative information system.* Washington, DC: American Public Welfare Association.

Weisbord, M. R. (1993). *Discovering common ground: How future search conferences bring people together to achieve breakthrough innovation, empowerment, shared vision, and collaborative action.* San Francisco: Berrett-Koehler.

Zill, N. (1993). The changing realities of family life. *Aspen Institute Quarterly, 5*(1), 48-50.

Families and Work

The Importance of the Quality of the Work Environment

Ellen Galinsky

By and large, companies have been providing work-family assistance to prevent family problems from interfering with their employees' productivity on the job. Nevertheless, there has been virtually no attention to improving the quality of work environments, including social relationships at work, as a means of helping employees balance work and family life. New research reveals that this could be one of the most effective ways to reduce work-family conflict and stress among employed parents and to guard against poor developmental outcomes for children.

Context

There is no question of the rapidity of change in family life: 54.5 percent of mothers of children under three years old are in the labor force (U.S. Department of Labor, 1992), as compared to 34 percent in 1975 (U.S. Department of Labor, 1975). In fact, mothers typically take only twelve weeks off for childbirth (Bond, Galinsky, Lord, Staines, & Brown, 1991). An even higher number of the mothers of preschoolers (children from three to five years old) are in the labor force—63.3 percent—as are 75.3 percent of the mothers of school-age children (six to thirteen years old) and 77.5 percent of the mothers of teenagers (fourteen through seventeen years old) (U.S. Department of Labor, 1992). While some may think that the influx of mothers into the work force does not have much impact on the demographics of the work force, this is not the case: 42 percent of all wage earners and salaried workers have children under eighteen living at home (Galinsky, Bond, & Friedman, 1993).

Changes in the workplace have been equally dramatic. According to a nationally representative study of the U.S. work force conducted in 1992 by the Families and Work Institute, 42 percent of workers had experienced downsizing in their companies during the preceding year, and 28 percent had witnessed cutbacks in the numbers of managers. Likewise, 18 percent had experienced the effects of a merger or an acquisition of their companies, and 24 percent had experienced a change in the top leadership. With such rapid change, business's slow recovery from the recession, and an increasingly competitive business climate, it is not surprising that 18 percent of employees think that they will experience a temporary layoff during the coming year, and 17 percent suspect that they will lose their jobs altogether (Galinsky, Bond, & Friedman, 1993).

In focus groups, employees report that downsizing — cutbacks in "fat" throughout the company and in the managerial ranks, to render the company lean, mean and competitive — has increased their work load. In fact, both men and women in the U.S. work force report working longer hours than they wish. Men work an average of 45.8 hours per week and would prefer to work 40.3 hours. Women work 39.8 hours but wish they were working 34.7 hours (Galinsky, Bond, & Friedman, 1993). Phrases like *time famine* have become commonplace, and books like *The Overworked American* (Schor, 1993) have hit the best-seller list. According to the Families and Work Institute's National Study of the Changing Workforce, 80 percent of workers agree that their jobs require working very hard, and 65 percent agree that their jobs require working very fast. An astounding 42 percent of U.S. workers feel "used up" at the end of the work day, and 40 percent feel tired when they get up in the morning and have to face another day on the job (Galinsky, Bond, & Friedman, 1993).

Likewise, the family has felt the repercussion of these changes. For the first time, the number of cats in U.S. households has surpassed the number of dogs: everyone knows that cats take less time. Families with children engage in "tag-team parenting" and fantasize about "quality time" the way they used to fantasize about "and they got married and lived happily ever after." There is even a book for parents on the one-minute bedtime story. Overall, 66 percent of parents with children eighteen and under say they do not spend as much time with their children as they would like to, and 15 percent of employed parents say they never or rarely (once a week or less) do things with their children for "fun and recreation." There are 17 percent of parents with children under thirteen years old who experience "a lot" or "quite a lot" of conflict in balancing work, family, and personal life, while another 43 percent experience some conflict. Not surprisingly, workers with children exhibit higher levels of stress and are not coping as well as other workers (Galinsky, Bond, & Friedman, 1993).

Assumptions and Reality: Findings from Research

These changes in work life and family life have given rise to numerous commonly held assumptions about the causes of work-family problems, the kinds of work-family assistance business is providing, and the impact of this assistance on productivity and family stress. Fortunately, a growing number of studies examine the new social realities in the workplace and in family life, enabling an assessment of the validity of current assumptions.

Assumption: Maternal employment is, in and of itself, harmful to women and their families.
The corollary of this assumption is that if women would just return to their rightful place by the home fires, family problems would abate. This assumption posits that belt tightening would make a return to the home possible. That may be true for some families, but it certainly is not true for most. Dual-earner employed women contribute, on the average, 40 per-

cent of their family income. Among married women with children under six years of age, 54 percent feel it would be extremely difficult or quite difficult not to have a paid job, and only 3 percent feel it would not be difficult at all (Galinsky, Bond, & Friedman, 1993).

Also underlying this assumption is the belief that juggling multiple roles is inherently a problem. Crosby (1991) writes of the societal image of "the bedraggled Mrs. Juggler whose supermom cape has become badly tattered" (p. 66). Yet the research tells another story. It is becoming clear that the benefits of having multiple roles tend to outweigh the problems: women who juggle multiple roles are generally less depressed, higher in self-esteem, and happier (Crosby, 1991; Baruch & Barnett, 1987; Repetti, 1987). As employed parents report, having something go well in one part of one's life can compensate for problems in another area. Although much of this research has compared employed with nonemployed women, it stands to reason that employment per se is not the critical factor; it is having more than one focus in one's life that can bring satisfaction. It is also true that employment is not always satisfying—jobs can be gratifying or stressful, sources of pleasure or of pain.

Similarly, the research on how children are affected when their mothers are employed initially concentrated on comparisons of employed and at-home mothers, setting out either to prove or to disprove that employment caused harm (Bronfenbrenner & Crouter, 1982). After several decades of research, social scientists have concluded that maternal employment per se is not a robust variable. There are variations in home life, job life, and child care, and these variations affect children more than the fact of whether or not their mothers work (Howes, et al., in press).

Assumption: The logistics of employment, particularly child care, are the source of work-family conflict.

In speeches, when audiences are asked to guess the leading sources of work-family problems for employed parents, typical guesses are child care, guilt, and too much to do at home in too little time. Research has revealed that child care does have an impact on parents. Some studies have examined the impact of parental satisfaction with child care on parental well-being. The results of these studies are mixed. For example, a substudy of the National Child Care Staffing Study (Whitebook, Howes, & Phillips, 1990), with a sample of 441 mothers in forty-six centers in Atlanta, found that it is maternal satisfaction with how child-care arrangements meet the adults' needs (hours, cost, location, flexibility in covering parents' work schedules, and opportunities for parental input), not the children's needs (opportunities for learning, and so on), that has an impact on maternal stress and work-family conflict (Shinn, Galinsky, & Gulcur, 1990).

By contrast, the National Study of the Changing Workforce found that working parents who are more satisfied with their child-care arrangements are more likely to be satisfied with how they are doing as parents, are happier with their relationships with their spouses or partners, feel more successful in their personal and family lives, are more satisfied with their lives in general, are less stressed, and are coping better than parents who are less satisfied (Galinsky, Bond, & Friedman, 1993). Similarly, the breakdown of child-care arrangements (such as when the child-care provider is sick or does not show up) has a very negative effect on mothers' and fathers' well-being (Galinsky, Bond, & Friedman, 1993).

Other analyses of the substudy of the National Child Care Staffing Study enabled a comparison of how the actual quality of child care, as measured by standardized assessments using trained observers, affected maternal well-being. The findings revealed that parents were most affected by the nature of the relationship between their children and the children's teachers and by the frequency of staff turnover. When teachers are more detached, insensitive, or chaotic, mothers feel lonelier while their children are in care and miss their children more (Shinn, Phillips, Howes, Galinsky, & Whitebook, 1990). In addition, staff turnover explained between 18 and 31 percent of the variance in mothers' feelings about leaving their children in care. Higher staff turnover is linked to feelings of maternal inadequacy, loneliness, and the sense that the child may not benefit from being in child care.

Although child care does have an impact on parents' well-being, stress, and their ease in balancing work and family life, studies reveal that other factors are just as significant (and perhaps even more significant). Whenever audiences are asked to guess the "leading" sources of work-family conflict for employed parents, they tend to focus on the logistics of managing work and family life, rather than on the nature of jobs themselves. Among the job characteristics that have been found to be most significant are demanding and pressured jobs, heavy work loads, job insecurity, long hours, lack of job autonomy, lack of control over work schedules, unsupportive relationships with supervisors and co-workers, an unsupportive social climate, and a discriminatory atmosphere (Galinsky, Bond, & Friedman, 1993; Repetti, 1993; Karasek, Gardell, & Lindell, 1987; Bromet, Dew, Parkinson, & Schulberg, 1988; Hughes, 1988; Rose, Jenkins, & Hurst, 1978; Piotrkowski & Crits-Cristoph, 1981; Beehr, King, & King, 1990; Repetti, 1987; Greenberger, Goldberg, Hamill, O'Neil, & Payne, 1989). These job characteristics also affect marital relationships and children's development. A study of 522 employees of Merck & Co., Inc., revealed that workers in demanding jobs, with little support from their supervisors for managing their work and family responsibilities, reported that they frequently came home from work in a bad mood and with little energy for their families. This "spillover" from work life to family life was in turn statistically linked to more tension in their marriages. Excessive work hours were also associated with more marital tension (Hughes, Galinsky, & Morris, 1992).

An obvious question is whether job-related psychological distress also affects children. Addressing this question was possible in the Atlanta substudy of the National Child Care Staffing Study because data were collected on 206 children, as well as on their mothers. The results indicated that when mothers have demanding jobs (the measure in this study defined a demanding job as requiring the employee to work very fast and hard for very long hours), their children are less likely to be developing optimally. In American children of European descent, parents' demanding jobs were associated with poorer social-emotional development and with poorer adaptive language. In African American children, parents' demanding jobs were associated with the children's spending more time aimlessly wandering about than being engaged in constructive activities while in child care (Howes et al., in press).

A qualitative study of union workers supports the finding that the nature of jobs themselves and unsupportive relationships at work are strongly linked to problems in managing work and family responsibilities. When asked what the union could do to improve the quality of their family life, children six to eight years old were most likely to say that helping the family have more time together would be "nice," but more important was having their parents come home from work less "wired." When the interviewers asked the children what caused their parents to come home wired, most of the children seemed to know. The children mentioned things that were bothering their parents at work: a new boss who was a "jerk," a boss who was asking the parent to do "stupid things," incompetent co-workers who made it necessary for the parent to pick up the slack by doing more work, tension on the assembly line, and so forth. The children then described different techniques for handling parents who were wired. One teenager said that she got into the bathtub right away, since that was a safe haven and her parents would not intrude. By the time she was out of the tub, the tension had blown over. Another child said that he picked a fight right away, since he knew there would be an eventual fight, and he "might as well get it over as soon as possible" (Galinsky, Hughes, Love, & Bragioner, 1987).

The nature of parents' jobs affects family life in other profound ways, including parenting skills. Greenberger & O'Neil (1991) found that fathers and mothers with complex and challenging jobs were warmer, more responsive, and more likely to have firm but flexible disciplinary styles, especially with their sons.

In sum, most people think of the logistics of managing work and family as having the greatest impact, but they are unaware that the nature of jobs themselves and of relationships at work strongly affect parents' ability to balance work and family responsibilities, marital relations, and their children's development. This knowledge, however elucidating, creates real cause for concern: long hours and demanding jobs are commonplace. As the National Study of the Changing Workforce reveals, 43 percent of employees feel that they are asked to do excessive amounts of work, 65 percent say their jobs require them to work very fast, and 80 percent say that their jobs require working very hard.

Assumption: Companies increasingly provide work-family assistance to help employees balance job and family responsibilities.

For the most part, this assumption is valid. In 1978, an estimated 110 companies provided child-care assistance, while 5,600 companies did so in 1990. There are two kinds of work-family assistance that companies provide: work supports and family supports. Work supports are programs and policies that enable the employee to be at work without distraction from family responsibilities. In other words, these supports are focused on the company, although they are very helpful to the employee. Work supports include assistance in finding and paying for child care. Family supports are programs and policies that enable the employee to spend more time at home; in other words, these policies support family life. They include flexible time and leave policies, as well as the opportunity to work at home. Figures 6.1 and 6.2 compare the work supports and family supports that companies report providing with those that employees report having available at their companies.

As these two figures make clear, companies are more likely to provide and employees are more likely to have access to family supports than work supports. However, the simple presence of flexible time and leave policies does not necessarily mean employees can freely use them. Usage is typically dependent on the permission of the supervisor. Although most employees state in needs assessments that greater flexiblity or flextime would be an enormous help, it is striking that just over one-quarter of employees (29 percent in both employee studies) have the ability to set their arrival and departure times. Even when they are available, taking advantage of these policies can jeopardize

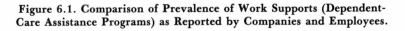

Figure 6.1. Comparison of Prevalence of Work Supports (Dependent-Care Assistance Programs) as Reported by Companies and Employees.

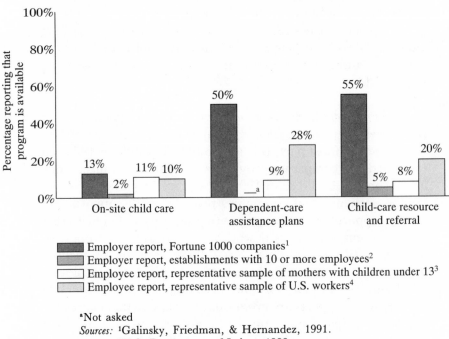

Employer report, Fortune 1000 companies[1]
Employer report, establishments with 10 or more employees[2]
Employee report, representative sample of mothers with children under 13[3]
Employee report, representative sample of U.S. workers[4]

[a]Not asked
Sources: [1]Galinsky, Friedman, & Hernandez, 1991.
[2]U.S. Department of Labor, 1988.
[3]Miller, 1992.
[4]Galinsky, Bond, & Friedman, 1993.

one's job or career: "Choosing flexible work options often carries a price. Even though part-time work, home-based employment, and job sharing allow parents to better balance job and family responsibilities, these options are often accompanied by lower wages, less opportunity for advancement, and less access to other employee benefits" (Employee Benefit Research Institute, 1992, p. 15).

A study conducted by the Families and Work Institute at four Johnson & Johnson (J&J) companies in 1990 found that although J&J offered very generous time and leave policies, 44 percent of employees thought that they paid a price for using these policies. Two years later, while that figure had gone down significantly, 32 percent (or one out of every three employees) still felt that taking advantage of the flexibility the company offered

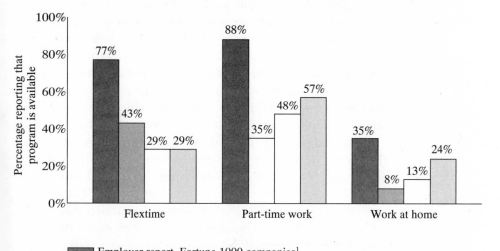

Figure 6.2. Comparison of Prevalence of Family Supports
(Flexible-Time Programs) as Reported by Companies and Employees.

■ Employer report, Fortune 1000 companies[1]
▨ Employer report, establishments with 10 or more employees[2]
□ Employee report, representative sample of mothers with children under 13[3]
▨ Employee report, representative sample of U.S. workers[4]

Sources: [1]Galinsky, Friedman, & Hernandez, 1991.
[2]U.S. Department of Labor, 1988.
[3]Miller, 1992.
[4]Galinsky, Bond, & Friedman, 1993.

would jeopardize their careers (Families and Work Institute, 1993a). Another Families and Work Institute study of parental leave found that the large majority of women cannot afford to take long leaves, even when these are offered by their employers. In fact, 19 percent of low-income women returned to work before the medically advised six weeks after childbirth was over (Bond, Galinsky, Lord, Staines, & Brown, 1991). Thus, although family supports are more prevalent than work supports, there are very real obstacles to using them.

A second problem is that the most privileged employees have greater access to work-family assistance than their less privileged counterparts. Analyses of the National Child Care Survey of 1990 found that 39 percent of the women in professional occupations had access to at least one child-care benefit, as compared to 11 percent of women in service jobs and 15 percent of women in production jobs. Similarly, 35 percent of women earning over $20 per hour were offered at least one child-care benefit, compared to 16 percent of women earning less than $5 per hour. Women with higher levels of education were three times more likely to have access to child-care benefits than women with less than high school education. The pattern of access to flexibility or family supports is more complex than access to work supports or child-care assistance, since flexibility usually carries with it lower wages and more dead-end jobs. For example, women earning less than $10 per hour were more likely to have the option of working part-time, whereas more highly paid and educated women had greater access to unpaid leave and flextime (Employee Benefit Research Institute, 1992).

This pattern of unequal access becomes dramatically visible in analyses conducted for the Families and Work Institute's National Study of the Changing Workforce. Access to dependent-care assistance was measured by calculation of how many of the following plans were available to workers: child-care resource and referral, elder-care resource and referral, employer-sponsored child-care services, child-care vouchers, and flexible spending accounts for dependent care. Scores ranged from 0 to 5, with the overall average being lower than 1 (0.66). As shown in Figure 6.3, more advantaged workers — managers and professionals, workers who earn more, and workers with more education — have greater access than other workers, and employees of larger organizations have much greater (but still quite limited) access to dependent-care assistance than employees of smaller organizations.

Access to flexible time and leave policies was measured by calculation of how many of the following policies or benefits were available to each respondent: paid vacation days, choice in setting times to start and end the work day, extended lunch hours for taking care of personal business, ability to work extra hours some days in order to take time off on others, ability to work at home on a regular basis, part-time work or job sharing, time off for childbirth and parenting, and time off to care for a sick child or family member. Scores ranged from 0 to 8. As can be seen in Figure 6.4, more advantaged workers — managers

Figure 6.3. Number of Dependent-Care Programs Received (Maximum = 5).

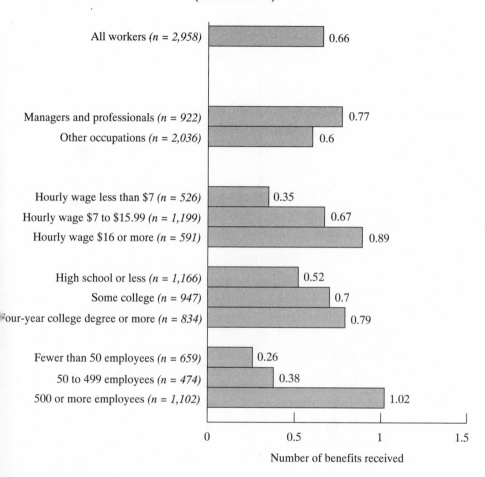

Note: All comparisons were statistically significant at $p < .0001$.
Sources: Families and Work Institute, 1993a, 1993b.

and professionals, workers who earn more, and workers with more education — again have greater access than other workers, although the discrepancies tend to be smaller than for dependent-care benefits. In addition, minority workers report less access to flexible time and leave policies than nonminority workers.

Figure 6.4. Number of Flexible-Time and Leave Benefits Received
(Maximum = 8).

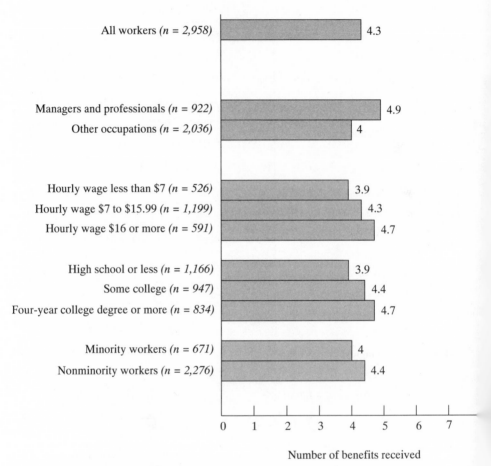

Number of benefits received

Note: All comparisons were statistically significant at $p < .0001$.
Sources: Families and Work Institute, 1993a, 1993b.

No differences were found by gender, age, dependent-care
responsibilities, or organizational size (number of employees nationwide).

  In sum, although companies in the U.S. have become significantly more responsive to the needs of families, in reality

there is differential access to the use of these programs. What is happening is that the gulf between the "haves" and the "have nots" in our society is being widened even more by reliance on the corporate sector to assist employees in meeting their family responsibilities.

Assumption: Work-family programs are win-win propositions, good for the employee and good for the company.

Is this assumption justified? Most companies and work-family consultants say so, but this claim has never been reliably tested until recently. Several new studies have begun to shed light on the impact of work-family assistance.

The National Study of the Changing Workforce found that workers who are offered more traditional fringe benefits (health insurance, pension plans), more flexible time and leave options, and/or more dependent-care assistance are more committed to doing their jobs well, are more satisfied with their jobs, and take more initiative at work. Workers with more flexible time and leave options and more dependent-care benefits also feel more loyal to their employers and are more committed to helping their employers succeed. However, this study found no connections between *access to* these programs (program use was not measured) and employees' well-being (Galinsky, Bond, & Friedman, 1993).

The longitudinal study of four Johnson & Johnson companies conducted by the Families and Work Institute (1993a) was also able to investigate the impact of work-family programs on the company and on employees. We found that users of the Johnson & Johnson Child Development Centers worry less about their children while at work than a comparable group of non users (J&J employees who would like to use the on-site centers but are not currently doing so). In addition, child-care problems are less likely to be viewed as negatively affecting productivity for women users of the on-site centers (but not for men users). This is undoubtedly due to the fact that the men with children in the on-site centers take greater responsibility for their children than do men using community child-care arrangements. They, not their wives, bring their children to the centers in the morning, end work promptly on time to pick their children up in the late afternoon, and are the ones called if the children become ill during the day. Despite the fathers' sense that there are negative productivity repercussions for using the centers, however, no measurable effects on productivity were actually found in this study. Furthermore, both women and men users of the centers feel that the Johnson & Johnson work-family program is "very important" in the decision to stay with the company.

An examination of the impact of flexible time and leave policies revealed that users are also more likely than nonusers to feel that these family-supportive policies are "very important" in the decision to stay with the company. Moreover, users are "much more likely" to recommend J&J as a place to work. Users also miss half as much work time as the work force as a whole—two days per year versus four days. These policies provide more relief for men than for women, however. Male employees who use these policies report less spillover from their jobs into family life than male nonusers, whereas women users report more spillover. Perhaps these policies provide just enough assistance for men, who tend to have less family responsibility, but not enough for women, who bear the lion's share of family work.

Thus the research to date reveals that work-family programs are basically a win-win proposition, although the results show stronger effects for companies than for employees, a finding that stands to reason. Programs vary in quality and in the intensity of intervention, and families vary in their need for this assistance.

Assumption: The solution to assisting families at work is the development of family-responsive programs.
The focus of the work-family field has been on the development of programs. Research at the Families and Work Institute indicates that the evolution of work-family assistance at a company tends to go through several stages. In stage 1, companies concentrate on child-care programs. Although the picture that most readily comes to mind is an on-site child-care center, companies are far more likely to provide help to employees in locating or in paying for child care than they are to construct an on- or near-site center. Among Fortune 1000 com-

panies, 13 percent have centers, compared to 55 percent offering child-care resources and referral and 50 percent offering dependent-care assistance plans (that is, salary-redirection accounts enabling employees to pay for child care with pretax dollars). In stage 2, companies enlarge the definition of dependent care to include elder care and also turn to the provision of more flexible time and leave policies, generally reviewing what they already have in place and expanding it to meet the needs of employees with family responsibilities (Galinsky, Friedman, & Hernandez, 1991). In stage 2 and stage 3, employers also typically begin to realize that programs and policies will not be effective in a vacuum. A leave policy in a hostile environment, where employees will be shunted into career limbo if they use the policy, may exist on the books but is not really available. This knowledge has led to the development of supervisory training programs, and 10 percent of large employers now train supervisors in how to handle the work-family concerns of employees. Providing managerial training is seen as a prevention strategy, enabling supervisors to learn how to use their discretionary power wisely. These training programs teach managers and employees to use a problem-solving process that attempts to accommodate the needs of employees and employer alike.

Studies reveal that the focus on improving supportive relationships at work has a more beneficial impact on employees than simply providing programs. In the Johnson & Johnson study, employees — both men and women — who rate their supervisors as more supportive, fair, and helpful when work-family problems arise are less stressed, experience less spillover from work into family life, and feel that they are more successful in balancing work and family life. They are also more loyal to the company, more likely to recommend J&J as a place to work, and more satisfied with their jobs. In addition, they report that family and personal matters interfere with work less often.

As assessment was also made of the impact of working in a company culture seen as supportive to employees' work-family concerns (in other words, one that does not force employees to choose between family and job and does not jeopardize them if they need to put their families ahead of their jobs). The results indicate that employees — both men and women — who experience the company culture as more family-friendly have the same positive outcomes as those with supportive supervisors: less stress, less work-family spillover, and less conflict in balancing work and family. In fact, these findings hold true regardless of whether the employee has a supportive supervisor. This suggests that the larger work environment affects employees independently of the attitudes and behavior of their immediate supervisors (Families and Work Institute, 1993a).

Next, an examination was conducted of which workers were the most likely to perceive their work environment as family-friendly. They fall into two groups: employees who report that the work-family benefits they have used met their needs, and those wih supportive supervisors. A finding consonant with the research revealing that job characteristics are strongly linked to work-family conflict is that employees who find the environment most responsive to their family needs are those who believe that they have more opportunities for promotion and who do not have high-pressure, stressful jobs. Surprisingly, they are also people with fewer family responsibilities. Women, employees with larger numbers of children under sixteen at home, and employees with more elder-care responsibilities are less likely to see the company as family-friendly. Perhaps they put heavier demands on the company to meet their needs, exceeding what the company can do and is willing to offer (Families and Work Institute, 1993b).

A study of a mid-size automotive gasket company, Fel-Pro, Inc., in Skokie, Illinois, also well known for its extensive family benefits program, came to similar conclusions. Conducted by University of Chicago researchers, this study found that those employees who use and appreciate Fel-Pro's benefits are more likely to want to remain with the company, to have better performance ratings by their supervisors, to have fewer work grievances, to be more open to organizational change, and to have participated more in the company's total quality management efforts. The researchers feel that work-family assistance can be seen as a foundation on which to build support for total quality management (Lambert, et al., 1993). As in the analysis of the Johnson & Johnson data, this study assessed which workers are most likely to feel that the company is supportive of them. The study's ten-item scale of organizational support, unlike that used in the J&J study, had no items on work-family support; rather, it was focused on the extent to which employees viewed the company as valuing their contributions. The results indicate that workers who use and appreciate Fel-Pro's benefits, who have challenging jobs with opportunities for promotion, and who have less job stress are those who feel that the company is more supportive of them. For men (but not for women), having a supportive supervisor and supportive co-workers is also linked to greater perceived organizational support. The study concludes (p. 81) that the basic design of workers' jobs is a critically important factor, and that "family-responsive policies must be considered only one part of the larger organization context that affects worker performance. These policies cannot fully compensate for poorly designed jobs, insensitive supervisors, or unsupportive colleagues."

Similarly, the National Study of the Changing Workforce found that employees with heavier work loads have more trouble balancing work with family and personal life, experience more work-family conflict and negative job-to-home spillover, are more stressed, and are coping less effectively than other workers. By contrast, employees with more autonomy in their jobs and more social support from supervisors, co-workers, and the workplace culture are more successful in balancing work with family and personal life, experience less work-family conflict and negative job-to-home spillover, are less stressed, and are coping more effectively than other workers. In addition, workers who feel less secure in their jobs, believe that they have experienced discrimination in their current workplaces, or feel that workers of their own gender or race have less opportunity for advancement report more negative job-to-home spillover, more stress, and less effective coping than other workers (Galinsky, Bond, & Friedman, 1993).

Although it is commonly assumed that work-family assistance is a matter of implementing programs and policies, these three new studies make it clear that this is a partially false assumption. Supervisory support and a family-friendly culture have a greater impact on the employees' family life and on the company's bottom line than does the mere use of work-family programs. Of course, these factors are not truly mutually exclusive. Johnson & Johnson and Fel-Pro helped to create a family-responsive environment by providing a range of work-family programs. In addition, Johnson & Johnson specifically trained supervisors in handling work-family issues. In fact, over the course of the two-year study at J&J, supervisors were viewed as increasingly supportive of employees when work-family problems arose. In this two-year period, the negative spillover from work in-to family life also decreased (Families and Work Institute, 1993a).

Another important finding from the new research is that, just as the nature of jobs is the leading source of work-family conflict, work-family programs cannot make up for badly de-signed, stressful jobs or poor work relationships. Families and Work Institute studies show that the supervisors who are best at managing work tasks (such as having clear expectations and good communication, and recognizing a job well done) are also best at handling work-family issues (Galinsky, Bond, & Fried-man, 1993).

Implications of Work-Family Research

The obvious conclusion to be reached from this research is that companies should expand the definition of the term *work-family* to encompass attention to the nature of jobs and supervisory re-lationships. In fact, this is one of the characteristics of stage 3 in the evolution of corporate work-family programs. In stage 3, a company's decision makers try to bring their initiative to bear on managing a more diverse work force, developing family-supportive policies, and enhancing the quality of products and services (Galinsky, Friedman, & Hernandez, 1991). In prac-tice, this is easier said than done, as a new study conducted by the Families and Work Institute reveals. In this case study of a leading company, it was possible to observe the implementa-tion of work-family programs and policies at sites remote from the corporate headquarters where these policies were created. The findings show that this company's efforts involving three major initiatives — on quality, diversity, and work-family rela-tionships — were acknowledged by some as integrated but were quite separate in practice. They were housed in different depart-ments, with different staff members responsible for them. At-tempts to bring them together did not succeed. For example, the work-family initiative was largely seen as white women's issue, while diversity was seen as a minority issue. Both were less mainstream than quality, which was seen as a white male initiative. Furthermore, since women more or less had responsibility for the work-family initiatives and minorities had responsibility for diversity, both groups were reluctant to see a merger with the quality initiative, since it might mean sharing newfound turf and power. As a result, these initiatives were sent out into the field as separate programs, which prompted an executive in one division of the company to refer to all these programs as "the reign of terror of human resources." According to Dana Friedman, copresident of the Families and Work Institute, it is little wonder that supervisors feel swamped: one day, they are supposed to be sensitive to family concerns; the next, to issues of race and gender; and the next, to producing the highest-quality products. All the while, they are trying to meet production schedules in an increasingly pressured economy.

Packaging these initiatives as programs does not always work. James Levine, project director of the present study, reports that when "diversity" is seen as encompassing only race and gender, it can elicit a backlash at a site where the real tension is between older and younger workers. Likewise, when a work-family program is viewed merely as offering assistance in finding child care, it becomes irrelevant at a site where workers rely on their extended families for child care.

The lesson of this study is that human resources programs, whether in large or small companies, are more effective if they are custom-designed. More important, these programs are inextricably linked because at their core they all have to do with the nature of jobs and with how workers treat one another at whatever level of the hierarchy. Yet this knowledge may be quite difficult to put into action because a number of deep-seated beliefs will have to be dislodged before change is possible, including beliefs about time, work, and work-family (see Exhibit 6.1).*

*The author is grateful to Lotte Bailyn, Deborah Kolb, and other members of the Massachusetts Institute of Technology Collaborative Research Project staff for their innovative thinking on the subject of deep-seated beliefs as expressed in companies at various stages.

Exhibit 6.1. Deep-Seated Beliefs That Must Yield to Change.

Beliefs About Time
   Time equals commitment.
   Presence (that is, number of hours at work) equals productivity.
   Time is an infinite resource.
   Time belongs to the work organization.

Beliefs About Work
   The work of managing is not legitimate, "real" work.
   People issues and work issues are different.
   Work that is invisible (such as managing) is less central to the functioning of
     the organization.
   Managing by crisis is the norm.
   The individual contributor is the hero.
   People have to sink or swim.
   Success is measurable, and what is not measurable cannot be managed.
   If it isn't unpleasant, it isn't work; people who are having fun are taking advan-
     tage of the organization.

Beliefs About Work-Family Relationships
   Work-family issues are not legitimate issues.
   It is an individual decision to have a family; therefore, it is the individual's
     responsibility to handle work-family problems.
   If there are work-family problems, the best response is to leave it to the man-
     ager to make accommodations, primarily for the best performers.
   If you give employees an inch, they'll take a mile.
   Accommodations should be made primarily for short-term family crises.
   All employees must be treated the same; equity is crucial.
   Employees must sacrifice their personal needs to get ahead.
   There is no connection between the work-family problems of employees and
     the company's productivity.
   Work-family solutions are only programs and have nothing to do with the way
     people treat one another.

    A new set of beliefs is coming to the fore in stage 3 companies:

Working smart, not working long, equals productivity.
It is better to focus on work tasks than on work time.
Manage by results.
Manage by empowering, rather than by controlling.
Manage by planning, not by reacting to crises.
Managing people is real work and is crucial to business profitability.
Change the notion of equity (treating everyone the same) to equality (treating
   everyone fairly).
People perform better when they are not hampered by personal pressures.
Flexibility is a competitive issue and a management tool.
Quality means responding to the needs of "internal" customers—employees.

Nevertheless, it will not be easy to move away from the old beliefs about time, work, and work-family issues. Both the fast pace of business change and the competitive global market call for and militate against such change. The increasing use of technology, the development of information highways, and "anytime, anyplace offices" (whereby employees travel everywhere with their computers and other information-exchange devices) are transforming the nature of work, but often the work-family "champions" at a company are not powerful enough to be in on the relevant discussions. All the same, the success of the workplace of the future will call for the integration of work skills with people skills.

When the movement that is called *work-family* or *work-life* began, a decade ago, few if any of the pioneers envisioned that their mission would lead to changing assumptions about work itself and to the creation of social support in the workplace. Clearly, however, that is the task of the next decade. Interestingly enough, the demographics support this task. The National Study of the Changing Workforce conducted by the Families and Work Institute shows that workers all over the country may be reaching a turning point. They want to put more emphasis on their own development and on family life. More so than in the past, they are willing to make sacrifices at work on behalf of their families and personal life. In fact, 34 percent of all workers report that they are willing to make "a lot" of sacrifices toward this aim. Among young workers with children, 60 percent report that they are willing to make "a lot" of sacrifices for personal and family life. It is possible that we are moving into a period in which employees will expect their employers to respond to their family needs. It is even possible that the focus of work-family efforts will shift away from simply providing programs or policies and toward building a high-quality work environment and the social support that workers need to care for their families and be productive. There are clear indications that this would be good for children and good for their parents.

References

Baruch, G. K., & Barnett, R. C. (1987). Role quality and psychological well-being. In F. J. Crosby (Ed.), *Spouse, parent, worker:*

On gender and multiple roles (pp. 63-73). New Haven, CT: Yale University Press.

Beehr, T. A., King, L. A., & King, D. W. (1990). Social support and occupational stress: Talking to supervisors. *Journal of Vocational Behavior, 36,* 61-81.

Bond, J. T., Galinsky, E., Lord, M., Staines, G. L., & Brown, K. R. (1991). *Beyond the parental leave debate: The impact of laws in four states.* New York: Families and Work Institute.

Bromet, E. J., Dew, M. A., Parkinson, D. K., & Schulberg, H. C. (1988). Predictive effects of occupational and marital stress on the mental health of a male workforce. *Journal of Organizational Behavior, 9,* 1-13.

Bronfenbrenner, U., & Crouter, A. C. (1982). Work and family through time and space. In S. B. Kamerman & C. D. Hayes (Eds.), *Families that work: Children in a changing world* (pp. 39-83). Washington, DC: National Academy Press.

Crosby, F. J. (1991). *Juggling: The unexpected advantages of balancing career and home for women and their families.* New York: Free Press.

Employee Benefit Research Institute. (1992). The distribution of family-oriented benefits. *Issue Brief, 130,* entire booklet.

Families and Work Institute. (1993a). *An evaluation of Johnson & Johnson's work-family initiative.* New York: Author.

Families and Work Institute. (1993b). Unpublished data from *An evaluation of Johnson & Johnson's work-family initiative.* New York: Author.

Galinsky, E., Bond, J. T., & Friedman, D. E. (1993). *Highlights: The national study of the changing workforce.* New York: Families and Work Institute.

Galinsky, E., Friedman, D. E., & Hernandez, C. A. (1991). *Corporate reference guide to work-family programs.* New York: Families and Work Institute.

Galinsky, E., Hughes, D., Love, M., & Bragioner, P. (1987). *The family study.* New York: Families and Work Institute.

Greenberger, E., Goldberg, W. A., Hamill, S., O'Neil, R., & Payne, C. K. (1989). Contributions of a supportive work environment to parents' well-being and orientation to work. *American Journal of Community Psychology, 17,* 755-783.

Greenberger, E., & O'Neil, R. (1991). *Characteristics of fathers' and mothers' jobs: Implications for parenting and children's social development.* Irvine: University of California, Program in Social Ecology.

Howes, C., Sakai, L. M., Shinn, M., Phillips, D., Galinsky, E., & Whitebook, M. (in press). Race, social class, and maternal working conditions as influences on children's behavior in child care. *Journal of Applied Developmental Psychology.*

Hughes, D. (1988). Relations between characteristics of the job, work-family interference, and marital outcomes. *Dissertation Abstracts International, 49,* 4053B.

Hughes, D., Galinsky, E., & Morris, A. (1992). The effects of job characteristics on marital quality: Specifying linking mechanisms. *Journal of Marriage and Family, 54,* 31–42.

Karasek, R., Gardell, B., & Lindell, J. (1987). Work and nonwork correlates of illness and behavior in male and female Swedish white-collar workers. *Journal of Occupational Behavior, 8,* 187–207.

Lambert, S., Hopkins, K., Easton, G., Walker, J., McWilliams, H., & Chung, M. S. (1993). *Added benefits: The link between family-responsive policies and work performance at Fel-Pro, Inc.* Chicago: University of Chicago, School of Social Service Administration.

Miller, B. (1992). *The distribution of family oriented benefits* (Issue Brief, 130). Washington, DC: Employee Benefit Research Institute.

Piotrkowski, C. S., & Crits-Cristoph, P. (1981). Women's jobs and family adjustment. *Journal of Family Issues, 2,* 126–147.

Repetti, R. L. (1987). Individual and common components of the social environment. *Journal of Personality and Social Psychology, 52,* 710–720.

Repetti, R. L. (1993). Common stressors: The effects of workload and the social environment at work on health. In L. Goldberger & S. Breznitz (Eds.), *Handbook of stress* (pp. 368–385). New York: Free Press.

Rose, R. M., Jenkins, C. D., & Hurst, M. V. (1978). *Air traffic controller health change study.* FAA Report No. AM-78-39. Washington, DC: Federal Aviation Administration.

Schor, J. B. (1993). *The overworked American: The unexpected decline of leisure.* New York: Basic Books.

Shinn, M., Galinsky, E., & Gulcur, L. (1990). *The role of child care centers in the lives of parents.* New York: Families and Work Institute.

Shinn, M., Phillips, D., Howes, C., Galinsky, E., & Whitebook, M. (1990). *Correspondence between mothers' perceptions and observer ratings of quality in child care centers.* New York: Families and Work Institute.

U.S. Department of Labor, Bureau of Labor Statistics. (1975). Unpublished data from the *Current Population Survey.* Washington, DC: U.S. Government Printing Office.

U.S. Department of Labor, Bureau of Labor Statistics. (1988). *BLS reports on employer child care practices* (News Release USDC 88-7). Washington, DC: U.S. Government Printing Office.

U.S. Department of Labor, Bureau of Labor Statistics. (1992). Unpublished data from the *Current Population Survey.* Washington, DC: U.S. Government Printing Office.

Whitebook, M., Howes, C., & Phillips, D. A. (1990). *Who cares? Child care teachers and the quality of care in America.* Final report, National Child Care Staffing Study. Oakland, CA: Child Care Employee Project.

□ 7 □

Family Support Programs in Black Churches

A New Look at Old Functions

Cleopatra Howard Caldwell
Angela Dungee Greene
Andrew Billingsley

In a changing society, families of various structures and social classes are less and less able to provide completely and independently for their members. Given reductions in state and federal assistance programs to help needy families during the 1980s, access to formal family assistance programs is diminishing (Burt & Pittman, 1985; Palmer & Sawhill, 1984). Edelman (1989), among others, has called for public, private, and community-based interventions as a way of decreasing the already high odds against the survival of African American children and their families. According to Hill (1989), there are three primary challenges that African American families must successfully meet if they are to achieve parity with White families by the twenty-first century: attaining economic self-sufficiency, strengthening and stabilizing their families, and developing viable and healthy communities. One institution already in place, with the ability to address each of these challenges, is the network of approximately 75,000 Black churches in existence today.

African American families traditionally have relied on

Funding for the project on which this chapter is based was provided through grants from the Ford Foundation and the Lilly Endowment.

Black churches to provide religious and spiritual guidance, as well as emotional, economic, and social support. No other institution in the history of the African American community has garnered more respect and devotion than the Black church. Taylor, Thornton, and Chatters (1988) found that 82 percent of African Americans believed that the church has helped the condition of African Americans, while a recent national poll reported that an overwhelming majority of African Americans (87 percent) viewed Black churches as effective organizations for representing the interests of African American communities ("Who Speaks for Black America?", 1992).

With the growing number of social problems facing African American families today, the viability of Black churches as family support systems is indeed an important topic. The nature of current family support programs sponsored by Black churches, and the characteristics of these churches and their senior ministers, are discussed in this chapter. We begin by examining the historical social service role of Black churches in African American communities and how it has changed over time. We then present preliminary findings from our ongoing research on what contemporary Black churches are doing to assist families. We include a discussion of service gaps that these programs may not be addressing. Finally, we offer suggestions, based on our findings, for expanding the presence of Black churches in the family support movement.

The Historical Social Service Role of Black Churches

The combined influences of African traditions and the desire for independent self-expression propelled African Americans to organize their own churches in the late eighteenth century (Smith, 1988). From its origin as a separate and unequal element in the White church structure of the eighteenth century, the Black church developed by the late 1700s into a network of independent congregations in the southern and northeastern portions of the United States. While worship activities continue to be the fundamental function of the church, it is not the only emphasis of most Black churches. Since their inception, organized Black churches have provided various forms of support and services to their individual members and to the broader African American community. It is difficult to separate the practice of religion from the response to social problems within the African American community. As Sullivan (1978) says, "The church in the Black community is more than a religious institution. It is also a social movement. It is a community organization. It is a formulator of practical solutions to everyday living and psychological problems. To Black people in America, the church is a pervasive influence even for those who are not active members or participants" (p. 59).

The dual responsibility of the Black church, to serve the spiritual and practical needs both of its members and of the community at large, is evident as far back as 1787 and the founding of the Free African Society by Richard Allen, Absalom Jones, and others. The Free African Society was a benevolent organization that provided charitable services within a slave society prior to the establishment of the First African Methodist Episcopal church in Philadelphia, in 1794 (Mukenge, 1983). With limited access to the resources of the larger society, Black churches have filled a service void for African American families from the time of slavery to the present.

The vitality of the Black church as a social service institution is due in part to its African origin. Adaptability was a key element in ancient African culture, which enabled Black religion to be transformed into the particular forms that arose in the New World, based on the needs of slave communities. Unlike other ethnic groups that came to this country to gain freedom of religious expression, African Americans were brought to this country as workers, and attempts were made to strip them of their family and formal religious roots. Consequently, informally organized Black churches became the backbone of the very survival of African American slave families, as reflected in spirituals and creative methods of family recognition.

The first African Baptist Church of Savannah, Georgia, is generally considered to be the oldest organized Black church in America. It was established in 1777, nearly one hundred years before emancipation. During the early to middle twentieth century, social scientists began documenting the role of the Black church as a central feature of African American group life. For example, in a study of 609 urban and 185 rural Black churches during the late 1920s, Mays and Nicholson (1933) described the sizable presence of the urban Black church, which reflected, in part, the Black migration to urban areas after the turn of the twentieth century. Community outreach was a prominent feature of urban churches of that era. In descending order of prevalence among the 609 urban churches, the following community support programs were available: poverty relief, recreational work, food for the unemployed, benevolent societies, free health clinics, cooperation with Y.W.C.A. and Y.M.C.A. programs, Girl Scouts, Boy Scouts, kindergartens, and day nurseries. Frazier (1974) provides evidence of the continued influence of the Black church as a family support system. The multiple functions of the Black church include its role as an economic cooperative, an educational institution, a political organization, and an agency for social change, as highlighted in Frazier's study.

After World War II, with the rise of urban communities in the North and the mass migration of African Americans from the South to the North, secular organizations began to assume some of the social service functions for which Black churches had been responsible. However, the political activist role of the church reached its peak during the civil rights movement of the 1960s. Subsequently, secular Black organizations, such as the National Association for the Advancement of Colored People and the National Urban League, which were established in the early twentieth century, came to prominence, and the role of the Black church as the institutional focal point in African American community life was somewhat diminished (Lincoln & Mamiya, 1990). Since these organizations were developed with the support of African American ministers, and since ministers' involvement in these groups has always been substantial, Lincoln and Mamiya (1990) have described the interaction between Black churches and these secular organizations as reflecting a partial differentiation between religious and secular institutions, rather than a total separation of church and worldly activities. The relationship between Black churches and secular community organizations tends to be more cooperative than conflictive, which has resulted in the church's maintaining some social responsibility to and influence in the African American community at large.

The Black church's renewed community-outreach role in the 1980s was fueled in part by the conservative reign of the Reagan administration. The 1980s began an era of drastic withdrawal of support from the public social programs that had benefited minorities and the poor. Consequently, in every sphere of life, the disparity between White and African American families widened (Phillips, 1990; Palmer & Sawhill, 1984; Peterson & Lewis, 1986; Burt & Pittman, 1985; Edelman, 1987; Children's Defense Fund, 1990; Dewart, 1990). What role can contemporary Black churches play in improving the quality of life in Black America?

In a comprehensive analysis of the history of the Black church, Jones (1991) concludes that because of their voluntary nature, the very survival of Black churches is dependent on how they "contribute to the enhancement of the quality of life in the communities they serve" (p. 16). Thus contemporary Black churches must be prepared to deal with the persistent problems affecting African American families in modern-day America. This position was the impetus that led to the establishment of the Congress of National Black Churches (CNBC) nearly a decade ago. The purpose of CNBC is to enable churches in the historically Black denominations to make a greater collective impact on the social, economic, and political well-being of Black communities throughout the nation. The Congress of National Black Churches represents six denominations: the African Methodist Episcopal Church, the Christian Methodist Episcopal Church, the Church of God in Christ, the National Baptist Convention of America, Inc., the National Missionary Baptist Convention of America, and the Progressive National Baptist Convention, Inc. These denominations combine resources in an effort to meet some of the challenges facing African American families today. This collaborative effort is one of the best examples of churches working together to support families. For instance, Project Spirit is one family support program sponsored by a consortium of fifteen churches that are part of the Congress of National Black Churches. Operating in Oakland, Atlanta, Indianapolis, and Washington, DC, this program is designed to foster parents' involvement in the educational and enrichment activities of their children through tutorials, skill development, and life-enhancement sessions (see Billingsley & Caldwell, 1991, for more details). In an evaluation of Project Spirit, McAdoo and Crawford (1991) report that the parents and children who participated found it helpful for strengthening their family relationships.

Many Black churches today remain strong, independent, economically viable self-help institutions, ready and able to assist African American families (Sullivan, 1978; Lincoln & Mamiya, 1990). The types of family assistance these churches provide exemplify an idea of self-help that can be divided into two categories: support and advocacy (Durman, 1976). In a recent study of the family-oriented community-outreach programs in 216 northeastern Black churches, Billingsley and Caldwell (1991) found that these churches sponsored more than 900 family assistance programs and were indeed a viable support system for contemporary families. These churches provided tangible aid and programs to strengthen families that were not members of the church. Needs across the life cycle were addressed. Children and youth, adults and families, and the elderly were targeted as beneficiaries of these efforts.

The directly supportive role of Black churches in strengthening African American families is the focal point for the research results reported in the next section. Our larger study, called the Black Church Family Project, in which 635 northern Black churches participated, provides the data for the section that follows.

The Black Church Family Project's Conceptual Model

The study reported in this chapter is an outgrowth of our long-standing interest in the family and the church as strong interactive institutions that are mutually enhancing in their influence on African American communities. We were particularly interested in how contemporary patterns of interaction may strengthen both institutions. African American families have viewed the church as a viable part of their social network, offering support from individual church members (Taylor & Chatters, 1986, 1988) and a variety of institutional services and resources (Mays & Nicholson, 1933; Lincoln & Mamiya, 1990). This study focuses on the social service role of the Black church. The primary thesis is that Black churches are mediators that buffer and enhance the relationship between the family's informal social network and the larger formal societal network.

The basic conceptual model for the Black Church Family Project is presented in Figure 7.1. This model assumes that the church is positioned between the family and the formal system of service delivery. The church's placement close to the family reflects its interdependence with the African American community. The proximity of the Black church to the African American family places it in an optimal position to provide assistance to families and to serve as a referral network to formal social

Figure 7.1. Family Support Model: Church as Mediator.

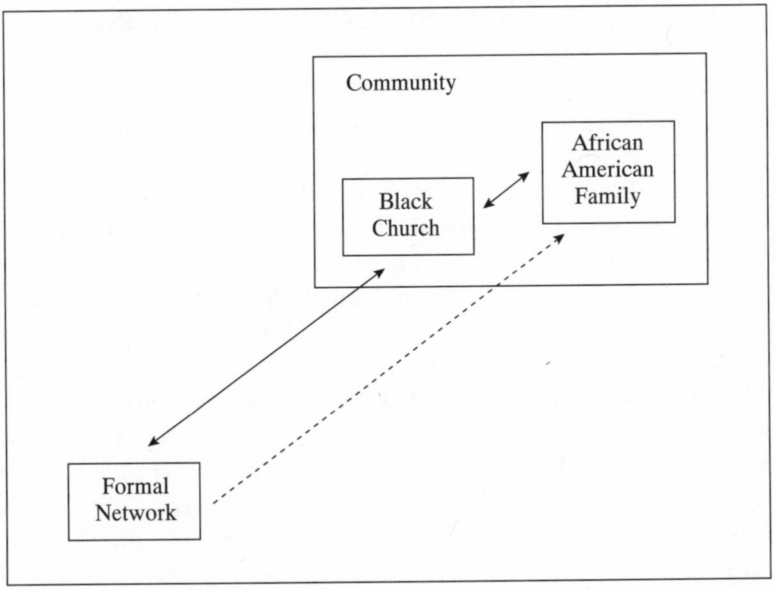

service institutions, as necessary. The solid arrow between the Black church and the family reflects the reciprocal relationship between families and churches. Although the distance is greater, there is also a reciprocal relationship between the formal service delivery system and the church. This distance is indicative of both real and perceived barriers between African American communities and the larger society. However, this link between churches and the formal service delivery system provides the basis for the church's potential to assist and nurture families through cooperative efforts with other community institutions. The unidirectional broken arrow between the formal network of service delivery and the African American family represents a tenuous relationship between the two institutions, reflecting the declining resources available to the family from the formal service delivery system (Caldwell, Greene, & Billingsley, 1992). The conceptualization of the Black church as a social service institution is a good example of an ecological approach to developing family support programs (Kagan & Shelley, 1987). We tested this model with data from the Black Church Family Project.

A Description of the Black Church Family Project

The Black Church Family Project is an exploratory study designed to identify and describe family and community support programs that are available within a nationally representative sample of Black churches. The specific outreach programs of interest are those that satisfy the following requirements: (1) their programmatic objectives and activities are designed to enhance and support the functioning of African American families; and (2) they include an identifiable outreach component that offers services to persons who are not church members (Caldwell, Chatters, Billingsley, & Taylor, in press). The church sample was drawn by means of the basic sampling strategy developed for the National Survey of Black Americans (NSBA) at the Institute for Social Research, University of Michigan. The NSBA sample itself was drawn according to a multistage area probability procedure, designed to ensure that every Black household had an equal chance of selection for the study (for specific details see Jackson, 1991).

For the Black Church Family Project, the desired total sample size of 1,500 churches was allocated across the four geographical regions of the country (the northeastern, north central, southern, and western regions) in proportion to the number of African American households in each region. In addition, denomination was used as a major stratifying variable for the study. Given the uncertainty inherent in estimating eligibility and response rates for Black churches, a replicated sampling procedure was used. This approach resulted in a final sample of 315 churches in the northeastern region and 320 churches in the north central region. Each interview was taken with the senior minister or with a knowledgeable church representative designated by the senior minister. Interviews were conducted by telephone and were approximately thirty minutes long (Caldwell, Greene, & Billingsley, 1992). To date, this is the most extensive and systematic study focusing on the outreach efforts of Black churches.

Churches in the Sample

The churches in this sample range in age from 1 to 203 years, with a median age of 37 years. Most are stable fixtures in their communities. Half have been at their current locations for twenty years or more, and 74 percent have moved two or fewer times in their history. The majority of churches (75 percent) are in neighborhoods that are described as mostly or all Black. The largest portion of the 635 churches is Baptist (44 percent), followed by Methodist (13 percent), Pentecostal (11 percent), Church of God in Christ (7 percent), and Apostolic (4 percent) churches. The remaining denominations include a variety of other Protestant religious groups, such as Episcopalian, Presbyterian, and Seventh Day Adventist. Worship services are held on at least a weekly basis in almost all of these churches (99 percent); 63 percent of the churches occasionally or frequently sponsor nonreligious activities.

Where social class is concerned, 58 percent of the respondents report that their congregations comprise both working-class and middle-class persons, 31 percent state that their congregations are exclusively working class, and only 8 percent indicate that their congregations are middle class. Less than 3 percent of congregations refer to their members as being poor or low-income people. Number of members in the congregation ranges from as few as 6 to as many as 5,000. Approximately half the churches have 162 members or more. Finally, an impressive 62 percent of these congregations entirely own their church structures, and an additional 28 percent are in the process of purchasing their buildings. Only 8 percent of the churches in this study are renting their church structures (for more details on sample description, see Caldwell, Greene, & Billingsley, 1992; Billingsley & Caldwell, 1991; Caldwell, Chatters, Billingsley, & Taylor, in press).

Types of Outreach Programs

Of the churches in the sample, 67 percent, or 426, sponsor at least one outreach program targeted to the wider community. A total of 1,804 community-outreach programs are provided by the 426 churches that have such activities. The majority (51.2 percent) of these programs are family support programs, which address the needs of the family as a unit (family counseling, food and clothing distribution) or the needs of adult family members (adult literacy, support groups for men and women). Demonstrating a substantive commitment to children and youth, roughly one-third (31.3 percent) of the churches' programs specifically target this population. The majority of these programs are basic educational and academic support programs, such as Head Start and after-school tutorial programs, complementing the efforts of educational institutions. Programs for recreational and cultural awareness are also prominent among the activities for children and youth. With only 15 percent of the churches' youth programs devoted to substance abuse, and with 3 percent and 2 percent, respectively, addressing AIDS awareness and other health-related services (Rubin, Billingsley, & Caldwell, in press), some of the tougher adolescent health issues of today often are not being confronted through available church programs. Most church-based programs for youth are diversionary in nature, their goal being to provide a protective environment so that youth can avoid trouble.

Community development programs comprise 9 percent of church activities and include community-based projects designed to improve the economic condition of the community or to provide communitywide services, such as those related to health, housing, or social action. The churches in this study seem to provide less for the needs of the elderly, with only 8 percent of the identified church-based programs targeted to this group (Caldwell, Chatters, Billingsley, & Taylor, in press). In an analysis of a subset of church-based family support programs, we found that the majority of program participants were poor families from the local community, and that these programs were staffed mostly by female volunteers and financed through donations from church members (Caldwell, Greene, & Billingsley, 1992).

Programs to Enhance Family Functioning

The results reported in this and subsequent sections of the chapter reflect 1,685 family support programs sponsored by 419 churches. Because of our focus on direct services to families, we have limited our definition of *family support program* to those programs that address a specific need of the family unit or of individual family members. Thus we have included such programs as family counseling services, programs for food and shelter, and adult support programs for men and women. We have also included programs for adults, children, youth, and the elderly. We have excluded the 119 economic development programs sponsored by these churches.

There are at least two basic functions that families are expected to provide for their members: instrumental functions and expressive functions (Billingsley, 1968). The instrumental functions include providing for basic life-sustaining needs, such as food, shelter, and clothing. The expressive functions include providing for the emotional, intellectual, and spiritual development and well-being of family members. Other family needs, such as basic education, child care, and health-related support, incorporate aspects of both instrumental and expressive functions (Caldwell, Greene, & Billingsley, 1992). For this study, three functional categories for which churches could provide assistance were examined: (1) instrumental functions only, (2) expressive functions only, and (3) a combination of instrumental and expressive functions. Results indicate that almost half of all programs sponsored by churches provide for the instrumental needs of the family. Church programs designed to meet the expressive needs of family members account for 28 percent of the programs, while 27 percent support instrumental-expressive functions.

Six dimensions of family support were also investigated to further clarify specific types of church-based programs being offered. As presented in Table 7.1, these dimensions are (1) counseling and intervention, (2) social recreation, (3) basic needs assistance, (4) income maintenance, (5) education and awareness, and (6) health-related activities. Dimensions 1 and 2 comprise the expressive category; 3 and 4, the instrumental category; 5 and 6, the instrumental-expressive category (Caldwell, Greene, & Billingsley, 1992). Basic needs assistance is by far the most available service provided by churches. Almost half of all churches in the study sponsored food and clothing distribution programs for families. Regardless of geographical region, if a church had only one family support program, it was likely to be a food or clothing distribution program. These programs could range from seasonal efforts, such as food and clothing drives at holiday time, to more elaborate, permanently housed food pantries and thrift-clothing stores.

The Church as Collaborator
with Secular Service Agencies

We found support for our conceptualization of the Black church as a mediator between the African American family and the formal system of service delivery. Referral to formal service agencies is evident in programs designed to meet basic family needs through several means. Contact with the formal system of service

Table 7.1. Instrumental and Expressive Functions
Provided by Church-Based Family Support Programs.[a]

Expressive	Instrumental	Instrumental-Expressive
Counseling and intervention (18%)	Basic needs assistance (40%)	Education and awareness (18%)
Family counseling	Food distribution	Academic tutoring
Aid to the incarcerated	Clothing distribution	Child care
Prisoners and their families	Emergency financial aid	Bible classes for nonmembers
Women's services	Referral center	African American culture classes
Child welfare	Shelter for the homeless	
Parenting/sexuality	Nonshelter services	College financial aid
Youth at risk	Home care	Performing and visual arts classes
Other	Meals on Wheels	Head Start
	Other	Mentoring
		Denomination-sponsored college
		Basic education
		Life skills
		Other
Social recreation (10%)	Income maintenance (6%)	Health-related activities (8%)
General recreation	Low-income housing	Substance abuse counseling
Scouting	Financial services	General health services
Fellowship/social	Youth employment	AIDS-related services
Other	Other	Other

[a]$n = 1,685$
Source: Caldwell, Greene, & Billingsley, 1992.

delivery was described as simple family referrals to more appropriate professionals and more structured collaborative programs between churches and specific social agencies. Nearly 71 percent of churches with community-outreach programs actively collaborate with a wide range of secular community agencies. The overwhelming majority of churches maintain working relationships with the local police and welfare departments, local schools, and hospitals and prisons, as well as with health, housing, and recreation departments. Many of these programs involve helping families make more effective contact with these community agencies. Others use the church as the service site (for example, health screening programs operated in conjunction with public health departments). Although churches rarely function as centralized referral centers without also maintaining some continued involvement with families, we found that the willingness of congregations to work with community agencies provided the potential for establishing more formalized arrangements with local agencies trying to serve hard-to-reach families in need.

Characteristics of Churches with Family Support Programs

The characteristics of churches that sponsor family support programs are explored as a way of identifying other churches that may be responsive to either initiating or expanding such efforts in the future. The results of our chi-square analyses suggest that northern churches sponsoring family support programs have several distinct characteristics. These churches tend to be at least forty years old and have larger memberships than churches that do not sponsor such programs (see Table 7.2). Further, churches with between 50 to 74 percent female members are also more likely to have family programs. Congregations that are perceived as mostly composed of working-class members are less likely to sponsor family support programs than either mostly middle-class or both working- and middle-class churches.

The staffing pattern of the church has also emerged as an important determinant of whether a church provides family support programs. Specifically, churches with no paid clergy (including the senior minister) and those with no paid staff other than the senior minister are the least likely to offer family support programs. Moreover, churches with two or more unpaid clergy are more likely to have such programs. Collectively, these findings suggest that churches with greater resources are more likely to sponsor family support programs.

Past research has highlighted the prominent role of the church as a focal center for a number of community activities

Table 7.2. Characteristics of Churches with
Family Support Programs.

	% Yes	% No	N	X^2	Cramer's V/Phi
Demographics					
Congregational Age					
<1–40 years	60.5	39.5	339	14.20***	.15
41–75 years	69.9	30.1	156		
76+	78.0	22.0	132		
Membership Size					
6–70	38.4	61.6	146	91.02***	.38
71–175	61.6	38.4	185		
176–400	76.4	23.6	157		
400+	88.3	11.7	145		
Percentage of Female Members					
<50%	56.5	43.5	62	10.15*	.13
50–74%	72.3	27.7	285		
75%	61.4	38.6	277		
Social Class of Congregation					
Working Class	57.2	42.8	194	13.34**	.15
Both Working & Middle Class	70.0	30.0	370		
Middle Class	79.6	20.4	49		
Staffing Patterns					
Number of Paid Clergy					
None	48.9	51.1	188	40.72***	.25
One	70.7	29.3	352		
Two+	79.6	20.4	90		
Other Paid Staff					
No	55.4	44.6	305	30.83***	.22
Yes	76.4	23.6	322		
Number of Unpaid Clergy					
None	60.0	40.0	105	6.24*	.10
One	60.1	39.9	138		
Two+	69.8	30.2	387		
Other Characteristics					
Frequency of Nonreligious Activities					
Rarely	42.7	57.3	232	71.93***	.34
Occasionally	68.7	31.3	217		
Frequently	86.5	13.5	185		

Table 7.2. Characteristics of Churches with
Family Support Programs, Cont'd.

	% Yes	% No	N	X^2	Cramer's V/Phi
Building Ownership Status					
Renting	40.4	59.6	52	17.44**	.17
Buying	66.1	33.9	180		
Own	69.5	30.5	394		

*p < .05
**p < .01
***p < .001

(Mays & Nicholson, 1933; Frazier, 1974). More recent studies have indicated that this role for the contemporary Black church has been somewhat diminished because African Americans have had greater access to the resources of the larger society ever since the gains of the civil rights movement (Lincoln & Mamiya, 1990). Nevertheless, many churches continue to open their doors to community groups, as necessary. The churches that frequently conduct nonreligious activities at church are also those that are more likely to provide family support programs.

One of the best indicators of the strength and independence of a Black congregation is its ability to purchase its church building. Our findings indicate a distinct difference between congregations that are renting their church buildings and those that are either buying or already own their church homes. Specifically, congregations that are renting their buildings are less likely to provide family support programs to the community than congregations that are buying or have already purchased their buildings.

Senior Ministers in Churches with Family Support Programs

In our earlier work (Billingsley & Caldwell, 1991; Caldwell, Greene, & Billingsley, 1992; Caldwell, Chatters, Billingsley, & Taylor, in press), the influence of senior ministers on the development of church-sponsored family support programs was evident. Therefore, we examined the demographic character- istics and out-of-church activities of senior ministers from north- ern churches with family support programs. We found that the senior ministers from churches with family support programs are younger ($p < .05$), with seminary or Bible college training ($p < .001$) and more formal education ($p < .001$) than senior ministers from churches that do not operate family support pro- grams. We also found that senior ministers who are not em- ployed outside the church ($p < .01$) and those who are involved in community activities ($p < .001$) are more likely to pastor churches that sponsor family outreach programs than those who have outside employment and those who have no out-of-church church activities.

The results of this study also highlight the continued in- volvement of African American ministers in secular commu- nity organizations. Senior ministers who are actively involved in the community typically are members of the National As- sociation for the Advancement of Colored People, the Urban League, and local ministerial alliances. Collaborative efforts be- tween these groups and the Black church have a long tradition, especially regarding political activism in support of human rights.

Suggestions for Expanding Black Churches' Social Service Presence

Previous research has documented the importance of Black churches to the survival of African American families through- out history (Mays & Nicholson, 1933; Johnson, 1934; Lewis, 1957; Frazier, 1974; Lincoln & Mamiya, 1990). The results of this study support the idea that the Black church continues to be a vital institution within African American communities. It represents more than a narrowly defined religious institution exclusively concerned with spiritual matters. The contemporary Black church is an extensive, strong, independent, economically viable, well respected self-help institution in the African Ameri- can community that spans a broad range of social classes and embraces a wide range of denominational affiliations. Most Black churches function as comprehensive and viable support systems for their members and the community at large. The contemporary Black church is a center of voluntarism in that the majority of church-based community-oriented support programs are operated by volunteers. Further, the Black church, through its physical and social presence in the African American community, can play a major role in harnessing the resources of the larger society and the African American community to ameliorate some of the perplexing social problems facing African American families today.

In this chapter, we have focused on documenting the historical role of Black churches in addressing community needs. We have also described Black churches that sponsor family support programs and identified the specific types of assistance that these churches provide through their organized outreach efforts to families in their communities. In this regard, 67 percent of the 635 northern churches in the study sponsored at least one community-outreach program. We found that most Black churches do actively engage in sponsoring outreach programs for children, youth, and families, but few of them target the elderly as a focal group for services. This finding was surprising, since the elderly comprise a large portion of congregational memberships, and since a large percentage of elderly African American people are poor.

It may be that the needs of African American elderly people are being met effectively by established health and human service agencies, or through more informal sources of assistance, such as families, friends, and neighbors. Indeed, the importance of kinship networks in the lives of older African Americans has been emphasized consistently in the social science literature (Walls & Zarit, 1991; Taylor, 1986; Gibson, 1982). Variations in whether the elderly have access to informal assistance are also evident. Taylor (1986) found that elderly people who have adult children are more likely to receive informal assistance than elderly persons without children, while Gibson (1982) found that older African Americans are twice as likely as Whites to use friends and neighbors in coping with emotional problems. However,

Neighbors and Jackson (1984) found that older persons are less likely to seek help exclusively from informal resources, which suggests that reliance on family and friends alone is not the most plausible explanation for the churches' lack of programs for elderly people.

In an examination of the role of the church as part of the informal social network of elderly African Americans, Walls and Zarit (1991) report that elderly African Americans sought assistance from Black churches before seeking formal help. Further, Taylor and Chatters (1986) have identified frequency of church attendance as an important predictor of the amount of assistance received, and they found that only 20 percent of elderly church members reported receiving nonreligious forms of assistance from the church. Thus the needs of the elderly may be only partially addressed by established church programs. Since we know that female volunteers provide much of the staffing for church programs, it may be that, within the church structure, the elderly are more likely to be providers than recipients of church-based services. Even though the results of our study indicate that the elderly as a group are not a special programmatic focus for most church activities, the general family support programs may be beneficial to senior citizens as well. Future efforts should explore whether the churches' lack of programs for the elderly is an indication of unmet needs or an indication that the formal service delivery system or community-based groups for senior citizens are better serving the needs of elderly African Americans.

We found several dimensions of support provided through church-based programs, including programs that addressed the emotional and instrumental needs of the participants. Approximately 50 percent of the programs offered were designed to meet basic instrumental needs (food, clothing, shelter). Instrumental services were prominent among churches with very few programs, as well as among churches with extensive community-outreach activities.

With respect to sponsorship of family support programs, characteristics that distinguished the more active churches from the less active or inactive churches had to do with the churches' resources and the senior ministers' backgrounds. These characteristics included the church's being older, having a larger congregation, perceiving its congregation as being mostly middle class or both working class and middle class, having a large female membership and ministerial staff, and owning its church building. The senior ministers from these churches were younger and highly educated, with Bible college or seminary training. They also were not employed outside the church and were very involved in community activities. With this prototype of the kind of church most likely to sponsor family support programs, agency planners can approach local churches that have these characteristics and try to involve them in outreach efforts targeting African American families. However, the financial burden of engaging in such activities may be overwhelming for many churches. To encourage more Black churches to work cooperatively with community institutions in providing a variety of family support programs, public and private funding sources must reevaluate their granting procedures, so that these procedures will not intimidate churches interested in developing and gaining external financing for family support efforts.

The majority of churches in this study relied on their congregations to develop and finance family support programs, for several reasons. They often wished to avoid intrusive government regulations, but they also were sometimes unable to negotiate the grantsmanship process, or they lacked knowledge about external funding sources and experts available for assisting in program development initiatives. With funding from the Lilly Endowment, the Howard University School of Divinity has established a clearinghouse of information to assist churches interested in learning how to develop, operate, and finance various family support programs. Similar projects should be initiated throughout the country to help provide an organizational base for coordinating such activities, with the primary goal being to increase the long-term prevalence of church-based family support programs.

The results of this study offer insight into the great unrealized potential of the Black church to provide an infrastructure for coordinating and furnishing an array of family support services within African American communities. With a conservative estimate of 75,000 Black churches in this country and more than 24 million churchgoers (Lincoln & Mamiya, 1990), Black churches are uniquely positioned to assume this responsibility effectively. Because the vast majority of church-based service providers and program participants are African American, many of the cultural barriers that often inhibit effective service delivery and long-term participation by African Americans could be minimized. These barriers include lack of transportation, mistrust of professionals, and issues of cultural sensitivity and appropriateness of services. They could be addressed by involving Black churches as intermediary, indigenous service delivery systems.

Most church-based programs are staffed by volunteers (Caldwell, Greene, & Billingsley, 1992), and so the potential for establishing both rapport and continuous contact with families is far greater than in most social service programs and health care settings. Therefore, church-based family support programs could be a cost-effective strategy for service delivery, one that should be explored further. It is not that churches could or would be willing to replace the formal system of service delivery. Rather, agencies working in conjunction with churches could expand their outreach efforts, and their long-term success rates could be improved with help from Black churches, especially with respect to hard-to-reach families.

The greatest strengths of the Black church as a family support system are its visibility and its stability in African American communities. This approach may not be appropriate for everyone, but the church still enjoys the allegiance of large numbers of African Americans, which makes it a credible source of information and service for many churchgoers and nonmembers alike. The expansion of Black church-based family support programs will require commitment and collective effort on the part of service delivery systems, policy makers, and congregations willing to expand or initiate such programs.

References

Billingsley, A. (1968). *Black families in White America*. New York: Simon & Schuster.

Billingsley, A., & Caldwell, C. H. (1991). The church, the family, and the school in the African American community. *Journal of Negro Education, 60,* 427–440.

Burt, M. R., & Pittman, K. J. (1985). *Testing the safety net: The impact of changes in support programs during the Reagan administration.* Washington, DC: Urban Institute Press.

Caldwell, C. H., Chatters, L. M., Billingsley, A., & Taylor, R. J. (in press). Congregational characteristics and social support programs for the elderly in Black churches. In M. A. Kimble et al. (Eds.), *Handbook on religion, spirituality, and aging.* Minneapolis, MN: Augsburg Fortress Publishers.

Caldwell, C. H., Greene, A. D., & Billingsley, A. (1992). The Black church as a family support system: Instrumental and expressive functions. *National Journal of Sociology, 6,* 21–40.

Children's Defense Fund. (1990). *A vision for America's future: An agenda for the 1990s.* Washington, DC: Children's Defense Fund.

Dewart, J. (1990). *The state of Black America 1990.* New York: National Urban League.

Durman, E. C. (1976). The role of self-help in service provision. *Journal of Applied Behavioral Science, 12,* 433–443.

Edelman, M. W. (1987). *Families in peril: An agenda for social change.* Cambridge, MA: Harvard University Press.

Edelman, M. W. (1989). Black children in America. In J. Dewart (Ed.), *The state of Black America 1989* (pp. 63–76). New York: National Urban League.

Frazier, E. F. (1974). *The Negro church in America.* New York: Schocken Books.

Gibson, R. (1982). Blacks at middle and late life: Resources and coping. *Annals of the American Academy of Political and Social Science, 464,* 79–90.

Hill, R. B. (1989). Critical issues for Black families by the year 2000. In J. Dewart (Ed.), *The state of Black America 1989* (pp. 41–61). New York: National Urban League.

Jackson, J. S. (Ed.). (1991). *Life in Black America.* Newbury Park, CA: Sage.

Johnson, C. S. (1934). *Shadow of the plantation.* Chicago: University of Chicago Press.

Jones, L. (1991). The organized church. In W. Payne (Ed.), *Directory of African American religious bodies* (pp. 1–19). Washington, DC: Howard University Press.

Kagan, S. L., & Shelley, A. (1987). The promise and problems of family support programs. In S. L. Kagan, D. R. Powell, B. Weissbourd, & E. F. Zigler (Eds.), *America's family support programs: Perspectives and prospects* (pp. 3–18). New Haven, CT: Yale University Press.

Lewis, H. (1957). *Black ways of Kent.* New York: Van Rees Press.

Lincoln, C. E., & Mamiya, L. (1990). *The Black church in the African American experience.* Durham, NC: Duke University Press.

McAdoo, H. P., & Crawford, V. (1991). *The Black church and family support programs.* New York: Haworth Press.

Mays, B. E., & Nicholson, J. W. (1933). *The Negro's church.* New York: Russell and Russell.

Mukenge, I. R. (1983). *The Black church in urban America: A case study in political economy.* Lanham, MD: University Press of America.

Neighbors, H., & Jackson, J. S. (1984). The use of informal and formal help: Four patterns of illness behavior in the Black community. *American Journal of Community Psychology, 12,* 629–644.

Palmer, J. L., & Sawhill, I. V. (Eds.). (1984). *The Reagan record: An assessment of America's changing domestic priorities.* Cambridge, MA: Ballinger.

Peterson, G. E., & Lewis, C. W. (Eds.). (1986). *Reagan and the cities.* Washington, DC: Urban Institute Press.

Phillips, K. (1990). *The politics of rich and poor: Wealth and the American electorate in the Reagan aftermath.* New York: Random House.

Rubin, R. H., Billingsley, A., & Caldwell, C. H. (in press). The role of the Black church in working with Black adolescents. *Adolescence.*

Smith, E. D. (1988). *Climbing Jacob's ladder: The rise of Black churches in eastern American cities, 1740–1877.* Washington, DC: Smithsonian Institution Press.

Sullivan, L. H. (1978). *The church in the life of the Black family.* Valley Forge, PA: Judson Press.

Taylor, R. J. (1986). Receipt of support from family among Black Americans: Demographic and familial differences. *Journal of Marriage and the Family, 48,* 67–77.

Taylor, R. J., & Chatters, L. M. (1986). Church-based informal support among elderly Blacks. *Gerontologist, 26,* 637–642.

Taylor, R. J., & Chatters, L. M. (1988). Church members as a source of informal support to elderly Black adults: Family, friends, and church members. *Social Work, 31,* 432–438.

Taylor, R. J., Thornton, M. C., & Chatters, L. M. (1988). Black Americans' perceptions of the sociohistorical role of the church. *Journal of Black Studies, 18,* 123–138.

Walls, C. T., & Zarit, S. H. (1991). Informal support from Black churches and the well-being of elderly Blacks. *Gerontologist, 3,* 490–495.

Who speaks for Black America? (1992). *Detroit News and Free Press* series, February 23–25.

□ 8 □

Family Support
and Criminal Justice

Ann Adalist-Estrin

Skyrocketing crime rates over the last decade have led researchers in pursuit of the antecedents of delinquency and criminality, and thus to a heightened awareness of the social conditions
likely to place individuals, families, and whole populations at
risk for involvement in the criminal justice system. The factors
continuously highlighted as correlates of persistent delinquency
and criminal behavior are poverty and economic deprivation,
school failure and truancy, parental addictions, inconsistent
parenting, and the absence of reciprocal emotional relationships
with available caring adults (Wolfgang, Seller, & Figlio, 1977;
West & Farrington, 1973; Tremblay, 1986). When we consider
these findings in relation to what we know about the effects of
teenage pregnancies (Children's Defense Fund, 1988), maternal addiction (Brooks, Zuckerman, Bamforth, Cole, & Kaplan-
Sanoff, in press) and long-term effects of sexual abuse (Herman,
1992; Putnam, 1989; Rohsenow, Corbett, & Devine, 1988), it
becomes evident that certain distinct social factors are directly
linked to criminality, and clusters of risk factors and combina-
tions of stressors mutually intensify the effects.

One parental characteristic associated with offspring's
delinquency and criminality, parental incarceration, is seen as

"the most striking and most consistent" (Rutter & Giller, 1984), yet little attention is paid to the children of incarcerated parents or to the parenting role of inmates. According to Jesness (1987), "While our predictions are not perfect, they are sufficiently accurate to be taken seriously and used in practice" (p. 156).

The family support literature (most notably Dunst, Trivette, & Thompson, 1990; Weissbourd & Kagan, 1989; Weissbourd, 1990) sets forth principles and premises that have generated effective practices in a wide variety of settings. Theoretical concepts and practical strategies have been integrated into the systems of education, social services, health, mental health, and child-abuse prevention. Such merging of disciplines and perspectives is essential to providing the intensive programming necessary for breaking the cycle of disadvantage that leads to criminal behavior (Schorr & Schorr, 1988).

In contrast, the criminal justice system is often viewed by professionals and the public alike as a depository for the results of social and human service program failures, rather than as an allied discipline in combatting risk factors affecting children and families. This attitude lacks both wisdom and forethought. The time has come to shift the focus of crime prevention away from locks, weapons, and accelerated prison construction. Rather, increased efforts to forestall the disruptions in the lives and development of children and families that lead to crime are called for, with parental incarceration consistently included as a significant risk factor. The available research data, the perspectives of practitioners, and the experiences of families converge to attest to the critical need for an integration of our knowledge base and for an intentional focus on the parenting roles of inmates and on the effects of incarceration on their children and families. This requires a reordering of social priorities that goes beyond the rhetoric of maintaining family ties and includes collective commitment to supporting the growth and development of relationships within inmates' families.

This chapter focuses on the collaboration between family support and criminal justice as a viable means of achieving this goal. Such collaboration requires examination of the settings in which offenders are held, the demographics related to inmates' families, the significance of the parenting role to post-release adjustment, and programmatic responses to the stated needs of the families of offenders.

The System of Custody

America imprisons nonpolitical offenders at a higher rate than any other Western industrialized society (Currie, 1985). Commonly held purposes for incarceration are (1) to confine those deemed dangerous, as protection for society; (2) to punish or dole out aversive consequences; (3) to deter inmates from committing future crimes (and deter others from criminality) by highlighting negative aspects of incarceration; and (4) to rehabilitate, or restore to a prior state of well-being, through education, training, and counseling.

Increasing recidivism rates in the late 1970s contributed to a shift in corrections that saw the concept of rehabilitation fall from favor in America (Adams, 1977; Martinson, 1974). A "nothing works" philosophy negated the confident optimism of rehabilitation models of the 1960s. The 1980s brought a surge of interest in causation theory and an emphasis on the sociological factors affecting criminal rehabilitation. Programs were designed to target job and skills training, drug and alcohol rehabilitation, and housing. Budgetary considerations, politics, hard-line law-and-order policies, and an emerging penology, all focused on managing large numbers of "disreputable" and/or violent people, have made confinement, punishment, and "warehousing" of criminals primary goals of the correctional system for the 1990s (Feeley & Simon, 1992; Fleisher, 1989; Irwin & Austin, 1987).

These goals are carried out in three types of settings: jails, prisons, and community-based facilities. Bartol (1991) clearly describes each setting:

> Jails are operated by local (city or county and sometimes state) governments to temporarily hold those who are awaiting trial or sentenced to confinement for a specific period of 1–3 years. It is often estimated

that on any given day, 50% of any jail population is likely to be awaiting trial and not yet convicted.

Prisons are operated by State and Federal Governments to hold persons sentenced under state and federal laws to sentences of more than one year. All prisons are classified by levels of security needed to maintain confinement. In the United States, approximately 40–50% of the prison population is held in maximum security, 37–40% in medium and 10–23% in minimum . . . .

Community based facilities are operated by public or private organizations (under government contract). They often hold prisoners for less than 24 hours of each day to allow them to work or attend school. (p. 349)

These distinctions affect program designs and delivery of services to those in custody.

People in Custody

It is estimated that 3.2 million people are under correctional supervision in the United States on any given day. This includes adults in prisons and jails, juveniles in public and private institutions, and adults and juveniles who are on probation or parole. Bartol (1991) provides further valuable data: 64 percent of adult inmates have experienced prior incarceration as juveniles, adults, or both; there is substantial evidence that a small number of those in custody (8–10 percent) actually commit over 50 percent of all crimes; and close to 55 percent of all recidivists return to prison on parole violations.

The inmate is likely to be between fifteen and twenty-four years old (male), between twenty and thirty-five years old (female), of ethnic minority, unmarried or in an unstable relationship, and raised in poverty or earning less than $10,000 per year at the time of arrest. Inmates often report having grown up with chemically dependent parents who themselves had been incarcerated, and even conservative estimates reflect extensive histories of physical or sexual abuse in inmate populations (Bloom & Steinhart, 1993; Stanton, 1980; West & Farrington, 1973). Although rates of reported substance use or addiction vary, the inmates' stories continually reflect histories of physical and sexual abuse, the pursuit of numbness (via drugs or alcohol) that follows in the wake of such abuse, and the criminal behavior that chemical dependence often requires.

Descriptive documentation is available on the general characteristics and backgrounds of offenders, but not enough information is available on family commitments or the parenting roles, attitudes, or perspectives of prisoners. Such data are needed to combat the "arguments at large" that prisoners are neither connected to nor interested in their children. We do know that of the 80,000 women currently incarcerated in United States jails and prisons, (U.S. Department of Justice, 1991), approximately 76 percent of them have at least two children, and over 50 percent of these incarcerated mothers were primary caregivers of their minor children prior to incarceration (Bloom & Steinhart, 1993). A single study focused on male inmates as parents did find that incarcerated fathers often had a clear sense of commitment to their role as parents, with aspirations to improve their parenting skills despite long periods of separation from their children (Hairston, 1989).

Children of Those in Custody

There are approximately 1.5 million children of incarcerated parents in the United States (Center for Children of Incarcerated Parents, 1992). The loss of a parent to incarceration can precipitate trauma, disruptions, and chaos that few children experience without serious consequences. These include anxiety, hyperarousal, depression, bedwetting, eating and sleeping disorders, behavior and conduct disorders, attention disorders, and prolonged developmental regression (Center for Children of Incarcerated Parents, 1992; Fishman, 1982; Morris, 1965; Stanton, 1980). Recent data suggest that some children may suffer from posttraumatic stress disorder (Center for Children of Incarcerated Parents, 1992; Jose-Kampfner, 1990).

Children of offenders have often been parented by adults who themselves have had long histories of trauma. Often present at the arrest of their parents, these children may suffer the trauma of separation in a context of violence and brutality (Center for Children of Incarcerated Parents, 1992; Stanton, 1980). Such separations from parents are often prolonged and involve multiple placements (Hadley, 1981; Stanton, 1980), which create a disturbing and previously unrecognized potential source of traumatic stress (Doyle and Bauer, 1989).

Equally disturbing is the related phenomenon of increased intergenerational crime rates (American Correctional Association, 1990; U.S. Department of Justice, 1991). Research indicates that children of prisoners are five to six times more likely to become incarcerated than their peers (Barnhill, 1991). Children of offenders are clearly at risk and need support if they are to escape a legacy of criminality.

Families on the Outside

Writings on the experiences of prisoners' families were pioneered by Pauline Morris in the early 1960s. Her study of the wives and families of 824 male inmates in England (Morris, 1965) identified the eight areas of concern most often mentioned by women interviewed. These are (in order of frequency), money, raising children alone, general loneliness, fears about the husband's release, housing, hostility from friends, isolation within the community, and fears related to the husband's treatment while incarcerated.

More recent works (Fishman, 1990; Shaw, 1992; Swan, 1981) shed additional light on the complex psychological and sociological processes involved in maintaining a relationship with a loved one who is behind bars, but the concerns and difficulties experienced by women with partners in prison have changed little since the Morris study. Partners of male offenders are still left to raise the children alone, struggling to earn a living, often changing residences, and sometimes experiencing stigmatization in the community, all while navigating a course through an often hostile and unfamiliar criminal justice system. In the midst of this potentially desperate picture, a note of optimism is heard in Swan's study (1981) of African American families, which concludes, "Most of the women in our sample considered their families to be strong in spite of the men's imprisonment; that is, both prisoners and their wives felt a concern for family unity and cooperation" (p. 87).

While the source of information on families of incarcerated men has traditionally been the women left on the outside to care for home and children, data on families of incarcerated women have been less available. This is partly because of the difficulty involved in finding family members of female prisoners, who receive fewer visits and are often more hesitant to openly discuss and reveal the details of family life. A notable and recent exception is found in Bloom and Steinhart (1993). This work is based on data gathered from questionnaires completed by 440 prisoner-mothers at correctional facilities in eight states and the District of Columbia. Collectively, respondents reported having 870 children under the age of eighteen. Significant among these findings were statistics related to the legal and physical custody of children before and during the incarceration of their mothers: 73 percent of the women surveyed had custody of their children prior to imprisonment, with 77 percent reporting that they were living with their children at the time of arrest. Incarcerated mothers who were mostly young and single seemed to rely on family members for child-care assistance before, during, and after imprisonment. Surprisingly, few children of incarcerated mothers were in foster care. Maternal grandmothers were most often caring for the children of female prisoners (Bloom and Steinhart, 1993; Hairston, 1991). However, 19 percent of the children in Hairston's study did live with the father during the mother's incarceration.

Regardless of specific custodial arrangements, women who are imprisoned worry about their children and mourn the separation from them. They plan to reunite with their children and assume child-rearing responsibilities, some for the first time (Hairston, 1991). In spite of these intense reactions to separation and deep concerns about maintaining contact with their children, few incarcerated women receive visits from their children

(Baunach, 1985; Hairston, 1991; Hairston & Hess, 1988). Many reasons for this are offered in the literature, the most significant being organizational policies (Hairston, 1989), distance of correctional facilities (Baunach, 1985; Bloom and Steinhart, 1993) and relationships between the incarcerated parent and the children's caregiver (Baunach, 1985; Hairston, 1989; Koban, 1983).

A slightly different picture emerges for male inmates. Hairston's work (1989) indicates that approximately one-half of the fathers studied were visited by their children; 62 percent of the married inmates received regular visits, whereas 20 percent of the single fathers and 42 percent of divorced and separated fathers visited with their children regularly. Hairston (1989) finds that "a sizeable group of families make a concerted effort to maintain family ties and preserve parental bonds" (pp. 28–29). This may suggest that partners (particularly spouses) of male inmates may be more willing or able to maintain ties to the prisoner than partners or family members of female inmates. These visiting patterns may also reflect the additional obstacles created by the increased distance of female correctional facilities from urban areas.

Three realities prevail: (1) male and female inmate parents do see themselves as parents and are open to and in need of support in that role; (2) incarcerated parents, especially mothers, actually see their children rarely; and (3) visiting conditions are most often not conducive to family interaction.

Without adequate contact, it is clear that the feelings of ambivalence, conflict, and role confusion that affect incarcerated and custodial parents are left unacknowledged by the very systems designed to serve them: education, social welfare, health, and mental health. Rather, the inmate, the child, the custodial parent, the foster parent, the grandparent, or the guardian is left to establish equilibrium in the aftermath of trauma in a criminal justice system that is focused on punishment and unable to address the dynamic and reactive process that is occurring within the family.

Going Home: The Parenting Role

Release from prison often creates a major crisis for the inmate and the family (Fishman & Cassin, 1981). The homecoming is most likely shrouded by financial stress, continued poverty, major shifts in the roles and responsibilities of family members, and many unresolved feelings of anger and resentment.

A parent's ability to cope and to maintain a balance between instinct and knowledge is significantly influenced by his or her own development, experiences, and relationships (Benedek, 1970). Parenting at its best is stressful and often challenging. It also offers an opportunity to rework internal conflicts and experience the joy of healthy attachment. When inmate parents are deprived of the parenting role while imprisoned (as most are, by virtue of the goals of incarceration), such opportunities and the relationships and skills they often yield are eliminated. Upon a parent's release, then, the trials and frustrations of parenting have potentially negative outcomes of disastrous proportions for the parolee, who is unable to understand the behavior and reactions of family members, has never learned or has forgotten effective parenting skills, and may feel unattached, abandoned, or rejected by children who are themselves adjusting and may be angry, confused, or testing limits. Faced with an overwhelming sense of failure, parolees often resort to coping strategies that are illegal, abusive, or self-destructive.

Researchers, scholars, and clinicians over the last decade have repeatedly indicated the need to design and implement programs that (1) maintain continued contact between inmates and families, (2) structure visiting to facilitate family interaction, (3) provide a forum for inmates to process emotional reactions to visits, and (4) clarify, highlight, and strengthen the parenting role (Barry, 1985; Fishman, 1982; Hairston, 1989; Bloom & Steinhart, 1993). Without such programs, inmates leave prison armed with fantasies and illusions about renewed relationships. They are filled with the energy and anxiety that come with long periods of withholding emotions. They often face financial hardship and the threat of continued substance abuse, and they often lack experience in engaging effectively in relationships. Consequently, their adjustment is in jeopardy.

Programmatic Responses to the Needs of Prisoners and Their Families

The research can provide us with some information, albeit scant, about the needs of offenders and their families. The framework of family support provides a set of principles from which to develop programs that can meet these needs within criminal justice settings. But how do we actually unite, on the one hand, a system that, by design, eliminates freedom, power, and choice from the lives of those within it and, on the other hand, principles that are set forth as a paradigm of collaboration, empowerment, and equality, with a primary focus on community building?

The answer lies in the ways in which family support programs have begun to meet the needs of inmates, parolees, and their families. The question "What do you and your family need and want from family support programs?" has been posed to groups of inmate parents in California, New York, Illinois, Kansas, Pennsylvania, New Jersey, Delaware, and the Provinces of Manitoba, Saskatchewan, and Quebec (Adalist-Estrin, 1993a). A compendium of the responses follows:

The Need for a Voice

> *I want to be heard, to feel like my opinions about parenting and life in general count — that gives me hope.*
>   Inmate father in Pennsylvania

Inmates across North America struggle with powerlessness and cry out to be heard, to be given legitimate choices, and to be confined with dignity. Family support programs afford inmates an opportunity to share concerns, as well as a chance to influence decisions related to group process and program management.

The Family Resource Center at the State Correctional Institute at Graterford, in Pennsylvania, opened in 1985 and traces its inception to the persistence and initiative of the inmates, who, with Episcopal Community Services and the prison administration, have designed and implemented programs that encourage and support fathers' involvement with their families, encourage their continued responsibility as fathers, improve the quality of institutional visits, furnish information about fatherhood, and encourage community support in the achievement of the center's goals. The center is open during visits. Coordinated parenting groups — one group inside the institution, for the inmate parent, and one in the community, for the custodial parent — are an additional component. This model suggests that empowering inmates to be responsible not only for their families but also for their programs gives them a voice and contributes to their overall effectiveness as parents and as people.

The Need for Understanding Child Development

> *It's really hard to decide whether my child's acting like this because he's four years old or because he doesn't know me or because his mom's spoiling him.*
> Inmate father in New Jersey

Incarcerated parents repeatedly voice concerns about the well-being of their children. Access to information on child development, parenting skills, parenting at a distance, and the effects of incarceration on children is crucial. Project H.I.P. (Helping Incarcerated Parents) is a collaborative project of the Maine Department of Corrections and the University of Southern Maine. The program is designed for male and female inmates at the Maine Correctional Center and includes parenting education, parent-child activities, support groups, and transportation assistance. One unique aspect of this program allows for once-a-month parent-child activity sessions, facilitated by a child development specialist for the incarcerated parent and his or her child, without the other parent. For inmate parents, these opportunities to extend their knowledge base are critical. All too often, however, parent education in criminal justice must take the form of talking about skills rather than learning them through practice.

The Need for Contact

> *I want to change her diaper or make a peanut-butter sandwich or even discipline her well.*
> Inmate mother in Illinois

Visits are seen as essential to the development and maintenance of attachment and to the well-being of prisoners' children. Visits can offer inmates the opportunity to parent, to practice skills, and to make use of their knowledge. When inmates must connect with their families through a glass, however, frustration replaces comfort. When visits are not long enough for children to adjust to the environment, they act out their anxiety, and when adults are not given sufficient privacy to discuss feelings and deal with conflict, the relationships are challenged. The visits feel incomplete. Many inmates and family members prefer not to suffer through it. Clearly, inmate parents feel acutely the effects of visiting policies that alienate and frustrate relationships: "If contact between the offender and the family is a key to success upon release, the prison system should be operated to maximize this contact — not frustrate it — as is usually the case" (Mustin, 1988, p. 6).

To that end, the pioneer Prison MATCH (Mothers and Their Children) program was initiated in 1978. The program operated the nation's first in-prison children's center at the Federal Correctional Institution in Pleasanton, California. The center was designed to provide a developmentally appropriate play environment for inmate parents and their visiting children. It also served as a training program for inmates interested in future employment in child-care programs. Each year, the center accommodated approximately 400 parents and 1,500 children, from newborns to sixteen-year-olds. Staffing patterns reflected the program's emphasis on collaboration among inmates, community professionals, volunteers, and correctional staff. Additional program components included parent education, social service, crisis intervention, and transportation services. The coordination of these services was deemed essential, in many cases, since arrangements for children's visits would necessitate the inclusion of foster parents, community caregivers, the courts, and social service agencies.

In 1981, the program was expanded to include inmate fathers. In 1989, Prison MATCH lost its funding and ceased operation. Its emphasis, however, on inmate participation and project ownership, and its focus on building strengths and acknowledging cultural diversity, made it a cornerstone model of correctional-based family support. A number of spinoff programs are noted in Cannings (1990).

Such programs as Parents and Children Together (PACT) in Fort Worth, Texas, and Prison Parents and Their Children (PATCH), in Missouri, are modified replications of the California model and could serve as beacons guiding other correctional facilities toward visiting policies and practices that promote and enhance the emotional health and well-being of families. Community-based programs that artfully facilitate visiting — by organizing transportation, housing, financial assistance, and parent-child activities — are also vital to the overall goals of maintaining family contacts. Private, nonprofit programs, such as Outside Connection, in Kansas, and Friends Outside and Centerforce, both in California, have championed services for visiting support and do much to advance the overall goals of family support.

Extended visiting programs, longer-than-regulation visiting hours, and overnight, weekend, or weeklong camp visits are slowly emerging as viable visiting formats in correctional facilities for women. These are rarely if ever designed for male inmates and their children (Cannings, 1990), and similar programs are needed for incarcerated fathers. Meanwhile, we can look to those that are available for women as essential models for increased program development for women and men alike. The Dwight Correctional Center for Women, in Illinois, has completed a three-year study of its Camp Celebration. This innovative weekend visitation program offers inmate mothers an opportunity to camp in private tents on prison grounds, cook three meals a day for their children, and enjoy traditional camping activities. Preliminary results of the study indicate that, as a result of the camp experience, inmate mothers felt they had increased their parenting skills, were closer to their children, and felt more positively toward the correctional staff members involved in the project (Higgins, 1990). Another landmark program, the Nursery, in the Bedford Hills (New York) Correctional Facility, is the oldest such program in the country. The Nursery houses female inmates who have given birth while incarcerated. Mother and infant can stay together until the child's first birthday. Other elements of the Bedford Hills program are a children's playroom and a parenting center.

Focused, sustained contact with children is necessary for the children's optimal development and essential if inmate parents are to use visiting periods to do the work that ongoing dynamic relationships require. Without this contact, inmates, their partners, and their children are not prepared for the adjustment process after release.

The Need for Release Preparation

> *I see my family every week, and we say, 'Hello. I love you. I miss you.' We chat and then say goodbye. No one wants to deal with painful and difficult issues.*
> Inmate father in Manitoba

This "on hold" phenomenon of family relationships leaves the intensity of family life, as well as feelings of betrayal, resentment, and anger about the crime and imprisonment, to be dealt with after release. Acknowledging the complexity of the needs of inmates and the enormity of the task of preparing them to reenter society, some family support programs have successfully combined such components as parent education, support groups, counseling, community outreach, and advocacy. Many now also include weekend and overnight family visiting, as a form of release preparation. A notable example of integrated family prerelease support programming with pre- and post release services, is *Continuité famille après des détenues* (CFAD, Family Continuity After Imprisonment) in Montreal, Quebec. Participants in the two-day visit programs must attend parent-education workshops regularly, and each overnight visit is followed by a mandatory discussion session designed to focus on the children's behavior and feelings and on the inmates' reactions and concerns related to the visit. Released inmates continue their involvement with the program's personnel through phone contacts and a drop-in center.

The Women's Activities and Learning Center (WALC), housed in the Central Unit of the Topeka (Kansas) Correctional

Facility, is also designed to provide programs that strengthen inmate mothers' relationships with their children and increase chances of the mothers' positive reintegration into their families after release. Special child-centered visiting areas, which include kitchens for inmates' use and playgrounds, are available, as are parent-education programs and special family events.

These family support programs build on the strengths of inmate parents and offer opportunities to focus on the obstacles likely to be encountered in the community.

The Need for Continuity of Services

I have no idea how I'll continue to find this kind of support when I get out.
Inmate mother in Kansas

Glasser (1992) presents findings related to the effects of a parenting program in Connecticut. Unlike other data positively correlating family relationships with reduced recidivism (Hairston, 1988; Holt & Miller, 1972), her report could not substantiate any link between a parent program for imprisoned mothers in Connecticut and reduced recidivism. The data collected showed that while the parenting program offered inmate mothers valuable support and education, as well as positive opportunities for visiting and communicating with their children, the benefits did not appear to reduce the women's chances of going back to prison. One key to discovering what it will take to prepare inmates for life in the community is the questions Glasser's report raises about how community agencies receive the inmates referred to them.

Family support programs in the community that focus on or are sensitive to the unique needs of ex-offenders are scarce. No comprehensive model for continuity of services exists yet in the United States. A groundbreaking conceptual model for community collaboration and integration of services does exist, however, in the Justice Resource Centre, in Winnipeg, Manitoba, Canada. One component of the center, operated by the John Howard Society of Manitoba, is its family support program, run by ex-offenders. It was established to provide a forum for the parents and family members of offenders. Since the John Howard Society also operates inside Manitoba prisons, the Justice Resource Centre provides the bridge to the community, which otherwise would not be available to families.

In the United States, as of 1989, there were over one hundred family support programs in thirty-nine states providing information and education to parent-inmates and facilitating opportunities for parent-child visits (National Resource Center for Family Support Programs, 1992). Few data are available on community programs that offer family support opportunities, specifically to custodial parents and parolees, and it is highly likely that countless numbers of family support programs in rural, inner-city, and suburban communities are encountering families for whom incarceration has become a life crisis.

Programs were mentioned here illustratively and chosen as representative of an emerging frontier of family support. These programs, as well as many others that were not mentioned, both encourage and challenge us. They offer models of empowerment necessary to instil the confidence and competence that are essential if inmates are to be effective and successful as parents and to advocate on their own behalf (Pizzo, 1987), both within the correctional facility and upon release.

Connecting the Systems

Existing programs also challenge us to continue reframing the principles of family support, in order to further integrate them into the criminal justice system. Empowerment, respect, and equality can occur when incarcerated parents are seen as the experts in our search for solutions, and when inmates play key roles in program planning, even in the context of a paradigm predicated on an imbalance of power and including elements of risk to those involved. Community building may mean challenging the personal and social networks of offenders and facilitating a rejection of street culture. Although the voluntary component of family support most often can be carried into a criminal justice model, there will often need to be mandatory components and limit-setting processes to enhance responsibility and counteract the potential for rule infractions, such as transference of contraband. What we know about crime and about criminals, their children, and their families gives us the responsibility to continue modifying and adapting the principles and practices of family support, designing programs that maintain contact between inmates and their families, clarifying, highlighting, and strengthening the parenting roles of inmates. Consequently, key program and policy imperatives exist.

Recommendations

1. *Family support programs should be available inside correctional facilities.*

Lessons learned from existing programs indicate that the criminal justice system can effectively enlist the support of community family resource programs to design and implement activities that provide information, support, counseling, and training, and identify basic, easy-to-read parenting resources, both general and incarceration-specific, for inclusion in prison libraries.

2. *Program designs must be carefully scrutinized for relevance to the offender population and to specific cultural and ethnic norms.*

Most traditional parent-education models ignore the realities of inmates' lives and fail to account for legacies of loss, abuse, poverty and powerlessness. When the content and format of family support programs are irrelevant and thus ineffective, we risk contributing to a continuing cycle of failure for inmates and their families. Such program failures also contribute to the "nothing works" mentality of the opponents of family support.

3. *Visiting must be conducive to optimal family interaction, within the parameters of security.*

Contact visits, flexible time frames, and consideration of families' work and school schedules are necessary. Child-oriented play areas for visiting, policies that allow for the practicing of parenting skills, opportunities for extended visiting, and creation of programs that provide a forum for the processing of emotional reactions to visits are all essential.

4. We must redefine the concept of prerelease programming to include continued contact between inmates and their families throughout incarceration.

Factors at work within the family, from the time of arrest to the time of release, do affect postparole adjustment. Family support programs can minimize the effects of incarceration and optimize prospects for effective reentry into the community by providing ongoing support and counseling. The final stages of this process can address specific concerns related to custody, housing, and employment.

5. Correctional officers and prison administrators need to be engaged and involved in the family support process for themselves, as parents.

This is necessary before changes in judgments, attitudes, and behavior can occur and an optimal level of support and cooperation can be attained.

6. Community family support programs are necessary for prisoner-family adjustment.

Paroled offenders and their families are in a most vulnerable position and consequently in the most need of family support services that are intentional in their design and that remove obstacles to the process of adjustment by building on strengths and promoting parenting and advocacy skills.

7. Existing programs in the broader community can do much to assess the effects of incarceration on families.

Language and programming that reflect awareness, understanding, and acceptance of incarceration as a real and present concern within the community can be welcoming to an often hidden population of families of offenders. Such programs can assist families in advocating for services and resources that enable them to care for their children and maintain and sustain a relationship with the incarcerated family member.

8. Whenever possible, community alternatives to incarceration should be considered in the sentencing of primary-caregiver parents of young children.

Sentencing options in the criminal justice system should be expanded, in light of the need to avoid unnecessary separations for young children and their parents. Family support programs in the community can play an important role in this process, since residential and nonresidential community correctional programs can include or be connected to family support services.

9. *There is an urgent need for a national data base that focuses on gathering comprehensive statistics related to inmates and their families.*

The dearth of such information severely limits program implementation and advocacy. Data collection and scholarly study of the parenting and family statistics of offenders, evaluative studies of family support programs, and longitudinal studies of postrelease family functioning are sorely needed (Hairston, 1990).

The Challenge of Change

There are obstacles inherent in the implementation of the recommendations made here. There are also obstacles to the overall advancement of a family-focused agenda in the corrections and criminal justice systems.

We are limited by historical perspectives.
1. Family support has not yet adequately found its way into the mental health and drug- and alcohol-treatment program models to which family-oriented criminal justice programs are often inextricably tied.
2. Criminal justice and corrections have not yet developed a rehabilitational category for family support, and family support has yet to consistently include criminal justice in its categories of systems affecting children and families.
3. The word *rehabilitation,* which implies restoration to a previously functional state, is irrelevant and useless in describing a population for which previous states and relationships have often been less than functional. Efforts focused on creating attachments have yet to replace those whose goals are rooted in a traditional rehabilitative process (Adalist-Estrin, 1993b).
4. Substantive efforts to provide family support have heretofore targeted female offenders. The vast majority of family support programs are designed for incarcerated mothers.

These programs are vital and certainly mirror the "free" community, where far more women than men engage in family support programs. This also reflects the reality that men typically have not been the primary caregivers of their children before incarceration, as women are most likely to have been. Providing support to incarcerated parents is a social policy issue related to male and female offenders alike, however. As such, it charts a course toward humane corrections and increased public safety. If this is viewed merely as a women's issue, existing and future programs for men and women alike will be jeopardized.

We are limited by public opinion
and ubiquitous prejudice.

1. The average American shows righteous indignation when it comes to criminals (Fleisher, 1989). Public opinion is definitely not sympathetic to offenders. Family support programs often appear too humane and evoke resentment from law-abiding citizens, who believe that criminals are being rewarded by such programs. Proponents of punitive corrections operate from the belief that deprivation and aversive conditions will "teach a lesson."

2. Inmates in the United States are disproportionately poor and from ethnic minority groups. Thus racism joins forces with fear and resentment, disconnecting the offender population from the parent population at large and inhibiting interest in the possible interface of criminal justice and family support. These prejudices permeate the criminal justice system, creating an atmosphere of tension for inmates and one of stigma for families as they encounter policies that frequently go beyond what is necessary for security and cause feelings of humiliation and degradation. These biases also contribute to the pervasive perception that the children and families of offenders are irrelevant, thus rendering them invisible individually, in their schools and communities, and collectively, in the eyes of policy makers and the general public. Combatting the presence of these forces is indeed a challenge for the family support field.

The Promise of the Future

Prisoners, their children, and their families need access to one another through reformed visitation policies, community programming, alternatives to incarceration, and postrelease support systems if they are to withstand the impact of incarceration. Family support principles and practices have begun to set the stage for program development within the criminal justice system, and advocates continue to promote a family support presence within corrections and criminal justice. These efforts also promote family support programs as critical components of rehabilitation, rather than as rewards, and can highlight issues, concerns, and strategies affecting male and female offenders alike.

The future holds promise for further collaboration and will require sustained efforts to focus public attention on the plight of children of incarcerated parents, the role of families in the rehabilitative process, and the effects of this process on reduced crime and increased public safety. Whose responsibility is it to advance the integration of family support into the criminal justice system? Ambrose Bierce (1967) defines *responsibility* as "a detachable burden easily shifted to the shoulders of God, fate, fortune, luck or one's neighbor." This responsibility must be acknowledged, accepted, and shared by the inmates, their families, treatment providers, departments of corrections, welfare administrators, and policy makers, and by family support practitioners and researchers and administrators at the local, state, and national levels. Indeed, shifting this burden fails everyone.

References

Adalist-Estrin, A. (1993a). *Interviews with inmate parents.* Unpublished manuscript.

Adalist-Estrin, A. (1993b, October). *Moral development and attachment: Disruptions that create cycles of criminal behavior.* Paper prepared for the Fourth North American Conference on Family and Corrections, Quebec City, Canada.

Adams, S. S. (1977). Evaluating correctional treatments. *Criminal Justice And Behavior, 4,* 323–340.

American Correctional Association. (1990). *The female offender: What does the future hold?* Washington, DC: St. Mary's Press.

Barnhill, S. (1991). *Three generations at risk.* Atlanta: Aid to Imprisoned Mothers.

Barry, E. (1985). *Children of prisoners: Punishing the innocent.* Youth Law News, 6(2), 12–18.

Bartol, C. R. (1991). *Criminal behavior: A psychosocial approach.* Englewood Cliffs, NJ: Prentice-Hall.

Baunach, P. (1985). *Mothers in prison.* New Brunswick, NJ: Transaction Books.

Benedek, T. (1970). Parenthood during the life cycle. In E. J. Anthony and T. Benedek (Eds.), *Parenthood: Its Psychology and Psychopathology* (pp. 185–206). Boston: Little, Brown.

Bierce, A. (1967). *The enlarged devils dictionary.* New York: Doubleday.

Bloom, B., & Steinhart, D. (1993). *Why punish the children? A reappraisal of the children of incarcerated mothers in America.* San Francisco: National Council on Crime and Delinquency.

Brooks, C., Zuckerman, B., Bamforth, A., Cole, J., & Kaplan-Sanoff, M. (in press). Clinical issues related to substance abuse–involved mothers and their babies. *Journal of Infant Mental Health.*

Cannings, K. (1990). *Bridging the gap: Programs and services to facilitate contact between inmate parents and their children.* Ottawa, Canada: Ministry Solicitor General.

Center for Children of Incarcerated Parents. (1992). *Children of offenders.* Report No. 6. Pasadena, CA: Pacific Oaks College.

Children's Defense Fund. (1988). *A call for action to make our nation safe for children: A briefing book on the status of American children in 1988.* Washington, DC: Author.

Currie, E. (1985). *Confronting crime.* New York: Pantheon.

Doyle, J. S., & Bauer, S. K. (1989). Post-traumatic stress disorder in children. *Journal of Traumatic Stress, 2*(3), 275–288.

Dunst, C. J., Trivette, C. M., & Thompson, R. B. (1990). Supporting and strengthening family functioning: Toward a congruence between principles and practice. In D. G. Unger and

D. R. Powell (Eds.), *Families as nurturing systems: Support across the life span* (pp. 19–44). New York: Haworth Press.

Feeley, M., & Simon, J. (1992). The new penology: Notes on the emerging strategy of corrections and its implications. *Criminology, 30*(4), 449–474.

Fishman, L. (1990). *Women at the wall: A study of prisoners' wives doing time on the outside.* Albany: State University of New York Press.

Fishman, S. H. (1982). The impact of incarceration on children of offenders. *Journal of Children in Contemporary Society, 15,* 89–99.

Fishman, S. H., & Cassin, C.J.M. (1981). *Services for families of offenders: An overview.* Washington, DC: U.S. Department of Justice, National Institute of Corrections.

Fleisher, M. (1989). *Warehousing violence.* Newbury Park, CA: Sage.

Glasser, I. (1992). Parenting programs for imprisoned mothers. *Practicing Anthropology, 14*(3), 17–21.

Hadley, J. (1981). *Georgia women's prison inmates and their families.* Atlanta: Georgia Department of Offender Rehabilitation.

Hairston, C. F. (1988). Family ties during imprisonment: Do they influence future criminal activity? *Federal Probation, 52*(1), 48–51.

Hairston, C. F. (1989). Men in prison: Family characteristics and parenting views. *Journal of Offender Counselling Services and Rehabilitation, 14*(1), 23–30.

Hairston, C. F. (1990). *Prisoners, families and children: Building a national data base.* Indianapolis: Indiana University School of Social Work.

Hairston, C. F. (1991). Mothers in jail: Parent-child separation and jail visitation. *Affilia, 6*(2), 9–27.

Hairston, C. F., & Hess, P. M. (1988, April). *Regulating parent-child communication in correctional settings.* Paper presented at the First National Conference on Family and Corrections, Sacramento, CA.

Herman, J. (1992). *Trauma and recovery: The aftermath of abuse, from domestic abuse to political terror.* New York: Basic Books.

Higgins, J. (1990). *Camp Celebration research report.* Dwight, IL: Illinois Department of Corrections.

Holt, N., & Miller, D. (1972). *Explorations in inmate family relationships.* Sacramento: California Department of Corrections.

Irwin, J., & Austin, J. (1987). *It's about time: Solving America's prison-crowding crisis.* San Francisco: National Council on Crime and Delinquency.

Jesness, C. F. (1987). Early identification of delinquent-prone children: An overview. In J. D. Burchard & S. N. Burchard (Eds.), *Prevention of delinquent behavior* (pp. 140–157). Newbury Park, CA: Sage.

Jose-Kampfner, C. J. (1990). *Post-traumatic stress disorder in children who witnessed their mother's arrest.* Unpublished manuscript.

Koban, L. A. (1983). Parents in prison: A comparative analysis of the effects of incarceration on the families of men and women. *Research in Law, Deviance and Social Control, 5,* 171–183.

Martinson, R. M. (1974). What works — questions and answers about prison reform. *Public Interest, 35,* 22–54.

Morris, P. (1965). *Prisoners and their families.* London: Allen & Unwin.

Mustin, J. (1984). *The family: A critical factor for corrections.* Paper presented at the 29th Annual Southern Conference on Corrections: Tallahassee, FL.

National Resource Center for Family Support Programs. (1992). *Family support programs and incarcerated parents.* Chicago: Family Resource Coalition.

Pizzo, P. (1987). Parent-to-parent support groups: Advocates for social change. In S. L. Kagan, D. R. Powell, B. Weissbourd, & E. F. Zigler (Eds.), *America's family support programs: Perspectives and prospects* (pp. 228–242). New Haven, CT: Yale University Press.

Putnam, F. (1989). *Diagnosis and treatment of multiple personality disorder.* New York: Guilford Press.

Rohsenow, D., Corbett, R., & Devine, D. (1988). Molested as children: A hidden contribution to substance abuse? *Journal of Substance Abuse, 5,* 13–18.

Rutter, M., & Giller, H. (1984). *Juvenile delinquency: Trends and perspectives.* New York: Guilford Press.

Schorr, L. B., & Schorr, D. (1988). *Within our reach: Breaking the cycle of disadvantage.* New York: Doubleday.

Shaw, R. (1992). *Prisoners' children: What are the issues?* London: Routledge.

Stanton, A. (1980). *When mothers go to jail.* Lexington, MA: Lexington Books.

Swan, L. A. (1981). *Families of Black prisoners: Survival and progress.* Boston: G.K. Hall.

Tremblay, R. E. (1986). *Prediction and prevention of juvenile delinquency in early childhood: The Montreal longitudinal study.* Montreal, Quebec, Canada: University of Montreal.

U.S. Department of Justice, Bureau of Justice Statistics. (1991). *Prisoners in 1990.* Washington, DC: Author.

Weissbourd, B. (1990). Family resource and support programs: Changes and challenges in human services. In D. G. Unger & D. R. Powell (Eds.), *Families as nurturing systems: Support across the life span* (pp. 69–89). New York: Haworth Press.

Weissbourd, B., & Kagan, S. L. (1989). Family support programs: Catalysts for change. *American Journal of Orthopsychiatry, 59*(1), 20–31.

West, D. J., & Farrington, D. P. (1973). *Who becomes delinquent.* London: Heinemann.

Wolfgang, M. E., Seller, J. T., & Figlio, R. M. (1977). *Delinquency in a birth cohort.* Chicago: University of Chicago Press.

□ Part Three □

PROGRAMMATIC CHANGE AND FAMILY SUPPORT

□ 9 □

Supporting
the Family Support Worker

Frances Stott
Judith S. Musick

Just as parents need support from other people and institutions, so too do staff serving families need support from their programs. This is particularly the case for this generation of family support programs, faced as they are with new challenges from many quarters. These challenges have their roots in external forces, such as chronic funding shortages, as well as increased family and community disorder. Greater numbers of families are currently coping with the strains of raising children in reduced and uncertain economic circumstances. Communities at all socioeconomic levels are increasingly unsafe places to raise children. Drug use, crime, and many forms of violence exist at levels that far surpass those of earlier generations. More single women are raising children, more women are working, and extended family members are less available for child care and support.

It is equally true, however, that many difficulties originate within the programs themselves, largely as a product of staff members' being underprepared for the realities of family life today. As a result of poorly thought-out practices (especially those regarding the parent-child relationship) and the lack of deliberate mechanisms to provide staff support, family support workers are often well intentioned but overwhelmed. Family support staff

189

today, no matter with whom they are working, need a broad repertoire of knowledge and skills and a perspective that takes account of the multiple psychosocial, biological, and cultural factors affecting human behavior and relationships. The purpose of this chapter is twofold: to examine program structure as supportive or unsupportive of staff development, and to consider the influence on practice of personal characteristics of staff members themselves. The focus is on programs serving families with children from birth to the age of three.

Who are family support workers? When a program's mission is to address a range of concerns pertaining to both children and parents, the question of staff competencies is more complex than in traditional settings, where professionals work with children *or* with parents, and where the roles and goals are more narrowly defined. Typically, clients come to the latter type of program with specific needs (help for a disabled child, day care, psychotherapy, and so on). These needs are then addressed through traditional professional roles (teacher, child development specialist, social worker) designed to meet explicit, delimited goals. Further, it is generally the child *or* the adult who is the initial focus (with the notable exception of family therapy, which requires highly skilled therapists).

Although today's emphasis on family and service integration means that traditional educational and social service institutions are more family-centered, family support programs are nevertheless — by design — less narrowly and rigidly prescribed. Preventive and proactive in nature, they deliberately seek to cut a wider swath. Reaching a wider range of families while the children are still young, these programs have the potential to set the parent-child *relationship,* as well as the parents' and the child's own personal development, on a more positive course. Under the right circumstances, a family support program can serve as a catalyst, enabling parents to feel better and gain positive momentum over time as they learn to seek and use new resources (Halpern, 1990b).

At the same time, one strength of these programs is also a significant source of their weakness: their flexibility and diffuse-ness of purpose make them very difficult to staff. Where greater adaptability, openness, and desire to reach a broader population are found, there is also greater potential for misguided effort. For example, a young mother initially comes to a family support program seeking companionship, resources for her child, or just a place to be out in the world. She may also be aware, at some level, of a problem between herself and her child. How this is recognized and dealt with by staff has the potential for ameliorating or further harming their relationship. Although the philosophy undergirding family support programs emphasizes strengths and health, rather than deficits and pathology, today's families bring many problems to family support programs. These present formidable barriers that staff must overcome, and they must do this without losing sight of longer-range, proactive goals for children and families. All too often, in spite of the best intentions, staff simply respond from moment to moment, to crisis after crisis. It takes staff who are very knowledgeable and confident in themselves — as people, not just as providers — to avoid becoming purely reactive in the face of such challenges.

Certain attributes have already been identified as characteristic of effective family support workers. These include such personal qualities as commitment to a dialogue with participants and the ability to establish relationships with children and families; a capacity for empathy and warmth; concern, compassion, sensitivity, and respect for the varied values and ways of diverse families and cultures; and flexibility and receptivity. In addition to these personal qualities, there are general characteristics, such as a store of information and knowledge, that are highly relevant to this work.

Such a list is only the beginning, however. Relationships, compassion, and knowledge carry different connotations across different contexts. What are the *motives* behind any particular staff member's relationships with participants? What are the assumptions underlying the work a program purports to do? Family support work is not simply a product of personal endowment, training, or prescribed practice. It is a complex and dynamic process. Nested within a particular community and institution, with particular cultural and programmatic norms and practices, the "work" of family support programs is constantly being created and re-created through interaction with participants and staff.

Program Structure

Since the issue of staffing encompasses both programmatic and personal characteristics, we will consider each in turn. We begin with program characteristics: as already suggested, they provide the guiding structure and "holding" environment within which staff carry out their work.

A program's practices are the natural outgrowth of its structure—or lack thereof. Just as inadequate resources, unrealistic goals, heavy caseloads, and inordinate administrative demands exact a heavy toll on workers, unquestioned practices lead to feelings of futility and anger on the part of staff (Fields, 1992). Conversely, the well-structured program becomes a "program family" as staff collaborate to achieve its well-articulated goals. This sense of community provides support to staff for their own personal and professional growth (Gilkerson & Young-Holt, 1992).

Good programs have a structure that is articulated on a number of different levels, providing support and guidance for staff, who then pass this on to families. Family support programs require clear administrative structures for developing program philosophy and goals and for providing clear role definitions, job descriptions, and boundaries. They must also have incremental benchmarks to let staff know that they are accomplishing something meaningful for the participants. Such a structure logically holds workers accountable for realistic, realizable goals. In doing this, it lessens the chances that they will feel defeated, confused, or overwhelmed. Embedded in this structure is a system of clinical supervision and a process for resolving conflict between staff and participants, and among staff members themselves. Service providers require a sense of what they are expected to do every day, as well as a forum to which they can bring triumphs and defeats.

Program Philosophy and Goals

While staff may come from different disciplines and have different theoretical orientations, there should be some common conceptual framework shared by all. This framework is derived both from the program's particular mission and philosophy and from a knowledge of theory-based "best practices." Once a program's mission and philosophy are clarified, these can be used to guide program development. The process of program development then further articulates the model.

Part of the original rationale for family support programs was derived from social support theory emphasizing informal helping (see Chapter Two, this volume; Unger & Powell, 1990). In recent years, additional principles from other fields have been assimilated into this tradition, some of which are particularly well suited to families with young children. A number of family support programs have incorporated aspects of clinical infant intervention, especially those tenets and practices that address psychological obstacles to adequate parenting in the early years (Fraiberg, 1980; Provence & Naylor, 1983; Greenspan et al., 1987; Greenspan, 1992).

The attempt to bring together disparate theoretical motifs has not been without its difficulties, however. Indeed, in some ways the wedding of informal social support and clinical intervention creates an uneasy marriage. Although it may be a marriage that makes good sense in theory, in practice it has been difficult to establish clear goals for programs seeking to integrate these two approaches. All too often, mission statements are too general: "to increase participants' effectiveness as parents"; "to improve the parent-child relationship"; "to enhance child development"; "to prevent child abuse." Although statements such as these are usually refined with more detailed guidelines by individual programs, particularly in response to a funding source, they are often not realized in day-to-day practice.

When programs are based on several traditions, the model may remain poorly articulated. If the assumptions underlying the model remain implicit, staff members inevitably find themselves working at cross-purposes with the program goals, or with each other. For example, one program may assume that there is a body of child-rearing knowledge that parents need to know; others may assume that parents mainly need emotional support, friendship networks, and concrete services, such as job training; still others are designed to ensure children's and parents' basic well-being during times of extreme stress or crisis.

Despite the services that logically follow from each of these assumptions, staff often feel ineffective because problems remain in the basic parent-child relationship. They have proceeded on the misguided notion that offering education and social support is sufficient to *change* relationships. This notion then gets translated into ineffective practice and unrealizable goals. In reality, the goal of profound change in parenting is derived from the principles of clinical infant mental health, which consider the complexity of relationship problems. As Anders (1989) states, "Given the limited psychological autonomy of infants before three years of age, we feel it unlikely that psychopathology can be sustained in the individual infant. It seems improbable also that an infant's disturbance is caused solely by an adult's disorder, since, in the absence of the infant, the adult's distress may disappear. Moreover, a disturbance in an infant may be present in relation to one parent and not the other. The conclusion is inescapable: most psychological and behavioral syndromes of infancy disturbance occur in the context of relationships" (pp. 125–126). Such clinical notions as these may be incorporated into a program without awareness of the operational implications involved. An infant mental health approach utilizes direct intervention to reverse maladaptive parenting; it does not presume that support and education alone are enough to change parenting capacities and behavior acquired through a lifetime of experience in a particular family and social world and reinforced by current circumstances (Halpern, 1990b, p. 304). Further, this model of addressing the *relationship* also takes the contribution of the child into consideration, which requires the ability to assess the many aspects of infant and toddler development and to understand their meaning to the parent. In recognizing that relationships transcend individual characteristics, this model is careful to avoid undermining them through such intervention practices as competing with the mother in an effort to "show her the right way to deal with her baby." Finally, while there are various approaches to parent-infant therapies, they all require trained staff and careful attention to the source of clinical information (for example, the mother's representations of the baby, the baby's medical history or behavior) and the therapeutic modalities employed (Stern-Bruschweiler & Stern, 1989).

Let us say that a support program's central mission is to strengthen the parent-child relationship. In this model, children stay in the room with their parents. When staffed by experienced and well-supervised child development specialists and social workers, programs such as this are similar in practice (as well as in philosophy) to those offered in infant mental health settings. Staff have sophisticated understanding of the multiple determinants of parenting, which include parents' psychological factors (such as their history of being parented), social context factors, and child characteristics. They bring this knowledge to bear in assessing parent-child relationships, offering limited interventions, and in serving as a vehicle for referral to more intensive clinical services (Bertacchi & Coplon, 1989).

A more typical family support approach might offer separate services for the child and the parent, with separate staff for each. This model lends itself to the provision of education and support for parents (including linkage to other services) and developmentally appropriate experiences for the children. If it is well structured and supervised, this model can have a salutary effect on parental motivation, attitudes, and behavior.

The lens through which all family support staff view their work must be wide enough to encompass the enormous complexity of human behavior, taking into account the influences of family, community, social, economic, biological, cultural, and psychological factors on parents and their children (Belsky & Vondra, 1989; Michaels & Goldberg, 1988). Further, they must recognize how the *transactions* taking place between and among these variables affect both parents and children (Sameroff & Fiese, 1990). Program staff also have the difficult task of building on the strengths that families bring with them — their resiliency, their resourcefulness, and, often, their extraordinary coping abilities.

Ultimately, staff members must develop their own personal working theories. This is as it should be, as long as they are conscious of how the assumptions underlying these theories affect their responses to and relationships with the participants they serve. Personal working theories also need to fit in with clearly articulated program goals. Not all programs can or should work with the same model, or with the same philosophy and goals. These are necessarily determined by the unique needs of each community and of each group of staff members. What matters most is that a program model clearly articulate its assumptions and treatment approaches. Without such articulation, staff feel at sea. Puzzled by issues they cannot understand, they remain dependent on familiar techniques, which at best address few aspects of multifaceted problems (Fields, 1992).

Articulation of Staff Roles and Functions

A natural outgrowth of program philosophy and goals, staff roles are a cornerstone of program structure. Yet the relative vagueness of family support goals can lead to difficulties in this domain. Katz's discussion (1980) of contrasts between the functions of mothering and those of teaching has clear relevance to staff roles in family support programs. She notes that the functions to be fulfilled by mothers are diffuse and limitless, whereas those of teaching are specific and limited. There is little about young children that is not in the parent's purview, while the functions of the teacher are limited to a technically defined sphere. The younger the child, however, the wider the range of functioning for which adults must assume responsibility. Because family support programs serve infants and their families, and because of their broader purview in relation to their more traditional program counterparts, a broader and more diffuse set of functions is often promoted.

All infant and family programs require clear role definitions to clarify various job functions, job descriptions, and decision-making domains. Directors and other administrative staff need to be conversant with the relevant disciplines and related competencies required for staffing the program. Just as there must be flexibility in program goals and philosophies in order to meet the needs of various families and communities, so too must there be flexibility in staffing patterns. The following are suggested staff roles and functions for family support programs.

Administrator/Clinical Supervisor. The administrator or director is responsible for accountability within the system, ensuring appropriate and effective service for program participants, by helping develop the program's mission and philosophy, and ensuring staff professionalism. This includes performance appraisal and the firing of staff, as necessary. This is often quite difficult for female directors, especially when they see themselves as choosing this work in order to help others. Female directors often experience difficulty in being assertive, recognizing their own anger, being clear about expectations, and establishing and enforcing rules so that expectations are met (Bertacchi & Stott, 1991). The director is also usually responsible for the budget and often is at least partly responsible for fundraising. This endless and often thankless task can distract the director from the "real" work of the program, leaving little time or energy for attention to the content and structure of daily practice.

Yet administrative policies are what either support or interfere with how a program's objectives are operationalized. If, for example, providers are expected to work with an unreasonably high number of families, or are discouraged from staying involved with families for a reasonable time, how can they possibly form enabling relationships with participants? If outreach is undervalued, home visits will wane. If competition with outside agencies and institutions interferes with cooperation, necessary service linkages will never be forged.

Program policy must also value and incorporate regular clinical supervision. Although directors may assume that they themselves should provide clinical supervision, it might be better to delegate this function to skilled, experienced others (Gilkerson & Young-Holt, 1992). It is critical, however, that the director make certain that ongoing supervision is in place. This means allocating funds and time for supervision to occur, hiring someone competent to supervise, and incorporating supervision into job descriptions.

Directors and supervisors need leadership skills, including the ability to comfortably facilitate group process, mediate staff problems and problems with clients, and help staff see what is possible through conflict resolution, problem solving, and decision making. Program leaders should also be critical consumers and appliers of professional information and literature.

The supervisor must have knowledge of the supervision process. While this seems obvious, many supervisors in family support programs rose to their present positions because they were effective with children or were capable administrators, not because of their specific training in clinical supervision. Supervision is an intensive and time-consuming process designed to teach, solve problems, and help staff effect changes, including outward changes (such as those involving skills) and inward changes in the use of the professional self (see Fenichel, 1991, 1992, for a discussion of supervision in programs for infants and families).

Supervisors in family support programs should have the capacity to provide supervision around the powerful psychological issues evoked when one is working with young children and their parents, particularly those unconscious, preverbal issues stemming from parents' and staff's own experiences as children and parents. Supervisors also need to understand such psychological phenomena as transference and countertransference, which may distort the way staff perceive and relate to participants. Finally, a good supervisor must have at her fingertips a portfolio of strategies for promoting the self-worth and development of staff.

Family Specialist. Each family support program needs at least one person whose competencies include working well with parents. Such competencies consist of interviewing and observation skills and techniques of determining family functioning, such as knowledge of external and internal boundaries, family power and decision making, communication, gender roles, family myths, and intergenerational issues. The family specialist also needs a sense of parenthood as a developmental process, and of the dynamics that take place between parents and partners. They should also be sensitive to the family's culture and values and to family strengths, weaknesses, resources, and needs. Since it often falls to the family specialist to deal with abuse and domestic violence, these staff members especially should be familiar with appropriate procedures, both for reporting and for dealing with the family in the most helpful way.

Child Development Specialist. We also believe that at least one member of a family support team should have formal knowledge of child development and should be capable of effectively planning for infants, toddlers, and their families. Indispensable skills for work with infants and toddlers include a working knowledge of development and of risk. The child development specialist should be able to observe infants with a focus on the underlying developmental processes, rather than on the appearance of individual milestones in all domains. She should be able to assess strengths (protective factors, coping strategies, and adaptive behaviors), as well as developmental status and needs, and be able to conduct a psychosocial assessment of the infant or toddler in his or her family context. The child development specialist should be able to develop naturalistic programs that support infant and toddler development and that fit into ongoing family patterns and existing community resources, capitalizing on child and family strengths and coping abilities. Finally, she should be aware of early intervention programs in the community that serve children with special needs.

The Role of the Paraprofessional. Much of the direct service in family support programs is provided by paraprofessional workers living in or near the communities that house the programs. The needs of a family can sometimes be met most appropriately by individuals who are familiar with the economic and cultural aspects of that family. At the same time, there are also problems with relying too heavily on lay staff, especially untrained and unsupervised lay staff working with families and communities where there are multiple risks. These problems are less the fault of paraprofessionals than of the unrealistic expectations of program administrators. Paraprofessionals are often asked to take on roles for which they are not prepared.

One problem is that many paraprofessionals, especially those in isolated, impoverished communities, lack direct access to mainstream institutions and organizations that are vital pathways to success for program participants. For example, in order to succeed in the wider world, adolescent parents need models and mentors to bring them there, literally as well as symbolically. These must be people who are comfortable being there themselves.

An equally troublesome problem, and one harder to remedy, is that lay workers, like professionals, may be hampered by their own inadequately resolved problems around sexual and reproductive behavior, relationships to men, child-rearing practices, family violence, assertiveness, or autonomy. These issues can cause strong psychological reverberations for workers when they threaten to bring to awareness painful feelings that have been denied or repressed. Issues such as these are particularly hard for staff members who had (or still have) serious problems in these domains themselves (Musick & Stott, 1990).

Even if they are not struggling with such psychological issues, paraprofessional workers may be affected by unacknowledged (and unexamined) ambivalence or conflict around personal change or success and perhaps around "outgrowing" their own partners, families, and friends. After all, many lay staff were once in similar circumstances themselves.[1] Lacking supervised clinical experiences — experiences designed to help professionals manage countertransference and other psychological reactions — these home visitors, parent-group leaders, community mothers, mentors, and child-care or youth workers are more likely to fail inadvertently in helping a participant because of their own unrecognized feelings.

As we have said before (Musick & Stott, 1990), there is a phenomenon apparent in many of the interactions between staff and participants: certain subjects simply are not raised, or at least are not raised or discussed consistently, possibly because these issues are too close to home. Halpern (1990a) calls these "domains of silence." It is difficult to deal straightforwardly with someone else's problem if it is one's own problem as well. It is hard to bring someone else beyond where you yourself have gone. Confronting domestic violence in a participant's family may be too stressful for the worker who was (or perhaps still is) a victim of it herself. Family planning and contraceptive issues may be taboo topics for the woman who was herself a mother of several children before she was twenty. If a home visitor disregards a parent's harmful child-rearing practices because she lacks formal knowledge about child development, that is one type of problem comparatively easy to remedy. But if she avoids intervening because of her own personal discomfort, the situation is more complex (Musick & Stott, 1990). Perhaps she was raised in the same way that the parents in her program are raising their children. Intervention problems such as these are magnified when professional-level staff (directors and supervisors) hesitate to set clear preventive goals for the paraprofessional because they also feel uncomfortable with such taboo and strongly value-laden topics as family planning.

It is critically important for professional and paraprofessional staff alike to have clear roles and responsibilities and for ongoing training and supervision for both groups to be in place, particularly when a program serves families in disadvantaged and high-risk communities, where a broader range of skills is required. While the paraprofessional can serve as a bridge to the community, she should not be expected to fulfill roles for which she is not prepared. At the same time, her experience and knowledge of the ways of the community can be invaluable assets to a program. The paraprofessional is often in the best position to do outreach and, with adequate preparation and supervision, to do direct service as well. If the skills and strengths that paraprofessionals bring to their work are recognized and valued sufficiently within the program, there will be effective collaboration between the two groups of staff. One approach, for example, is to pair a professional with a paraprofessional home visitor or group facilitator. Under the right circumstances, each will gradually learn from the other and grow, and the participants will be the beneficiaries of their collaboration and mutual respect.

Characteristics Essential for Family Support Staff

Personnel for family support programs should be wisely re-cruited. There are personal qualities on which there should be no compromises. Staff should be caring, intuitive people who are capable of developing positive relationships with others. They should also have the capacity for reflection about themselves and their work and should be open to new ways of thinking and do-ing. Most of all, they need to be emotionally strong people with a good deal of common sense.

Work with young children and families requires people who are authentic and comfortable with the full range of feel-ings. Considerable harm can be done by saintly do-gooders who take on personal responsibility for all the misery in the world. This holds for every level of staff, from the director to the paraprofessional worker. Staff who are not psychologically needy can serve as realistic models in ways that are nonthreatening. They can objectively mediate between child-rearing (and other) norms of a family's reference group and those of other groups.

Since family support is fundamentally a cultural enter-prise, staff must have an awareness of the meaning of culture. The day-to-day activities, child-rearing practices, and patterns of discourse among family members reflect cultural beliefs about use of interaction patterns, organization of activity, and use of space and time. If staff understand the social and political context in which their program is embedded and can recognize and be sensitive to differing patterns, they can respect and use the multi-ple perspectives and points of view converging in their program.

Some of the necessary competencies may already be part of a staff member's repertoire when she first comes to a family support program. Others are largely acquired within the con-text of the particular program. Learning is a ongoing process, one that occurs through experience, supervision, collaboration with colleagues, in-service, and continuing education.

Ability to Translate Theory into Practice

Formal knowledge of theories and a common conceptual frame-work are necessary, but they are not sufficient. A family support worker must see how these apply to real individuals and families. It is one thing to understand theory; it is often quite another to work effectively with people who act in ways that are quite different from what a textbook has suggested. Although it is useful to be able to place what one observes in this work within some conceptual framework, experience may result in the need to revise one's hypotheses.

To move from theory to practice is a complex and indirect process. Knowledge about early language development does not automatically tell us how to structure a language curriculum for infants and toddlers. We cannot simply take a concept such as "motherese" (the way in which adults modulate their voices and use fewer words when they speak to infants) and create a language-facilitating environment. Motherese is largely an *unconscious* behavior. Program developers and staff must *consciously*, deliberately, construct programmatic analogues to such naturally occurring parental behaviors.

In a similar vein, theories about early emotional development (Ainsworth, 1978; Stern, 1985) cannot be directly applied in work with families. Theories such as these are concerned with parent-child relationships; staff are not parents (even though they sometimes fulfill parentlike roles). As Schafer (1991) points out, "We are not professional early mothers; we are rather professionals who understand the implications of early motherhood. Learning the difference between these two visions of the profession is, I submit, the crucial task" (p. 13). Thus, in using theories of parent-child relationships, staff must be prepared to use what is helpful to them for understanding the relationship and promoting the best interests of the family, not for trying to be a "better" mother.

Clearly, effective family support workers also understand and respect individual differences. Recognizing the unique endowment, culture, and set of circumstances that each child and family brings to a program, they realize that no single theory or set of practices is useful for all families across all contexts. Obviously, the deeper the understanding, the broader and more flexible the set of programmatic responses. As the saying goes, "If all you have is a hammer, every problem is a nail."

Ability to Form Helping Relationships

Forming helping and enabling relationships is a complex and
often arduous process, especially when one is working with individuals from ethnic, cultural, and socioeconomic groups different from one's own. It calls for a degree of maturity—for the
ability to care but never collude, and the ability to provide wise,
informed support. Not everyone is able to form, let alone maintain, such a relationship. Winnicott's (1971) definition of the
essential traits of people suitable for working with children and
families can be applied to the helping relationship required for
family support staff.

  *Capacity to Identify with the Participant Without Loss of
Personal Identity.* Family support workers are often asked to
respond empathically to the needs of parents who may be (or
be perceived as) neglectful or rejecting of their helpless infants.
Sometimes young or unreflective staff find themselves embroiled
in unhealthy overidentifications with infants. The resultant anger
toward parents impedes progress, at best; at worst, it creates
further problems in the parent-child relationship. Conversely,
overidentification with a parent can result in colluding with,
sanctioning, and even exacerbating maladaptive parenting.

  Being clear about personal identity helps staff maintain
clear boundaries when participants present material that is beyond the scope of family support. Winnicott (1971) provides
a wonderful example:

> The client will bring and display (though at first
> in a tentative way) the current problem or the emo-
> tional conflict or the pattern of strain which obtains
> at this moment of the client's life. I think that this
> is true if one simply listens to the story of the per-
> son sitting next to one on a bus journey; if there
> is any kind of privacy the story will begin to evolve.
> It may be just a long tale of rheumatism or of in-
> justice at the office, but already the material is there
> for a therapeutic consultation . . . . Obviously it
> would be *irresponsible* to turn neighbors on a bus

journey into clients who would inevitably become
dependent, needing further opportunities or else
suffering a sense of loss at the bus stop. (p. 7; emphasis added.)

It is equally irresponsible to encourage confidences or enter-
tain "therapeutic ambitions" when one is not trained or in a
position to follow through with a program participant. Often
it is sufficient simply to listen, keeping in mind that not every
problem has an immediate solution. Nevertheless, someone on
the staff should be skilled enough to know when a referral is
warranted: "If you don't know what to do, you should know
who to tell" (Emily Fenichel, personal communication, June
1993).

Capacity to Contain Conflicts and Wait for Resolution.
One must master one's own anxiety in order to modulate that
of a parent. This can be a very difficult task. One must be able
to listen, understanding that listening *is* doing something. In
family support work, there is a fine line between offering a parent advice (What should I give Amanda to eat? How do I toilet
train Robbie?) and knowing when simply to listen, sensing that
issues other than the obvious are operating. (Maybe mother has
an eating disorder. Maybe father always needs to be in control.) There is an art to not rushing in to "fix" problems — to
going slowly, listening, suggesting, waiting.

Capacity to Avoid Retaliating When Provoked. When one
is angry with children or parents, or perhaps frustrated by not
being able to help, it is tempting to interpret their behavior to
them, or otherwise retaliate. For example, one might say to a
mother who is being punitive to her child, "You know, Mrs.
B., I think Sally just reminds you of your sister, and you know
you can't stand her." It is likewise tempting to exert one's power
as a staff member — by showing a parent the "right" way to feed
her child, for example. Establishing a relationship involves sharing control, encouraging the other to actively play his or her
part. Mutual definition of goals is difficult but extremely worthwhile. Staff should be neither domineering nor passive, and they
should encourage parents to be the same.

Self-Reflection and Self-Knowledge

The capacity for self-reflection and self-awareness is often the difference between a good and a not-so-good family support worker. It is this capacity that enables a worker to enter into healthy relationships with others and recognize her reactions to difficult families, without acting on them. Reflection, or stepping back, from hands-on work develops professionals and greatly improves services to children and families.

Self-awareness gives the family support worker an accurate assessment of her own cultural and personal values, attitudes, and beliefs. If, for example, she has never used center-based infant care herself, will she be ambivalent or negative about multiple caregiving for the families with whom she works? Above all, self-knowledge is critical for staff who carry the burden of their own unresolved childhood pain or the burdens of guilt, anger, or helplessness in the face of troubled families. The resulting need to rescue — empathy gone awry — may hurt families more than help them.

It is in the context of supervision that reflection takes place. It is the supervisor who helps the staff member struggle with problems of identity, relationships, and so on, and develop a clearer vision of the work. Yet staff often do not feel entitled to supervision. One explanation suggests that staff may feel ambivalent about supervision, even when it is designed in an atmosphere of mutual respect and trust. At some level, staff may worry about professional ineptitude or about revealing too much of their personal issues:

> The most salient challenge to "selling" supervision is the lack of entitlement many of these practitioners feel. They see supervision as something for them, rather than their clients, and they are not as important as the people they serve. In order to really institutionalize good supervision and mentorship programs . . . education [will be needed] on how supervision translates to better care for the clients, so that practitioners feel entitled to ask for this help. (Fenichel, 1992, p. 153)

While there are programmatic and attitudinal obstacles to reflective supervision, it is not a luxury but rather a critical necessity in family support programs. Supervision is the very mechanism that supports the staff, so that the staff can in turn support the participants.

Case Examples

The following vignettes illustrate how — and why — family support programs are fertile soil for the cultivation of some of the problems already discussed. They also illustrate the interplay of training, supervision, and conceptual approaches to staffing.

Vignette 1

Asked about her work in a family support program, Kathy said, "Let me start at the beginning. Even though I had a college degree, it was in English, so it was difficult for me to find a job. Eventually, I found a job as a legal secretary and slowly worked my way up to being a paralegal, and did that for many years.

"During this time, I found out that I would never be able to have children. Soon after I found this out, I went to work at a family support program. Its purpose was supposedly to prevent child abuse, and many of the families were there because the court had ordered them to be in a program to improve their parenting. They attended parenting classes, GED programs, groups to make crafts and discuss their problems, and so on. When the moms came to the program, they could also drop their kids off in a separate room for children, and that's where I worked.

"I stayed there for two years, because I needed the work and I loved kids, but I always had a funny feeling that somehow we weren't doing the right thing. You know, looking back, I have to say that the program really ruined those children. I'm not kidding. We took toddlers who were developing reasonably well, until they got to us, and by never setting limits, or else getting *really* angry, we turned them into children who were out of control — all the while, somehow creating barriers between them and their parents. It wasn't until I moved and went to work at the place I work now that I figured out what was wrong at the other program.

"I can't tell you how much I love this job. It makes me feel great. It is completely different from the program where I used to work. My supervisor now is really terrific. The first thing she did was help me see how much pain I had felt, and never acknowledged, about not being able to have children myself. I was then able to understand why I had been drawn to this work.

"At my first job, the head of the children's program had a master's in child development. She believed her calling in life was to 'rescue' these children from their parents. She encouraged me to feel that I was like the kids' mother — in fact, a much *better* mother. I had no idea that I was meeting my own needs at the expense of both the children and their mothers.

"My supervisor now is helping me see what being a primary provider really means. At the first program, I thought it meant that I was number one in 'my' kids' lives. I never knew what it meant for a program to be truly family-centered — that my job is to help support the whole family. I can't tell you how much better I feel today. Not only do I feel personally effective, I can see that the children *and* parents are thriving in this program."

Vignette 2

Miriam, a social worker, was the director of an inner-city family support program. Because of a shortage of funds and a strong desire to be truly community-based, the program was staffed by neighborhood women. None had ever worked in this type of program before.

One of these women, who had several children of her own, told Miriam that she was concerned about Richard, a one-year-old in the children's room where she worked. He didn't crawl, didn't even try to speak, and seemed very different from the other infants his age. Miriam observed Richard and agreed that, indeed, he did appear to be delayed in his development.

She consulted with Yvette, the parent-group worker, who had a good relationship with Mrs. S., Richard's mother. Yvette reported that Mrs. S. periodically came to her for reassurance that Richard was okay, since she could see that he was not doing the same things as the other babies in the room. Yvette felt that it was important to reassure Mrs. S. about Richard. She and Miriam both felt that Mrs. S. clearly did not want—and was not ready—to hear that something was the matter with her child, and they agreed to hold off saying anything that might upset her and interfere with her relationship with Richard, which was just beginning to improve after a very rocky start. In the meantime, however, Richard was getting older and falling farther behind.

Commentary

In both vignettes, we saw lack of clarification of program philosophy and goals—particularly of what it means to be *family-centered*. In the first vignette, the guiding principle in work with children seemed to be to enhance their cognitive and language development—at the expense of looking at social-emotional development or at the nature of teacher-child and parent-child relationships. In the second vignette, we saw a program that was too focused on the mother, with no appreciation that parental identity struggles always include the child. That is, by focusing on Mrs. S's denial of Richard's problem, Yvette and Miriam failed to meet the needs of either mother or son. Richard needed someone to see that he might be developmentally delayed, that he needed an evaluation and quite possibly early intervention services. Mrs. S. needed help with her anxiety about Richard, and some help in doing what was in his (and her) best interest.

Staff roles played themselves out in both cases in several ways. In vignette 1, Kathy's misguided mission to be a "professional early mother" (Schafer, 1991) was reinforced by the program's assumptions. Staff in the children's room were encouraged to believe that it was they who truly cared for these children. Such role confusion clearly led to disastrous results, both in terms of the children's development and in terms of dividing rather than supporting the family. It also contributed to the staff's feeling unsupported and incompetent.

In vignette 2, we saw the opposite phenomenon: staff were overidentified with Mrs. S. They seemed to operate under the assumption that they were building a relationship of trust by not troubling Mrs. S. too much, allowing her to maintain her illusions and move at her own pace yet not really addressing her concerns.

The family support specialist who is confused about her role may find herself placating parents rather than facing difficult feelings and issues. While Mrs. S.'s seeking of reassurance and her partial denial may help her cope with her anxiety about Richard's development, she — and he — are also suffering. Gently letting Mrs. S. know that Richard may need to be evaluated will not be easy. But staff must be willing to issue invitations to Mrs. S. to speak about her child's development or at least hear what they are saying. Perhaps when Mrs. S. comes to Yvette with some question, Yvette can ask Mrs. S: "What do you see?" This is not the same as demanding that she immediately acknowledge that something is wrong. Staff also need to be willing to communicate to Mrs. S's unconscious — that is, to assume that she has heard on some level, and that the message will be available to her consciousness when she can tolerate it. In this way, Mrs. S. and Miriam (or Yvette) may be able to reach a *mutual* decision about Richard's need for evaluation before too much time has passed.

Although the staff had formed a good relationship with Mrs. S., it was not a truly respectful one. A respectful relationship is always based on the assumption that a parent wants what is best for her child, even when this may involve some temporary personal discomfort. Family support programs do not purport to offer therapy, but staff can make themselves available to listen and participate in a parent's concerns. They can help contain her anxiety and validate her concern that something may be wrong with her child.

Situations such as Richard's — and there are many such situations in family support programs — also point to the need for a program to have a child development specialist as part of the team, a professional who can at least conduct preliminary assessments of children about whom there are concerns, speak with confidence about her impressions, and talk about the need (if there is one) for further developmental evaluation.

The defining role of supervision is apparent in both cases. In the first case, supervision made the critical difference between how Kathy functioned — and felt about herself — in the two different programs where she worked. Proper supervision provided a transforming experience, one that enabled her to recognize the way her own agenda (her infertility) played itself out in her work. Through supervision, Kathy became aware of her search for a new basis of self-esteem, and of how that search led her to compete with and set herself against parents who needed all the support and cooperation they could get. Under the false assumption that she was largely (if not wholly) responsible for "her" children's development, she felt compelled to be infinitely nurturing and selfless — a dangerous assumption and an unrealistic goal. Only with excellent supervision was she able to see the importance of setting limits and promoting children's independence, for their sake and hers. This also enabled her to maintain a life of her own away from her job.

High-quality supervision, along with in-service and continuing education, could have greatly enhanced the quality of service in the program described in the second vignette. Clearly, the director herself had not been able to reconcile the conflicting agendas of the child-care and parent-support staff, or to simultaneously address the needs of both parent and child — to be for both the parent and the child. Supervision would have helped Yvette to understand and accept that she, as well as Mrs. S., was dealing with ambivalence and fear. Staff are in a position to provide guidance and support for families. Intelligent, sensitive supervision enables them to gain support for themselves. This includes some perspective on themselves and on the motives underlying their attitudes and actions.

In this chapter, we have been attempting to bring to light a potential weakness in the new and growing field of family support. That weakness lies in the ever-present danger that families' vulnerabilities may be magnified by those of their helpers.

Families come to programs for good reasons. They crave guidance and support even as they sometimes seem to resist it. They look to us to provide direction for them — as parents and partners, students and workers, sons, daughters, and friends. When we miss opportunities to provide this direction, we compound the problems we purport to solve. When we seize opportunities to provide this direction, we enable families to build better lives for themselves and their children.

A family support program can be only as good as its staff, but its staff can be only as good as the program structure that supports them. Individual staff members form growth-promoting and sometimes healing relationships with children and families. Although the commitment, character, and skills of staff matter greatly, these are always played out within a system, one whose structure and practices either magnify or diminish staff's potential to be put to good use.

It is the rare program that can devote sufficient attention, with sufficient intensity, to all the domains relevant to all participants. This is just one of the reasons why no program can by itself be the answer to such complex social problems as intergenerational poverty or serious parenting disorders. Realistically, few family support programs are comprehensive. Most tend to devote more attention either to the child or to the parent(s), or to emphasize one domain of parental functioning over another. Programs — people, for that matter — typically do most what they are equipped to do best. What is of paramount importance is that programs recognize what it is they *can* do, acknowledge their limitations, and develop their missions, philosophies, and practices accordingly. While doing this, they must also keep in mind the families to whom their efforts are directed. The clinically informed approaches so essential for understanding and working with troubled or multiproblem families are not necessarily appropriate for those who are less distressed.

There are many hard realities facing all families today, as well as the programs that endeavor to help them. At the same time, we must remember that to help one family — even a little — is to make a monumental difference, one that ultimately reverberates in the lives of many people. In order for this to happen by design rather than by chance, those who provide growth-fostering support and direction to others must also receive it themselves.

Note

1. Paraprofessionals are not by any means a homogeneous group. For younger staff members, being employed (or volunteering) in a program may be only a stop on the journey to choosing and working toward a career. There are middle-aged and older women who want to do something for families in their communities, after having successfully raised their own families. There are also lay workers for whom a community-based program is the first job after many years of being on public assistance; indeed, such a job is often the ideal way to make the transition from welfare to work. The new worker is still in the community where she feels comfortable, and she does not have to go abruptly from a familiar to a faraway world. She can enter the world of work with people similar to herself. She can be herself, surrounded and supported by people who understand her experience, as she allows the work experience to gradually socialize her into a new role and self-image (Toby Herr, personal communication). If she still has a troubled life herself, however, the job may be beneficial for her but less so for the families she is supposed to be helping (Musick, 1993).

References

Ainsworth, M. (1978). *Patterns of attachment.* Hillsdale, NJ: Erlbaum.

Anders, T. F. (1989). Clinical syndromes, relationship disturbances, and their assessment. In A. J. Sameroff & R. N. Emde (Eds.), *Relationship disturbances in early childhood* (pp. 125–144). New York: Basic Books.

Belsky, J., & Vondra, J. (1989). Lessons from child abuse: The determinants of parenting. In D. Cicchetti & V. Carlson

(Eds.), *Child maltreatment: Theory and research on the causes and consequences of child abuse and neglect* (pp. 153–202). New York: Cambridge University Press.

Bertacchi, J., & Coplon, J. (1989). The professional use of self in prevention. *Zero to Three, 9*(4), 1–7.

Bertacchi, J., & Stott, F. M. (1991). A seminar for supervisors in infant/family programs: Growing versus paying more for staying the same. *Zero to Three, 12*(2), 34–39.

Fenichel, E. (1991). Learning through supervision and mentorship to support the development of infants, toddlers, and their families. *Zero to Three, 12*(2), 1–6.

Fenichel, E. (Ed.). (1992). *Learning through supervision and mentorship to support the development of infants, toddlers and their families: A source book.* Arlington, VA: *Zero to Three*/National Center for Clinical Infant Programs.

Fields, B. (1992). Towards tenacity of commitment: Understanding and modifying institutional practices and individual responses that impede work with multi-problem families. In E. Fenichel (Ed.), *Learning through supervision and mentorship to support the development of infants, toddlers and their families: A source book* (pp. 125–131). Arlington, VA: *Zero to Three*/National Center for Clinical Infant Programs.

Fraiberg, S. (1980). *Clinical studies in infant mental health.* New York: Basic Books.

Gilkerson, L., & Young-Holt, C. L. (1992). Supervision and the management of programs serving infants, toddlers, and their families. In E. Fenichel (Ed.), *Learning through supervision and mentorship to support the development of infants, toddlers and their families: A source book* (pp. 113–119). Arlington, VA: *Zero to Three*/National Center for Clinical Infant Programs.

Greenspan, S. I. (1992). *Infancy and early childhood.* Madison, CT: International Universities Press.

Greenspan, S. I., Wieder, S., Lieberman, A., Nover, R. A., Lourie, R. S., & Robinson, M. (Eds.). (1987). *Infants in multirisk families: Case studies in preventive intervention.* Madison, CT: International Universities Press.

Halpern, R. (1990a). Community-based early intervention. In S. J. Meisels & J. P. Shonkoff (Eds.), *Handbook of early child-*

hood intervention (pp. 469–498). New York: Cambridge University Press.

Halpern, R. (1990b). Parent support and education programs. *Children and youth services review, 12,* 285–308.

Katz, L. G. (1980). Mothering and teaching: Some significant distinctions. In L. G. Katz (Ed.), *Current topics in early childhood education* (pp. 3, 47–63). Norwood, NJ: Ablex.

Michaels, G., & Goldberg, W. (1988). *The transition to parenthood: Current theory and research.* New York: Cambridge University Press.

Musick, J. S. (1993). *Young, poor and pregnant: The psychology of teenage motherhood.* New Haven, CT: Yale University Press.

Musick, J. S., & Stott, F. (1990). Paraprofessionals, parenting, and child development: Understanding the problems and seeking solutions. In S. J. Meisels & J. P. Shonkoff (Eds.), *Handbook of early childhood intervention* (pp. 651–667). New York: Cambridge University Press.

Provence, S., & Naylor, A. (1983). *Infants and parents: Clinical case reports, No. 2.* Madison, CT: International Universities Press.

Sameroff, A. J., & Fiese, B. H. (1990). Transactional regulation and early intervention. In S. J. Meisels & J. P. Shonkoff (Eds.), *Handbook of early childhood intervention* (pp. 119–149). New York: Cambridge University Press.

Schafer, W. M. (1991). The professionalization of early motherhood. *Zero to Three, 12*(2), 10–15.

Stern, D. N. (1985). *The interpersonal world of the infant.* New York: Basic Books.

Stern-Bruschweiler, N., & Stern, D. N. (1989). A model for conceptualizing the role of the mother's representational world in various mother-infant therapies. *Infant Mental Health Journal, 10*(3), 142–156.

Unger, D., & Powell, D. (Eds.). (1990). *Families as nurturing systems: Support across the life span.* New York: Haworth Press.

Winnicott, D. W. (1971). *Therapeutic consultations in child psychiatry.* New York: Basic Books.

Family Support and Care of the Elderly

Program and Policy Challenges

Benjamin H. Gottlieb
Monique A. M. Gignac

This chapter focuses on programs and policy issues surrounding family support of the elderly. It gives explicit recognition to the importance of viewing family support within a life-course perspective, rather than restricting its scope to the contributions that parents make to their children's health and welfare. The investments that family members make in one another's lives have a continuous character, although their forms of expression and their functions change at different life stages, and in response to differing needs and stressors that arise during these periods. Moreover, from a public policy perspective, initiatives that strengthen the family's contribution to the care of the aged are as vitally important as those that buttress the family's nurturance of children. Both sets of initiatives have the common aim of keeping families together and fostering the support and mutual aid that sustain them.

The main goal of the chapter is to describe and critically consider programs and services that have been designed to assist families with the care that they provide to elderly relatives. Therefore, the bulk of our review centers primarily on inter-

Both authors contributed equally to the writing of this chapter.

generational and spousal caregiving. It does not address the formal supports and public services provided directly to the elderly through financial outlays and services administered by government agencies or by private nonprofit organizations. In short, our attention is narrowed to the nexus between the informal care offered by the principal family caregiver and the programs and services extended to these caregivers by the agencies and institutions of the community and the state.

We begin by highlighting the aging trends that make family care of the elderly an urgent public policy issue. We then consider the many demands that are placed on family caregivers and their impact on the caregiver's health and well-being. Next, we concentrate on a range of programs and interventions that have been designed to meet the needs of family caregivers, touching also on the factors that affect the use of these services. In addition, we briefly consider selected issues surrounding the evaluation of these initiatives, with special attention to the criteria that have been used to gauge their impact on the caregiver. The chapter concludes by discussing the twin themes of control and support in the relationship between family members and the professionals who provide care to older people, and by raising several broader issues in this realm of public policy.

Aging of the Population

Any discussion of the policy issues surrounding family care of the elderly must be informed by information about the aging trends in North America. These trends spotlight present and potential demands placed on the family in its role as the principal provider of support for the elderly.

In the United States and Canada, as a function of both increased longevity and declining fertility rates, the proportion of the population aged sixty-five and older is rising rapidly. In Canada, this segment of the population grew from 10 percent in 1981 to 12 percent in 1991 (Statistics Canada, 1992), while in the United States, it grew from 11 percent in 1980 to 12.6 percent in 1990 (American Association of Retired Persons, 1991; Subcommittee on Human Services, 1987). In raw numbers, older Americans increased by 5.7 million persons in the last decade (American Association of Retired Persons, 1991). It is projected that by the year 2031, approximately 21 percent of all Canadians will be over the age of sixty-five (Statistics Canada, 1984), while in the United States, 21.8 percent of all Americans will be in this age group by the year 2030. A final statistic reveals just how rapid the rise of the elderly population will be: by 2030, there will be about 66 million older persons in the United States, two and one-half times their number in 1980 (American Association of Retired Persons, 1991). In both countries, the oldest of the old—those eighty-five and over—is the group growing at the fastest rate. Even with life-style changes and the advances in disease prevention and treatment that are redefining the age range of old age, this segment of the elderly population will undoubtedly require the greatest care.

A Portrait of Caregivers and Caregiving

Who currently provides informal care to elderly family members? What does eldercare entail? The Informal Caregivers Survey, a component of the 1982 National Long-Term Care Survey conducted by the U.S. Bureau of the Census, presents a national portrait of those who provide informal care to the elderly (Stone, Cafferata, & Sangl, 1987). The study was based on a random sample of approximately 36,000 Medicare enrollees who were screened to determine whether they had a long-term problem with at least one activity of daily living. Those who received help from an informal (unpaid) caregiver were included in the subpopulation sampled for the Informal Caregivers Survey.

Data from the final sample of approximately 2,000 respondents revealed that 72 percent of all caregivers were women and 28 percent were men. Adult daughters comprised 29 percent and wives constituted 23 percent of all caregivers. More husbands (13 percent) than sons (8.5 percent) assumed caregiving responsibilities. The average age of the daughters, 52.4 years, fell into the prime years of employment. Caregiving wives averaged sixty-nine years of age. More than 60 percent of the daughters lived in the same household with their elderly relatives, and

43.5 percent of them were employed. Because the wives' mean age places them in the retirement years, fewer than 10 percent of them were employed (Stone, Cafferata, & Sangl, 1987).

Although no comparable Canadian data base provides national estimates of the number of family eldercare providers and their characteristics, the 1990 General Social Survey reports on the characteristics of those who provide care to parents who are over the age of sixty-five and who live outside the caregiver's household. These statistics are highly congruent with those cited for the United States, testifying to the overrepresentation of middle-aged women among those providing eldercare. Specifically, the survey revealed that 58 percent of intergenerational caregivers were daughters and 42 percent were sons. However, whereas 19.4 percent of the sons between the ages of forty-five and sixty-four provided personal care to their parents at least once a week, almost one-third of the women (32 percent) provided such personal care. Gender differences were even more pronounced when it came to assisting elderly parents with unpaid housework. Only 3.1 percent of the middle-aged sons provided such assistance at least once a week, while 28.5 percent of middle-aged daughters did unpaid housework for their elderly parents so frequently. As to their employment status, the data revealed that 56 percent of the middle-aged daughters and 7 percent of the daughters who were over the age of sixty-five were employed while fulfilling their caregiving responsibilities. Not surprisingly, 93 percent of the middle-aged sons were in the paid work force (Statistics Canada, 1990).

Demands of Caregiving

In addition to providing the personal care and doing the household chores that constitute the most labor-intensive aspects of eldercare, family members often are called on to assist their aged relatives with transportation, legal and financial affairs, home maintenance, shopping, and the administration of medications. Moreover, the greater the decline in the elderly person's functional capacity, the more likely it is that the caregiving network will expand to include a variety of formal care providers (Soldo,

Agree, & Wolf, 1989). The greater the number of professional services provided to the care recipient, the more time and energy are required from the caregiver to ensure that they are properly orchestrated and effectively delivered.

The care of relatives with chronic cognitive impairments, such as dementia, poses even greater hardships on the caregiver. People with dementia require constant monitoring because of their disorientation, and many show symptoms of mental and behavioral disturbance that are distressing to their caregivers. They may be suspicious and belligerent toward others, refuse to cooperate, engage in repetitive verbal or overt behavior, and cling to the caregiver even though they may no longer recognize him or her. In addition, because of disturbances in their sleep-wake cycle, persons with dementia may prevent their caregivers from getting the rest they need so badly (Light & Lebowitz, 1989).

Finally, in addition to demands associated with the personal care of the aged and those stemming from the cognitive and behavioral problems that they may have, there is evidence that caregiving creates a set of secondary dislocations in the caregiver's life (Gottlieb, 1989). Aside from having to withdraw from paid employment, caregivers may have less time available for leisure pursuits, continuing education, volunteer activities, and socializing with friends. As Pearlin and his colleagues observe (Pearlin, Mullen, Semple, & Skaff, 1990), they may become captives of their caregiving role, cut off from contacts with valued sources of support. Collectively, these personal costs may take a profound toll on the caregiver's mental and physical well-being.

In fact, in the past ten years, a great deal of evidence has accrued that testifies to the risks that eldercare constitutes for the mental and physical health of caregivers. A review of this research is beyond the scope of this chapter, but the weight of the evidence shows that subjective burden, occasioned by the demands and repercussions of caregiving, is what has the strongest bearing on health outcomes; that is, disturbances in the caregiver's psychological, social, and physical functioning arise only when the *objective* demands of caregiving are *subjectively* perceived as burdensome. Subjective burden tends to be most intense among those who care for relatives with symptoms of dementia, and it results from their exposure to the cognitive and behavioral deterioration of a loved one (Horowitz, 1985; Light & Lebowitz, 1989; Montgomery, Gonyea, & Hooyman, 1985; Zarit, Reever, & Bach-Peterson, 1980). Moreover, those caring for relatives who display symptoms of dementia are at particularly high risk for emotional and physical exhaustion (Deimling & Bass, 1986; George & Gwyther, 1986; Light & Lebowitz, 1989).

Naturally, characteristics of the caregiver (age, health, financial resources, coping behavior, relationship to recipient) and of the caregiving context (coresidence, functional status of the care recipient) have the capacity to mediate or moderate the impact of the burdens placed on the caregiver's health (Haley, Levine, Brown, & Bartolucci, 1987; Vitalaiano, Maiuro, Ochs, & Russo, 1989). The degree of strain experienced by principal caregivers also depends on the assistance that is available from other family members and from the community.

But, and perhaps most important, the meaning that caregivers derive from their activities and the significance that they attach to their relationships with their elderly relatives can mitigate the strain of caregiving. Caregiving is a voluntary activity, typically prompted by feelings of loyalty and affection toward family members, as well as by a sense of responsibility for their welfare. Norms of mutual support and reciprocity are deeply embedded in family relations. When illness and dependency occur, feelings of commitment and obligation to family members can spur caregiving quite independently of affection (Hagestad, 1982; Howowitz & Shindelman, 1983a). Further, caregiving can bind together family members' invisible loyalties and can be a source of great satisfaction and reward. Hence, provision of care for a loved one is not invariably regarded as burdensome and does not necessarily lead to distress. It may be an expression of the generational and marital interdependence that lies at the heart of family relationships. The challenge is to ensure that policies and services are designed in ways that sustain rather than deplete family members' energy and commitment to one another.

Programs and Services for Family Caregivers

A variety of services and interventions have been designed to
help individuals maintain their elderly relatives at an optimal
functional level and mitigate strain or subjective burden. Exhibit 10.1 organizes these initiatives into three main classes:
caregiver-centered programs, which provide education, training, and
support directly to caregivers, in order to enhance their knowledge, skills, and emotional well-being; *service-centered programs,*
which augment the caregiver's contribution to the care of elderly
family members; and *financial compensation programs,* which remu-
nerate caregivers or offset certain costs that they incur. Whereas
caregiver-centered programs aim to fortify the caregivers by

Exhibit 10.1. Programs for Family Caregivers of the Elderly.

Caregiver-Centered Programs

    Information, education, and training: provide information and education about
        physical, psychological, legal, and financial aspects of caregiving, as well
        as training in caregiver skills

    Counseling: provides services ranging from unstructured, client-centered pro-
        grams, which help family members deal with the problems of caregiving,
        to more structured interventions

    Support groups: provide caregivers with an opportunity to discuss various aspects
        of caregiving with others in similar situations

Service-Centered Programs

    Home care: provides in-home nursing and therapeutic services, as well as assis-
        tance with activities of daily living (for example, bathing)

    Homemaker services: provide assistance with routine housecleaning and may in-
        clude help with meal preparation, shopping, or home maintenance and
        repairs

    Respite care: provides caregiver with temporary relief or rest from caregiving
        activities; includes *in-home respite, day care,* and *institutional respite*

    Day hospitals: provide rehabilitation for older persons and some training for
        caregivers

Financial Compensation Programs

    Indirect financial support: includes a range of options, such as tax deductions,
        tax credits, and low-interest housing loans

    Direct financial support: includes cash allowances to family members as payment
        for caregiving services, or vouchers with which caregivers can purchase for-
        mal services

---

enlarging and reinforcing their personal resources, service-centered programs aim to unburden caregivers either by substituting formal for informal support or by supplementing informal support with formal services (Berry, Zarit, & Rabatin, 1991; Edelman & Hughes, 1990; Noelker & Bass, 1989; Pillemer, MacAdam, & Wolf, 1989). Although we describe the formal services separately in this section, an emphasis on greater service coordination has resulted in the circumstance that multiple services often are provided under one auspice. For example, respite care may include information, education, and training, as well as emotional support for family members.

Information, education, and training services allow family members to maintain their roles as caregivers over time by providing them with the additional information and skills necessary for them to adjust to changes in the condition of their elderly relatives. An example of one such program is the Education and Family Support Services (E&FSS) unit of Good Samaritan Hospital and Medical Center in Portland, Oregon (Heagerty, Dunn, & Watson, 1988). Since 1979, E&FSS has trained caregivers to communicate effectively with their older relatives and to provide personal care without jeopardizing their own needs. A caregiver resource center, containing books and videotapes on such topics as the physical, psychological, legal, and financial aspects of caregiving, is also maintained.

Counseling services range from relatively unstructured, client-centered approaches, which help family members with the emotional demands and family repercussions of caregiving, to more structured interventions. Counseling is often sought when caregiving produces family conflict, when the caregiver is faced with decisions about whether to continue or surrender the role, and when caregiving is complicated by tensions in the relationship with the care recipient (Toseland, Rossiter, Peak, & Smith, 1990; Zarit & Zarit, 1982). Research comparing individual and group interventions has found that individual counseling enabled caregivers to discuss a wider range of personal problems, helped them remain more problem-focused, and produced greater reduction in psychological symptoms than group interventions (Toseland, Rossiter, Peak, & Smith, 1990).

However, many individuals report feelings of isolation and lack of support in their roles as caregivers. As an alternative to individual counseling, *support groups* provide empathic understanding and the opportunity to form a support network of peers. In a critical review, Toseland and Rossiter (1989) present seven topics addressed in most caregiver support groups: (1) information about normal and abnormal changes in the aging process; (2) the emotional impact of caregiving on family members; (3) self-care for caregivers; (4) problems with interpersonal relationships; (5) the development and use of outside supports; (6) practical home-care skills; and (7) the group as a source of caregiver support. Many support groups are time-limited, consisting of six to eight sessions of one and one-half to two hours each. Support groups may be led by professionals or by individuals with personal experience in caring for an older relative, or leadership may be shared by professionals and non-professionals.

Generally, participants report high satisfaction with support groups (Toseland & Rossiter, 1989; Wasow, 1986; Wright, Lund, Pett, & Caserta, 1987). They feel less alone in their situations, gain a sense of hope and optimism from the group experience, learn new ways of handling problems, and value the opportunity to vent their fears, frustrations, and doubts in a supportive and understanding social context. Many come away with a greater sense of what is possible for them to control in the caregiving context, and of what lies beyond their control. Above all, the group validates their feelings and affirms the value of the caregiving role. However, as we shall report later, more rigorous efforts to evaluate the impact of support groups have produced less positive results.

Practically, in order for caregivers to attend support groups, arrangements must be made for the care of their relatives. Without such coverage, attendance tends to be poor, and the group suffers from lack of cohesion. In addition, the group's composition must be carefully considered. In order for the members to identify with one another, they must be in relatively similar stressful circumstances. For example, whenever possible, it is advisable to form groups that are homogeneous in terms of the nature of the relationship between the caregiver and the recipient (daughters and sons versus spouses), the type and extent of the care recipient's impairment (frail elderly versus dementia sufferers), and the overall context of caregiving (home-based versus institutional). Effective leadership is also needed to ensure that the process is satisfying for all participants. Support groups may suffer if one or two members dominate the group's discussion, or if the discussion is allowed to dwell on the burdens and negative emotions aroused by caregiving (Wright, Lund, Pett, & Caserta, 1987; Wasow, 1986).

In-home assistance, in the forms of *home care* and *homemaker services,* is one of the most frequently identified service needs of caregivers (Zimmer & Sainer, 1978). *Home care* usually refers to in-home nursing, personal care, and therapeutic services, such as physiotherapy and occupational therapy. *Homemaker services* provide assistance with housecleaning, meal preparation, and other household chores. During the time when the service provider is in the home, the caregiver can rest, turn to other maintenance activities, or engage in activities outside the home. These services can be expensive if used regularly (Brody, Saperstein, & Lawton, 1989). Medicare provides in-home health care services only to persons "whose conditions render them essentially immobilized" (Blieszner & Alley, 1990, p. 99).

One of the fastest-growing formal supports for family caregivers is *respite care.* Kaye and Kirwin (1990) note that more than 2,000 adult day-care programs serve over 70,000 older persons in the United States. Respite care is often defined broadly as "any service or group of services that provides temporary periods of relief or rest for caregivers away from the patient" (Brody, Saperstein, & Lawton, 1989, p. 41). In addition to providing relief, respite may also improve the functioning or enhance the social involvement of older individuals, and it may delay or prevent their institutionalization (Berry, Zarit, & Rabatin, 1991; Brody, Saperstein, & Lawton, 1989; Hughes, Junker, & Krauss, 1987; Kaye & Kirwin, 1990; Lawton, Brody, & Saperstein, 1989; Montgomery & Borgatta, 1989). As a result, respite care has been viewed with a great deal of optimism by many policy makers, despite early reports of underutilization by potential clients and a tendency for caregivers to delay using respite care until they can no longer manage their relatives (Brody, Saperstein, & Lawton, 1989; Hughes, Junker, and Krauss, 1987; Montgomery & Borgatta, 1989).

Respite care generally falls into one of three categories: in-home respite, day care, or institutional respite. In-home respite includes visits by a trained caregiver who comes into the home on an occasional or regular basis. Typically, visits occur during the day, but some services provide periodic weekend or evening support. The advantages of in-home respite are that it can be more flexible than other types of respite care, it can be used with older individuals who are more severely impaired, and it is provided in the older person's familiar environment. But regular in-home respite care tends to be more expensive than the other two respite arrangements, and the quality and training of in-home caregivers may vary a great deal (Brody, Saperstein, & Lawton, 1989).

Day programs represent a second type of respite arrangement. Here, the older person travels to a day-care center on a regular basis and has an opportunity to socialize with other participants in a friendly and safe milieu. These respite programs vary a great deal in their daily and weekly hours of operation; but, in a typical arrangement, an individual attends once or twice a week, from midmorning to midafternoon. Although day-care centers are usually less costly per hour than in-home respite care, one Canadian study of twenty-two day programs found that the vast majority cannot supply the number of hours of respite needed by caregivers who are employed on a full-time basis (Gottlieb & Johnson, 1992). In addition, it can be taxing for caregivers to get their relatives ready to attend day-care centers (Brody, Saperstein, & Lawton, 1989). Transportation must be arranged, and elderly persons who suffer from dementia may become even further confused by having to enter a novel environment. Moreover, many caregivers may be reluctant to enroll their relatives in center-based respite programs because of their fear of entrusting their relatives to institutional authorities. Particularly when respite programs are affiliated with or physically housed in long-term care facilities, the programs may be viewed with trepidation, as stepping-stones toward long-term placement.

The third type of respite care is institutional respite. This form of care is used on a short-term basis, when substitute care is needed for vacations or for emergencies that call the caregiver away. Institutional respite offers a block of time away from caregiving, as well as the comfort that comes from the knowledge that the care recipient is in a safe environment. However, many caregivers are reluctant to leave their relatives because of feelings of guilt or fears about the adequacy of the care (Brody, Saperstein, & Lawton, 1989). Again, the cost can also be prohibitive.

Day hospitals are less widely available than other types of formal support and are generally used for a limited period of time. They aim to provide rehabilitation for older persons and some education and training skills for family caregivers. They are not intended to serve a respite function. One of the advantages of day hospitals is that, by making occasional visits into the community, care recipients and their caregivers can adjust to the idea of using other community supports like respite care (Provincial Senior Citizens Advisory Council, 1989).

Financial support involves either indirect compensation to caregivers, such as tax deductions or credits and low-interest housing loans, or direct payments in the form of wages to caregivers, or vouchers with which caregivers can purchase formal services. Tax incentives have the advantages of universal coverage and administrative simplicity (Pillemer, MacAdam, & Wolf, 1989). However, they may be most beneficial to those in the middle or higher income brackets and consequently may not be targeted to those persons with the greatest financial need (Pillemer, MacAdam, & Wolf, 1989; Rivlin & Wiener, 1988). Direct compensation to informal caregivers has been hypothesized to result in more continuity and a better quality of care for the elderly than schemes based exclusively on the provision of formal services. Informal care does not involve the obstacles frequently faced by formal programs, such as high job turnover, restrictive hours of operation, and inability to access clients in remote areas (Keefe & Fancey, 1992; Rivlin & Wiener, 1988).

Nevertheless, there is concern that the quality of care to older individuals may actually be more variable because formal support staff are unable to ensure the quality of services (England, Linsk, Simon-Rusinowitz, & Keigher, 1990). Others point out that such compensation undermines the altruistic motives of family members in helping their relatives (Keefe & Fancey, 1992) and that public money would now be used for help that otherwise would have been provided free (Arling & McAuley, 1983). Finally, caregivers themselves report preferring other services, such as home care or homemaker services, to economic support (Horowitz & Shindelman, 1983b).

Use of Formal Support Programs

In order to ensure that needed services actually reach family caregivers, it is necessary to publicize these services, increase access to them, and foster their utilization. The fact is that many caregivers never access formal support systems at all. Others are confused by the sheer multiplicity of agencies, charging policies, and eligibility criteria and by the lack of service coordination. Still other caregivers delay their use of services until the situation has deteriorated to the point where agency staff have little choice but to encourage placement in long-term care.

Facilitators of and barriers to service use can be organized into three categories: *predisposing factors, enabling factors,* and *need factors* (Andersen & Newman, 1973; Bass & Noelker, 1987; Wister, 1992; Yeatts, Crow, & Folts, 1992). Predisposing factors include age, gender, ethnicity, education, religion, and the attitudes of caregivers toward service use (Wister, 1992; Yeatts, Crow, & Folts, 1992).

For example, in their study of caregivers with demented relatives, Collins and her colleagues (Collins, Stommel, King, & Given, 1991) identified five distinct sets of attitudes toward service use. The first encompassed the caregivers' concern with the opinions of others. Many caregivers believe that other family members frown on the use of formal services or would view the use of services as a sign that the caregiver was reneging on her responsibilities. The second factor reflected the caregivers' lack of confidence in the formal support system. Often caregivers do not believe that professional service agents will render the high quality of care they seek for a family member. Third, caregivers varied in their views toward reliance on informal care; that is, they differed in their readiness to solicit aid from and mobilize family members and friends, as opposed to the community service system. Fourth, caregivers differed in their need to function independently of formal support. Many were confident in and proud of their ability to care for others without transferring any responsibilities to outside services. Finally, family caregivers ranged in their basic attitudes toward the government's role or responsibility in helping them and their relatives.

Enabling factors embrace a variety of variables related to the accessibility and cost of formal services. They include the caregiver's and older relative's income, the availability of formal services, the availability of additional informal support (like other family members and friends), transportation needs, and the urban or rural character of the community. Some of the barriers to entry into the service network, as well as gaps in caregivers' knowledge of available services, can be redressed through concerted efforts to educate primary referral agents (Bass & Noelker, 1987; Wister, 1992; Yeatts, Crow, & Folts, 1992). For example, family physicians and hospital staff are often the first to be consulted when the elderly experience health problems, and therefore they need to be trained to make accurate referrals to community services (Fortinsky & Hathaway, 1990).

Outreach and case management, along with service access, can also help families consider the full range of options available to them by targeting resources to those most in need and most able to benefit from them. Services for outreach, case management, and access assess the needs of both the elderly person and his or her caregiver and provide assistance in obtaining, coordinating, and monitoring the chosen formal supports. Case management is typically offered at the community level, although in recent years a number of private companies have come into being. These companies can often coordinate services across the United States and are especially beneficial to family members trying to care for relatives from afar.

The use of formal support is also related to the real and perceived needs of caregivers and their family members for these services (Bass & Noelker, 1987). Need factors relevant to service use among older individuals relate to their illness or levels of impairment. Need factors pertaining to service use among caregivers include their need for assistance with caregiving tasks, their need to learn new skills to manage the changing demands of their relatives' illnesses, and their need for relief from the burdens of caregiving.

Evaluation of Formal Support Programs

Evaluation of the impact of formal support on the well-being of family caregivers is among the most formidable tasks facing policy makers, health professionals, and researchers. The scope of this task is reflected in the sheer number of criteria that have been used in outcome evaluations. For example, psychological outcomes have included measures of burden, stress, depression, coping, problem solving, life satisfaction, and health attitudes (Berry, Zarit, & Rabatin, 1991; Edelman & Hughes, 1990; Haley, Brown, & Levine, 1987; Lawton, Brody, & Saperstein, 1989; Toseland, Rossiter, Peak, & Smith, 1990). Researchers have also examined changes in the behavior-management skills of the caregiver and changes in the size and assistance of the caregiver's support network (Haley, Brown, & Levine, 1987; Kaye & Kirwin, 1990; Wright, Lund, Pett, & Caserta, 1987; Zarit, Anthony, & Boutselis, 1987). Continued employment, additional leisure time, and involvement in other life spheres have been used to gauge the impact of respite care (Berry, Zarit, & Rabatin, 1991; Gottlieb, 1992; Kaye & Kirwin, 1990). Numerous studies have also examined whether such service initiatives as support groups and day programs extend the length of time the elderly remain in the community. In short, delayed institutionalization has been used as a criterion of program effectiveness (Lawton, Brody, & Saperstein, 1989; Greene & Monahan, 1987).

The impact on the caregiver of any single type of service program has been equivocal. For example, studies of the outcomes of support groups have not yielded consistent ameliorative effects on measures of caregiver burden, stress, and depression (Toseland & Rossiter, 1989). The same is true of respite programs (Lawton, Brody, & Saperstein, 1989). Within the scope of this chapter, it is impossible to review the evaluative data that have been brought to bear on the service programs listed in Exhibit 10.1. However, it is important to discuss briefly the basis for choosing relevant and appropriate outcomes and to comment on the difficulties that attend evaluation of services in support of family caregivers.

First, questions can be raised about the appropriateness of the criteria that have been used to judge the "success" of formal services. Is it reasonable to expect caregivers, who are dealing with the ongoing demands of caring for an older relative with a progressively debilitating illness, to experience less depressive affect or less anxiety as a result of their participation in an eight-week support group? Can respite care provide the needed relief when the service is available only half a day per week? Given these scenarios, the prospects for "success" seem bleak. Many caregivers do, however, report high levels of satisfaction, increased acceptance of their own feelings and limitations, an ability to find meaning in their role, heightened self-efficacy, and more hopefulness about the future, yet few measures have been developed to tap these changes in caregivers' self-appraisals.

Second, problems of cointervention plague researchers who attempt to evaluate formal support; that is, caregivers often make use of a variety of informal and formal support services to assist them in their caregiving role. As a result, it is difficult to evaluate the impact of any one service program. Similarly, any single program is not equivalent in its intensity or "dosage" to other programs in the same class. For example, center-based respite services differ a great deal in the ancillary services they offer (education, training, counseling, support groups) and in caregivers' participation in them. Again, understanding the impact of such a service is hampered by the inability to tease apart those aspects of the program that may or may not be helpful to caregivers. It follows that greater precision is needed in measuring the effects of services that are provided to caregivers, through the use of appropriate measures, carefully matched comparison groups, and longitudinal designs that capture the changing needs of family caregivers.

Control and Support in the Relationship Between Informal and Formal Care

Programs and services for family caregivers need to be critically examined from broader perspectives as well. An agency must carefully consider the stance it takes toward family caregivers, weighing the effects of its actions on the caregivers' personal well-being as well as on their continued provision of optimal care to their elderly relatives. Twigg (1989) draws out the implications of these two stances toward caregivers: "They represent essentially the difference between a focus on carers as co-workers and carers as clients. In the latter model, carers have outcomes per se and their morale is one of the final ends of the system. In the former, carer outcomes are only intermediate outcomes, part of the means to the end of client satisfaction and care, which are regarded as the final outcomes" (p. 64). But, as Twigg points out, even when the agency fully recognizes that its first responsibility is to safeguard the well-being of caregivers, it cannot ignore caregivers' need to maintain their own involvement in the care of their relatives. Therefore, professional service providers must find ways of enhancing caregivers' quality of life without forcing them to surrender the caregiving role.

How can agencies balance these competing objectives, allowing family caregivers to have a meaningful role in the care of their relatives while protecting them from undue harm? Principally, the state must provide the full range of programs and services outlined earlier, in order to supplement (and, as needed, substitute for) family care on a temporary or permanent basis. In this way, certain pressures can be taken off the caregiver before his or her resources are overtaxed, and tasks that are too difficult to be performed or too disruptive of other domains of the caregiver's life can be transferred to paid helpers. Ultimately, a policy of "shared care" will succeed only if homemaker, respite, and home-care agencies view the family as the unit of planning, letting its needs dictate the appropriate mix of supplementary and substitutive arrangements. The welfare of older people, their families, and the larger society is best served by a policy that enlarges the service arrangements in ways that optimize family choice and support.

Choice and support are also the two critical dimensions for assessing the particular relations between professional service providers and family caregivers. The issue of choice revolves around decision making, while the issue of support concerns perceptions of what is helpful to the family. The two themes overlap the larger issue of autonomy and control.

When professional service providers become involved with family caregivers, there is the risk that they will ignore or overstep boundaries. Specifically, there is the danger that, in their zeal to create a constructive alliance with family caregivers, professionals will attempt to dictate their functions, direct their activities, and convert them into "case managers." Paradoxically, by teaching caregivers how to manage their time more effectively, and by usurping the care tasks that family members view as properly within their own orbit, professionals may undermine the caregivers' confidence in their native skills and deny them the satisfaction gained from the care they render. In this sense, dynamics of control enter into the relations between the two parties and can subvert the mutual provision of aid and increase the strain on the caregiver and on the caregiving relationship. Moreover, when professional expertise is substituted for experiential knowledge, the complementary roles and functions of the informal and formal sectors are threatened. When informal caregivers are supplanted or made over in the professional's image, the virtues of a system of "shared care" are eclipsed.

The issue of control is related to the theme of support, because each party's helping efforts can miscarry when they are constrained. Neither professionals nor family caregivers wish to be told how to care for the elderly by persons who are perceived not to have the "standing" to do so. For example, Kaye (1985) asked a sample of sixty-seven home-care workers to comment on the strengths and limitations of informal supporters who were involved with their elderly home-care clients. He found that 43.5 percent of the workers stated that family members, friends, and neighbors interfered with the home-care service by trying to specify the type of work performed. Moreover, the workers felt that relatives in the household complicated their jobs more than relatives who lived in the community did. These data suggest that, far from seeing themselves as accountable to family caregivers, the service providers viewed them as obstructions to their work. Similarly, although there is little doubt that family caregivers need assistance with personal-care tasks, as well as relief from them, they do not wish to be told when and how to render care, and they want more say about the tasks that they are relieved of and the scheduling of such relief. For example, many caregivers who use day programs lament the fact that the hours of the programs do not suit their employment schedules, and many resent the other requirements that they must meet in order to qualify for the program (such as participation in a caregivers' support group). In short, too often, professional services are offered in a way that is constraining.

Finally, we must concede that avoidance of institutional placement is not the single most significant criterion for judging the success of long-term care policies. In some family circumstances, institutional placement may be the best solution, safeguarding the health of caregivers and their elderly relatives. For example, in their study of caregiving to demented elderly persons, Levin, Sinclair, and Gorbach (1983) found that the death or institutionalization of the elderly relative contributed the single greatest improvement to the mental health of the caregiver. However, institutional placement does not invariably terminate the provision of informal care; it does so only when authorities deny caregivers continued involvement in decisions that affect their relatives, and when they make no provision for family members to participate in the personal care of their relatives. It follows that here, too, the staff of institutions need to adopt policies and practices that invite the continued participation of family caregivers in numerous roles and activities, encouraging them to have as much involvement as they wish.

Broader Policy Issues
Surrounding Family Care of the Elderly

It is essential to recognize that the state has a paramount influence on the family's very involvement in the care of older people. As Walker (1991) points out, it has a direct influence by providing certain kinds and levels of compensation and benefits to those caring for dependents. Indirectly, it influences the burden of care that the family must shoulder by regulating the kinds and number of substitutive services it makes available and by formulating the rules that govern public eligibility for and access to such services. It follows that in jurisdictions where the state makes more services available, families that are not moved to volunteer their care will not feel coerced to do so, and those that do volunteer will have the assistance they require. In jurisdictions where the care of the elderly depends largely on informal and voluntary efforts, some families will feel coerced, and others will be left without the support they need to moderate the burdens of care and to relieve their strain. Therefore, the question of whether the family enlists itself or is drafted into caring for an older person reflects policy options that ultimately affect the quality of life for older people, their families, and the larger society. Everyone's interests and welfare are best served by a policy that enlarges the service arrangements.

An effective social care system requires greater administrative flexibility than now exists, however. Principally, more flexibility will mean the development of a service delivery system in which health and social services are unified, not simply coordinated. It will also require the creation of service brokerage agencies that will have the authority and the mechanisms to command the full spectrum of community and institutional resources that families need during different stages of their caregiving careers. At the same time, unless the restrictive eligibility criteria that apply to the use of needed services are removed, such brokerages will be frustrated in their efforts to serve their clients. For example, if home care is contingent on the presentation of medical certification, or if financial restrictions limit the length of enrollment in day-care centers, then a substantial portion of those families that require support will go without it.

Finally, programs and services must be designed in ways that address the mutually limiting effects of women's participation in eldercare and employment. On one side, eldercare curtails women's entry into, and their tenure and upward mobility in, the sphere of paid employment. On the other side, there is evidence that women's participation in the paid labor force reduces the time they devote to eldercare (Boaz & Muller, 1992). The latter authors observe, "As an increasing number of young women become committed to career employment, fewer of them are likely to provide the level of informal care that has enabled the frail elderly to be maintained in the community up to now" (p. 158). In fact, with women likely to account for the majority of labor-force growth in the coming years, it is estimated that by the year 2000 three-quarters of all women in the age group most likely to be called on to care for the elderly (forty-five to sixty years old) will be employed in the United States (Gibeau, Anastas, & Larson, 1987). Hence, the costs to women, calculated in terms of both economic and psychological privation, are high, in many cases outstripping the potential benefits, to the state and to the family, of the informal care they render.

Accordingly, programs must be designed in ways that afford greater harmony between employees' job and their family responsibilities. Employers are challenged to institute different kinds of flexible work arrangements and employee assistance programs that are tailored to the needs of an older work force that faces the joint demands arising from the domestic and job spheres. At the same time, public policy makers are challenged to create services that complement and sustain the substantial contribution that families make to the care of older persons, while also recognizing the family's need for respite, ongoing support, and financial security. The social foundations of an effective and humane policy for the care of the elderly cannot rest on strictly private and informal arrangements (Minkler, 1983); they must be firmly grounded in the combined resources of the family and the state.

In Sweden, three principles underlie social legislation affecting service provision to the elderly: the principle of *normalization,* meaning that the elderly should live in as normal a setting as possible; the principle of *self-determination,* meaning that they should have options and involvement in decisions affecting their welfare; and the principle of *influence and participation,* meaning that the elderly should be active participants in society as a whole. A similar set of principles might be applied to those who provide family care to the elderly, forming a credo to guide the planning and design of services in support of caregivers. The caregiver should live as normal a life as possible, maintaining his or her involvement in other valued roles and activities. The caregiver should also have a range of options for, and control over, the resources that aid in maintaining a satisfying quality of personal life and optimal care for an elderly relative.

References

American Association of Retired Persons. (1991). *A profile of older Americans.* Washington, DC: Author.

Andersen, R. M., & Newman, J. F. (1973). Societal and individual determinants of medical care utilization in the United States. *Millbank Quarterly, 51,* 95–124.

Arling, G., & McAuley, W. (1983). The feasibility of public payments to family caregiving. *Gerontologist, 23,* 300–306.

Bass, D. M., & Noelker, L. S. (1987). The influence of family caregivers on elders' use of in-home services: An expanded conceptual framework. *Journal of Health and Social Behavior, 28,* 184–195.

Berry, G. L., Zarit, S. H., & Rabatin, V. X. (1991). Caregiver activity on respite and nonrespite days: A comparison of two service approaches. *Gerontologist, 31,* 830–835.

Blieszner, R., & Alley, J. M. (1990). Family caregiving for the family. *Family Relations, 39,* 97–102.

Boaz, R. F., & Muller, C. F. (1992). Paid work and unpaid help by caregivers of the disabled and frail elderly. *Medical Care, 30,* 149–158.

Brody, E. M., Saperstein, A. R., & Lawton, M. P. (1989). A

multi-service respite program for caregivers of Alzheimer's patients. *Journal of Gerontological Social Work, 14,* 41–74.

Collins, C., Stommel, M., King, S., & Given, C. W. (1991). Assessment of the attitudes of family caregivers toward community services. *Gerontologist, 31,* 756–761.

Deimling, G., & Bass, D. (1986). Symptoms of mental impairment among elderly adults and their effects on family caregivers. *Journals of Gerontology, 41,* 778–784.

Edelman, P., & Hughes, S. (1990). The impact of community care on provision of informal care to homebound elderly persons. *Journals of Gerontology, 45,* 74–84.

England, S. E., Linsk, N. L., Simon-Rusinowitz, L., & Keigher, S. M. (1990). Paying kin for care: Agency barriers to formalizing informal care. *Journal of Aging and Social Policy, 2,* 63–86.

Fortinsky, R. H., & Hathaway, T. J. (1990). Information and service needs among active and former family caregivers of persons with Alzheimer's Disease. *Gerontologist, 30,* 604–609.

George, L. K., & Gwyther, L. P. (1986). Caregiver well-being: A multidimensional examination of family caregivers of demented adults. *Gerontologist, 26,* 253–259.

Gibeau, J. L., Anastas, J. W., & Larson, P. J. (1987). Breadwinners, caregivers, and employers: New alliances in an aging America. *Employee Benefits Journal, 12,* 6–10.

Gottlieb, B. H. (1989). A contextual perspective on stress in family care of the elderly. *Canadian Psychology, 30,* 596–607.

Gottlieb, B. H. (1992). Quandaries in translating support concepts to intervention. In H.O.F. Veiel & U. Baumann (Eds.), *The meaning and measurement of social support* (pp. 293–309). Washington, DC: Hemisphere.

Gottlieb, B. H., & Johnson, J. (1992). *Organizational and program characteristics of 22 respite/day programs.* Unpublished manuscript, Department of Psychology, University of Guelph, Ontario, Canada.

Greene, V. L., & Monahan, D. J. (1987). The effect of a professionally guided caregiver support and education group on institutionalization of care receivers. *Gerontologist, 27,* 716–721.

Hagestad, G. (1982). Parent and child: Generations in the family. In T. Field, A. Huston, H. Quay, L. Troll, & G. Finley (Eds.), *Review of human development* (pp. 485–499). New York: Wiley.

Haley, W. E., Brown, L., & Levine, E. G. (1987). Experimental evaluation of the effectiveness of group intervention for dementia caregivers. *Gerontologist, 27,* 376–382.

Haley, W. E., Levine, E. G., Brown, S. L., & Bartolucci, A. A. (1987). Stress, appraisal, coping, and social support as predictors of adaptational outcome among dementia caregivers. *Psychology and Aging, 2,* 323–330.

Heagerty, B., Dunn, L., & Watson, M. A. (1988). Helping caregivers care. *Aging, 358,* 7–10.

Horowitz, A. (1985). Family caregiving to frail elderly. In M. P. Lawton & G. Maddox (Eds.), *Annual review of gerontology and geriatrics* (Vol. 5, pp. 194–246). New York: Springer.

Horowitz, A., & Shindelman, L. (1983a). Reciprocity and affection: Past influences on current caregiving. *Journal of Gerontological Social Work, 5,* 5–20.

Horowitz, A., & Shindelman, L. W. (1983b). State and economic incentives for family caregivers of the elderly. *Health Care Financing Review, 5,* 25–33.

Hughes, R. C., Junker, L., & Krauss, C. (1987). Challenges and successes in developing an in-home respite program. *Journal of Gerontological Social Work, 11,* 47–57.

Kaye, L. W. (1985). Home care for the aged: A fragile partnership. *Social Work, 30,* 312–317.

Kaye, L. W., & Kirwin, P. M. (1990). Adult day care services for the elderly and their families: Lessons from the Pennsylvania experience. In A. Monk (Ed.), *Health care of the aged: Needs, policies, and services* (pp. 167–183). New York: Haworth Press.

Keefe, J. M., & Fancey, P. (1992, October). *Which is more beneficial to caregivers: Financial compensation or formal services?* Paper presented at the Canadian Association on Gerontology annual educational and scientific meeting, Edmonton, Alberta.

Lawton, M. P., Brody, E. M., & Saperstein, A. R. (1989). A controlled study of respite service for caregivers of Alzheimer's patients. *Gerontologist, 29,* 8–16.

Levin, E., Sinclair, I., & Gorbach, P. (1983). *The supporters of confused elderly persons at home.* London: National Institute of Social Work.

Light, E., & Lebowitz, B. D. (1989). *Alzheimer's Disease treatment and family stress: Directions for research.* Publication No. (ADM)89-1569. Washington, DC: U.S. Department of Health and Human Services.

Minkler, M. (1983). Blaming the aged victim: The politics of scapegoating in times of fiscal conservatism. *International Journal of Health Services, 13,* 155–168.

Montgomery, R.J.V., & Borgatta, E. F. (1989). The effects of alternative support strategies on family caregivers. *Gerontologist, 29,* 457–464.

Montgomery, R. J., Gonyea, J. G., & Hooyman, N. R. (1985). Caregiving and the experience of subjective and objective burden. *Family Relations, 34,* 19–26.

Noelker, L. S., & Bass, D. M. (1989). Home care for elderly persons: Linkages between formal and informal caregivers. *Journals of Gerontology, 44,* 63–70.

Pearlin, L. J., Mullen, J. T., Semple, S. J., & Skaff, M. M. (1990). Caregiving and the stress process: An overview of concepts and their measures. *Gerontologist, 30,* 583–594.

Pillemer, K., MacAdam, M., & Wolf, R. S. (1989). Services to families with dependent elders. *Journal of Aging & Social Policy, 1,* 67–88.

Provincial Senior Citizens Advisory Council. (1989, January). *Support services to family caregivers of older Albertans.* Background paper prepared for the 1988 annual report of the Provincial Senior Citizens Advisory Council. Edmonton: Alberta Senior Citizens Secretariat.

Rivlin, A., & Wiener, J. (1988). *Caring for the disabled elderly: Who will pay?* Washington, DC: Brookings Institution.

Soldo, B. J., Agree, E. M., & Wolf, D. A. (1989). The balance between formal and informal care. In M. G. Ory & K. Bond (Eds.), *Aging and health care: Social science and policy perspectives* (pp. 193–216). London: Routledge.

Statistics Canada. (1984). *The elderly in Canada.* Statistics Canada Catalogue No. 99-932. Ottawa: Minister of Supply and Services.

Statistics Canada. (1990). Housing, Family and Social Statistics Division. *General social survey. Cycle 5: Family and Friends* (machine-readable data file). Ottawa: Author.

Statistics Canada. (1992). Freedom 65. *Census of Canada: Focus for the Future, 6,* 2.

Stone, R., Cafferata, G. L., & Sangl, J. (1987). Caregivers of the frail elderly: A national profile. *Gerontologist, 27,* 616–626.

Subcommittee on Human Services of the Select Committee on Aging, U.S. House of Representatives. (1987). *Exploding the myths: Caregiving in America.* Committee Publication No. 99-611. Washington, DC: U.S. Government Printing Office.

Toseland, R. W., & Rossiter, C. M. (1989). Group interventions to support family caregivers: A review and analysis. *Gerontologist, 29,* 438–448.

Toseland, R. W., Rossiter, C. M., Peak, T., & Smith, G. C. (1990). Comparative effectiveness of individual and group interventions to support family caregivers. *Social Work, 35,* 209–217.

Twigg, J. (1989). Models of carers: How do social care agencies conceptualise their relationship with informal carers? *Journal of Social Policy, 18,* 53–66.

Vitaliano, P. P., Maiuro, R. D., Ochs, H., & Russo, J. (1989). A model of burden in caregivers of DAT patients. In E. Light & B. D. Lebowitz (Eds.), *Alzheimer's Disease treatment and family stress: Directions for research* (pp. 267–291). Publication No. (ADM) 89-1569. Washington, DC: U.S. Department of Health and Human Services.

Walker, A. (1991). The relationship between the family and the state in the care of older people. *Canadian Journal on Aging, 10*(2), 94–112.

Wasow, M. (1986). Support groups for family caregivers of patients with Alzheimer's Disease. *Social Work, 31,* 93–97.

Wister, A. V. (1992). Residential attitudes and knowledge, use, and future use of home support agencies. *Journal of Applied Gerontology, 11,* 84–100.

Wright, S. D., Lund, D. A., Pett, M. A., & Caserta, M. S. (1987). The assessment of support group experiences by caregivers of dementia patients. *Clinical Gerontologist, 6,* 35–39.

Yeatts, D. E., Crow, T., & Folts, E. (1992). Service use among low-income minority elderly: Strategies for overcoming barriers. *Gerontologist, 32,* 24–32.

Zarit, S. H., Anthony, C. R., & Boutselis, M. (1987). Interventions with care givers of dementia patients: Comparison of two approaches. *Psychology and Aging, 2,* 225–232.

Zarit, S. H., Reever, K. E., & Bach-Peterson, J. (1980). Relatives of the impaired elderly: Correlates of feelings of burden. *Gerontologist, 20,* 649–655.

Zarit, S. H., & Zarit, J. M. (1982). Families under stress: Interventions for caregivers of senile demential patients. *Psychotherapy: Theory, Research and Practice, 19,* 461–471.

Zimmer, A. H., & Sainer, J. S. (1978, November). *Strengthening the family as an informal support for their aged: Implications for social policy and planning.* Paper presented at the thirty-first annual scientific meeting of the Gerontological Society, Dallas.

$\square$ **11** $\square$

Addressing the Challenges of Diversity

Eugene E. Garcia

The global transformations influencing our own nation are mounting. We continue, in analysis after analysis of our economic, employment, social, educational, and environmental problems, to conclude that without a global perspective, we are unable to understand the nature of and the solution to these national challenges. It is quite apparent in such analyses that our globe is shrinking daily. Incidents in one corner of the globe are influencing events in far-reaching corners, through direct or indirect pathways. It is becoming essential that we attend very directly to the linguistic and cultural diversity that resides in our global neighbors. Without such an understanding, we make our own solutions trivial and set them on a course for failure.

This reality of global diversity and interrelatedness pertains directly to our own nation's families and their support networks. Our country is an amalgamation of families from diverse cultural and linguistic backgrounds. This trend of ethnic and racial population diversification continues most rapidly among our young and school-age children. California has already been transformed into a minority-majority state; 52 percent of today's students come from "minority" families, and in less than two score years, 70 percent of California's students will be non-White, and one-half of them will speak a language other than English on their first day of school. Nationwide, White, non-Hispanic student enrollment has decreased since 1976 by 13 percent, or a total of 5 million students. As the overall total of the U.S. student population has decreased from 43 million to 41 million students (prekindergarten to grade twelve) since 1976, the following demographic student indicators have become educationally and socially significant:

- Minority enrollment, as a proportion of total enrollment in elementary and secondary education, rose from 24 percent in 1976 to 30 percent in 1986.
- As a proportion of total enrollment, Hispanics increased from 6.4 percent in 1976 to 10 percent in 1986. The number of Hispanic students increased from almost 3 million in 1976 to more than 4 million in 1986, an increase of 45 percent.
- During this same period, Asian/Pacific Islander students increased from 535,000 to 1,158,000, an increase of 116 percent (National Center for Education Statistics, 1991).

The demographic transformation that has become more evident in the last decade was easily foreseen at least that long ago. Our future growth in diversity is just as predictable: in forty years Whites will be a minority in every category of public life. Unfortunately, these emerging majority ethnic and racial-background children and families continue to be placed at risk in today's social institutions.

The National Center for the Study of Children in Poverty (1990) has provided a clear and alarming demographic window on these at-risk populations. Of the 21.9 million children under six years of age in 1987 who will move slowly through society's institutions — family, schools, the workplace — 5 million (23 percent) were living in poverty. Although fewer than 30 percent of all children under six years of age were non-White, over 50 percent of these children in poverty were non-White. In addition, these children continue to live in racial and ethnic isolation. Some 56 percent lived in racially isolated neighborhoods in 1966; 72 percent resided in such neighborhoods in 1987; 61 percent of these children in poverty live in concentrations of poverty, where 80 percent of the population is poor.

With regard to schooling, high school or equivalent completion rates are alarming for these emerging majority student populations. In 1989, the high school completion rate for the U.S. population was 81.1 percent for nineteen-year-olds, 86.5 percent for twenty-four-year-olds, and a very respectable 86 percent for twenty-nine-year-olds. For Blacks and Hispanics, the rate of completion in all age groups was close to 60 percent (U.S. Department of Commerce, 1991). With regard to academic achievement, in 1989 30 percent of thirteen-year-old students were one grade level below the norm on standardized achievement levels. However, this differed significantly for emerging majority and White students: 27 percent for White students, 40 percent for Hispanic students, and 46 percent for Black students.

Much more eloquent than any quantitative analyses of this situation have been the more intensive case studies, which dramatically tell the disheartening educational stories of these underserved populations (Kozol, 1991; Rose, 1989; Wong-Fillmore, 1991). These expository in-depth studies have found evidence of serious disruption of individual, family, and community functioning occurring when young children from non-mainstream backgrounds encounter the schooling process. Academic achievement is the most uninteresting effect of the overall circumstances for many of these children. It is quite evident, either quantitatively or qualitatively, that the plight of culturally and linguistically diverse populations in the United States is highly problematic — socially, economically, and educationally.

This portrait of vulnerability has been a historical reality for culturally diverse children and their families in the United States. The term *culturally diverse* is a relatively new one. Of course, it shows little appreciation of the diversity among such identified U.S. populations; that is, it is quite evident that such identified populations (African Americans, Mexicans, Mexican Americans, Puerto Ricans, Cubans, Chicanos, Latinos, Southeast Asians, Pacific Islanders, Filipinos, Chinese) are quite heterogeneous linguistically and culturally, both within and between categories. However, health, social, economic, and educational indicators, which have documented the vulnerability of these populations, have generated social, economic, and educational programs, related research, and a wide range of intellectual discussion regarding the at-risk educational circumstances of these populations (Barona & Garcia, 1990). Combined with the contemporary educational zeitgeist, which embraces equity, attention to the unrealized success of culturally diverse children and their families has been significant. The major thrust of any such efforts aimed at these populations has been centered on identifying why such populations are not succeeding and on how social institutions can be reformed or restructured to meet this significant challenge (Barona & Garcia, 1990; Comer, 1986; Schorr, 1989).

The initiatives targeted at these populations have been synonymous with endeavors aimed at the "poor," the "lower class," "immigrants" the "underclass," and "underachieving" and "disadvantaged" groups. As Gonzalez (1990) has documented, these children and families are usually perceived as "different" — foreigners, intruders, immigrants, who speak a different language or dialect and hold values significantly different from the so-called American mainstream. These perspectives have led policy makers (including the U.S. Supreme Court) to highlight the most salient characteristic of the student — the racial and language differences — in their attempts to address the historical social, educational, and economic "failures" of these populations. A discussion of risk factors, both within and outside the contexts in which these children and families reside, will be presented in this chapter, along with recent conceptual and empirical information of particular relevance to the "effective" community support services for this growing population of children and families. Specifically, the chapter will address the following topics:

- An overall demographic assessment of factors related to the services to and for culturally diverse populations, including issues of poverty, family stability, language diversity, and immigrant status.

- A particular analysis of the new understandings, and related implications for more effective service delivery.

It seems appropriate to conclude that, as cultural and linguistic diversity increase in our society arithmetically, the social challenge increases geometrically, and possibly exponentially. The U.S. society of tomorrow will be transformed by our responses to a number of pressing variables and agendas. One of the most significant will be how to provide adequate support programs for the array of families in tomorrow's society.

Global Perspective

According to Hobbs and Lippman (1990), demographic and social changes swept through the developed world between 1965 and 1990 that deeply affected the world of children. Changes occurred in the composition of families; in the family income and public resources available to them; in their risks of death, illness, or injury; in the level of education they were likely to attain; in the number and types of jobs available to them; and in the way they formed their own families. The report of the Center for International Research (Hobbs & Lippman, 1990) presents comparable data on the current status of children and youth in each of these areas for the United States and other selected countries, providing a comparative perspective on the well-being of youth in the United States.

This report presents comparable international figures on the status of children and families in the following areas: basic demographic trends, family composition and marital dissolution, the economic status of children, education, labor-force participation, and family formation. In this first attempt, broad indicators of the basic well-being of children and families, based on national statistics, are presented. National-level statistics enable comparisons between children and families in countries as a whole. The countries were classified by development categories, according to the United Nations scheme. The developed countries include all of North America and Europe, the Soviet Union, Japan, Australia, and New Zealand. The developing countries include Africa, Asia (except Japan), Latin America and Oceania (except Australia and New Zealand).

The developed countries selected for analysis in the report were chosen for their comparability with the United States, demographically and economically, and for the quality of the data available. The specific developed countries studied were the United States, Australia, Canada, France, West Germany, Hungary, Italy, Japan, Norway, Sweden, the Soviet Union, and the United Kingdom. The following developing countries were also included for the purpose of comparison with the developed countries when data were available: the People's Republic of China, India, Israel, and Mexico.

Countries that are similar economically — and, in many cases, politically — could be expected to produce similar environments and outcomes for children and youth, yet this is not the case. Major differences were found between the United States and the other countries:

- The United States has the highest yearly rate of both marriage (10 per 1,000 population) and divorce (21 per 1,000 married women) among the countries studied.
- Almost 1 out of 4 children in the United States lives in a single-parent family, a higher rate than in the other countries studied.
- Teenage fertility is highest in Hungary and the United States (52 and 51 births, respectively, per 1,000 women between fifteen and nineteen).
- The United States had, around 1980, the highest percentage of children in poverty (17 percent), even after tax and transfer benefits were applied.
- Poverty rates were higher among children in single-parent families than among children in all other family types.
- The United States had near the highest poverty rates among families with children (14 percent), even after tax and transfer benefits were applied.
- Poor families with children in the United States had the lowest earnings, compared with poor families in other developed countries studied, except for Australia.

- At least 99 percent of poor families with children in the developed countries received government assistance, compared to 73 percent in the United States.

To many parents in the United States, this comparative analysis — which suggests our nation's retreat from our youth and families — would be quite surprising. Every study of parental attitudes toward children and children's future indicates a strong belief that children should be a priority. Concomitantly, U.S. citizens express strong support as a whole for the enhancement of family life and education, preschool through postsecondary. Such values are considered a foundation of this nation's present and future vitality. Yet there is no mistaking where we stand as a nation with regard to indicators of these core values. Relatively speaking, we are lagging scornfully behind our brother and sister nations. We put up with more poverty, fail to support all families in need, and spend less on education.

Special concern for children and their families is universally significant and is reflected in the institutions we create to serve them, such as the surveys, studies, and census data used to determine what types of monies, political clout, and importance should be given to groups. In the United States, unpacking these racial, cultural, and regional differences is particularly instructive. Doing so presents a particularly intriguing portrait of our society, which is increasingly affecting our schools most directly, but also the fabric that will either bond the society together or form even greater intrasocietal boundaries, resulting in even further cultural, linguistic, educational, and economic polarization.

This dichotomy can occur at the most trivial levels. For example, the U.S. Bureau of the Census, in its attempts to document racial and ethnic heterogeneity, arrived at a set of highly confusing terms that place individuals in categories: White, White non-Hispanic, Black, and Hispanic (with five subcategories of Hispanics). Unfortunately, outside of the census-specific meanings of these terms, they are for the most part highly ambiguous and nonrepresentative of the true heterogeneity that the bureau diligently seeks to document. Therefore, it is im-

portant to note at the outset of this discussion that these categories are useful only as the most superficial reflection of our
nation's true diversity. I do not know many census-identified
Whites, Blacks, or Hispanics who believe that they truly are
White, Black, or Hispanic. But, given the forced-choice responses allowed in census questionnaires, they are constrained
by these choices. Racially and culturally, we are not "pure" stock,
and any separation by the Bureau of the Census, the Center
for Education Statistics, or other social institutions that attempt
to address the complexity of our diverse population is likely to
impart a highly ambiguous sketch.

   Having consented to this significant restriction with regard
to efforts aimed at documenting population diversity in this country, I must still conclude that an examination of the available
data in this arena does provide a fuzzy but useful portrait of
our society and of the specific circumstances of various groups
within our nation's boundaries. That sketch is one of consum-
mate vulnerability for a Hispanic population that has grown
significantly in the last two decades and will grow substantially
in the decades to come. On almost every indicator, non-White
and Hispanic families, children, and students are at risk, likely
to fall into the lowest quartile on indicators of well-being: family stability, family violence, family income, child health and
development, and educational achievement.

Family Income and Poverty

When families and students are labeled with the "at risk" epithet,
there is only one thread between them and society's institutions.
As fibers of the thread wear, the results are vivid: poor students
are three times more likely to become dropouts than students
from more economically advantaged homes (National Commission on Children, 1991). According to the National Center for
the Study of Children in Poverty (1990), 14 million children
and youth under the age of eighteen (approximately 20 percent
of our total population in this age category) resided in circumstances of poverty in 1986. This was an increase of some 2 million since 1975. Of this increased total, 6.5 million, or 45 percent, were non-White and Hispanic. Table 11.1 presents exact

Table 11.1. Children and Youth
Eighteen Years Old and Younger in Poverty.

Race/Ethnicity	(Numbers in Millions)					
	1975	1986	1996	2006	2016	2026
Total	12.3	14.2	16.4	19.3	23.1	27.9
White, non-Hispanic	6.7	7.7	8.8	10.1	11.5	13.2
Total Minority	5.6	6.4	7.6	9.2	11.5	14.7
Black	3.8	4.0	4.2	4.4	4.5	4.7
Hispanic	1.7	2.4	3.4	4.9	7.0	10.0
	Percentages of Poor Children by Ethnicity					
	%	%	%	%	%	%
Total	100.0	100.0	100.0	100.0	100.0	100.0
White, non-Hispanic	54.8	54.4	53.6	52.1	50.0	47.2
Total Minority	45.2	45.6	46.4	47.9	50.0	52.8
Black	31.5	28.5	25.5	22.5	19.7	16.9
Hispanic	13.7	17.1	20.9	25.4	30.3	35.9

Source: U.S. Department of Commerce, Bureau of the Census (1991).

numbers and percentages of children and youth in poverty for 1975 and 1986 and related projections through 2026. Projections in this table indicate that, unless poverty is contested in very direct ways, the number of children and youth in poverty will nearly triple by the year 2026, and almost three-fourths of those children and youth will be non-White and Hispanic.

The overall family earnings of these families over the next decades are another fiber ready to tear. All families in this category have experienced and are projected to experience a decrease in economic capability. Particularly vulnerable again will be families headed by persons who are non-White and Hispanic. By the year 2026, the median family income for non-White and Hispanic families will be $10,000 per year. Children in families with income below the poverty level are nearly twice as likely to be held back a grade level as their more advantaged classmates, and as young people from low-income families enter the labor force to earn additional income for themselves or their families. While work experience during adolescence can have positive effects, recent research indicates that working more than half-time during the high school years can undermine academic performance (National Commission on Children, 1991). As for those students from non-English-speaking home environments, over 90 percent in 1984 met poverty guidelines, which allowed them to receive free or reduced-price lunches (Development Associates, 1984).

The inevitable conclusion that can be drawn from these income data is that children and their families, particularly those from non-White and Hispanic ranks, are being forced to add additional weight onto the economic and social fibers that can enhance or abate their social, economic, and educational status. Today's challenge is to ease the tension in the fibers while continuing to provide the support services we provide to families. Clans that continue to grow culturally and keep on diversifying their linguistic modes are the same population that will come to seek services from institutions that are already identified as disadvantageous.

Understanding the Challenge

Making sense of the demographic and income data within the realm of socially related domains is like trying to make sense out of baseball by exploring only the vast array of statistics that we as Americans compile about our national sport. As we all know, no one can obtain a clear understanding of the game by just examining those statistics, no matter how comprehensive, strategic, or ingenious those numbers are. However, we utilize demographic statistics much as we use baseball statistics, to help us understand the nature of the social service enterprise through descriptions of the status or well-being of the teams and individual players. In the demographic analysis presented in this chapter, specific status indicators for specific groups and individuals have been presented with the understanding that such descriptions can add some depth, but not total understanding, to the challenge that today's and tomorrow's social service providers face.

Following with the baseball metaphor, what do these descriptive data tell us about that challenge? It is unmistakable that the children and families who will populate our society, who will "play the game," will be radically different with regard to race, culture, and language within a relatively short period. In less than four decades, one-half of our population will be non-White and Hispanic, with half of the children of this population speaking a language other than English. A professional receiving training today will likely be responsible for services to a more diverse population than at any other time in the history of this country. These growing populations of children and families will undertake their quest for a place in this society with several strikes against them. They are and will be coming to bat from social and economic circumstances that will likely leave them more vulnerable to the various pitches they will be asked to hit. Those pitches include an increasingly global competitive climate in which family and social stability, combined with educational success, is an absolute must, and a world in which our fundamental knowledge base is growing exponentially.

They are likely to be underequipped, not with the best money can buy but only with the least that society is willing to allow itself not to spend on other endeavors or to spend differentially on other players. They are likely to be coached by individuals who do not meet the highest standards, or by coaches who themselves are learning the game as they are given major coaching responsibilities. Moreover, many of these players will require coaching in a language that is not their own. They will need to acquire knowledge of the game along with the language and culture in which the game is immersed.

Yet these same data unequivocally indicate that the future of the game rests with them. As they emerge as the majority of players, their success is our success and their failure is our failure. They must succeed. We have no other alternative short of disbanding the game. There is no doubt that we have the resourcefulness to continue playing the game. The challenge lies in improving skills and communication, to make this contest beneficial for all those involved. We must learn to redefine our individual and group expectations while reevaluating embedded notions about ourselves and the other participants. We must learn to understand not only the context of the cultures that others come from but also where we come from ourselves.

Cultural Context

The traditional notions of culture, used by functionalist anthropologists in their analysis of behavioral patterns and normative customs of groups, fall into two categories. The *group culture* is generally understood as the system of understandings (values, prescriptions, proscriptions, beliefs and other constructs) characteristic of the individual's society. The group culture can be a positive tool, when understood properly, but it can also become a tool to stereotype and discriminate, even unintentionally. The *individual-oriented culture* is the person's own participation in and practice and understanding of the traits of the culture. As an individual, the person can follow, reinvent, or ignore practices passed along by other members. Individuals construct the group, and the group follows the individual. The relationship is a mutual understanding, where the individuals are the hub of the culture, and the group culture channels all the traits to all those members who want them.

Group Culture

This concept, in its technically anthropological meaning, was first defined by Edward Tylor, in 1871, as "that complex whole which includes knowledge, belief, art, law, morals, custom, and other capabilities and habits acquired by man as a member of society" (cited in Kroeber & Kluckhohn, 1963, p. 81). Since Tylor's time, a great variety of definitions of culture have been advanced by anthropologists. These definitions commonly attempt to encompass, as did Tylor's, the totality (or some subset of the totality) of humanity's achievements, dispositions, and capabilities, and virtually every anthropologist considers culture to be something learned, transmitted from generation to generation.

Most definitions of culture include another social dimension: the notion that culture is something that members of a group have in common. A recently published anthropology textbook states, for example, that behaviors and ideas may be considered cultural only insofar as they are shared among members of a social group (Nanda, 1980). This formulation is useful for anthropological comparisons between societies or subgroups within societies. Its basic assumption, however, is that of uniformity in the cultural equipment of individual members of societies and their subgroupings. In this formulation, the ontological locus of culture is some kind of group.

At the same time, all anthropologists acknowledge that members of all sorts and sizes of societies display differences in their behaviors and ways of thinking and valuing; that is to say, societies are characterized to some extent by intercultural heterogeneity. But such discussions remain most often at the level of the group, as in statements about the "looseness" or "tightness" of societies' cultural systems. When these researchers proceed to write ethnographies, deep descriptions, and analyses of groups, they tend to ignore interindividual variations as they abstract what they apparently consider to be "an essential homogeneity from the background noise of insignificant diversity" (Schwartz, 1978, p. 419).

Along these lines, anthropologist Ralph Linton has defined culture as "the sum total of ideas, conditioned emotional responses and patterns of habitual behavior which the members of [a] society have acquired through instruction or imitation and which they share to a greater or lesser degree" (quoted in Kroeber & Kluckhohn, 1963, p. 82). Although acknowledging that cultural items (ideas or learned behavioral habits) need not be totally shared by everyone in a group, in this concept it is nevertheless the property of sharing that defines the domain of culture.

This emphasis on shared traits is relevant to any consideration of the conceptual requirements of understanding the role of culture with respect to support services. This emphasis on shared traits leaves little if any room for the conceptual recognition of each individual's individuality within the framework of the concept of culture. Individuality becomes the domain of psychology, relevant only to discussions of personality, while the concept of culture is reserved for behavioral and ideational features of the individual's group. The latter might be appropriate to the goal of educating (or reeducating) a group, as in modernization programs applied by developing countries to their peasant populations. But keep in mind that the focus of support services is to nurture individuals and their families, not to judge the traits or culture of the entire ethnic group.

The relevance of this problem lies in the possible consequences of the group-oriented concept for the perceptions and expectations of professionals in their interactions with culturally and linguistic diverse families. It is my contention that a group-oriented notion of culture may distract professionals' attention from important culture-generating processes, in and outside of the support networks. The connection between families' and professionals' interaction and the group-culture concept derives from the fact that assumptions about families' "culture," whether right or wrong, stereotype the families and thus preclude the flexible, realistic, and open-minded quality of individual-professional interaction needed for competent delivery of services. This possibility becomes more apparent when one realizes that the majority of individuals providing services might try to Americanize instead of support the family.

Picture, if you will, a situation where a professional is perplexed by some action or response on the part of a minority person. If the professional has studied some of the anthropological ethnographies of the individual's ethnic culture, he or she may leap to an interpretation of the person's behavior in terms of idealized or modal characteristics attributed to that culture. To construe an individual's behavior solely on the basis of generalizations about group traits is to stereotype the individual, no matter how valid the generalizations or how disinterested one's intentions may be. It would be better for the professional to pursue the meaning of the person's behavior in the way anthropologists most often come to understand the people they study. Even though they write about cultures in collective terms, they come to know about them through observation of individuals. Of course, the professional's efforts to understand the individual could (and should) benefit from knowledge of cultural orientations that are widely or typically held in the person's ethnic community. But this inventory of knowledge should be viewed only as background information. The question of its applicability to the particular person should be treated as inherently problematical. Many studies in education (for example, Rodriguez, 1989; Tharp & Gallimore, 1989) caution educational personnel against hasty ethnographic and cultural generalizations of students, on the grounds that all linguistic and cultural groups are continuously undergoing significant cultural changes.

Carter's research (1968) into the effects of teachers' expectations on student learning and classroom behavior — namely, that Chicano students may sometimes actualize in their behavior the negative expectations held of them by teachers — confirms the concerns expressed here. It may be expected, of course, that this pattern would be less likely among teachers who have elected to teach in Spanish/English bilingual and bicultural settings. It should be noted, however, that many teachers teach in bilingual and bicultural settings that may not be formally designated as such. And even minority teachers may be considered to be in some ways culturally different (generational and acculturational differences) from children in their own ethnic groups. This observation is not recent. Guerra (1979) points to linguistic and other cultural variations both within (student-student) and between (student-teacher) generations of bilingual populations. Likewise, Cuellar (1980) argues that one's understanding of the meaning and value of culture and language must take account of the fact that "a community's characteristics reflect the composition of the different generational cohorts in the different age strata" (p. 198). Within the same cultural group, individuals may not have a group concept of practices but may recognize and practice those traits individually.

Individual-Oriented Culture

An early expression of the individual-oriented concept of culture is seen in the work of the anthropologist J. O. Dorsey. Sapir (quoted in Pelto & Pelto, 1975, p. 1) wrote the following of Dorsey's orientation: "Living as he did in close touch with the Omaha Indians, [Dorsey] knew that he was dealing, not with a society nor with a specimen of primitive man . . . but with a finite though indefinite number of human beings who gave themselves the privilege of differing from each other not only in matters generally considered as 'one's own business' but even on questions which clearly transcended the private individual's concerns."

Advocates of the individual-oriented approach to culture frequently describe a society's culture as a pool of constructs (rules, beliefs, values) by which the society's members conceptually order the objects and events of their lives. The participation of individuals in this pool is seen as variable. Spiro (1951), for example, has distinguished between the cultural "heritage" of all members of a society (that which has been made available to them by their predecessors) and each individual's particular cultural "inheritance" (that portion of the group's heritage that he or she has effectively received, or "internalized," from the past). Schwartz (1978) has stressed that the individual also manipulates, recombines, and otherwise transforms his inherited constructs; this, together with the outright creation of new constructs, is a major source of culture change. The individual's own portion of a society's culture is called by Goodenough (1981) a "propriocept," by Wallace (1970) a "mazeway," and by Schwartz (1978) an "idioverse." For these anthropologists, this constitutes the ontological locus of culture.

For some of the anthropologists employing an individual-oriented concept of culture, "the private system of ideas of individuals *is* culture" (Pelto & Pelto, 1975, pp. 12–13). Other individual-oriented anthropologists, however, reject the implication of such a notion of individual cultures. As they see it, the contents of one subjective system cannot be considered a culture. Like Schwartz, these theorists consider a cultural system to consist of all the constructs available to a society's members. Nevertheless, the society is itself not the locus of culture; its individual members are. The culture is a distributive phenomenon in that its elements are widely distributed among the individual members of a society. A major implication of this distributive model of culture is a rejection of the traditional assumption of cultural homogeneity. It implies that each individual's portion of the culture differs in some ways from those of the other members.

Schwartz's model of culture takes into account both the sharing and nonsharing of cultural constructs between members of a society, and he argues that both are functionally essential to the viability of any society. Diversity, he argues, increases a society's cultural inventory — what any individual could contain within his head would make up a very small culture pool — and commonality permits communication and coordination in social life. In Schwartz's words, "it makes as little sense to depict the distribution of a culture among the members of a society as totally heterogeneous and unique in each individual as it did to argue for complete homogeneity. We must dispense with the *a priori* assumption of homogeneity, but, similarly, we are not served by an *a priori* assumption of heterogeneity" (Schwartz, 1978, p. 438).

Schwartz's formulation is the most appropriate model of culture for addressing issues of cultural diversity as it relates to providing services to families, since it permits, within the framework of culture, simultaneous recognition of a family's ethnic culture (that is, such families share with their ethnic peers constructs that are not shared with out-group members) and those characteristics that define each family as unique (all families are in some ways different from their ethnic peers). It also permits recognition of traits shared with members of the larger culture, such as those acquired through acculturation.

Acculturation is a crucial variable in the analysis of ethnic minorities in plural societies, and its process contributes significantly to the heterogeneity of ethnic cultures. Writing of U.S. Hispanic culture, Bell, Kasschau, and Zellman (1976) note, for example, that among Chicanos "many have ancestors who came to North America several centuries ago, but others are themselves recent immigrants. Hence, a simple cultural characterization of [this] ethnic group should be avoided" (p. 7). These authors also caution against a simplistic view of the process of acculturation, noting that it "may not be linear, in the sense that one simply loses certain Mexican attributes and replaces them with Anglo attributes" (pp. 31–32). The process may be characterized more by complex patterns of combination and by ongoing recombination than by simple substitution. Therefore, degrees of acculturation among individuals contribute to the cultural heterogeneity of any ethnic population (which is to say, the uniqueness of its members).

Some people are likely to respond to the individual-oriented conception of culture with the question "What about customs?" Chicanos, for example, might point out that they recognize certain *costumbres* that distinguish them as a group from the larger society. This points to a realm of culture that is highly shared and more likely to belong to the public sphere than to the individual's subjective orientation. Referring to the "layered" nature of culture, Paul (1965) has observed that "What we call customs rest on top and are most apparent. Deepest and least apparent are the cultural values that give meaning and direction to life. Values influence people's perceptions of needs and their choice between perceived alternative courses of action" (p. 200).

What I am emphasizing here is the problematical nature of the variability and sharing of values and other constructs as internalized by individuals. Such courses of action reflect the unique set of life experiences by which individuals accept or reject societies' processes of adaptation. In America, that process is called *Americanization*. Our nation, as a pluralistic country, must deal with the cultural diversity among groups and with the variation that exists within those groups.

Americanization

Historically, Americanization has been a prime social institutional objective for culturally diverse families and their children (Elam, 1972; Gonzalez, 1990). Americanization practices were adopted whenever the population's diversity rose significantly in a community. This adaptation established special programs and was applied to both children and adults in urban and rural communities. The desired effect of Americanizing children and families was to socialize and acculturate the diverse community. In essence, if social service institutions could teach these students English and American values, then social and educational problems could be averted. Ironically, social economists have argued that this effort was coupled with systematic efforts to maintain disparate conditions between Anglos and minority populations. Indeed, more than anything else, past attempts at addressing the "Black, Hispanic, Indian, Asian, etc., social problem" have actually preserved the political and economic subordination of these communities (Spencer, 1988).

Coming from a sociological theory of assimilation, Americanization has traditionally been recognized as a solution to the problem of immigrants and ethnicity in the modern industrialized United States. Americanization was intended to merge small ethnic and linguistically diverse communities into a single dominant national institutional structure and culture. Thomas and Park (1921) argued that the immigrants' Old World consciousness would eventually be overcome by modern American values. Although I will not provide here a detailed review of the literature regarding the historical circumstances of the many immigrant populations that came to the United States, I will rely on recent analysis by Gonzalez (1990) and Spencer (1988). According to Gonzalez (1990), there were important distinctions between European immigrants and other immigrant experiences regarding assimilation. First, the Americanization of the non-European community has been attempted in a continuously highly segregated social context. Black, Hispanic and other non-White families are more segregated today than three decades ago. Secondly, assimilation of these groups had both rural and urban aspects, whereas the European experience was overwhelmingly urban. Third, this assimilation was heavily influenced by the regional agricultural economy, which retarded a "natural" assimilation process. Finally, slaves and immigrants from Africa, Mexico, Puerto Rico, and other Latin and Asian countries could not escape the effects of the economic and political relationship between an advanced industrialized nation, the United States, and semiindustrialized, semifeudal nations and territories, the latter increasingly under the political and economic sway of the United States. This relationship led to a very constrained immigration pool, with only farm and low-skilled labor immigrating continuously to this country. None of the contributory European nations had such a relationship with the United States, and thus their national cultures tended to be judged more on an equal footing with nations and territories struggling to realize their interests against the nationalism of a rising world power. This factor alone would have made for a significant modification in the objectives and in the way Americanization was applied to non-European communities.

It can be argued that Americanization is still the goal of many programs aimed at culturally diverse families and children (Weis, 1988; Rodriguez, 1989). Americanization for these families, unfortunately, still means the elimination not only of linguistic and cultural differences but also of an undesirable culture. Americanization programs seem to assume a single homogeneous ethnic culture in contact with a single homogeneous modern one, and the relationship between the two is not that of equals. The dominant community, enjoying greater wealth and privileges, claims its position by virtue of cultural superiority (Ogbu, 1987). In one way or another, nearly every culturally diverse child, whether born in the United States or elsewhere, is likely to be treated as a foreigner, an alien, or an intruder. The Los Angeles school superintendent voiced a common complaint in a 1923 address to district principals: "We have the [Mexican] immigrants to live with, and if we Americanize them, we can live with them" (Spencer, 1988). Unfortunately, even today the objective is to transform the diversity in our communities into a monolithic English-speaking and American-thinking and acting community. This attitude was recently articulated by a California superintendent who has received national and state distinction for his efforts in a district serving a large number of African American, Mexican American, and Asian American students: "We've got to attend to the idea of assimilation and to make sure that we teach English and our values as quickly as we can so these kids [and their families] can get in the mainstream of American life" (cited in Walsh, 1990, pp. B1-4). The superintendent is echoing the Americanization solution articulated over and over again over the last century. It is important to note that the dropout rate for non-White students in his school district was recently reported as being over 40 percent (Matute-Bianchi, 1990).

The Americanization solution has not worked. Moreover, it depends on the flawed notion of group culture. The Americanization solution presumes that culturally different families and their children are culturally flawed as a group. To fix them individually, we must act on the family or on the individual as a member of a cultural group. By changing the values and language of the group, we will have found the solution to the social, economic, and educational problems of the individuals who represent these groups. In essence, the groups should melt into one large and more beneficial American culture. The previous discussion, regarding group versus individual-oriented concepts of culture, suggests that our social service efforts have been responding quite ignorantly with regard to the processes in which individuals and groups come together to form culture and to show that understanding should in turn inform service providers. The challenge facing providers with regard to culturally diverse children and families is not to Americanize them. Instead, it is to understand them and act responsively toward the specific diversity that they bring and the goals of social and economic success for all families.

Public and private organizations have attempted to address this significant challenge. United Way of America articulates a set of standards for effective services to children and families. These standards attempt to address the issue discussed in this chapter by acknowledging the grounding of support services in family and community diversity. I summarize these in Exhibit 11.1. These standards serve as a simple checklist for the numerous agencies reaching out to our diverse communities. However, the recognition of such standards alone will not meet the challenge without attention to related initiatives that must be launched, nor should we consider one organization's effort to address the issue as the only manner of dealing with this challenge.

Meeting the Challenge

It is not enough to understand diversity and respect individuality. We must also be keenly aware of the fact that our culturally

Exhibit 11.1. Standards for Effective Services.

Effective services for children and families . . .

1. Have an undivided focus on serving the needs of children and families
2. Take a long-term view of their work with children and families and of their own operations
3. Are rooted in the community they serve and fully reflect community diversity
4. Employ extraordinarily persistent outrech efforts and an intensive, personalized, culturally respectful service plan for those participants most at risk
5. Attend to the needs of parents and caregivers as well as children
6. Provide or facilitate access to a comprehensive array of services to meet the particular needs of the individual child and family
7. Foster and reward participant-staff relationships that are grounded in mutual respect, trust, and caring
8. Attract and support the development of staff and volunteers who are highly skilled, well trained, and very effective in helping community residents
9. Have adequate, stable, and flexible support and an adaptive management orientation
10. Specify long-term and short-term outcomes and assess results regularly

---

Source: United Way of America, 1992, p. 25.

diverse populations have been and continue to be highly vulnerable in today's society. The current efforts are a positive push in the right direction. It is in all our very best interests for them to succeed. Our diversity can elevate us to a new plateau or plunge us to new depths.

Let us recognize the present circumstances and the magnitude of the challenge. A call to arms and a plan of action are imperative. We must acknowledge the differences between and within cultures, diverge from the Americanization concept, and ensure that support services for culturally diverse populations go hand in hand with their expectations and go by their norms. Allow me to be so bold as to suggest several ingredients that can accomplish all three goals.

Personal Commitment

We need not be fooled by any liberal or conservative rhetoric. We have not achieved educational equality for our culturally diverse populations. If we are to make any substantive progress, we will need further resolve. It is often said that with universal prenatal care, Head Start, school choice, and the like, we have solved or soon will solve the problems of at-risk, linguistically and culturally diverse populations. Please do not misunderstand: these contributions may be important, but our own past suggests that we should remain doubtful about any miracle cures. No new interventions, reorganizations, or resources will satisfactorily address this problem unless the individuals who implement these initiatives are deeply committed to the enterprise. The change that is necessary must be fueled by the type of social energy that sent us forward in the past with vigorous and consistent resolve. As in the New Frontier and War on Poverty eras, we must grasp the importance of this challenge.

More than a decade ago, President Jimmy Carter warned of a crisis of commitment in America, a warning that proved politically disastrous for him but was repeated in the successful presidential campaign of Bill Clinton. A broad spectrum of the nation's social and intellectual leaders are concluding that Carter was right. In fact, they say, the crisis has deepened.

A consensus has emerged that lack of confidence in the future, and in one another as Americans, lies at the heart of our ills as a nation. A nation that passed much of the 1970s in the aftermath of Vietnam, in search of its soul and its self, spent the 1980s in what many see as a self-consuming materialism and now is entering the 1990s in a cynical, dispirited mood. According to Bok (1990), "There is disturbing evidence to suggest that most forms of responsibility toward others have eroded in recent decades." Moreover, the percentage of people who feel that most individuals in power try to take advantage of others has doubled over the last two decades and now exceeds 60 percent. One source for this analysis is *The Cynical Americans*, by Kanter and Mirvis (1989). On the basis of a national survey of attitudes, the authors conclude that "the tendency to behave cynically is being reinforced to an unprecedented degree by a social environment that seems to have abandoned idealism and increasingly celebrates the virtue of being 'realistic' in an impersonal, acquisitive, tough-guy world. In citizen and country alike, there seems to be a loss of faith in people and in the very concept of community. A recent national survey found that 43 percent of Americans — and more than half of those under age twenty-four — believe selfishness and fakery are at the core of human nature" (p. 143). Big majorities of those sampled say they feel most people lie if they can gain by it, sacrifice ethical standards when money is at stake, and pretend to care about others more than they really do.

Some have argued that we have lost the ability to inspire our children. Others go so far as to say that we have lost the ability to inspire ourselves. Inspiration is the mother and the father of resolve. We cannot afford to be without it. We will need inspiration, resolve, commitment, and passion. To borrow from Jaime Escalante, the noted educator featured in the popular film *Stand and Deliver,* we will need *ganas* — the will to overcome great challenges.

Knowledge of What Makes a Difference

We will also need a new knowledge base. Recent research has redefined the nature of our culturally diverse students' educational vulnerability. It has destroyed both stereotypes and myths and laid a foundation on which to reconceptualize present educational practices and launch new initiatives. This foundation recognizes the homogeneity and heterogeneity within and between such populations. No one set of descriptions or prescriptions will suffice. However, it is worthwhile to consider a set of intertwined commonalities, which deserves particular attention. This foundation has been established by recent research, which has documented effective practices with linguistically and culturally diverse students in selected sites throughout the United States. These descriptive studies have identified specific programs that serve minority families, children, and students.

The results of these preliminary studies provide important insights with regard to general organization, development, academic achievement in content areas like math and science, and the perspectives of students, teachers, administrators, and parents. Interviews with classroom teachers, principals, and parents have revealed an interesting set of perspectives regarding the education of the students in these schools. Service providers were highly committed to the children and families they served. They perceived themselves as innovators, utilizing new theories and philosophies to guide their practice, and they continue to be involved in professional development activities, including participation in small-group support networks. They also had a strong, demonstrated commitment to communication and dialogue and felt that they had the autonomy to create or change the systems in which they worked, even if the solutions did not meet exact bureaucratic guidelines. They had high expectations for all those they served and also acted as advocates for their clients. They rejected any conclusion that their clients were culturally disadvantaged.

Leadership

A new knowledge base and commitment are not enough. We will also need leadership, particularly leadership that recognizes the following interlocking domains.

Knowledge Transmission. We will need to disseminate new knowledge to those who can utilize it. This requires training, retraining, and more retraining. Individually and institutionally, new knowledge must be appropriated by those in the field. It is of no use for researchers to share their knowledge only with themselves. New avenues for knowledge dissemination and appropriation are required. Leadership in this domain is also required.

Skill Development. New knowledge alone does not automatically lead to a new set of practices. New knowledge must be transferred and translated to specific service contexts. Time and energy must be devoted to the collaboration required to develop new skills. Moreover, these skills must be evaluated in the field—they must prove effective. We will need to hold ourselves and others automatically accountable. This requires leadership in both knowledge dissemination and skill development.

Disposition for Leadership. "Many are called, but few will self-select." Needed to meet this challenge is a generation of leaders who are willing to sacrifice, work very hard and long, take risks, learn from failure, rise above frustration, shift paradigms, and collaborate with and support their colleagues. Those who cannot or will not do these things should step aside, minimize obstruction, and otherwise ensure that if they cannot be part of the solution, they will not be part of the problem.

Affective Engagement

We will need leadership that embraces our culturally diverse children and families, adopts them, nurtures them, celebrates them, and challenges them. "They" must become "us." Anything short of raw advocacy, every minute, hour, and day, will not suffice. We must not give up hope. Too many of these families have given up hope in themselves.

Mostly, service providers need to act. Presidents and governors proclaim and set national goals; practitioners need to move beyond such proclamations. The task at hand is not just to see the future but to enable it. With inspiration, knowledge, and leadership, we can enable the future for our culturally diverse families and children and for our present and future culturally diverse society.

Professional Challenge

Professionals trained over a decade ago were not encumbered by the challenges facing preservice professional candidates today. They did not need to be ready to respond to the challenge presented by a highly diverse population. Moreover, few individuals from the ranks of the emerging majority succeeded academically themselves a decade ago, and so they were not and are not in the professional ranks. For example, in the 1987–88 school year, of the 2.6 million public and private school teachers and the 103,000 school administrators, over 88 percent were White. Fewer than 12 percent were non-White and Hispanic: 8 percent were Black, 3 percent were Hispanic, and fewer than 1 percent were Native American, Alaskan Native, Asian, or Pacific Islanders. In the same academic year, non-White and Hispanic academic enrollment was at 30 percent (National Center for Education Statistics, 1991).

It remains quite evident that the vast majority of professional service providers and administrators are White and will continue to be White in the near future, while the non-White and Hispanic proportion of the population continues to increase rapidly. It is difficult to identify specific attributes that have served diverse populations of children and their families effectively, but, in the educational domain, Dwyer (1991) identifies four areas where good teachers excel: content knowledge, teaching for student learning, creating a classroom community for student learning, professionalism. Villegas (1991) suggests that good teachers incorporate culturally responsive pedagogy into their classrooms.

Concern about the effectiveness of professionals is not new. Unfortunately, very little attention is given to the attributes of the professional and paraprofessional staff members who implement the myriad models and program types omnipresent in the service of diverse populations. Typically, attention to the characteristics of staff members is restricted to years of service and extent of formal training received (Olsen, 1988), yet most researchers will grant that the effect of any intervention is directly related to the quality of that intervention's implementation by service providers.

Even with quite universal acceptance of the necessity to train and assess professionals on competence in meeting the needs of culturally diverse children and families, the present modes of training and assessment are highly problematic. The data are quite clear with regard to the problems of individual assessment of professional competence. Current professional assessment can be criticized on several levels (McGahie, 1991; Shimberg, 1983; Sternberg & Wagner, 1986):

1. Evaluations usually address only a narrow range of practice situations. Professionals engage in very complex planning, development, implementation, problem solving, and crisis management. These endeavors do not usually require technical skills and knowledge, which are easily measured.

2. Evaluations are biased toward assessing formally acquired knowledge, probably because of the preponderance of similar outcomes measures. We assess professionals as we assess students, even though we have differing expectations.

3. Despite the presumed importance of practice skills, evaluations devote little attention to their assessment. With regard to service aimed at highly diverse families, we do have some understanding of specific skills that might be necessary, but the lack of specific research in this domain makes it difficult to articulate the exact skills that would be recommended as candidates for assessment.
4. Almost no attention is given to what have been identified as the disposition and affective domains of the service provider. In recent analyses of effective teaching, these attributes were identified as being as significant as content knowledge and practice skills (Pease-Alvarez, Espinosa, & Garcia, 1991; Villegas, 1991).

Moreover, assessment instruments are subject to severe violations of reliability and validity. Feldt and Brennan (1989) have demonstrated that components of measurement error are highly inconsistent in the area of professional assessment. Similarly, test validity is a fundamental problem for professional assessment (Berk, 1986). Keep in mind that inferences about professional competence or ability to practice are actually inferences about specific constructs. This is the old and dangerous chicken-and-egg problem. We construct an assessment, and soon we are willing to say that whoever scores at a particular level is competent. At the base of this assessment, however, is the legitimacy of the constructs that generate the assessment. We lack any definitive body of research and knowledge about the constructs that signify good teaching in general and good teaching with culturally diverse students in particular. That knowledge base is developing but it is not yet substantive (Garcia, 1991).

In noneducational areas, the knowledge base is close to nonexistent. Professionals who are now serving minority families are being evaluated by what McGahie (1991) refers to as the "connoisseur model." This model carries certain presuppositions, which are relevant to services for diverse children and families:

• Not all features of professional practice can be quantified.
• There is no one best answer to a professional problem or question.

- Connoisseurs are unbiased, fair in rendering decisions, and, given their demonstrated competence and commitment to the profession, are the most effective evaluators of professionals.

The connoisseur model is routinely used in a number of professional assessment endeavors, as in the performing arts. We would never imagine using a test to determine the winners of Academy Awards. In fact, to determine "Teacher of the Year" honors within local districts, at the state level, and even at the national level, connoisseurs are called on to serve as judges. They are asked to use their varying experience and expertise to identify the best teachers. Closer examination of our present mode of evaluating professional training programs indicates that the connoisseur model is the primary model in operation. Experts — fellow psychologists, social workers, early childhood educators — are sent to evaluate the effectiveness of a training program. In turn, local program experts, acting as connoisseurs, evaluate individual candidates.

The connoisseur model can be used to scaffold a model for training and assessing the competencies of professionals who, more and more, will face the challenges of a diverse population. Unfortunately, given the rapid growth of this diverse population and our own professional unpreparedness, we are creating this method at the same time we are using it. In the process, we train our own set of experts and connoisseurs and the diverse families themselves. Over time, as we develop a large corps of connoisseurs, it will be possible to utilize this model, and it is likely to become the only and best appropriate one. At present, however, it is not possible to implement this model on any large scale with any hope that it will be either reliable or valid.

In summary, the expertise of professionals whose task is to meet the challenges of diversity is highly questionable. These individuals have not been well prepared. We are beginning to react to that challenge. Many of you are reading this chapter because of your interests, concern, and the specific professional obligations that will be yours in the service-related professions. It is important to recognize that we are struggling together in this enterprise. We are far from achieving the service expertise that will effectively meet the growing challenges of diversity. However, that challenge is not dissipating, and you will probably be called on directly to assist in developing and implementing service initiatives that will meet the challenge. You will not be just an actor in this domain; you will be strategically involved in writing the script.

Within the global economy, the family and its support networks must be reinforced to face the challenges of the future. Families in our nation face countless adversities, by the mere fact of being culturally and linguistically distinctive. This country's past must be contained in the past, and the generation of a better future must begin with all of us. We cannot just hope that, somewhere along the path, all families will reach an axis where family support is equally available to all. We must work and learn about the contexts in which the families of the future will operate and we will address their needs.

Current global, demographic, and income trends are pointing toward a future world more diverse than we ever imagined, and with unheard-of linguistic challenges. The families of tomorrow will bring with them new agendas and, if history is any indicator, they will reject Americanization as the only means of being American. The fusion of conceptual insights, new research, and improved practices is allowing us to meet the challenge with a new vision and new hope for the future.

References

Barona, A., & Garcia, E. (1990). *Children at risk: Poverty, minority status and other issues in educational equity*. Washington, DC: National Association of School Psychologists.

Bell, D., Kasschau, P., & Zellman, G. (1976). *Delivering services to elderly members of minority groups: A critical review of the literature*. Santa Monica, CA: Rand Corporation.

Berk, J. (1986). *Culture clashes throughout the ages*. Albany, NY: State University of New York Press.

Bok, D. (1990). *Universities and the future of America*. Durham, NC: Duke University Press.

Carter, T. P. (1968). The negative self-concept of Mexican-American students. *School and Society, 96,* 217–219.

Comer, J. (1986). Home-school relations as they affect the academic success of children. *Education and Urban Society, 16,* 323–337.

Cuellar, J. B. (1980). A model of Chicano culture for bilingual education. In R. Padilla (Ed.), *Ethnoperspectives in bilingual education research. Vol. II: Theory in bilingual education* (pp. 246–269). Ypsilanti, MI: Department of Foreign Languages and Bilingual Studies, Eastern Michigan University.

Development Associates. (1984). *Final report: Descriptive study phase of the national longitudinal evaluation of the effectiveness of services for language-minority, limited-English-proficient students.* Arlington, VA: Author.

Dwyer, C. (1991). *Language, culture and writing.* Working Paper No. 13. Berkeley: Center for the Study of Writing, University of California.

Elam, S. (1972). Acculturation and learning problems of Puerto Rican children. In F. Corrdasco and E. Bucchini (Eds.), *The Puerto Rican community and its children on the mainland* (pp. 146–162). Metuchen, NJ: Scarecrow Press.

Feldt, L. S., & Brennan, R. C. (1989). Reliability. In R. L. Linn (Ed.), *Educational measurement* (3rd ed., pp. 105–146). New York: American Council on Education.

Garcia, E. (1991). Bilingualism: Second-language acquisition in academic contexts. In A. Ambert (Ed.), *Bilingual education and English as a Second Language: A research annual* (pp. 181–217). New York: Garland.

Gonzalez, G. (1990). *Chicano education in the segregation era: 1915–1945.* Philadelphia: Balch Institute.

Goodenough, W. H. (1981). *Culture, language, and society* (2nd ed.). Menlo Park, CA: Benjamin/Cummings.

Guerra, M. H. (1979). Bilingualism and biculturalism: Assets for Chicanos. In A. Trejo (Ed.), *The Chicanos: As we see ourselves* (pp. 129–136). Tucson: University of Arizona Press.

Hobbs, F., & Lippman, L. (1990). *Children's well-being: An international perspective.* Washington, DC: United States Department of Commerce, Bureau of the Census.

Kanter, D. L., & Mirvis, P. H. (1989). *The cynical Americans: Living and working in an age of discontent and disillusion.* San Francisco: Jossey-Bass.

Kozol, J. (1991). *Savage inequalities: Children in America's schools.* New York: Crown.

Kroeber, A. L., & Kluckhohn, C. (1963). *Culture: A critical review of concepts and definitions.* New York: Vintage Books.

Matute-Bianchi, E. (1990). *A report to the Santa Clara county school district: Hispanics in the schools.* Santa Clara, CA: Santa Clara County School District.

McGahie, W. C. (1991). Professional competence evaluation. *Educational Researcher, 20*(1), 3–9.

Nanda, S. (1980). *Cultural anthropology.* New York: Van Nostrand Reinhold.

National Center for Education Statistics. (1991). *The condition of education* (Vols. 1 & 2). Washington, DC: United States Department of Education.

National Center for the Study of Children in Poverty. (1990). *Five million children: A statistical profile of our poorest young citizens.* New York: Columbia University.

National Commission on Children. (1991). *Beyond rhetoric. A new American agenda for children and families.* Washington, DC: U.S. Government Printing Office.

Ogbu, J. (1987). *Minority education and caste: The American system in cross-cultural perspective.* San Diego, CA: Academic Press.

Olsen, L. (1988). *Crossing the schoolhouse border: Immigrant students and the California public schools.* San Francisco: California Tomorrow Policy Research.

Paul, B. (1965). Anthropological perspectives on medicine and public health. In J. K. Skipper, Jr., and R. C. Leonard (Eds.), *Social interaction and patient care* (pp. 256–289). Philadelphia: Lippincott.

Pease-Alvarez, L., Espinosa, P., & Garcia, E. (1991). Effective schooling in preschool settings: A case study of LEP students in early childhood. *Early Childhood Research Quarterly, 5*(3), 153–164.

Pelto, P., & Pelto, G. H. (1975). Intra-cultural variation: Some theoretical issues. *American Ethnologist, 2*(1), 1–45.

Rodriguez, C. E. (1989). *Puerto Ricans born in the U.S.A.* Winchester, MA: Unwin Hyman.

Rose, M. (1989). *Lives on the boundary.* New York: Free Press.

Schorr, L. B. (1989). *Effective services for children and families*. Cambridge, MA: Harvard University Press.

Schwartz, T. (1978). Where is the culture? Personality as the distributive locus of culture. In G. Spinder (Ed.), *The Making of psychological anthropology* (pp. 243–267). Berkeley: University of California Press.

Shimberg, B. (1983). What is competence? How can it be assessed? In M. R. Stern (Ed.), *Power and conflict in continuing professional education* (pp. 17–37). Belmont, CA: Wadsworth.

Spencer, D. (1988). Transitional bilingual education and the socialization of immigrants. *Harvard Educational Review, 58*(2), 77–106.

Spiro, M. E. (1951). Culture and personality: The natural history of a false dichotomy. *Psychiatry, 14,* 19–46.

Sternberg, R. J., & Wagner, R. K. (Eds.). (1986). *Practical intelligence*. New York: Cambridge University Press.

Tharp, R. G., & Gallimore, R. (1989). *Challenging cultural minds*. London: Cambridge University Press.

Thomas, S. V., & Park, B. (1921). *Culture of immigrants*. Cambridge, MA: Newcome Press.

U.S. Department of Commerce, Bureau of the Census. (1991). *Current Population Reports*. Series P-60. Washington, DC: U.S. Government Printing Office.

United Way of America. (1992). *Indicators of effective community service programs*. New York: Author.

Villegas, A. M. (1991). *Culturally responsive pedagogy for the 1990's and beyond*. Princeton, NJ: Educational Testing Service.

Wallace, A.F.C. (1970). *Culture and personality* (2nd ed.). New York: Random House.

Walsh, J. (November 14, 1990). Local school district receives recognition. *San Francisco Chronicle*, p. B1–4.

Weis, L. (1988). *Class, race and gender in American education*. Albany: State University of New York Press.

Wong-Fillmore, L. (1991). When learning a second language means losing a first. Early Childhood Research Quarterly, *6,* 323–346.

12

Funding
Family Support Programs

Judy Langford Carter

Funding for community-based family support programs and the family-supportive approaches they pioneered has changed dramatically since the earliest days of the first programs. From the beginning, however, funding for these hard-to-pigeonhole programs has been as creative and diverse as the programs themselves — pulling together funds from diverse sources, crossing categorical funding lines, mixing public and private funds, and building on what participants could bring or raise. The sources of ongoing funding today are slowly becoming more reliable and institutionalized as programs stabilize in their communities and the ideas behind them are more widely understood. Public funds are more readily available from a variety of sources as the comprehensive, preventive family support approach is more widely used by public systems.

The most dramatic development in the public funding of family support programs is unfolding as this chapter is being written, and its full impact is not yet known. The federal budget agreement passed in August 1993 includes a capped entitlement that will provide $930 million for family preservation and family support services over a five-year period, beginning with fiscal year 1994. As the parameters and definitions of this law are

276

developed and the funds are distributed to states, the funding possibilities for community-based family support programs will undoubtedly increase.

Funding Initial Innovations: Largely a Private Affair

The earliest center-based family resource programs—such as Avance, in San Antonio; Family Focus, in Chicago; The Family Place, in Washington, DC; and Parents Place, in San Francisco—began in the late 1970s with support from individual donors, local charitable or religious organizations, and small grants from local foundations. For most of these pioneer programs, this support gradually grew into an eclectic mix of intensive fundraising, with individual donors, larger foundation funding, sometimes national foundations, and, in a few cases, some state contracts for certain services and payments by parents who used the services. Virtually none of the early center-based programs received public funding of any kind until several years after the programs were well established (Goetz, 1992).

One programmatic result of the lack of public institutional support was an intense focus, and a large staff effort within the programs, devoted to fundraising activities and issues. Local corporations, foundations, and United Ways were made aware of the programs through this vigorous effort and often provided substantial but short-term funding. Parent fundraising, systematic approaches to individuals, and large, well-publicized annual family events also led to widespread public knowledge about programs and increased possibilities for program outreach. In some communities, the payment of fees or tuition for some center services has contributed significantly to the budget, and to the variety of services that could be offered by a single program. Scholarships and sliding-scale fees, along with a number of free services, have traditionally made family resource centers available to all families in a community, even when charges were necessary for some services.

A second and more important programmatic result of limited funding was the unique development of each center's program into a responsive community institution. Forced to rely

on local fundraising efforts, programs developed interesting partnerships with a variety of human and financial resources in their
communities, which in turn influenced the direction that the
programs took. Ongoing, necessary efforts to forge linkages with
other service providers (including public ones), in order to serve
families effectively, made the programs more responsive to their
communities than they might have been with ongoing, long-
term funding for all their services. The neighborhood's sense
of ownership for its family resource center, reinforced by the
necessity for community financial support, has been a vital element in the program's successful integration into the fabric of
the community, an element that makes the center attractive and
physically and psychologically accessible and causes it to be
viewed as a positive hub of neighborhood activity for all kinds
of families.

Other early family-supportive programs that were not
based in community centers, such as Parents as Teachers (PAT),
Home Instruction for Parents of Preschool Youngsters (HIPPY),
and parent-education groups, were also supported in the beginning by private foundation funding, usually on a small scale.
Some of these programs (as well as some of the center-based
models), which developed training programs for staff or volunteers on a specific curriculum or model, have been able to win
contracts with public agencies in some states or with not-for-
profit organizations utilizing their models. These state contracts
have generally been used to support initiatives designed to reach
certain kinds of families receiving state services (for example,
teenage parents or recipients of public benefits).

Public Agency Funding
Discovers Family Support Programs

As family support programs grew in number and developed in
a wide array of community settings, the principles of program
flexibility and responsiveness positioned them to utilize a variety of different funding opportunities from federal, state, and
local sources. For example, when gang intervention and prevention funds became available through these sources, many fam-

ily support programs found that these programs fit easily into the missions they had evolved in their own communities. The programs themselves actively sought funding from these sources, but the funders benefited from using these well-established programs for providing the community-based services they needed to provide. In a similar way, teen pregnancy prevention funds, substance-abuse prevention funds, and maternal and child health outreach programs found effective partners in existing family support programs. Virtualy all family support programs today in low-income communities take advantage of these sources of discretionary funds to assist in their programming (Schorr, Both, & Copple, 1991).

Children's Trust Funds, established in some form in each state, provide funds for local child-abuse prevention programs through state-generated funds (usually income-tax refund check-offs) and Federal Challenge Grant funds from the National Center on Child Abuse and Neglect. Many of the programs funded through this mechanism turn out to be local family support programs. Wisconsin's Children's Trust Fund has managed to obtain legislatively appropriated funds, in addition to its original program funds, to support a network of eight family resource programs in that state.

In some states, public agencies with particular missions in mind have helped establish new family support programs, using the lessons learned from the early community-based programs and new state funding for these special initiatives. Oregon, Colorado, California, and Washington, among others, all have new initiatives at the developmental stage. Two examples will illustrate how a state can fund family support as a strategy for addressing different issues.

First, Oklahoma's Child Development and Parent Education Program, administered through the Oklahoma Department of Health, is available in forty-two counties. It began in 1974 as a primary prevention effort available to all families with children up to the age of three and was funded through the child-abuse and child-neglect challenge grant program. It has grown into a comprehensive program, which incorporates developmental screening for all children and early intervention services for families with handicapped children. Money for the program comes from the federal government, from the state early intervention funds, and from fees for child guidance clinic services. In addition to providing direct services through child guidance and child development staff, the program often works in partnership with Head Start programs, community organizations, day-care centers, and preschools (Goetz, 1992).

Second, Maryland, in an effort to address a very high teen pregnancy rate and the complications for mothers and babies that it represents, established and funded Friends of the Family, a statewide public-private partnership, in 1985. Friends of the Family developed and today supports neighborhood centers in thirteen high-risk communities, with comprehensive services for teen parents and their children and preventive programs for nonparenting adolescents. State funds, through the Department of Human Resources, and federal funds for a comprehensive child development program represent 70 percent of the funding for Friends of the Family. The remaining 30 percent comes from foundations, corporations, and individuals. The combination of public and private funds has been a particular strength for the program over time, allowing for necessary flexibility as the program has developed and creating an emphasis on program quality and staff development that is sometimes lacking in single-funder programs (Goetz, 1992).

Statewide Initiatives Gain Support

Many family support initiatives exist in many states, but three states have committed state funds to family support services for all families throughout those states. In all three cases, funding was obtained through linkages to the educational system and by means of the argument that families are essential in providing good environments for healthy child development, which in turn is essential for a child to be successful in school.

Minnesota was the earliest pioneer, with its Early Childhood and Family Education Program, which entered a pilot phase in 1971. In 1984, the state legislature authorized education funding for it in every school district throughout the state, through the community education division of the state department of education. From the beginning, the program was designed to provide parent education, parent-child interaction, and early childhood education for all families with children, from birth to the age of kindergarten enrollment. Programming options for local communities, provided in a number of different sites, include home visits; lending libraries for toys, books, and other materials; a variety of classes; family events, field trips, workshops, drop-in lectures; and parents-only programs in women's shelters and prisons and at work sites.

Missouri's Parents as Teachers program, now nationally replicated in many states, began with foundation funding in partnership with the Missouri Department of Education at a few pilot sites in St. Louis. All parents with children from birth to the age of three, regardless of income, were offered the opportunity to learn how to be more effective parents. As word of the successful program spread, legislators from all parts of the state were under pressure to make sure that children and families in their districts were offered the same opportunities. Even in a time of fiscal restraint and looming budget deficits, the Missouri legislature funded a statewide program to offer the program to all parents through the state department of education. Subsequent funding has added services and supports to the initial program for families living in poorer communities.

In 1990, the state supreme court in the commonwealth of *Kentucky* ruled that the state educational system was unconstitutionally discriminatory and had to be completely reconstructed by the state legislature. This school reform effort proved to be one of the biggest opportunities for family support programs in the country. As legislators grappled with designing a world-class educational system for the state from the ground up, they also acknowledged that even a world-class educational system would not be able to produce the results they wanted without some attention to the other aspects of children's lives and without attention to the issues that children bring with them into the school, which can be barriers to their full participation in the school system. As a result, the Kentucky Education Reform Act of 1990 included a new statewide program, with funding to go with it: a family resource or youth services center for every school where more than 20 percent of the children were eligible for free or reduced-price lunches. The implementation plan included the elements of family support that have been pioneered in many community programs around the country, and it built on earlier initiatives in Connecticut and New Jersey, which effectively linked schools with community-based programs and services.

Following Kentucky's lead, several other states have initiated family resource programs as adjuncts to their educational reform efforts, although none has done so yet on Kentucky's statewide scale. A currently emerging national initiative, in partnership with several states, promises to move funding or community-based family support to a different level, including (but not linked solely with) schools. In 1992, the Pew Charitable Trusts, in Philadelphia, offered fourteen states the opportunity to apply for funds for major planning and technical support, in order to completely reform their children's services along the lines of a general design developed by the Pew Charitable Trusts. The design drew from the best available knowledge about the effectiveness of preventive, comprehensive, developmental programs around the country. A central feature of the design envisioned for the states is the use of family centers as neighborhood hubs for all services provided for children and their families.

A number of other state initiatives are exploring additional strategies for reconfiguring and refinancing services, for developing new governance, information, and eligibility systems, and for developing and using new front-line practices, both in the family centers and in the new service systems. A major result of these developing initiatives will be examples of new funding options for family-supportive services at both the state and local level. The degree to which state governments are able to form effective financial and programmatic partnerships with local programs will also be a closely watched aspect of new initiatives as they develop over time.

Creative Financing Finds
Flexibility in Categorical Funds

One indication that the family support movement is truly a grass-roots movement is its overall lack of public funding until very recently. Programs that began in local communities, and that were funded locally, have been increasingly funded for specific purposes by state agencies, but there has been little coherent national definition of family support as a service, nor has there been funding for it from federal sources. One reason is that family support, as a comprehensive and flexible approach, defies the categorization that is part of time-honored practice in federal funding. It is not exactly education, although it can contribute significantly to it. It is not a health service per se, although it can enhance and extend health services. It is not a specific social service that can be delivered to a specific individual who can be defined as eligible for it.

In an era of fiscal restraint, when many existing services have been cut back and entitlement programs have come under increasing scrutiny, widespread funding for any new service, especially one that does not easily fit into a single category, has been unlikely. There are currently three different aproaches to dealing with the dilemma of finding and using categorical funds to finance comprehensive and flexible family support programs.

The first approach has been developed creatively by the programs themselves, which have patched together a complicated funding scheme using a variety of different sources of public funding to support overall programs. These programs are usually large and have relatively sophisticated administrative and fundraising experience. A look at a single example — the Beethoven Project, in Chicago — illustrates why such sophistication is necessary.

The Beethoven Project, also known as the Center for Successful Child Development, was the brainchild of philanthropist Irving Harris, an originator and longtime supporter of innovative child development strategies. The Beethoven Project's original goal was to provide all the necessary services for a cohort of infants, born in the catchment area of Beethoven Elementary School, to enter school at age five, developmentally ready to take full advantage of what the school had to offer. In the Robert Taylor Homes, relatively few children entered school in such a state. The challenges of providing full health services, parent education, emotional support, and the full range of other social services to families living in one of the country's most socially isolated, impoverished, violent, and gang-infested communities were considerable.

The program design was complex and comprehensive, utilizing the best available knowledge about community-based family support, child development, and outreach and engagement for hard-to-reach families. The center and a related infant-care facility were established in the housing development itself. The staff included a full array of medical, social services, and child development professionals, along with a strong outreach component of local women trained as family advocates.

The complicated funding mix that was created shows what is still involved today in order for a large comprehensive family support program to fully support its services. Federal money for the project came from a competitive discretionary grants program and from funding for a Head Start center related to the project. State money came through a contract under an infant-mortality reduction initiative, from an employment training contract, from funds for an infant-care center, and, later, from a state board of education early childhood education initiative. The Chicago Housing Authority provided the space rent-free and eventually upgraded building security through extensive renovation of the ground floor. Foundation funds were provided primarily by the Robert Wood Johnson Foundation (for an on-site medical clinic) and the Chicago-based Harris Foundation, with smaller grants from a variety of local and small national foundations. Other private funds from individuals and corporations were raised for renovation and furnishing of the two spaces used for the center. Administrative authority for the project was shared by the Chicago Urban League and the Ounce of Prevention Fund. This approach of mixing a variety of funds can sometimes work well, but it is far beyond the reach of many local programs and most state agencies looking for ways to finance family support services.

A second approach has opened up recently as expert financial analysts have begun to explore the possibility of states' more effectively using categorical federal funds for family-supportive services. In Kentucky, for example, the Center for the Study of Social Policy, with assistance from the Institute for Human Services Management, developed extensive recommendations for using existing sources of categorically defined federal money to help fund family support services that would be available through family resource centers. Some Medicaid funds available for outreach to Medicaid-eligible families, for example, could legally be used for outreach to the same families through the family resource center (Center for the Study of Social Policy, 1991b). This new avenue of financing is available to states, not directly to local programs; but, effectively used by states, it could provide a large proportion of funding for local programs, especially for centers in underserved areas where many families are eligible for federal programs (Center for the Study of Social Policy, 1991a). Options for financing services are currently being explored in many states, with assistance from these national resources.

The third approach to using existing funding streams for family support programs and services is the most revolutionary. Ultimately, it should provide the most money. This approach requires a wholesale policy shift, from funding only the relief and treatment of identified problems of individuals to funding the prevention of problems and the promotion of healthy families, as well as integrating services in order to provide a more commonsense, holistic approach to families' needs (National Resource Center for Family Support Programs, 1992). In the coming few years, the states participating in a variety of promising initiatives may provide examples of how states can make this critical shift. Other experiments in providing comprehensive and intensive services to families have been envisioned but rarely implemented.

The Iowa Family Development and Self-Sufficiency Demonstration Grant Program, initiated in 1988, represents one of the most comprehensive projects using family support principles as its core and utilizing federal assistance and job training money and Medicaid as its funding sources. A 1992 assessment of the program indicates that instituting intensive, long-term family-supportive strategies, primarily through the work of a family development specialist, can, over time, bring a variety of successes for the families most at risk for remaining dependent on the welfare system and other public systems. The capacity to align the funding streams more closely with families' overall needs is a continuing challenge to this program, as well as to other programs not so well established (Child and Family Policy Center, 1992).

The challenge of working out appropriate blending and shifting of the funding streams should be well worth the time and effort in the long run (Bruner, 1990). Even a brief look at listings of the federal money now being used to fund categorical services for children and families gives a clear picture of the large amounts involved — and of the large number of categories that could easily be utilized by families served in local family resource programs (see Levitan, Mangum, & Pines, 1989; Bruner & Carter, 1991; Pizzo, 1992).

A New Federal Perspective Promises New Investments

Growing evidence that preventive, comprehensive programs may be more cost-effective in the long term has inspired states to invest in them as a new strategy for facing the most complex problems: child-abuse prevention, reduction of teen pregnancy, reduction of infant mortality, and healthy development of babies born at risk for a number of problems. The initiative so far has come from the states, with growing pressure on the federal government to reduce the categorical funding barriers that prevent some state initiatives from fully utilizing existing federal resources and to begin directly funding some family support services.

There is also evidence that the federal government is poised to respond directly to the need for family support services. Four significant pieces of federal legislation, all passed in the last few years, have begun the process of making federal funding available to family support programs. Even with severe fiscal restraints on new spending for domestic programs, family support has gained recognition and support at the federal level. With a new presidential administration in office, an acknowledged commitment to strengthening and expanding investments in programs for healthy child development has already brought new funding and new attention to family support programs. These developments are likely to continue expanding the new funding opportunities for local family support programs and for state initiatives using this approach.

The first bill, which described comprehensive family support services to be demonstrated and researched with federal funds, was the Comprehensive Child Development Program, first authorized in 1988 at a level of $25 million per year. The program, which funded a total of twenty-four projects in 1989 and 1990 with five-year grants, was influenced by the Beethoven Project. These federal research projects were intended to fully test the results of providing long-term, intensive, comprehensive services for families at high risk. Grant awards averaged $1 million per year per program, with the number of families served in each program held at 120 randomly selected participants. The size of the budget, the intensity of the services, the targeting of specific families, and the establishment of a completely new program for this project are elements not likely to be found in typical community-based family support programs. But the concept of family support as a comprehensive, noncategorical approach that includes both parents and children was an important precursor of future federal funding of family support. (Congress increased the annual appropriation to $45 mil-

lion, beginning in 1992, to allow more grantees to be funded.)
The results of the original research project, due at the end of
the five-year period, will probably influence future funding for
family support, at least for this particular population of families (Hubbell et al., 1991).

The McKinney Homelessness Prevention Act, passed in
1990, included family support services as a strategy that could
be used to stabilize families, especially families that included
teen parents, and prevent them from becoming homeless. Funding was appropriated in 1991. Local programs first received
grant funds in the summer of 1992. Local community-based
programs, many of which had already been offering a variety
of family-supportive services, were eligible to apply directly for
this funding.

The Family Resource and Support Grants Program,
which offers states an opportunity to develop and support networks of local family support programs, was authorized for three
years as part of the Young Americans Act of 1990. The grants
program received an appropriation of $4.9 million in 1992, and
the first request-for-proposals announcement appeared in the
Federal Register in June 1993. Three states, out of forty-four that
applied in the initial round, were chosen to be recipients of
these funds. The large number of states that applied for the funds
is one indication of the growing interest in and need for federal
support to local programs. This grants program is likely to grow
as more states begin to develop partnerships with local programs
and use the networks of programs as a vehicle for state services.

The largest source of federal funding for family support
programs is one that is not yet fully defined. As part of the Clinton administration's 1993 budget agreement, almost $930 million (over a five-year period) was included to fund a capped entitlement for family support and preservation services through
the child welfare system. Each state is to receive a formula-determined portion of the funds, which will be used for family
support and family preservation, defined according to guidance

from the Department of Health and Human Services in the first year and official federal regulations in subsequent years. The guidance issued by the Department of Health and Human Services includes family support definitions that conform to the language used in the Family Resource and Support Grants Program. This will allow local programs to be providers of services, through some form of public-private partnership with state child welfare agencies in states that choose to pursue this plan.

Challenges to Program
Integrity as Funding Options Grow

Local family support programs have struggled financially for years to keep their doors open. They welcome the new interest and support on the part of the state and federal governments, but they are also legitimately concerned about the expectations that will come with these new funds, and which may change the program's original missions and purposes in unacceptable ways. There are several areas of concern:

- The bureaucratizing and standardizing of inherently unique and flexible programs that are responsive to the individual communities and families they serve
- The targeting of certain families to receive services in programs whose universal accessibility has been one of their greatest assets
- The expectation that family support will definitively solve the problems of severely dysfunctional families or take the place of more expensive treatment alternatives that many families will still need

Family support programs, as they have grown up in their own communities, have evolved individual outreach approaches, staffing patterns, governance structures that involve parents, and program activities and services unique to the programs' missions and targeted populations. The "luxury" of finding funds from a variety of private sources has allowed programs to set their own agendas and provide the services their participants want and need. Using public funds for some program elements, such as substance-abuse prevention or health education and outreach, has been a way to preserve the program's own core approach and let it use its own staff while providing needed services to families. Even linking up with federal service providers or public health nurses and providing these services at the program site still did not jeopardize the program's underlying mission; it allowed convenience and support for families and service providers alike. The first challenge in establishing public funding for family support services will be to preserve this unique and responsive approach, as well as neighborhood ownership of the programs, while ensuring the kind of accountability and program quality that public funding ought to require. For example, the commonwealth of Kentucky, in establishing its family resource and youth services centers, rejected a single-model approach in favor of an extensive community assessment and planning strategy for ensuring that centers would be responsive to local needs and governed by the families who participated in them (Kentucky Interagency Task Force on Family Resource and Youth Services Centers, 1992).

The second challenge will be to coordinate the targeting of public funding to the neediest communities and families with the traditional principle of universal access. Family support is a preventive strategy, which means that its services are by definition universally helpful to all families, long before any identified problems arise or any particular families can be considered eligible for services. However, public resources remain too scarce to ensure the same level of service to everyone, and so some targeting of public funds will undoubtedly occur. One compromise that has been effective in several pilot programs, such as Maryland's Friends of the Family and Illinois's Ounce of Prevention, is to target communities with high levels of risk factors that could be reduced by family-supportive services. Services through a family resource center are then available to all families in the identified community.

Other compromises have also been successful. Many family resource programs already serve a variety of families, those that are eligible to receive federal services as well as those that are not. There are several strategies for ensuring that the program serves everyone (for example, sliding-scale fees and scholarships for some services, a number of free programs open to all, and a significant outstationing of free community resources in the centers; see National Resource Center for Family Support Programs, 1992. With this configuration, all families can use some resources of the center, but those in need of more intensive services can also be provided for. In school-linked centers, which are intended to serve all parents of the children in a school, programming is often designed to appeal to the full spectrum of possible participants, and then special outreach and assistance strategies are developed for families that are reluctant or unable to come to the center. Managing the compromises involved in targeting has not been impossible for existing programs, but care must be taken to learn from these experiences. A major reason for the success of family resource centers that have reached out to families and become an integral part of community life has been their avoidance of deficit-oriented thinking: the programs have not been identified as places for "problem" families. Future funding decisions need to maintain the integrity of a services-for-all policy while providing for underserved communities through a sensitive, creative approach to targeting.

The third challenge is to resist any "overselling" of the program's benefits and to maintain strong support for funding necessary services outside the family support center. While family support has been shown to improve family functioning and educational achievement and reduce the chances for child abuse and neglect, it cannot take the place of substantive treatment for serious family dysfunctions. And, while one indication of success is that a well-established center often becomes the first stop when a family problem or issue arises, a center must still maintain a delicate balance between responding appropriately to the crises of its families and focusing on a preventive, long-term developmental program. Especially in a community with few traditional services for families, a family support center may become overwhelmed by the daily crises that families bring in. A family support center often coordinates other existing services (such as medical services or mental health services) for its families or serves as an interim or follow-up support system when families seek additional services not offered through the center. As a preventive, developmental resource, a family support program normally does not provide these more intensive treatment services itself unless it has a special component specifically dedicated to them. One potential pitfall of using public funding for family support programs would be an erroneous assumption that such programs can substitute for more intensive services or reduce the need for such basic family assistance as drug-abuse treatment or mental health services. These services must also be available, so that the family support program can support its families effectively. With more family support centers in place, the demand for some "outside" services may actually increase. This will be the case especially as family support centers are able to help families discover what resources they need.

The Partnership Goes On

Regardless of the new funding possibilities, the role of family support programs as partners with other service providers and other community resources will continue. In each neighborhood, family support is defined more by its approach and its responsiveness than by its specific services. The neighborhood and community role of a center is to lead the way for assessing the full range of support needed by families, matching them up with what already exists and then providing or facilitating or advocating for ways to fill the gaps. The unique structure and character of each community mandates a unique role for a family center in each one. Funding should continue to come from a variety of sources, and the programs should continue to focus on building the capacity of families to identify and fully utilize all the resources available to them.

References

Bruner, C. (1990). *Improving maternal and child health: A legislators' guide.* Des Moines, IA: Child and Family Policy Center.

Bruner, C., & Carter, J. (1991). *Family support and education: A holistic approach to early childhood education.* Denver: National Conference of State Legislatures.

Center for the Study of Social Policy. (1991a). *Leveraging dollars, leveraging change: Refinancing and restructuring children's and family services in five states.* Washington, DC: Author.

Center for the Study of Social Policy. (1991b). *Refinancing in Kentucky: Expanding the base for family resource and youth service centers.* Washington, DC: Author.

Child and Family Policy Center. (1992). *Making welfare work: A family approach.* Des Moines, IA: Author.

Goetz, K. (Ed.). (1992). *Programs to strengthen families: A resource guide.* Chicago: Family Resource Coalition.

Hubbell, R., et al. (1991). *Comprehensive child development program: A national family support demonstration.* Washington, DC, and Bethesda, MD: CSR, Inc., & Information Technology International.

Kentucky Interagency Task Force on Family Resource and Youth Services Centers. (1992). *Kentucky family resource and youth services centers guide for planning and implementation* (rev. ed.). Frankfort: Family Resource and Youth Services Center Branch, Kentucky Cabinet for Human Resources.

Levitan, S. A., Mangum, G. L., & Pines, M. W. (1989). *A proper inheritance: Investing in the self-sufficiency of poor families.* Washington, DC: Center for Social Policy Studies, George Washington University.

National Resource Center for Family Support Programs. (1992). *Keeping the lights on: Fundraising for family support programs.* Chicago: Family Resource Coalition.

Pizzo, P. D. (1992). *Financing family-centered infant child care.* Washington, DC: Zero to Three/National Center for Clinical Infant Programs.

Schorr, L. B., Both, D., & Copple, C. (Eds.). (1991). *Effective services for young children: Report of a workshop.* Washington, DC: National Academy Press.

□ Part Four □

POLICY CHANGE
AND FAMILY SUPPORT

13

Family Support
and Community Development

James Garbarino
Kathleen Kostelny

The role of social support systems in enhancing family functioning lies in the interaction of social nurturance and social control (Garbarino, 1987; Garbarino & Associates, 1992). Such support systems "provide individuals with opportunities for feedback about themselves and for validations for their expectations about others, which may offset deficiencies in these communications within the larger community context" (Caplan & Killilea, 1976, p. 41). When they occur as a matter of policy and program and are directed toward improving family functioning, these support systems constitute a form of intervention.

Two corollary premises are embedded in the concept of social support as a family intervention. The first is that the support provided can be internalized in some manner and thus have an effect beyond the period during which it is provided. The second is that the support provided can strengthen child rearing enough to have a meaningful effect on child health and development (Weiss & Halpern, 1991).

These concerns reverberate through all analyses of family support in the form of a series of recurrent questions: Can family support be a "treatment," or must it be a condition of life? Can family support succeed under conditions of high risk?

Is the neighborhood the appropriate unit of social analysis for conceptualizing and offering family support programs? Is neighborhood-based programming feasible among the neediest families, and in the neediest and most socially impoverished neighborhoods? Is it possible to "synthesize" neighborhoods? To what extent can and should social support programs for families be staffed, at least in part, by indigenous volunteers and/or paraprofessionals? To what extent can and should efforts be aimed at assisting neighbors in helping each other? In short, to what extent is neighborhood-based programming for families inextricably tied to issues of empowerment and community development?

These are the questions that underlie our analysis in this chapter. They drive us to consider a host of issues in social context. The focus of our analysis is thus the context for social support in neighborhoods and communities. To provide a basis for understanding these issues, we turn first to a brief historical review.

Historical Perspective

One of the origins of the family support "movement" lies in the settlement houses that were created as part of liberal reform movements in the nineteenth century — for example, Hull House, in Chicago (Halpern, 1990b). These settlement houses sought to provide a neighborhood focus and to serve a wide range of needs — ameliorative, preventive, and enabling. Staff lived in the settlement house, and the overall theme was one of establishing a center for promoting the culture, values, and resources of middle-class America among the poor and immigrant populations.

A second origin of the family support approach lies in the early concept of the visiting nurse. By sending nurses into the community, and by defining their role as "holistic," the visiting-nurse programs of the nineteenth and early twentieth centuries complemented the settlement house by incorporating the concept of "friendly visitors" and "mutual help" into day-to-day practice. Visiting nurses clearly bear a direct conceptual (and often historical) relationship with contemporary approaches to family social support, in which "community nursing" figures prominently (Froland, Pancoast, Chapman, & Kimboko, 1981; Kagan, Powell, Weissbourd, & Zigler, 1987).

From the 1930s through the 1950s, other neighborhood-based strategies emerged. One of these, the Chicago Areas Project, targeted reducing juvenile delinquency and general community breakdown by identifying natural community leaders who could mobilize other community members. Another neighborhood approach, developed by Saul Alinsky in his community organizing work, was more militant. This approach deliberately engendered conflict, to emphasize the power and control of institutions outside the community and with the goal of bringing the community together against these outside institutions (Alinsky, 1970).

From the 1950s through the 1980s, the Gray Areas program of the Ford Foundation was the prototype for many neighborhood-based initiatives (Halpern, 1991). Like earlier initiatives, this approach had its foundation in the idea that mainstream institutions and disenfranchised residents of poor neighborhoods had similar goals but were frustrated by not knowing how to achieve them either independently or together.

One of the Gray Areas programs, Community Progress, Inc. (CPI), was one of the most widely known programs. Based in New Haven, Connecticut, it was composed of a tightly knit group of young reform-minded professionals who knew one another and had developed the program. They deliberately excluded the leaders of large, established agencies, such as schools, social services, and health departments. One drawback, however, was that while the professionals were committed to neighborhood members' providing services, they did not encourage neighborhood members to participate in the planning process.

Current family support approaches include a wide and proliferating variety of programs and organizations designed to establish social support in the environment of families. These efforts are often called *family support and education programs* (for example, the Family Focus Program developed by Weissbourd and her colleagues), *social support networks* (Belle, 1989), *parent-*

education projects (for example, the New Parents as Teachers Program described by Pfannenstiel and Seltzer, 1989), or *home health visitor programs* (for example, the Elmira, New York, project described by Olds, Henderson, Tatelbaum, & Chamberlain, 1986, and by Olds & Henderson, 1989).

In the political and cultural climate prevailing in the United States since the 1970s, such efforts have had great appeal. They reflect private and local initiative. They play to themes of voluntarism that have received prominent political sponsorship. They echo recurrent themes of "empowerment" and "ownership" that are offered as a complement or even a substitute for increased public investment and control in local affairs (for example, as articulated by the Washington-based Enterprise Institute's Robert Woodson). And they seem consistent with the affinity for community- and neighborhood-based orientation that has intuitive appeal to so many in the public and private sectors. Before going any farther, however, we will undertake some clarification of what we mean by *neighborhood* and *community*.

Neighborhoods and Neighboring
in a Community Context

We define *community* as a geographical entity defined politically and psychologically by its members and by "outsiders." We recognize the importance of economic factors in defining communities — for example, the central role of a "primary economy" (dairy farming, regional banking, military industries, universities, and so on) — we also understand that communities typically encompass a number of discernible subunits, usually referred to as *neighborhoods*. The concept of neighborhood has a history as a focal point for research, theory, policy, and practice in the United States (Hawley, 1950; Warren, 1978). We rely on a standard definition of *neighborhood:* "a small geographic unit consensually identified" (U.S. Advisory Board on Child Abuse and Neglect, 1991).

The issue of size is problematic for rural areas, of course, once we move beyond small towns and villages to farms, ranches, and isolated dwellings. Nonetheless, most such efforts contain an attempt to limit geographical borders, most notably in terms of the walking distance of a young child (compare the "neighborhood walk methodology" of Bryant, 1985). Coupled with this spatial dimension is some effort to respect history (the evolution of residential patterns) and psyche (some sense of shared identity among the residents, as in a common inclination to "name" the neighborhood).

Such efforts have led to three elements in the definition of the term *neighborhood:* a social component, a cognitive component, and an affective component (Unger & Wandersman, 1985). Thus we see definitions of *neighborhood* (and *neighboring*) in terms of interaction patterns, a common understanding of boundaries and identity, and a set of shared feelings of belonging.

The social component of the neighborhood includes both informal social supports (emotional, instrumental, and informational) and social networks (links to other people). This social component is central in offering support and in providing resources for coping with stressors at both the individual level and the neighborhood level.

Some observers, however, have noted a shift in the function of neighborhoods. With advances in communication, technology, and transportation, neighborhoods have lost some of the important functions that they once had (Wellman, 1979). Many activities and relationships now take place outside a person's neighborhood. Such a view makes it necessary to consider "communities without propinquity" — that is, communities not limited by their geographical boundaries (Wellman, 1979). However, while people may belong to a variety of communities, depending on their interests, people will belong to only one neighborhood, based on where they live. Thus a neighborhood is a geographical area where people feel physically, although not necessarily socially, close to each other (Barry, 1991).

The cognitive component of a neighborhood refers to the thoughts or ideas that individuals have about their neighborhood's social and physical environment, and it can be used both to understand the neighborhood and to develop ways of dealing effectively with neighborhood issues. One aspect of neighborhood cognition involves a mental mapping process, resulting from repeated experiences in the neighborhood, which allows individuals to manage their neighborhood better. For example, cognitive mapping in dangerous neighborhoods would determine where people felt safe to walk or where they could interact socially with others without fearing harm.

A neighborhood also has an affective dimension, including a sense of mutual help, a sense of community, and an attachment to place. The sense of mutual help involves the belief that assistance is available when needed, even though neighbors are not frequently contacted. Indeed, when there is heavy actual use of neighborhood resources, it may well lead to a reduction in neighboring due to overload. Neighborhood support is thus best understood in terms of confidence, rather than in terms of utilization.

A sense of community encompasses feelings of membership and belongingness and shared socioemotional ties with others in the neighborhood. Attachment to place develops through analysis, by individuals, of the costs and benefits of living in their neighborhood, as compared with living in other neighborhoods.

Although most of the conceptual rhetoric surrounding the concept of neighborhood focuses on urban settings, many observers seek some way to incorporate rural settings (Fitchen, 1981). In rural areas, however, providing community-based programs is often problematic, for at least two reasons. First, rural communities are spread out, and so families often have difficulty getting to the programs. Second, there is a tendency to duplicate urban program models in rural communities, thereby disregarding the needs and characteristics of the rural population and disempowering the rural residents if these programs come under external control (Myers-Walls, 1992). Going still further, we must recognize that different ecologies generate different patterns of neighborhoods (for example, the rural area of the American West versus Appalachia; the organizational pattern of "old" urban neighborhoods in New England versus the diffused patterns of Sun Belt cities).

However we define *neighborhood,* we must struggle to understand the potential and actual impact of neighborhood-based programming in supporting families (Garbarino, Stocking, &

Associates, 1980). As we see it, the defining characteristics of a neighborhood-based approach are premised on the notion that deliberately engineered social support, provided during a formative period in child and family development, can buffer the child and the family against some of the psychological and social effects of poverty, promote personal development and psychological well-being, and stimulate healthy patterns of interaction, both within the family and between the family and the broader environment (Weiss & Halpern, 1991). In starker terms, it can be argued that deliberately engineered social support may be potent enough to alter insufficient or dysfunctional parenting capacities or styles acquired and reinforced through a lifetime of experience in a particular familial and social world.

Issues in Family Support as a Feature of Community Development

Our efforts to understand neighborhood-based intervention (Garbarino & Kostelny, 1992a, 1992b) have led us to a series of issues, which we believe are embedded in any effort to understand family support and community development.

Intuitive Appeal Versus Rigorous Grounding in Theory and Research

Does existing program evaluation strongly confirm the validity of the assumptions underlying community-based family support and education programs, or has their intuitive appeal in the current political and cultural climate sustained them in the absence of conclusive empirical evidence? If forced to answer this question, we would have to acknowledge that family support programs rest primarily on a foundation of faith. Few studies exist to address the validity of these approaches, particularly with high-risk families in high-risk communities.

Appropriate Matching of Services and Needs

What is the "market" for neighborhood-based family support efforts? A gross analysis might start with the following approx-

imation by Bernice Weissbourd (personal communication, 1992):
One-third of the families are functioning well without us; one-
third need and can profit from us; one-third are too troubled
to make good use of our program. While the exact percentages
in each category are open to question, the underlying analysis
seems valid because it recognizes that effectiveness depends in
part on an appropriate matching of services and needs.

Unless there is extraordinarily effective and charismatic
leadership, successful participation in a family-oriented social
support program requires participants who have moderate levels
of competence, organization, available resources, and continuing motivation. As has been said in analyses of Head Start, those
who have the most gain the most.

The same phrase may apply to neighborhoods. Can family
support programs operate from a neighborhood base if the neighborhood is socially and physically devastated? How much congruence is required among neighborhood-based institutions? Is
it enough to have a school? a church? Is an active business community necessary? Can we operate neighborhood-based programs in a ghost town?

This leads us always to look closely at a family support
program, to see whether it is reaching beyond the "easy" families and reaching beyond the "easy" neighborhoods. There is
always the danger that the program will simply open its doors
and the best families will walk in — the top third, to which we
referred earlier in our discussion. The lowest third are rarely
able and willing to participate in such programs. This is a particularly serious concern if we seek to employ family support
to prevent child maltreatment, because families involved in child
maltreatment are by and large drawn from this group, which
has the lowest levels of competence and motivation.

Consultation Versus Training

To what degree is it necessary and feasible to "train" natural
helpers and neighbors to function as family support systems?
This is one of the hot issues in the field of family support. One
camp emphasizes the need for professionals to serve as consul-

tants to natural helpers or "central figures"; projects conducted by Collins and Pancoast (1976) and their colleagues have adopted this approach. In their day-care information project, they identified women who were already the focal point of natural helping networks in the informal day-care referral system. They saw their goal as facilitating these natural helpers without interfering with their operations. They emphasized the existing knowledge and skills of the natural helpers, and the danger of disturbing their work through overt intervention. Thus consultation, rather than training, was the focus of their efforts.

By contrast, Danish et al. (1980) established a training program for preparing indigenous citizens to function on behalf of mental health promotion in their community. They emphasized the limitations of these natural helpers and the need to augment their skills and concepts. Thus training, rather than "mere" consultation, was the focus of their efforts.

Use of paraprofessionals has limitations, however. Halpern and Larner (1987) found that paraprofessionals encountered problems while assisting clients in the areas of health care, child care, and mental health services. Other problems may arise from overidentification with a client, excessive dependence on a client, projecting one's own situation onto a client, or low expectations (Austin, 1978). Parents are also sometimes reluctant to reveal personal matters to indigenous workers from the community, fearing loss of privacy (Olds & Henderson, 1989).

Still other professionals perceive traditional staff education and training programs for paraprofessionals from the community as inadequate for promoting change in parents and optimal development in children, particularly when such psychically loaded issues as sexual abuse are involved.

At the Ounce of Prevention programs in Chicago, for example, in addition to formal training, new strategies were designed to change the service provider by transforming the way she viewed and understood parents, children, and the parent-child relationship (Musick & Stott, 1990). The training protocol was restructured in terms of forming a relationship, to model the kinds of reciprocal, interactive roles that the professional staff expected the paraprofessional staff to fulfill with respect to the teen parents. Such a "chain of enablement" fosters positive growth in paraprofessional staff, so that they in turn can foster such growth in teen parents. This method of training paraprofessionals is designed to result ultimately in more enabling and nurturing parenting, through a structured, well-planned "trickle-down effect."

Domains of Silence

Are there topics and issues with which neighbors and/or indigenous paraprofessionals cannot deal because they are too personally threatening or culturally taboo? This issue extends the consultation-versus-training issue still further and is of special relevance to any consideration of the role of social support in preventing child maltreatment.

Two of the family issues most likely to invoke personal or cultural "domains of silence" (Halpern, 1990a) are sexuality and aggression. Any effort that aims to prevent child maltreatment through family support systems that rely on natural helpers must contend with the fact that matters of sex and violence are the least likely to be addressed successfully (or even addressed at all). The natural helper's own experiences of victimization, teenage sexual activity, and use of corporal punishment create powerful impediments to dealing openly with these issues, as the program's formal curriculum typically dictates (Halpern, 1990a; Musick & Stott, 1990). This is not to say that these two obstacles are insurmountable; indeed, both can be addressed.

The Ounce of Prevention programs concerning sexuality and teen mothers have found it possible to address issues of sexuality with indigenous helpers, but only after an extensive program of education and "processing." By the same token, the North Lawndale Family Support Initiative of the National Committee for Prevention of Child Abuse, also in Chicago, was able to open a dialogue with community members about the issue of corporal punishment, a dialogue that started from the sometimes fierce unwillingness of many parents (and natural helpers from the neighborhood) to acknowledge that a problem existed in the community with respect to corporal punishment (Lauderdale & Savage, 1991).

Selection Effects or Genuine Impact?

To what extent are neighborhood effects primarily self-selection effects and the results of exclusionary policies versus being results of the milieu represented in the neighborhood? All community and neighborhood analyses are potentially compromised on the basis of self-selection. Why are some people living in neighborhood A while others live in neighborhood B? Rarely is random selection the answer. The systematic grouping or exclusion of families on the basis of race, ethnicity, or income militates against efforts to understand family functioning (including child maltreatment) on the basis of neighborhood characteristics.

A study by Freudenburg and Jones (1991) of twenty-three communities experiencing rapid population growth found that all but two communities had a disproportionate increase in crime, suggesting that the changes in a community's social structure that accompany rapid growth result in a breakdown of social control. As the "density of acquaintanceship" (the proportion of a community's residents who know one another) decreases, criminal activity increases.

Another issue concerns outmigration from neighborhoods that are beginning to "turn bad." Such outmigration may have debilitating effects on social networks (Fitchen, 1981) and create still more confounding self-selection effects.

Beyond even these obvious selection factors, neighborhoods differ on the basis of "ethos." Some areas are more vital and coherent (Warren, 1978), while other neighborhoods are more problematic. A survey in South Carolina (Melton, 1992) revealed that on a scale of 1–7 — with 7 indicating high involvement — the average score for neighborhood residents was 2 + in response to the question "How involved are you in other people's children?" The same survey revealed that most people could not name one agency that had been particularly helpful on behalf of children.

Nevertheless, if intervention is straightforward in recognizing these analytical limitations, it may still be possible to go forward with prevention programs aimed at and through neighborhoods. We do know that context is important (as is self-selection and the content of "treatment"). For example, one recent study reports that youth whose families were relocated to subsidized housing in the suburbs were more than twice as likely to attend college as youth who were relocated to subsidized housing in inner-city areas (54 percent versus 21 percent), and 75 percent versus 41 percent found employment (Rosenbaum & Kaufman, 1991). Assuming that there were no systematic differences in who was relocated where, this result suggests a powerful social support effect on important life-course events (attending college and finding employment).

Research on the Link
Between Neighborhood and Family Support

Research has sought to explore and validate the concept of social impoverishment as a characteristic of high-risk family environments and as a factor in evaluating support and prevention programs aimed at child maltreatment. The starting point was to identify the environmental correlates of child maltreatment (Garbarino, 1976; Garbarino & Crouter, 1978; Garbarino & Gilliam, 1980). This provided an empirical basis for screening neighborhoods to identify high- and low-risk areas (Garbarino, 1987; Pelton, 1978, 1981, 1992). Poverty is associated with a significantly elevated risk of family problems, including child maltreatment.

From this flows a twofold conception of risk as it applies to neighborhoods and families (Garbarino & Crouter, 1978). The first aspect refers to areas with a high absolute rate of child maltreatment (based on cases per unit of population). In this sense, concentrations of socioeconomically distressed families are most likely to be at high risk for child maltreatment. For example, in one city (Omaha, Nebraska), socioeconomic status accounted for about 40 percent of the variation across neighborhoods in reported rates of child maltreatment.

The magnitude of this correlation may reflect a social policy effect. It seems reasonable to hypothesize that in a society in which low income is *not* correlated with access to basic human services (for example, maternal and infant health care), this correlation would be smaller. In a society totally devoid of policies to ameliorate the impact of family-level differences in social class, it might be even larger.

This hypothesis merits empirical exploration but is consistent with the observation that socioeconomic status is a more potent predictor of child development in the United States than in some European societies (Bronfenbrenner, 1979). This is evident in low infant-mortality rates in some poor European countries (for example, Ireland and Spain), rates lower than in the United States as a whole and much lower than among poor communities in this country (Miller, 1989). This point emphasizes the important fact that social support is a concept operating at the macrosocial level, not just at the neighborhood level (see Thompson, 1992).

It is the second aspect of high risk that is of greatest relevance here, however. High risk can also be taken to mean that an area has a higher rate of child maltreatment than would be predicted on the basis of its socioeconomic character. Thus two areas with similar socioeconomic profiles may have very different rates of family and child problems. In this sense, one is high risk while the other is low risk, although both may have higher rates of child and family problems than other, more affluent areas (see Garbarino & Sherman, 1980; Garbarino & Kostelny, 1992a). Unfortunately, this sort of community risk analysis is lacking in virtually all programmatic efforts aimed at preventing child maltreatment (indeed, in all areas where social support programs might be aimed at improved family functioning).

The Human Significance of Community Risk

What do low- and high-risk social environments look like? Answering this question is important if we are to understand the essential elements and likely outcomes of family support programs.

One recent development has been a refining of the meaning of social impoverishment, away from a simple concept of social support and toward a more complex phenomenon of social integration (particularly as reflected in employment and neighboring patterns — see Deccio, Horner, & Wilson, 1991, a study in Spokane, Washington; Bouchard, 1987, a study of Montreal neighborhoods; Sattin & Miller, 1971, a study of two neighborhoods in a Texas city; Garbarino & Kostelny, 1992a, a study of Chicago neighborhoods).

In the study of two economically similar neighborhoods in Spokane, it was found that the high-risk neighborhood had reported rates of child maltreatment more than two times higher than those in the low-risk neighborhood. Although differences in perceived social support were not found, differences in social integration were. For instance, the unemployment rate in the high-risk neighborhood was three times greater than that of the low-risk neighborhood. The average family income was a few hundred dollars higher in the high-risk neighborhood, but the percentage of families living below the poverty level was also larger in the high-risk neighborhood (26 percent versus 17 percent). Differences were also found in stability of residence, possession of a telephone, and vacancy rates. A greater percentage of families in the low-risk neighborhood had lived in their current homes for more than five years — 52 percent, versus 35 percent in the high-risk neighborhood. Moreover, there were three times as many families in the high-risk neighborhood who lacked telephones, by comparison with the low-risk neighborhood (absence of a telephone is both a cause and an effect of social isolation in the sense we are using here). Finally, the high-risk neighborhood had more than twice as many vacant housing units as the low-risk neighborhood — 16 percent versus 7 percent.

Community Influences on Family Support Programs

In high-risk communities, do social service agencies mirror the high degree of social deterioration characteristic of the families and the communities? Conversely, do we observe a strong, informal support network among social service agencies in low-risk communities? The answer to both questions, on the basis of interviews conducted with agency staff in two Chicago communities, appears to be yes (Garbarino & Kostelny, 1992a).

The general tone of the interviews in the high-risk community was somewhat depressed: people had a hard time thinking of anything good to say about the situation. The physical spaces of the programs themselves seemed dark and depressed, and a casual visitor could easily spot criminal activity. In the low-risk community, people were eager to talk about their community. They did list serious problems, but most of them felt that their community was a poor but decent place to live; "poor but not hopeless" was the way one respondent described it. The low-risk community also reported drug and crime problems, but they were not apparent to the casual visitor.

In the high-risk community, respondents knew less about the other community services and agencies that were available, and they showed little evidence of a network or support system, either formal or informal. (One exception, however, seemed to be the Family Focus Program: everyone knew about Family Focus, and the staff at Family Focus knew people in other programs by name.)

In the low-risk neighborhood, there were more services available, agencies knew more about what was available, and there were very strong formal and informal social support networks. The subjects in the low-risk area also reported strong political leadership from the local state senator (the high-risk community did not report positive feelings about political leaders).

In the high-risk community, the staff who were interviewed described a situation in which their agencies mirrored the isolation and depression of their community. In the low-risk community, the agencies mirrored the strong informal support network that existed among families in their community. They seemed hopeful because many of their families were hopeful. At least in terms of this study, it seems fair to say that the social service agencies in a community mirror the problems facing the community.

The final piece of evidence available to us in our analysis concerns child deaths due to maltreatment. Child deaths are a particularly telling indicator of the bottom line for families in a community. There were twelve child-maltreatment deaths reported for the two community areas we studied during the period from 1984 to 1987. Eight of these deaths occurred in the high-risk area, a rate of 1 death per 2,541 children. For the low-risk area, the rate was 1 death per 5,571 children. The fact that deaths due to child maltreatment were more than twice as likely in the high-risk area seems consistent with the overall findings of our statistical analyses and interviews. This is an environment in which there is truly an ecological conspiracy against children. As such, it directs our attention to the need to approach the concept of family support with our eyes open.

Such an open-eyed approach involves refusing to accept superficial, quick, conventional efforts. Anyone with an appreciation for the depth and pervasiveness of the social impoverishment in contemporary high-risk neighborhoods understands that social support must be part of a sweeping reform of the neighborhood and of its relations with the larger community.

Social impoverishment has rapidly escalated in many inner-city neighborhoods. For example, until the 1960s, the social organization of many inner-city black neighborhoods was enhanced by the presence of working- and middle-class families; these neighborhoods featured a vertical integration of different income groups (Wilson, 1987). By the 1980s, however, most of the middle- and working-class population had moved, leaving behind an underclass with few mainstream role models to help maintain the traditional values of education, work, and family stability.

Likewise, there was a breakdown in social control by members of these neighborhoods. For example, Dubow and Podolefsky (1982) suggest that for informal social control to be effective, a neighborhood must have a consensus on values or norms, be able to monitor behavior, and be willing to intervene, if necessary, when behavior is not acceptable. In socially impoverished neighborhoods, consensus on values and ability to monitor behavior are often lacking.

Social support must include an approach to psychosocial factors in the community that influence the ability and willingness of professionals and residents alike to make a public commitment to social support programs. Of particular concern in thinking about social support programs in socially impoverished neighborhoods is the impact of community violence on the public behavior of community resource people (Garbarino & Associates, 1992). The role of poverty is often considered in protective services decision making and in child-abuse prevention program design. The impact of community violence and social deterioration are often noted as social problems as well. But rarely are these factors considered in relation to the stresses they place on those providing services, especially in the context of pervasive violence.

Human service workers increasingly find themselves serving children and families who live in community environments that are chronically violent. These include some large public housing developments and socially deteriorated, low-income neighborhoods in cities across the nation. For example, over 100,000 children live in public housing projects in Chicago, where the rate of serious assault has increased 400 percent since the middle 1970s. Most of this increase is concentrated in neighborhoods already at risk because of poverty and family disruption. One of the regional directors of the Department of Children and Family Services in Chicago reported that at any given time at least two of his forty caseworkers are unable to work because of injuries sustained while going to and coming from the homes of the families they serve. Many more have experienced significant trauma and live constantly in fear because of having to investigate cases in the urban "war zone."

Trauma and fear are not limited to protective service workers, of course. We conducted a survey of sixty Head Start staff who worked in high-crime areas, and we asked them to describe things that had happened around the children's center that had made them fearful or upset. Over 60 percent of the staff had witnessed shootings and gang-related activities and listed these as the things that caused them the most fear. We believe that this level of violence undermines the foundation for neighborhood-based programs to support families. Our work points to some additional challenges as well:

- In many areas, parents are afraid to attend night meetings at school. How can a neighborhood-based program succeed if families are intimidated?

- One of the social workers who conducts home visits with parents of Head Start children described how she had had to take cover in the playground to avoid being hit by random bullets from two rival gang factions. She stated, "I was caught in the crossfire." Before the gunfire stopped, she witnessed the shooting of one young man. When the shooting stopped, she ran back to the children's center and reported the event to a co-worker, who listened sympathetically. "Then it was over," the social worker said. The next day, the same social worker had to resume her responsibilities. There was no intervention. How does this experience reverberate when she is faced with the prospect of reporting a case of child abuse to the protective services agency, knowing that any such report is viewed as collaborating with the law enforcement agencies and may bring violent reprisal? How can a neighborhood function as a support system when key players are traumatized?
- When a teacher at one center heard gunshots outside the classroom window, she and all twenty of the children got down on the floor. Although this teacher knew how to protect children in a crisis, she was unable to deal with the long-term consequences of the event, particularly the fear that it could happen again at any moment. How can she assess the likely impact of community violence on children who are also at risk for domestic violence and emotional neglect?
- At an after-school program, as some of the children were entering the building, shooting by gang members started nearby. One girl described crawling on her hands and knees to get to the center. Once the children were in the building, however, staff were confused about whether to talk about the event or ignore it and go about planned activities, since discussions often lead eventually to reports of domestic violence. How can the staff respond to community violence when they have not come to terms with domestic violence?

Professionals who deal with children of violence are often at a loss to know how to respond to them. For example, in training sessions involving Head Start staff from four major Chicago public housing complexes, the majority of the sixty participating staff expressed feelings of inadequacy related to being unable to help students deal with the violence they encounter in their daily lives. Many of these staff are "indigenous" to the communities they serve. How does this relate to prevention and protective services? Successful child-abuse prevention and child protective services must address the issues of powerlessness, traumatization, and immobilizing fear that impede effective family life and social development for a significant and growing proportion of children in areas with underclass populations (Garbarino, Dubrow, Kostelny, & Pardo, 1992).

It is also crucial to understand the needs of professionals who work in these environments. The professionals themselves often feel powerless, traumatized, and afraid. How do they make sense of prevention and protection missions in neighborhoods so violent that they fear for their own personal safety? How can they bring messages of family safety? Does everyone concerned accept lower standards for child protection in such environments? Do people fall silent when confronted with harsh and even violent child-rearing practices?

Halpern (1990a) has identified "domains of silence" as a significant impediment to the delivery of effective family services, most especially among paraprofessionals recruited from high-risk populations. This impediment is both significant and serious.

One further case study amplifies this point. We undertook a site visit to a nationally recognized family support and abuse-prevention program located in a major urban public housing project. The interaction between the program and the social environment resembled what we have observed in Cambodian refugee camps in eastern Thailand (Garbarino, Kostelny, & Dubrow, 1991). We were particularly struck by the fact that the professionals in both family support programs faced a very difficult psychological and political challenge that derived from the realities of power in both settings. In both the public housing project and the refugee camp, all "outsiders" left at the end of the business day. After dark, the setting was controlled by the gangs (in the Cambodian situation, they were more clearly political gangs, but they were gangs nevertheless). In the public housing project, the gangs had been known to set curfews for residents, as a demonstration of their power. Any decisions made or actions taken during the day had to be reconciled with the realities of who was in charge at night. People were afraid to come out of their apartments or to contest the power of the gangs. This is hardly a desirable environment in which to promote social support programs. It represents the tip of a horrible iceberg of community development issues that we must address in order to fulfill the promise of family support programs in our society.

Social Momentum and Peacekeeping

Our review has highlighted a number of important issues that we must face as we seek to enhance family support through neighborhood- and community-based interventions. These issues include several that cluster around the phenomenon of social momentum. Just as positive influences reinforce each other through a process of positive feedback, so also do negative influences conspire to undermine positive behavior and developments. This is particularly true of the highest-risk neighborhoods in urban areas, where negative socioeconomic and demographic factors interact with self-sustaining patterns of violence. As such, they create a highly negativistic sociocultural context in which family support systems are hard-pressed to exist, let alone enhance parental functioning and child development. For this reason, it will not be enough simply to introduce family support programs in a very limited way. It will also be necessary to link them to massive peacekeeping and socioeconomic development efforts. This will be an enormous challenge, but it is one that must be met.

References

Alinsky, S. (1970). Citizen participation and community organization in planning and urban renewal. In F. Cox et al. (Eds.), *Strategies of community organization* (pp. 216–226). Itasca, IL: Peacock.

Austin, M. (1978). *Professionals and paraprofessionals.* New York: Human Sciences Press.

Barry, F. (1991). *Neighborhood-based approach: What is it?* Background paper for the U.S. Advisory Board on Child Abuse and Neglect. Ithaca, NY: Family Life Development Center, Cornell University.

Belle, D. (Ed.). (1989). *Children's social networks and social supports.* New York: Wiley.

Bouchard, C. (1987). *Child maltreatment in Montreal.* Montreal: University of Quebec.

Bronfenbrenner, U. (1979). *The ecology of human development: Experiments by nature and design.* Cambridge, MA: Harvard University Press.

Bryant, B. (1985). The neighborhood walk: Sources of support in middle childhood. *Monographs of the Society for Research in Child Development, 50*(3).

Caplan, G., & Killilea, M. (Eds.). (1976). *Support systems and mutual help: Multidisciplinary explorations.* Philadelphia: Grune & Stratton.

Collins, A., & Pancoast, D. (1976). *Natural helping networks.* Washington, DC: National Association of Social Workers.

Danish, S., et al. (1980). *Helping Skills: A basic training program.* New York: Human Sciences Press.

Deccio, G., Horner, B., & Wilson, D. (1991). *High-risk neighborhoods and high-risk families: Replication research related to the human ecology of child maltreatment.* Cheney, WA: Eastern Washington University.

Dubow, F., & Podolefsky, A. (1982). Citizen participation in community crime prevention. *Human Organization, 41,* 307–314.

Fitchen, J. (1981). *Poverty in rural America: A case study.* Boulder, CO: Westview Press.

Freudenburg, W., & Jones, R. (1991). Criminal behavior and rapid community growth: Examining the evidence. *Rural Society, 56,* 619–645.

Froland, C., Pancoast, D., Chapman, N., & Kimboko, P. (1981). *Helping networks and human services.* Newbury Park, CA: Sage.

Garbarino, J. (1976). A preliminary study of some ecological correlates of child abuse: The impact of socioeconomic stress on mothers. *Child Development, 47,* 178–185.

Garbarino, J. (1987). Family support and the prevention of child maltreatment. In S. L. Kagan, D. R. Powell, B. Weissbourd, & E. F. Zigler (Eds.), *America's family support programs: Perspectives and prospects* (pp. 99–114). New Haven, CT: Yale University Press.

Garbarino, J., & Associates. (1992). *Children and families in the social environment* (2nd ed.). Hawthorne, NY: Aldine.

Garbarino, J., & Crouter, A. (1978). Defining the community context of parent-child relations. *Child Development, 49,* 604–616.

Garbarino, J., Dubrow, N., Kostelny, K., & Pardo, C. (1992). *Children in danger: Coping with the consequences of community violence.* San Francisco: Jossey-Bass.

Garbarino, J., & Gilliam, G. (1980). *Understanding abusive families.* Lexington, MA: Lexington Books.

Garbarino, J., & Kostelny, K. (1992a). Child maltreatment as a community problem. *International Journal of Child Abuse and Neglect, 16*(4), 455–464.

Garbarino, J., & Kostelny, K. (1992b). *Neighborhood-based programs.* Prepared for the U.S. Advisory Board on Child Abuse and Neglect. Washington, DC: National Center on Child Abuse and Neglect.

Garbarino, J., Kostelny, K., & Dubrow, N. (1991). *No place to be a child: Growing up in a war zone.* Lexington, MA: Lexington Books.

Garbarino, J., & Sherman, D. (1980). High-risk neighborhoods and high-risk families: The human ecology of child maltreatment. *Child Development, 51,* 188–198.

Garbarino, J., Stocking, H., & Associates. (1980). *Protecting children from abuse and neglect: Developing and maintaining effective support systems for families.* San Francisco: Jossey-Bass.

Halpern, R. (1990a). Community-based early intervention. In S. J. Meisels & J. P. Shonkoff (Eds.), *Handbook of early childhood intervention* (pp. 469–498). New York: Cambridge University Press.

Halpern, R. (1990b). Parent support and education programs. *Children and Youth Services Review, 12,* 285–308.

Halpern, R. (1991). *Neighborhood-based initiatives to address poverty: Lessons from experience.* Chicago: Erikson Institute.

Halpern, R., & Larner, M. (1987). Lay family support during pregnancy and infancy: The Child Survival/Fair Start Initiative. *Infant Mental Health Journal, 8*(2), 130–143.

Hawley, A. (1950). *Human ecology: A theory of community structure.* New York: Ronald Press.

Kagan, S. L., Powell, D. R., Weissbourd, B., & Zigler, E. F. (Eds.). (1987). *America's family support programs: Perspectives and prospects.* New Haven, CT: Yale University Press.

Lauderdale, M., & Savage, C. (1991, June). *Prevention strategies in the neighborhood environment.* Paper presented at the National Center on Child Abuse and Neglect Prevention conference, Washington, DC.

Melton, G. (1992). It's time for neighborhood research and action. *Child Abuse and Neglect, 16*(6), 909–913.

Miller, G. (Ed.). (1989). *Giving children a chance: The case for more effective national policies.* Washington, DC: Center for National Policy.

Musick, J. S., & Stott, F. (1990). Paraprofessionals, parenting and child development: Understanding the problems and seeking solutions. In S. J. Meisels & J. P. Shonkoff (Eds.), *Handbook of early childhood intervention* (pp. 651–667). New York: Cambridge University Press.

Myers-Walls, J. (1992). Natural helping networks: Using local human resources to support families. *Family Resource Coalition Report, 11*(1), 10–11.

Olds, D., & Henderson, C. (1989). The prevention of maltreatment. In D. Cicchetti & V. Carlson (Eds.), *Child maltreatment: Theory and research on the causes and consequences of child abuse and neglect* (pp. 722–763). New York: Cambridge University Press.

Olds, D., Henderson, C., Tatelbaum, R., & Chamberlain, R. (1986). Preventing child abuse and neglect: A randomized trial of nurse home visitation. *Pediatrics, 78,* 65–78.

Pelton, L. (1978). Child abuse and neglect: The myth of classlessness. *American Journal of Orthopsychiatry, 48,* 608–617.

Pelton, L. (1981). *The social context of child abuse and neglect.* New York: Human Sciences Press.

Pelton, L. (1992). *The role of material factors in child abuse and neglect.* Washington, DC: U.S. Advisory Board on Child Abuse and Neglect.

Pfannenstiel, J., & Seltzer, D. (1989). New parents as teachers: Evaluation of an early parent education program. *Early Childhood Research Quarterly, 4*(1), 1–18.

Rosenbaum, J., & Kaufman, J. (1991, August). *Educational and occupational achievements of low income black youth in white suburbs.* Paper presented at the Annual Meetings of the American Sociological Association, Cincinnati, OH.

Sattin, D., & Miller, J. (1971). The ecology of child abuse within a military community. *American Journal of Orthopsychiatry, 41*(4), 675–678.

Thompson, R. (1992). *Social support and the prevention of child maltreatment.* Washington, DC: U.S. Advisory Board on Child Abuse and Neglect.

Unger, D., & Wandersman, A. (1985). The importance of neighbors: The social, cognitive, and affective components of neighboring. *American Journal of Community Psychology, 13*(2), 139–169.

U.S. Advisory Board on Child Abuse and Neglect. (1991). *Creating caring communities: Blueprint for an effective federal policy on child abuse and neglect.* Washington, DC: U.S. Government Printing Office.

Warren, R. (1978). *The community in America.* Boston: Houghton Mifflin.

Weiss, H., & Halpern, R. (1991). *Community-based family support and education programs: Something old or something new?* New York: National Center for Children in Poverty, Columbia University.

Wellman, B. (1979). The community question: The intimate networks of East Yonkers. *American Journal of Sociology, 84,* 1201–1231.

Wilson, W. J. (1987). *The truly disadvantaged.* Chicago: University of Chicago Press.

14

Local Initiatives
in Support of Families

Norman B. Rice

We are all increasingly aware of the essential contribution that
families make to the economic, social, and cultural richness of
the community. Families are the lifeblood of our communities —
the place where dreams are born, children are nurtured, adults
find purpose, and life's challenges are weathered. For better or
for worse, the families we are born into (or choose) greatly influence our sense of our role in the world and our decisions about
whether and how we will contribute to the well-being of the community.

In recent years, government at all levels has struggled to
find its place in relationship to families. Because there is so much
to do to strengthen and support this vast resource, those in
leadership roles can sometimes feel overwhelmed by the magnitude of the task. They hear about promoting "family values"
and wonder what it means in practical terms for setting local
policies and carrying out local initiatives. They worry about the
costs of beginning major programs, the outcomes of which may
be difficult to assess.

But times are tough for American families, and cities and
towns are beginning to pay attention. At the same time that
the problems facing families have increased, state and federal

financial support for families has dwindled. Across all income brackets, families are experiencing serious strains. Cities are seeing at firsthand the impact of more than a decade of declining support for children and families (Center for the Study of Social Policy, 1992).

In recent years, there has been much talk about making traditional family values a high priority for our nation. Little has been done to support and strengthen families or to expand the concept of "family" to include the growing number of households that differ from the traditional two-parent structure. As a result, America risks perpetuating a cycle of defeat, where too many families and children are left permanently out of the mainstream, and where the mainstream does not show an acceptable degree of family well-being.

Cities have many reasons to take the lead in support of families and children, but first they should recognize the extent to which they are already involved in the lives of families. In every city and town in America, the policies and practices of local government affect family life, making it easier or more difficult for families to function. Traditional municipal services — sanitation, police and fire protection — exist to ensure a safe and healthy environment. Zoning and building regulations seek to develop and protect neighborhoods that function well. Parks and recreation departments offer opportunities for children and adults to enjoy leisure time, and sometimes they provide care for children while parents work. Community centers serve as focal points for neighborhoods.

Cities should be more deliberately involved in family support initiatives because they are most likely to reap the benefits of strong families, healthy children, and an active and involved populace. Cities may see those benefits in a stronger economy, safer neighborhoods, and greater citizen participation in the life of the community. Cities know better than any other level of government the consequences of not addressing problems. And while local governments, by comparison with other levels of government, have the most limited capacity to generate revenue to fund services and programs, cities are often in the best position to develop and carry out effective and responsive programs.

If ever the challenges facing families will be met, it will require a greatly expanded role for cities across the nation. No other level of government can respond as effectively, and none has as much to gain from this involvement.

While our system distributes power and responsibilities across the various levels of government in an often confusing and sometimes duplicative manner, the historical role of municipal government has been to ensure the public health and safety. Involvement in activities to support and strengthen families should be viewed as a natural expansion of this role. We can no longer afford to see such involvement as optional. Increasingly, the survival and health of a city will hinge on the quality of life it is able to create and sustain for its families.

A Call for Action

One of the first tasks of a community is to acknowledge, in policy and in practice, that families come in many shapes and sizes. An example of an inclusive definition is this one, from the City of San Francisco's Mayor's Task Force on Family Policy: "Family: A unit of interdependent and interacting persons, related together over time by strong social and emotional bonds and/or ties of marriage, birth, and adoption, whose central purpose is to create, maintain, and promote the social, mental, physical and emotional development and well being of each of its members" (p. 1). Defining the term *family* broadly and inclusively helps address the changing nature of the family structure and suggests a sharing of responsibility for the growth and development of all family members.

In addition to defining the family in broad terms, communities must also develop principles and goals to draw attention to family issues and guide actions. Local government can provide the leadership to begin this kind of community dialogue, and it can set a vision for its own actions across all aspects of government. What is essential is a commitment to all members of the community, regardless of circumstances, and an understanding of the capacity of all families and individuals to contribute.

In Seattle, an interdepartmental team was established to develop family support and development opportunities for action, which included goals and operating principles to guide the city's actions. Among the goals identified by the team were the following (City of Seattle Family Support Team, 1991, p. 1):

> The City shall focus its energy and efforts to improve the quality of life, making Seattle the best possible place for families of all economic levels to live, and shall strengthen its capacity to support a diverse array of families and individuals. The City shall strive to:
>
> 1. Promote physically and emotionally healthy families.
> 2. Assure that families living within our community can meet their basic needs and receive the support necessary to be self-sufficient.
> 3. Assure a safe environment throughout Seattle for families.
> 4. Develop opportunities for families to live, work, play and grow together in a multi-cultural environment that supports and promotes communication among all groups and individuals.
> 5. Work to attract and keep a diverse population in Seattle, which includes families with children, to ensure the city is a viable, dynamic community in the future.
> 6. Promote diversity within Seattle's neighborhoods and support neighborhoods that are economically, ethnically and culturally varied.
> 7. Educate the public, including youth, families and elders, on the changing needs of families.
> 8. Promote partnerships within the community to meet the diverse and changing needs of families.

What would a family-supportive city look like? Every city can set a vision that is truly family-focused: a city where neighborhoods would feel and be safe, and everyone would have access to open space, dynamic community centers, and a wide array of cultural, artistic, and recreational activities; a place where people could easily use public transportation and could work and play in environments that supported a mix of individual and family needs. The workplace would be flexible and family-friendly. People would be able to find housing they could afford, and building and land-use codes would encourage development with families in mind.

In this community, all people would share responsibility for protecting the natural environment, and business involvement in human development would be consistent and supportive. All families would have others who visited and supported them in their efforts to grow and thrive. When family members needed additional help, affordable health care and social services would be readily available.

School and city facilities would be open for community use after school and on weekends. Taking into account the many ways people learn, schools would support the development of every learner. Everyone would have the opportunity to learn skills for entering and returning to the job market. All families would have access to high-quality early childhood development programs, child care, and elder care, as necessary.

In this thriving community, all segments of the population — people of every age, both genders, all levels of ability, and every sexual orientation, race, and cultural background — would participate fully in the decision-making process and would work together to build a caring community.

A vision such as this one includes more than a city could ever hope to realize fully. But it is critical to set an ambitious agenda for supporting families. Without a plan, progress is unlikely. A recent survey by the National League of Cities found that just one in four cities had any kind of formal written policy or plan with regard to families (Born, 1989).

Leadership and Partnership

Even without developing a single new program, every city has the opportunity to make sure its services support rather than hinder families in carrying out their responsibilities. Making sure that city offices and services are available when and where people need them — on weekends and in the evenings, for example, or in neighborhoods instead of in downtown locations — can go a long way toward freeing parents' time to care for their children and participate in community affairs. Revising zoning regulations to allow accessory apartments in neighborhoods where they were previously not allowed can create affordable housing and result in better care for children. In Rockville, Maryland, a homeowner may seek a zoning exception to create an additional apartment in the house he or she occupies. With this kind of change in regulations, grandparents and other family members or caregivers can join a family and permit a more supportive environment for everyone. Cities can revise regulations regarding group homes, family day care, or child-care centers, to make operating these facilities in the community more attractive. Training city staff to recognize and respond to the needs of citizens in their many contacts every day is another way of supporting families without starting new programs.

But municipalities can do much more to create the conditions that allow families to function effectively. By definition, effective family support programs require planning at the level most immediately accessible to those who will use the services and programs. Local thinking is also needed to make sure that state and federal policies and programs make sense. The State of Washington, for example, is now closely watching the development of family support and resource programs at the local level. Washington's Family Policy Initiative is an effort to break down categorical funding arrangements that make it difficult for children and families to receive the services they need. The initiative recognizes the need for a grass-roots, community-based approach, rather than a top-down planning process.

Cities can be laboratories for innovations in programs, partnerships, and new ways of doing business. Local government can set up programs that are flexible and can respond to new or emerging needs. Cities may be able to take risks with funding and program development, risks that many other sectors of the community are afraid to try. Some years ago, for example, the City of Seattle recognized the need for a resource center where families could get information about child care and help with understanding their children's needs. In partnership with a private foundation and United Way of King County, the city set up a model program to test the feasibility of such a center. After a few years, it was clear that the program was viable and effective, and it was spun off as an independent nonprofit agency.

Local governments can form partnerships with local business, school districts, United Way and other charitable organizations, consumers, and the nonprofit service sector. Some of the best new programs for children have resulted from such partnerships. The City of Minneapolis, for example, works with the Minneapolis public schools, the county government, and other agencies in a program to provide comprehensive health services for teenagers in all the city's high schools. A few years ago, Seattle joined with King County government and suburban cities to form a consortium for looking at human services issues across jurisdictions. The partnership is called the Human Services Roundtable, and the members fund a private consultant to staff its decision-making process. One recent initiative was to assess the need for a countywide child-care information and referral system and to make recommendations for action. The assessment showed a high need for such a system and determined that a nonprofit agency should be formed to deliver a comprehensive child-care referral service. Several of the partners contributed funding to the newly formed agency, and smaller programs were folded into it. After only three years, the child-care resource program has expanded to include a comprehensive, countywide child-care referral program, a teen-parent hotline, increased referral information for before- and after-school care, resource information and training for child-care providers, and special training and support groups to promote culturally competent service delivery. The Human Services Roundtable is now developing a plan for a countywide home-visit program similar to Hawaii's Healthy Start Program, which is designed to reach at-risk parents at the time of their child's birth.

By not taking on some of these responsibilities, a city risks having families move to other places. Businesses will follow families out of the city, and new businesses will not find the city attractive. As a city loses its mix of residents, it can easily become a place where only economically disadvantaged families and households without children will live. Cities should continue to find creative ways of rebuilding their basic structures and attracting new services and businesses, all the while keeping an eye on how families are affected by change and growth.

Roles for Local Government

In most communities, the vital role of providing education for children and youth from kindergarten through twelfth grade is carried out by special-purpose districts. City governments, however, can take on the complementary challenge of ensuring that children are safe, healthy, and ready to learn. Across the country, local leaders have taken this challenge to heart by forming partnerships with school districts, business leaders, community members, teachers, and parents. These partnerships play a role in achieving the year-round educational goals of the community. Before- and after-school care, youth counseling and activities, tutoring and mentoring support, and summer activity programs have been developed to complement school services.

As an example of such an effort, shortly after the mayoral election of 1989 in Seattle, the mayor's office joined with other city leaders and school district leaders to sponsor a citywide education summit. In neighborhoods all across the city, people came together to offer ideas on how to strengthen the educational and social support system for families and children. Over two thousand residents pooled their collective wisdom to help the city and the school district begin the challenging task of improving the educational system. The effort led to the passage of a $58 million, seven-year levy for families and education. A major thrust of this and other city efforts has been to build on the strengths of the community. By opening new family support centers, latchkey programs, teen health clinics, and late-night recreation programs, the city has increased its commitment to family-focused services. Since the passage of the levy, the city has continued to build on that commitment by developing its cross-departmental Children and Youth Action Plan, to be implemented over a four-year period.

Family assistance requires more resources, but much can also be accomplished through better coordination of existing programs and resources. Increasingly, the various needs of families and children are interrelated, and so categorical or isolated efforts to assist families are no longer efficient or productive. A better approach would be "a system that cuts across and underlies all of the current categorical service programs. In this approach, support for families would be defined as an overarching social policy goal in itself, and program development would be done in the many, varied ways that could advance this goal. The specific programs that would emerge from this approach could be both free standing or incorporated within current health, social service, mental health, economic security, and education programs, but they would all be instruments of a clear public policy goal to establish more comprehensive supports for family functioning (Center for the Study of Social Policy, 1989, p. 20.)

A city can play either a leadership role or a supportive role in building these kinds of educational and family support partnerships. And the city can take on other roles as well, such as advocate and community leader, resource developer and funder, and planner and coordinator (see Exhibit 14.1). A city can provide technical assistance to community agencies and groups, work to develop strong neighborhoods, and promote economic vitality. Ann Arbor, Michigan, provides child-care scholarships for low-income families and has linked the program to its economic development efforts. A city can promote human rights, develop policies supportive of cultural and racial diversity, and act to enable all its citizens to contribute to and participate in the life of the community.

Whether or not a city takes a strong role in many of these areas, it can set an example as a model employer. Cities in America employ more than 2.5 million people. As a major employer, a city government can test family-supportive work models

Exhibit 14.1. Roles for Local Government.

Model employer
Advocate and community leader
Service deliverer
Resource developer and funder
Technical assistance provider
Planner and coordinator
Neighborhood developer
Economic developer
Policy maker
Public educator/information agent
Promoter of human rights and cultural diversity
Enabler of citizen contribution and participation

---

and policies, including flexible schedules, family-leave policies, part-time positions, child-care tax benefits or subsidies, and many other creative, forward-thinking, family-friendly practices. Each city has an opportunity to demonstrate its commitment to families through its workplace policies. Cities and other employers that have instituted innovative workplace initiatives are discovering that their employees are becoming more loyal and that attendance has improved (Families and Work Institute, 1993).

Barriers to Cities

With barely enough resources to fund such basic services as fire and police protection, politicians may be reticent to consider family support initiatives. More and more, however, they are recognizing the relationship between family concerns and such basic needs. Young people without opportunities for recreation and supervision are more likely to be a problem for police. Children left unattended are more likely to harm themselves or their environment. Lack of resources may be the biggest barrier to local action, but people are also beginning to see that not addressing family needs may result in even greater budget problems. The relationship between healthy families and healthy communities is becoming ever more clear.

Perhaps the biggest obstacle is a sense that the well-being

of children and families is someone else's responsibility — that of federal, state, and county governments or of the families themselves. Traditionally, cities do not have legal responsibility for the child and family programs most familiar to the public — child protection services, family income support, even schools.

Another barrier in some communities is lack of vision on the part of public officials and community leaders. Cities that have seen public safety and "bricks and mortar" as their primary responsibilities sometimes fear making the change to a more child- and family-focused policy framework. But lack of vision and fear of change can put a city in serious jeopardy of losing its rich mix of residents and commerce.

Confounding the fear of change is lack of a clear consensus, even among child advocates, about what should be done. The "family values" discussion of the past few years has fueled concern that families are being used as the scapegoat for failed public policies. There is also concern that the prevention orientation of family support programs may mean a move away from targeting services (a method used to focus resources and programs on those most in need), as well as concern that families with children will become a priority at the expense of other groups, such as single adults or the elderly. Cities often see these barriers as too significant to overcome, or they are content to use the lack of consensus as an excuse for inaction.

When cities and communities do take action, additional problems become apparent. As city officials, community members, and service providers begin the process of building coalitions and collaborative partnerships, they may find it more difficult and time-consuming than they had anticipated. Turf issues, fears about loss of funding, historical disagreements, and the challenges and costs of working together often stand in the way of moving to more collaborative ways of doing business. Coalitions and consensus building may take a great deal of time and energy, but the potential rewards far outweigh the short-term resource drain.

When local government decides to take the lead and chooses to build coalitions, yet another problem surfaces: the political environment encourages politicians and others to look

for quick fixes — single programs for solving complex problems —
but the reality is that individuals and families need different kinds
and levels of support throughout the life cycle. Problems that
develop over many years may take as many years to be resolved.
Changing the way the present system works, and investing in
those changes, may be much more beneficial than starting new
programs. System reform, however, requires significant commitment of resources over a very long time.

After making families a priority, local communities may
get bogged down in the complexity of the systems (government,
health care, education, human services) that need to be changed.
Those working in the public sector are well aware of the difficulty
of changing funding mechanisms and regulations and are even
more aware of how difficult it is to change another public system. The traditional ways of delivering services will need to be
changed, but it is not always clear how to begin the process.
As a result, leaders may become overwhelmed by the complexity and seriousness of the challenges. Concerted effort by many
people will be required to affect how and when services are delivered, how parents and family members will be involved in services, and how working conditions will change. The effort, however, can result in surprising and beneficial results for everyone.

Overcoming Obstacles

Many who have looked at implementing the principles of family support have commented on the need to start addressing issues as close to the family as possible. Local government is in
an ideal position, both to get close enough to families to understand their unique strengths and opportunities and to develop
strategies that will be attractive to people and cost-effective to
carry out.

Cities often have the ability to bring a variety of people
to the table to identify and solve problems. City government can
draw on the expertise of many workers, community agencies,
schools, churches, businesses, and community groups. The special concerns of minority families, and of others who may be isolated from mainstream services, can also be included more easily.

To begin the process of making change, local government can look at its services (such as police and fire protection, or recreation) in new ways and design workable solutions within those systems. Even without starting any new programs, cities can make all their services more accessible to and more supportive of families. By setting an example of a family-supportive work environment, a city can influence other employers to take similar steps.

Getting Started

In advancing a family support agenda, Seattle has learned several lessons, and a number of guidelines have emerged. Political, economic, and other contextual factors do vary from city to city, but these lessons may help inform local-level family support initiatives nationwide.

Begin the process at the beginning. A first step might be to assess the level of family-friendliness in city policies and practices. The opinions of employees and residents can serve as a valuable measure of City Hall's policies and regulations with regard to family needs. A city can ask itself what makes it a good place for families to live. How does each city service help or hinder parents in the task of ensuring their children's well-being?

Do the easy things first, to show success quickly. Making city services more accessible to and supportive of families can include relatively simple changes that have immediate public recognition and impact. For example, changing hours of operation of such key services as libraries and parks can greatly increase availability and convenience.

Gather advice from many people. City departments should strive to involve parents, the elderly, and young people as advisers in planning and reviewing specific city services. Personnel policies and practices should be revisited, with the goal of the city's becoming a model employer. Every sector of the work-place and community should be heard — people of a variety of incomes, racial and ethnic backgrounds, abilities, and ages.

Ask families to participate — and keep asking. There is no such thing as too much community involvement. An advisory group or a commission on children and families may be an effective ve-hicle for fostering such involvement. For example, Seattle's Chil-dren and Youth Commission provides a voice for young people in City Hall. In addition to speaking out on issues of concern to families, the twenty-member volunteer group, which includes youth members, has taken on numerous independent projects, devoting time and energy — the most precious resources — to solv-ing community problems. Seattle's Youth Involvement Network, which was inspired by strong youth-involvement initiatives in cities like New York, creates opportunities for young people to speak out on issues of concern and to participate in solving com-munity problems.

Build a broad community coalition. Input from a range of in-dividuals and groups can contribute to a vision statement sup-ported by the entire community. Most cities have had success-ful planning efforts on land use, transportation, safety, and other important concerns. The same resources and talents can be used in bringing the community together to plan the services and support needed to help families. In 1988, the City of Seattle embarked on a major planning effort, the result of which was the Policy Plan on Children and Youth. With wide participa-tion from the community and assistance from the Children and Youth Commission, the policy plan identified goals and stra-tegic options for city action.

Develop a plan for cooperation across levels and departments. Plan-ning efforts can be expanded when a city joins with other juris-dictions (county and state, especially). For example, city leaders could challenge parks and libraries to work together and create after-school activities for children. Likewise, city leaders could initiate a cross-departmental strategic planning process and de-cide together what steps to take on behalf of children and families.

Find a cause. Initially focusing on a single issue, such as reducing infant mortality or preparing children for school, can help galvanize community interest and involvement. The big picture can be overwhelming.

Identify high-quality community programs, and support them. Government cannot meet every need. Community-based agencies, schools, and other organizations may be able, with the city's support, to expand strong programs. Financial support from local government may help programs leverage other resources or increase program stability.

Pilot some innovative programs. Substantial change generally involves taking risks. Every community includes people with great ideas. Cities can take the lead to demonstrate program effectiveness. For example, Seattle has proudly demonstrated an innovative program in the schools and one at three city sites.

In the Family Support Worker Program, forty-two workers assist children in elementary schools with food, clothing, housing, after-school care, and access to health care and the social services they need. The program, which provides sustained support to many of Seattle's most vulnerable families, is funded by the City of Seattle and the local United Way. Administered by the school district, the Family Support Worker Program has active involvement of the funding partners in hiring, program planning, and evaluation.

As part of the Family Support Center Demonstration Project, funded by the recently passed levy for families and education, the City of Seattle opened three family centers in 1992. The centers are operated by community agencies in partnership with other service providers. The centers are warm, welcoming places where parents and children can find information, advice, support, and opportunities to learn about child development, parenting, and other topics. Local parents may form support groups or initiate other activities, such as family video nights or tutoring programs.

Take responsibility for one issue. A number of years ago, Seattle assumed a leadership role in child care. Local leaders consistently

identify child care as the service most needed by children, and
Seattle is one of many cities that have responded to this need
with child-care programs. The City's Comprehensive Child Development Program subsidizes child care for low-income working
families and provides training, health, nutrition, and other assistance to improve the quality of care for children throughout
the city. The program supports parents' efforts to work or complete training programs, and it ensures that children get high-
quality care.

Recognize your accomplishments. An upbeat, positive approach
to a serious challenge can help a great deal in gathering support. As a community begins to achieve success, recognition
of that success serves both to acknowledge the contributions of
individuals and groups and to spur on additional and increased
commitment to family support efforts.

The future of any city depends on the health and stability of its families. Whether a city will thrive or decline depends
on its capacity to be a place where children can grow and develop into healthy and capable adults, and where a high quality of life is maintained for people at all stages of life.

Government alone cannot guarantee such a capacity. It
can do so only in partnership with the most essential building
block of the community — families. Cities need the strength of
all their citizens to tackle the significant task of reinvesting in
families and building the foundation for a caring community,
one rich in cultural and ethnic diversity.

Even in times of limited resources, increasing demands,
and competing priorities, there is an opportunity to nurture and
support families. Even without new resources, communities can
evaluate and refine policies and practices in ways that support
employees and residents in their roles as members of families.
By reassessing not only what is done but also how it is done,
cities can improve the climate for families.

All over America, cities are beginning to take the lead
through powerful and innovative programs. Several examples

have been offered here to illustrate the diversity of approach. These initiatives are not unique. The possibilities are endless. We have been fortunate in this effort to have people in public service, and throughout the community, with a vision not just of the potential rewards for making such a commitment but also with an understanding of the cost of failing to do so. We are learning and beginning to act on those lessons. That in itself is cause for great hope.

References

Born, C. E. (1989). *Our future and our only hope: A survey of city halls regarding children and families.* Washington, DC: National League of Cities.

Center for the Study of Social Policy. (1989, April). *Public policy and family support and education: Challenges and opportunities.* Paper presented at the Public Policy and Family Support and Education Colloquium, Washington, DC.

Center for the Study of Social Policy. (1992). *The challenge of change: What the 1990 census tells us about children.* Washington, DC: Author.

City of Seattle Family Support Team. (1991, June). *Family support opportunities for action.* Seattle, WA: Author.

Families and Work Institute. (1993). *An evaluation of Johnson & Johnson's work-family initiative.* New York: Author.

Mayor's Task Force on Family Policy. (1990). *Approaching 2000: Meeting the challenges to San Francisco's families.* San Francisco: Author.

□ 15 □

State Government and Family Support

From Marginal to Mainstream

Charles Bruner

State governments often have been referred to as "fifty laboratories of democracy," to signify the richness of social policy experimentation and innovation that exists at the state level. Many if not most federal policies affecting children and families have their roots in earlier successful innovations at the state level.

The 1988 Family Support Act was based in large measure on a number of state welfare reform efforts, especially in Massachusetts, Washington state, and California. Medicaid expansions in 1989 and 1990 ensured greater perinatal coverage for pregnant women and infants and were based on a number of innovative, state-only perinatal programs that had shown the effectiveness of providing more comprehensive and more universal coverage for perinatal care. Most recently, the 1993 Family Preservation and Family Support Act has its antecedents in a large number of ambitious state initiatives to reduce reliance on out-of-home care by providing intensive, short-term family preservation services and to a similar number of state-funded family resource and support centers that have proved popular with state-level policy makers, the communities receiving support to establish those centers, and the residents who use them.

This innovation among states is expected to continue and

338

recently has received public support and encouragement from the federal government. President Clinton's experience as governor of Arkansas has made him sensitive to the need for flexibility in federal legislation and policy and the need to invite state-level innovations by making federal policies more flexible and responsive to states' adaptations.

The same innovation and experimentation that have occurred at the state level for addressing specific family and child issues — economic self-sufficiency under welfare reform, infant and child health under perinatal care, and avoidance of out-of-home placements of children through family preservation — are now being undertaken to achieve more general family well-being under family support. Governors and state legislatures are establishing new funding streams targeted to family centers for adolescent parents, prevention-oriented home-visiting services for families at risk for child abuse, school-community collaborations supporting family involvement, and parent-education services to strengthen the role of parents as first teachers.

Family Support and State Innovation: Rhetoric and Reality

Programmatically, centers and home-visiting services adhering to family support principles and designed to focus on prevention or investment, rather than on remediation or therapy, have been established or supported at the state level in a variety of professional agencies. They have become a part of some school reform efforts, as is the case with Kentucky's family resource and youth service centers. They have become a part of public health, as is the case with Hawaii's Healthy Start program. They have been free-standing, community-based new programmatic efforts with their own developing organizational bases, as is the case with Maryland's family support centers and their intermediary organization, Friends of the Family. They have been incorporated into demonstration efforts within welfare reform, as is the case with Iowa's Family Development and Self-Sufficiency Demonstration Grant Program. And they have been part of a state commitment to early childhood education and parent support, as is the case with Missouri's Parents as Teachers and Minnesota's Early Childhood Home Education Program. Finally, they have been established as new partnerships between the public and private sectors of government, as is the case with Illinois' Ounce of Prevention Fund programs (Bruner & Carter, 1991).

In addition to specific programmatic support and innovation, family support values themselves have been incorporated into state authorizations for existing programs within public health, public welfare, education and special education, child welfare, child mental health, and juvenile justice. State agency missions have been redrafted to reflect values associated with family support, incorporating the language of family-centered, individually tailored, community-based, preventive, and comprehensive services.

Increasingly, state policy makers recognize that the public sees families under increasing stress and wants government services to be less bureaucratic and more connected to the family's needs for supportive home and neighborhood environments. Further, state policy makers see the fragmented and categorical public service systems they operate as often working at cross-purposes to family support values, both by assuming a deficit-oriented approach to families and by treating individual problems in isolation and not as part of a family structure.

Adding to the momentum, the Council of Governors' Policy Advisors (CGPA) has supported year-long planning processes for key state and community leaders in fifteen states on family policy, and these leaders have taken substantial time out of their busy schedules to prepare family policy directions for their states. Uniformly, the results of these state planning teams have been a greater appreciation of the need for cross-system approaches to meeting family needs, as families define them, and of the need for public institutions to collaborate, both with one another and with community organizations in providing services that are more flexible, comprehensive, preventive, and family-friendly. Corporate leaders have been partners in many of these teams and have assumed leadership in their own right on behalf of state initiatives for children and families, adding both a "bottomline" perspective and a new ally for committing resources to meeting child and family needs. Specific state initiatives, as well as new operating philosophies, have resulted from the CGPA process (Chynoweth & Dyer, 1991).

At the rhetorical level in many states, it is clear that family support principles have come of age. Policy makers want to value and validate families. State politicians now seem almost as eager to wrap their arms around families as they always have been to kiss babies.

Beyond the rhetoric, however, there is much work to be done in the states to embrace family support principles at the practice level. At the same time that family policy statements are being developed and pilot family resource centers are being funded, out-of-home placements of children into foster care, mental health facilities, and juvenile detention and training schools have risen (American Public Welfare Association, 1993). The state posture toward youth gangs and drug rings often seems neither family-focused nor supportive of the belief that "all children can change," involving harsher sentencing and more waivers to adult court.

In addition to positive reforms, states also have taken the lead in more punitive welfare reform measures, designed to require families in public assistance to meet "performance standards" to receive assistance for their children, and designed to impose time limitations on receipt of public assistance. At the same time that policy makers are seeking to provide two-parent families of very young children with more "choice" about staying at home to care for their very young children (one of the rationales for adoption and expansion of the federal earned income tax credit), some state welfare systems are opting to tell single parents that they must join the work force when their infants are as young as three months old. There has been little discussion of the impact of such state welfare decisions on parent-child relationships or on child development, even though welfare policies affect some of the nation's most vulnerable families and children. The question is seldom debated of how a poor, single parent who works forty hours a week at minimum wage will have the energy to cook, clean, and clothe her toddler and still experience those precious moments of "quality time" that are so important to her and to her child's life. It is unlikely, at the least, that the government picking up child-care expenses and providing some form of medical coverage will address these fundamental needs for family support.

As this discussion suggests, the strong rhetorical emphasis on family and family support, and its reflection in demonstration programs and pilot "prevention" initiatives, does not necessarily extend to serving the most vulnerable families and the most troubled and troubling youth, who are found in more categorical and traditional service systems financed and regulated by the state.

In short, the fragmented system of services to families and children, the policy makers who have developed it, and the administrators who direct it—an amalgam composed of health, child welfare, education, juvenile justice, and mental health services, among others—all continue to reflect fragmented thinking about families and family policy. To date, with very few exceptions,[1] services incorporating family support principles have been marginal additions to a fragmented mainstream service system that does not espouse those values.

Challenges to State-Level Family Support

As the previous discussion concludes, it is clear that family support programs and the principles they embody have established a level of visibility and recognition at the state level that did not exist a decade ago. Moreover, state planning efforts and demonstration projects have been constructed to hasten the spread of these principles in two ways: through creation and expansion of new programs and services designed to embody these attributes, and through planning and fiscal incentives to incorporate these principles within (and across) mainstream systems.

The State Role in the Spread of Family Support

At some point, if family support principles and programs are to move beyond modest expansions of small-scale pilot or demonstration efforts, toward becoming universal, states must see the centrality of family support principles and programs to meeting the needs of children and families and improving child outcomes. As they have in other fields and practices, states will need to be the innovators and laboratories in developing family support practices to a level where they have the power to produce a systemwide impact on outcomes for children and families. Over the last decade, in tight fiscal times, programmatic expansions have been most likely to occur at the state level only when they have been specifically tied to producing results that benefit society's "bottom line."[2]

In fact, the challenge to the family support movement at the state level is to move, within at least a few pioneering states, from a breadth of appreciation for the potential value of more people doing family support work (as embodied in demonstration family support centers) toward a depth of commitment to providing such services, at least in a fairly large geographical area, for all families who can benefit from them. Such efforts at going to scale[3] are needed to test the true potential of family support for revitalizing families and children in the context of their communities, and especially in the context of poor neighborhoods. They also are needed to explore the potential for family support principles themselves to become more embedded within mainstream service systems.

Challenges to Realizing Family Support in the States

New efforts to expand family support at the state level will face multiple challenges. Not all the challenges of going to scale can be anticipated; but some, predicated on past experience, can be expected. This section discusses eight challenges in particular that pioneering state initiatives must face and build paths to overcome.

Many if not most current state programmatic family support initiatives are not tied to any vision for system reform, but a few have explicitly sought to define themselves as moving, over time, beyond a "demonstration" basis to becoming beachheads for broader system reforms and becoming pathfinders for eventual jurisdictionwide implementation. Among these are the state efforts supported under the Pew Charitable Trusts (Center for Assessment and Policy Development, 1991),[4] the Annie E. Casey Foundation's state-level service design efforts,[5] and some purely state-designed efforts. For these efforts, providers, advocates, and state and community policy makers eventually must seek to identify and address a variety of challenges in going to scale that do not necessarily arise in efforts to establish small-scale demonstration sites. These implementation challenges are fundamental ones, challenges that have been variously characterized as "reproducing the unique," "institutionalizing the deinstitutional," "mass producing warm, human interactions," and "moving from marginal to mainstream" (Bruner, 1991). As these characterizations suggest, the challenges of going to scale are more than quantitative. While individual, exemplary, community-based programs may coexist with other services, do demonstrable good, and even become sources of pride within neighborhoods and communities, universalizing them creates challenges different from the challenges faced in their initial creation and development.

Some of the issues and challenges that seem most important to address with state initiatives that have pretensions of going to scale are described below. They may seem formidable. They are not raised to deter action, however, but rather to further thinking on how to take effective steps and learn needed lessons in the innovation process. It will probably take a combination of insight and naïveté among states taking this pioneering role to truly further the adoption of family support principles and practices within publicly financed service systems.[6]

1. *Determining the size of the programmatic commitment needed (defining what it means to go to scale).* One of the biggest challenges confronting state efforts is in determining the level of commitment to family support programs that is needed. As stated earlier, moving from marginal to mainstream, or going to scale, means that family support services are broadly available and without barriers (geographical, cultural, or psychological) to ac-

cess. It means that when families need more comprehensive services and support than the program can provide, those are available as well. It means that the family support program can spend enough time with a family to ensure that the family's needs for support are met. And it means that the family support program provides significant outreach, in order to engage families.

This requires states to identify or define the intended population for family support services within the defined geographical service area and then provide sufficient resources to effectively serve that population. Hopefully, this means expanding the services beyond a small geographical area, to become communitywide or statewide services. It remains a fact, however, that most of the small, community-based initiatives so frequently cited as exemplary in their approach to families operate at well below this level, even within the neighborhoods they serve.

As an illustration, the widely and deservedly praised Beethoven Project in Chicago — a program that seeks to provide comprehensive services and support to families with children from the prenatal period to school age, in one of the nation's most distressed public housing projects — serves approximately 150 of the 900 families living in six of the forty-two high-rise buildings that comprise the project. It provides parent advocates, who give support to those families and broker other public services. The Beethoven Project also provides preschool programs and infant care, as well as some health services. Its total budget is approximately $1.5 million annually. It has a reputation as one of the country's most intensive, comprehensive, and ambitious programs, most nearly at scale within the area it serves.[7]

In fact, however, there are easily an additional 150 families within the six high-rise buildings that meet Beethoven's definition of service need and that could be recruited to participate, if Beethoven had the resources to serve them. There are waiting lists for its child-care services, and it sometimes cannot secure substance-abuse treatment slots, mental health counseling services, and other social services from community providers to meet the needs of its clients. Even in the six high-rise buildings it serves, the Beethoven Project is not universally available, despite its $1.5 million budget. While the Beethoven Project is an ambitious undertaking, and while much can be learned from its experiences in service design and working with families, it cannot meet many of the challenges that pioneering states need to face as they seek to move family support from the margins to the mainstream. The first challenge that states and participating communities may face, however, is simply in fairly defining the magnitude of the commitment they will need to make, at least if they hope to truly test the power of family support programs in helping improve outcomes for children.[8]

2. *Effectively targeting services for maximum impact.* A second challenge that states will face is in effectively targeting services to reach the families for which the services are intended, particularly those families for which support can provide the greatest impact. Exemplary community-based family support programs almost invariably find that they become sought-after by community residents. They create their own loyal clientele. They also recognize that if they continue to reach out to new residents and clients, they will have difficulty serving those with whom they already are involved. Their orientation to inclusiveness militates against their denying services to the marginally needy in order to seek out those in greater need.

Effectively focusing necessary services on those most in need — who also may be the most likely to be suspicious or initially uninterested in receiving support — represents a fundamental challenge and one that also, if not handled carefully by programs, can change the philosophy of the program itself. The goal is to serve such families, but in a normative and not a therapeutic sense.[9] At the same time, however, these harder-to-reach families are likely to be high-opportunity families — families that the new service philosophy of family support may still be able to reach and help, but that the mainstream service system has abandoned as unreachable.

If one of the goals is to produce an impact on child and family outcomes on a systemwide basis, clarity in approach and effective targeting of support is needed and probably requires development of a recruitment strategy that is successful in engaging those who are most socially isolated and distrustful. This may require a discipline in approach that focuses resources where they are most needed, rather than simply where the demand is most clearly articulated. With limited exceptions, most demonstration programs funded in part or in whole by states, after their start-up period, simply have not placed priority on developing techniques to enlist those most difficult to serve. The result is that much remains to be learned about what practices are most effective in engaging those families.

Moreover, to the extent that these families are recruited and do participate, they may change the character of the programs themselves. There is a distinct tension between serving those within even a very poverty-stricken neighborhood's network of mainstream families and also recruiting and serving those at or beyond the margins of what is considered generally acceptable by neighborhood norms.

3. *Ensuring access to needed outside services.* Exemplary, small-scale, community-based programs often develop considerable skill in networking with other, more mainstream public service organizations and securing for their clients a wide variety of other community services and support. If the exemplary program serves only a small portion of the potential number of clients for these other services, other public organizations may be able to accommodate the program's requests and demands, although these accommodations may come at the expense of serving other persons within the community. Exemplary family support programs may be successful in securing housing, drug treatment, training programs, Big Brothers or Big Sisters, and health clinic appointments because of their skill in being first in line and omnipresent.

As such programs expand toward scale, however, they are likely to lose much of this ability, as they now must compete against one another for inadequate outside resources. Again, the Beethoven Project is likely to be more effective in brokering public services outside its program for a large portion of its clients when it serves only 150 families in six high-rise buildings. If it served 2,100 families in all forty-two buildings in the housing project, its problems in securing slots would be much greater than they are today.

4. *Maintaining program quality and integrity.* When programs seek to expand to new locations or to expand within existing sites, they face challenges in maintaining some of their basic program features. The dramatic programmatic expansion required to truly test the power of family support in affecting outcomes on a systemic basis risks destroying one of family support's distinguishing features for families: its openness and intimacy, where everyone is on a first-name basis. As programs and agencies grow in size, they face challenges in retaining this sense of intimacy. Further, their inventors and leaders may not have the skills to manage larger organizational structures, however successful they were in designing the more intimate ones.[10] If they seek to expand through moving to new locations under new administration and leadership, the élan that made their flagship efforts successful may not be easily transported. Reconstructing this programmatic vision is difficult and involves the creation of the same type of staff and community involvement and ownership as existed in the original program and location.

Individual programs may demonstrate program efficacy, the ability of a well-constructed program to achieve results. To show program effectiveness, however, requires that a programmatic approach achieve results in a world where competent (but not exceptional) management can be assumed. Even when certain small-scale programs do show efficacy, expansion of these programs, with retention of the core elements that made them efficacious (often themselves the result of exceptional, dedicated staff), has proved to be quite problematic.[11]

5. *Maintaining program intensity and comprehensiveness (defining need for diverse families).* In one of the most common examples of "model drift" and program dilution, an exemplary program is discovered and then asked to expand and serve additional families. Moving from focused to more universal coverage frequently results in a much greater expansion in the number of

families served than in the amount of resources provided to serve them. One of the best illustrations of program expansion that consciously has sought to resist this tendency to dilute is family preservation services targeted to families at imminent risk for out-of-home placement. At the outset, the Edna McConnell Clark Foundation supported states in establishing and expanding family preservation services, but only as a very specific intervention, dependent on extremely small caseloads in order to produce results. Caseload size was seen as one of the critical elements distinguishing intensive family preservation services from other intervention strategies, and a reason for family preservation's effectiveness (Barthel, 1992). The ability of intensive family preservation services to make this distinction was based, at least in part, on its definition of a very focused target population: those families at imminent risk of having their children removed from them to out-of-home care.

As family support programs serve their focused populations, more diverse than for family preservation but often including those who are among the most socially vulnerable, the actual reach a family support program can have and still be effective with the families it serves needs to be established. All families may deserve some support, but some clearly need more intensive, comprehensive, and long-term support than others. At the same time, the natural tendency for workers is to provide help and support to those most willing and eager to receive it (precisely those who might be most likely to secure it for themselves even without the assistance of a family support program), which may be a very different set of families from those for whom the opportunity to "add value" by publicly funded family support is greatest. Experiences from such programs as the Beethoven Project, Hawaii's Healthy Start Program, and Iowa's Family Development and Self-Sufficiency Program suggest that the number of socially vulnerable families a single worker can effectively serve is quite small.[12]

6. *Moving from select to standard sites.* In addition to programmatic leadership and vision, most exemplary family support programs can point to a hospitable political climate as a

component of their success. Most demonstration or pilot programs select their sites precisely because the political climate and the leadership basis at the neighborhood and community level appear to exist or be capable of development. In broadly expanding family support, however, it is not possible to select only the most propitious sites. At the beginning, it may be well to "let one hundred flowers blossom," but as pioneering states move to incorporate family support broadly within their communities, they face new challenges, both in providing support to ensure that the conditions for the growth of the flowers exist and in setting standards for ensuring that efforts in practice adhere to family support principles and operate effectively. Neither of these tasks is an easy one, and both challenge the current way that states generally relate to communities.

7. *Addressing critical issues when program change means system change.* Ultimately, the family support program philosophy is at fundamental variance with many of the mores and practices within mainstream service systems. At some point when programs move from the margins to the mainstream, these new programs and their practices are likely to reach a critical mass that challenges the way existing systems serve families. If services sufficiently empower families, the families themselves will expect services from mainstream institutions — schools, social welfare agencies, employment offices, police departments, city hall — that are similarly respectful and empowering. The reaction of these institutions to such challenges to their authority has at least one recent historical referent that deserves study: the reaction to "maximum feasible participation" in the 1960s (Lehman, 1988).

In going to scale, it may be impossible to avoid system reform issues, even if those were not explicitly a part of the effort at the outset. The state will be faced with challenges of breaking down categorical and professional boundaries within its own regulatory and financing systems. In short, state efforts to go to scale are likely to fundamentally challenge the way the state does business in other mainstream service systems and the manner in which the state treats families, neighborhoods, and local governance structures in these systems.

8. *Designing new paradigms for evaluations of outcomes and impacts.* One of the strongest forces behind changing the current configuration of systems serving children and families is the recognition of the inability of the current system to produce good outcomes for a large number of children. Rhetorically, there is an emphasis on moving from a process-driven system to an outcome-driven one, with accountability measured on the basis of the "bottom line" for society. At the same time, however, a flexible, individualized, family-centered service strategy is likely to produce different outcomes for each of the different families it serves.

A first challenge in fairly evaluating such reform efforts is to develop an evaluation strategy that captures the very different changes that families make in the process of growth. Too often, evaluators tell programs, "I know that's what you do, but that's not what I measure," which results in evaluations that fail to examine whether such flexible, family-centered, individualized programs meet their own goals. Evaluation methodologies are only beginning to be adopted that take a broader perspective in measuring program impact than traditionally has been taken (Weiss & Jacobs, 1988; Weiss & Greene, 1992).

A second challenge in constructing an evaluation system relates to how family support services, designed to be inclusive and based in the neighborhood and the community, can be fairly evaluated, even when outcomes have been defined. Since these initiatives are based in part on their inclusiveness and their becoming a vital part of the neighborhood, as well as on their providing services to individual families, they deserve to be evaluated on the basis of their neighborhood, community, and individual impacts. Randomized trials, frequently cited as the only true way to determine program efficacy, violate one of the tenets of family support programs themselves: to be open and inclusive. In effect, this means that some states, at least in selected communities, must be pioneers in expanding family support services to scale, simply in order to fairly assess their capacity to affect outcomes for children and families at the societal level.

These evaluation issues are important because, increasingly, states are mandating evaluations of new services and pressing for outcome-based accountability systems. Unless this is done sensitively and in a very sophisticated manner — recognizing the many difficulties and complexities inherent in demonstrating an intervention's success in producing measurable changes on such multicausal outcomes as school performance, infant health, and social adjustment (Bruner, 1993) — evaluation runs the risk of proving a null hypothesis for some very promising initiatives. Both in capturing individualized program impacts and in assessing communitywide impacts, states must recognize that evaluation designs need to construct new tools of measurement and new approaches to evaluation itself.

The Next Step

The challenges facing pioneering states that seek to take the necessary next step in developing and testing the power of family support, both as a service for families and as a philosophy in serving families, are not separate and distinct but rather very interconnected. However daunting, they are challenges that cannot be avoided. They are the important issues looming on the horizon, if family support truly is to move beyond its perception as a marginal "add on" to the existing service system. It is critical that the potential for state-supported family support programs be viewed as involving more than isolated pilot programs that, from a political perspective, satisfy some constituencies and, from a programmatic perspective, may do some good.

   If the family support movement is to move forward, some states and their communities must take the lead in addressing these issues by moving from the margins to the mainstream. The federal government can play a leadership role in encouraging such actions, and many of the issues addressed here must first be played out at the community level, but the state level is where many of these challenges must be met and addressed head-on. Ultimately, it will take the commitment of states to ensure that the development of family support programs produces a robust, inclusive, and comprehensive family support system that itself will create the necessary demand for the development of more integrated and responsive services across all child- and family-serving systems. Even the most robust family centers cannot be wholly effective with the families they serve unless those families experience the same forms of support within other statewide publicly financed service systems — schools, welfare offices, health provider communities, and social service agencies. The challenge and opportunity facing state governments is to truly envision family support programs as part of the mainstream service system, accessible to all and with sufficient resources to press for needed changes in other systems as well.

Notes

1. Kentucky's family resource and youth service centers represent one of the broadest-based state initiatives in this respect, but the level of financial support provided for individual family resource and youth service centers is small. In some communities, it has proved to be a catalyst for leveraging resources from other systems, but state-level support alone does not provide any guarantee that centers will be able to provide the needed support to the families they are designed to serve. The same holds for such other statewide initiatives as Missouri's Parents as Teachers and Minnesota's Early Childhood Home Education Program. There are a number of valuable lessons that may be gleaned from some of these efforts, however. For a discussion of five exemplary statewide initiatives, describing the challenges to achieving such reforms on a statewide basis, see Bruner and Perrin (1993).

2. As noted earlier, over the last decade state policy makers have used the few new discretionary state funds available to them (or have redirected funds from existing programs and services) primarily for programs that could argue effectively for their long-term social-cost benefits. Perinatal health care programs were developed and funded on the basis of studies and simulations suggesting that, for every dollar invested in prenatal care, three dollars could be saved in later neonatal intensive care expenditures. Early childhood education programs were sold on the basis of the

results from the Perry Preschool Program and other high-quality early childhood education programs that had been studied. Family preservation services were adopted for the promise they showed in reducing more costly out-of-home placements. While the actual programs developed through state support did not always adhere to the models studied in the research, and while the research itself was not always definitive or methodologically exact, the fact remains that state policy makers not only voiced but also truly believed that the programs they developed not only would help families but also would lower societal costs for later care and treatment. For one delineation of these studies, see Select Committee on Children, Youth, and Families (1990).

3. As used here, *going to scale* means implementing, within a sufficiently large jurisdiction to encounter most obstacles to reform, a new service strategy, reaching a significantly large portion of its intended population to have the capacity to test the effectiveness of that strategy in improving outcomes on a systemwide basis. This definition is adapted from a Wingspread Conference convened in March 1993 by the National Center for Service Integration (National Center for Service Integration, 1993).

4. The Pew Charitable Trusts initiative is a ten-year partnership between the foundation and three states to design a system of inclusion for families with young children that is based on the availability of family support centers within neighborhoods that themselves are linked to any and all other needed systems of support for those families and their children. In the first years of the initiative, the states are expected to work with at least two communities that are substantially affected by poverty. An extensive set of materials explaining the initiative and describing strategies for reform is available through the Center for Assessment and Policy Development (Center for Assessment and Policy Development, 1991).

5. The Annie E. Casey Foundation has been a pioneer in seeking state-level system reform by using different entry

points into the service system and currently is operating initiatives in state-level child welfare reform (in Maryland, and with the Clark Foundation in Iowa, Missouri, and Tennessee), child mental health, family foster care, juvenile detention, and adolescent pregnancy prevention, as well as participating with a number of states around their own agendas.

6. In *The Golden Notebook*, by Doris Lessing (1962), one character refers to "the power of naïveté"—the progress that is possible if one goes into a situation without the baggage of conventional wisdom. In breaking paradigmatic thinking, leadership coupling naïveté with insight may move farthest in achieving change.

7. The Beethoven Project was used as the basis for the development of the federal government's Comprehensive Child Development Program Initiative, now operating in thirty sites around the country as demonstration projects of comprehensive, community-based family support programs (Hubbell et al., 1991).

8. One of the failings of many evaluations of family programs is that they define outcomes that the individual programs, however effective they may be at achieving their own goals, have no hope of demonstrating any impact on. If the goal of an initiative is truly to produce an impact on outcomes at the systemic level, then it must reach a sufficient portion of its intended population to affect outcomes systemwide. Since family support programs are based on an inclusive orientation to families that helps build neighborhood as well as family ownership of the programs, evaluations are based on individual family outcomes.

9. One of the powers of family support programs is that they characterize themselves not as interventions addressing the deficiencies of families but as part of a normative system of support for families. If family support programs become referral sources from other agencies and institutions, they also may become labeled by those in their neighborhoods and communities as treatment or welfare programs, and not as broadly inclusive loci of support.

10. In fact, the attributes that make people successful inventors often do not serve well to produce programmatic expansions, as the diffusion-of-innovation literature suggests.
11. Medical research makes clear distinctions between the efficacy and the effectiveness of an intervention. The more complicated the intervention, the more problematic it is to assume that efficacy in a highly controlled environment can be translated into effectiveness in the real world. For this reason, increasing emphasis is being placed on how processes and organizational structures — as well as specific programmatic elements — can be institutionalized in furthering family support. For an interesting discussion of this subject, see Carl and Stokes (1991).
12. Generally, caseloads of fifteen to twenty are seen by workers as ideal, with a recognition that within such caseloads there must be a mix of families that need only very occasional contact and those who need more intensive support (Bruner & Berryhill, 1992).

References

American Public Welfare Association. (1993). *Characteristics of children in substitute and adoptive care.* Washington, DC: Author.

Barthel, J. (1992). *For children's sake: The promise of family preservation.* New York: Edna McConnell Clark Foundation.

Bruner, C. (1991). Is change from above possible? State-level strategies for supporting street-level services. *TEAM: Early Adolescent Magazine, 5*(4), 29–39.

Bruner, C. (1993). *Notes on the role of outcomes in selling service system reforms.* Occasional Paper No. 1: Issues in Developing Comprehensive, Community-Based Service Systems. Des Moines, IA: Child and Family Policy Center.

Bruner, C., & Berryhill, M. (1992). *Making welfare work.* Des Moines, IA: Child and Family Policy Center.

Bruner, C., & Carter, J. (1991). *Family support and education: A holistic approach to school readiness.* Denver: National Conference of State Legislatures.

Bruner, C., & Perrin, J. (1993). *Going to scale: Developing com-*

prehensive state strategies to improve infant and child health. Des Moines, IA: Child and Family Policy Center.

Carl, J., & Stokes, G. (1991). Ordinary people, extraordinary organizations. *Nonprofit World, 9*(4–6), parts 1–3; (4), 8–12; (6) 21–26; (5) 18–26.

Center for Assessment and Policy Development. (1991). *The children's initiative: Making systems work.* Design document for the Pew Charitable Trusts. Bala Cynwyd, PA: Author.

Chynoweth, J. K., & Dyer, B. (1991). *Strengthening families.* Washington, DC: Council of Governors' Policy Advisors.

Hubbell, R., et al. (1991). *Comprehensive child development program: A national family support demonstration.* Washington, DC, and Bethesda, MD: CSR, Incorporated, and Information Technology International.

Lehman, N. (1988). The unfinished war. *Atlantic Monthly,* December 1988, pp. 38–45ff.

Lessing, D. (1962). *The golden notebook.* New York: Simon & Schuster.

National Center for Service Integration. (1993). *Proceedings of the Wingspread Conference.* Falls Church, MD: Author.

Select Committee on Children, Youth, and Families, U.S. House of Representatives. (1990). *Opportunities for success: Cost-effective programs for children update, 1990.* Washington, DC: U.S. Government Printing Office.

Weiss, H. B., & Greene, J. (1992). An empowerment partnership for family support and education programs and evaluations. *Family Sciences Review, 5*(1, 2), 131–149.

Weiss, H. B., & Jacobs, F. H. (Eds.). (1988). *Evaluating family programs.* Hawthorne, NY: Aldine.

Family Support
on the Federal Policy Agenda

Frank Farrow

This chapter describes an approach to developing federal policy that promotes family resource and support programs and principles. Until recently, such a discussion would have seemed unrealistic. The interest, energy, and innovation that have fueled the growth of family resource programs in the past decade have been concentrated almost exclusively at the local and state levels. Locally, thousands of programs emerged, not as the result of policy mandates but because of parents' own efforts and the work of community groups and nonprofit agencies. In the middle to late 1980s, a handful of state initiatives demonstrated that family resource and support principles could lead to politically visible, programmatically effective policies at the state level. (Missouri's Parents as Teachers effort, Maryland's Friends of the Family and family support centers, and Minnesota's Early Childhood and Family Education Program were early examples of strong state initiatives.)

Explicit federal recognition of family resource and support programs is more recent, however. In 1991, as part of Head Start reauthorization legislation, two small-scale initiatives were added in federal statute. A clearinghouse for family resource and support programs was funded through the Department of

Health and Human Services (DHHS), and authorization was created for a federal program to develop state networks of family resource and support programs. (The state network program, although authorized in federal fiscal year 1991, first received an appropriation in FFY 1993.) These legislative accomplishments have now been followed with passage of broader legislation, as part of the Omnibus Budget Reconciliation Act of 1993 (H.R. 2264), which provides funding to states for improvements in child welfare programs. It requires states to establish family support services, defined as "community based services to promote the well-being of children and families designed to increase the strength and stability of families . . . to increase parents' competence and confidence in their parenting abilities . . . and otherwise to enhance child development" (Section 431(a)(2)).

These stirrings of federal legislative interest in family resource and support programs may prove to be either first steps toward sustained, coherent federal policy in this area or merely superficial recognition of a currently popular service delivery trend. Which of these courses prevails depends on at least three factors:

- The development of a *policy framework* for defining family resource and support at the federal level, which is consistent and cuts across agency and jurisdictional boundaries
- A short-term and longer-range *federal strategy* for family resource and support, which matches the federal role to the evolving nature of family resource programs and policy at the state and local levels
- *Deeper levels of conceptualization, greater program experience, and more extensive evaluation* by the proponents of family resource principles and programs, so that the field can deliver on the expectations engendered by new federal policy and in turn generate the knowledge necessary to make the case for strong federal policy

This chapter addresses each of these issues. It suggests guidelines for incorporating family resource and support principles into federal policy and proposes a series of specific family-supportive federal action steps. At this early stage, the need is for discussions about federal policy in this area to become clearer and more concrete. On the assumption that it is useful to present an agenda with which others can argue, this chapter proposes one and invites others to propose theirs.

Policy Framework

Any consideration of federal policy for family resource and support principles and programs must first address the question of what family support is. This is the question most frequently asked by congressional staff and federal administrators, and its answer will determine much about future policy directions.

For the purpose of establishing a federal policy framework, the answer has three parts. Family support comprises the following elements:

1. The *underlying premise* that all families need support, and that all communities should and can support parents in their parenting roles.
2. A series of *principles* about how supportive resources for families are provided most effectively, which include parent ownership and involvement in programs; a partnership arrangement between family members and any program in which they participate; valuing of informal supports as well as formal services; flexibility in program design, based on community needs; and a unifying principle of respect for others — their diversity and unique strengths — that pervades all aspects of program design and operation
3. *Programs, policies, and systems* that are based on this premise, incorporate these principles, and are directed toward three goals: building parental skills; connecting families with the resources of the communities in which they live; and promoting, in partnership with parents, the full and healthy development of children

If this definition is accepted, it will suggest ways in which federal policy should and should not develop. Let us start with the "should nots."

Federal policy in this area must not become categorical, linked only to a single domain (whether that is the school system or a human service system) or narrow programmatic focus. Stating this, of course, is tantamount to saying that policy in this arena must follow a different course than for most other education or human service policies. At issue is whether policy around family resource and support initiatives can develop in a fashion that retains these programs' unique benefits to neighborhoods and communities, or whether this will become one more layer of an already complex, rigidly categorized, and often unresponsive service system.

Family resource and support programs are at their strongest in local communities when they are not the exclusive property of any one professional field but are able to respond to all parents and to diverse needs and are part of a network of informal supports and formal services that, together, assist parents and support children's healthy development. Programs' ability to span bureaucratic boundaries, and to be embedded within (not imposed on) local communities, is what gives them their appeal and power for parents.

Federal policy will undercut these strengths if it seeks to make family resource and support principles and programs the exclusive domain of any one system, whether that is the child welfare, public welfare, mental health, health care, housing, education, or employment and training system. (Family resource programs are now being discussed, somewhat proprietarily, in the context of federal legislation in most of these areas.) Similarly, the impact of these programs will be reduced if they become the province of only one of the congressional committees that have jurisdiction over health, human services, and education issues. If that occurs, the likelihood is that family resource initiatives will be identified as narrowly targeted to a limited range of families and problems.

The appeal of a narrowly programmatic approach to family resource programs poses the most immediate legislative danger. For example, as the popularity and the reputations of specific state-level family resource initiatives increase, the temptation is to introduce legislation at the federal level to replicate particular program models. Members of Congress justifiably take pride (and gain political benefit) from promoting funding nationally for their states' forms of family resource programs. In the normal course of events, the expected outcome within a few years would be one or more national mandates to replicate a certain "brand name" of family resource program.

If this approach prevails, an opportunity will be lost. The power of the premise and the principles underlying the family resource field will have fallen short of its potential. Rather than introducing genuinely new elements (and a new way of thinking) into the human service and education fields, this approach would propagate only another specific program. In the long run, this is not a favor to states, to communities, or to neighborhood programs themselves. Local communities would once again have to fit their needs into a specific program model, rather than customizing federal resources around the needs of individual communities. Further, at this early stage of family resource program development, this approach stifles innovation. Several states' models for family resource initiatives are indeed admirable, but none is fully developed, and none sets itself up as the exemplar for all others.

To avoid these pitfalls, federal policy should follow two major directions. First, the long-range goal should be to infuse the underlying premise of family support and its accompanying principles into a wide range of federal funding sources, particularly the entitlement statutes that are the foundations of our nation's human service and education systems. Federal policy should reorient the major expenditures of federal funds in a way that reflects and incorporates these principles. As examples, federally funded income-support programs should encourage funding of the family-supportive approaches that have been shown to help families move toward self-sufficiency. Federal child welfare policy should encourage family-supportive approaches and directions whenever possible, not only in preventive programming but also in the so-called traditional child welfare programs (protective services, foster care, and adoption). Federal health care reform should include a series of family support provisions that can help ensure that federal financing for health care strengthens families' own caregiving capacities, rather than undercutting them. The goal, over time, is to fuel the large engines of federal funding with family-supportive ideas and orientations, not just to have family resource initiatives as the "bells and whistles" of federal policy, affecting few communities and having little impact on how resources are made available to families.

Second, federal support for family resource initiatives should be structured in a way that promotes state, local, and parental ownership, knowledge, and responsibility for family supportive programming, rather than undercutting it. Thus, as federal policy makers seek to enhance family-supportive approaches, they should look at funding mechanisms that are less directive about how money gets spent but clearer about the purposes and outcomes that are to be achieved. Rather than specifying specific services in detail, federal funding should be available in a way that creates incentives for communities themselves to define their own preventive and developmental approaches.

Strong family support programs are built from the bottom up. They work only when local communities, and parents within those communities, feel ownership and fully participate in program design and operations. Federal initiatives related to family resource and support must institute mechanisms and timelines that allow parents to become involved, to develop their own approaches, and to implement these programs in a way that makes sense within their own communities. Operationally, this suggests that federal funding for such programs must allow longer lead times for community planning to occur, must ensure mechanisms for parental ownership and participation, and must view these initiatives as community development activities, not just as social service programs.

This approach also requires federal leadership in this field to focus not just on programmatic support. Given the early stage of evolution of family resource programs in many states, the federal government's role should emphasize capacity building, information sharing, training of providers and participants in family support efforts, technical assistance to promising program initiatives, and better assessment of program impact. In many jurisdictions, the infrastructure necessary to support family resource and support programs on other than a small scale does not exist. State agencies are not prepared to help guide local communities as they develop programs. Institutions of higher learning have not yet begun to train people in providing these services. Evaluators have only scratched the surface of assessing programs' impact (and still often apply unrealistic measures that either miss or misperceive what these programs are about). In short, the supports and resources that could enrich the family support movement are not there, and if their lack persists, programs will fall short of their goals. The federal government can play a creative role by beginning now to put in place the infrastructure necessary to strengthen state and local family resource initiatives.

If these guidelines are adopted, federal policy related to family resource and support should be openly opportunistic. It should take advantage of every chance that comes along to incorporate family-supportive principles into new legislative proposals and into legislation that is up for reauthorization. Rather than struggling, in this time of scarce resources, to install major new federal programs (a difficult task, in any case), policy makers and advocates will do better to seize upon major legislative vehicles and try to strengthen them through the introduction of family-supportive principles and program components. A number of major human service and education statutes are due for reauthorization in the next five years, and each of these should be scrutinized closely to see how it could be improved — that is, how its purposes could be better achieved — by the building of family-supportive program components into its fabric. This approach is consistent with the broad goal already enunciated: to infuse family support principles into federal policy, rather than add layers of new program initiatives.

Federal Strategy: A Family Support Agenda for the Next Five Years

Assuming that these general directions for federal policy are correct, how does this translate into a specific agenda for family support in the years ahead? As administration officials, congressional staff, state and local advocates, and other proponents of family resource programs decide what to do first, second, and third, what are the logical next steps? Which opportunities will have the most impact on local communities and the best outcomes for parents, given that all available opportunities cannot be pursued equally?

The answers to these questions will emerge as many people work together to develop a specific agenda. However, given the current needs in the family support field, the evolving nature of state and local programs, and the primitive state of research-based knowledge in this area, here are some suggested priorities.

1. *Increase information about family resource and support initiatives.* States and localities are eager for additional information about family resource program approaches and policy initiatives. Because program innovation in this field is so rapid, federal leadership is needed to ensure that information and technology transfer occurs equally rapidly. This is a low-cost, high-impact method for the federal government to assist the field at large and simultaneously to build states' and communities' capacity for administering strong programs.

The family support clearinghouse, currently authorized and funded within the Department of Health and Human Services, should be reauthorized with an expanded mandate and increased capacity. The purpose of the clearinghouse is to disseminate information about family resource programs, to identify effective models and share information about these models with a broad constituency, and to help educate the public about the values and characteristics of family support. It has dramatically increased information available nationally about family support programs. To make the most of this resource, however, its capacity should be expanded in the following ways:

- The statutory authorization for the clearinghouse should be lengthened from three to four years and made concurrent with Head Start reauthorization. (Given that the clearinghouse authorization is part of the Head Start reauthorization bill, it makes sense to consider it on the same legislative timetable.)

- The clearinghouse's capacity should be expanded to allow more sustained attention in three areas: family resource programs that are linked to schools and that help achieve national education goals; family resource initiatives that are related to the self-sufficiency of AFDC clients and other disadvantaged families; and family resource initiatives that benefit the families traditionally served by child welfare agencies. In each of these areas, new federal legislation is being or will be proposed, and state and local efforts are proliferating. As a result, the need for information about best practices and best program models is urgent. Material generated through the clearinghouse could help inform federal policy in these areas and build state and local capacity.

2. *Build the capacity of, and learn from, state family resource initiatives.* It is at the state level that the most serious development of family resource and support initiatives needs to occur. States can benefit from incentives and guidance to establish high-quality statewide networks of family resource programs that are well integrated with other health, social service, and education systems. If strong federal leadership can be provided for this task, many aspects of effective program development will have been addressed.

The framework for this work exists in the legislative authorization for state networks of family support. This should be viewed as one of the learning laboratories for broader federal policy. States' enthusiastic response to the related legislation suggests that the structure, parameters, and incentives of the legislation are sound. The definition of core family support services under this program, as well as its requirements for local community involvement, strong parental participation, and interagency collaboration in the design and oversight of state and local programs, should be prototypes for family-supportive approaches in other legislation.

In addition, this legislation creates the possibility of learning more about the implementation process for family resource initiatives. DHHS, the parent agency for this program, should make intensive technical assistance available to help the three to five pioneering states that, under this law, will implement high-quality program networks that are outcome-driven and linked to broader human service systems, rather than existing as isolated programs. In addition, DHHS should assess states' implementation experience carefully, adding substantially to the small body of implementation research about family resource programs.

3. *Demonstrate the value of family resource programs and principles as a vehicle for change in the child welfare system.* With passage of the Omnibus Budget Reconciliation Act (OBRA) of 1993, DHHS has a major opportunity to help states use family resource programs and principles to set new directions in child welfare services. This legislation is the first to explicitly suggest that states develop family resource programs as part of one of their long-established human service systems. The definition of family resource and support programs in the law is broad. It provides little guidance to states about how family resource programs differ from traditional services. However, DHHS can use this opportunity to suggest more innovative directions to states. Useful guidance to states could include the following elements:

- States should be encouraged to link family resource programs with other parts of a family-based continuum of care. While the new child welfare amendments in OBRA 1993 explicitly link family support and family preservation, in reality a host of other family-supportive approaches can be combined into an effective network of community support.
- States should be encouraged to build family resource program networks (using the funding provided through this legislation), not isolated programs.
- Federal implementation should emphasize training and technical assistance. DHHS should make as much material and information as possible available to states, providing hands-on technical assistance as well.
- The evaluation provisions of this law should be used to learn

more about the impact of family support programs, their possible linkages to family preservation, and their "fit" within the broader child welfare system.

4. *Introduce family resource programs and principles into major new and reauthorized federal legislation.* This should be the major legislative activity related to family resource programs and principles over the next five years. As new federal legislation reshapes the health, human service, and education fields, principles of family resource and support should be promoted, to ensure that changing federal policy will be responsive to parents, will be respectful of communities' and parents' prerogatives in program design, and will help build (rather than fragment) a coherent system of community services and supports.

Legislative targets for infusion of family resource and support principles include the following:

- *Welfare reform legislation* (likely to be introduced by the Clinton administration in FFY 1994). Family resource programs should be recognized and encouraged as part of the supportive network (also including child care, transportation, and other community services) that is necessary to help many families toward self-sufficiency. Family resource principles, incorporated as part of job training and placement programs, can also contribute directly to program effectiveness.
- *Health care reform.* A significant dimension of proposed health care reform should be the extent to which it is family-supportive (that is, the extent to which it recognizes and encourages the role of family members as caregivers and decision makers in all aspects of health care). As the health care reform debate proceeds (and as components of reform are implemented over the long term), family resource principles can suggest how care is best delivered. Family resource programs should also be considered for direct funding when they are part of a health education, outreach, and preventive care program.
- *Head Start reauthorization.* Many of the principles of family

resource programs are already included in Head Start's program structure (for example, parental participation requirements). As major expansion of Head Start programming for younger children is considered, however, even more extensive design specifications are needed to ensure that such programming will reflect the best practices of family resource programs. (It can be argued that all such programs should *be* family resource programs.). Because of the broad coverage and public acceptance of Head Start, the way that this legislation addresses family resource issues is a critical legislative watershed for the family resource field.

- *Education reform legislation.* The precise form of legislation to help states and localities restructure schools is still emerging. However, whether the vehicle is the Clinton administration's proposed bill or reauthorization of current statutes (such as reauthorization of Chapter I of the Elementary and Secondary Education Act), family resource and support principles must be a part of redesigning schools. Several of the most innovative state-level education reform efforts are demonstrating the importance of school-linked family resource programs, and emerging principles of parental participation and involvement in schools are similar in many ways to the principles governing strong family resource programs.

The challenge in all these areas will be for proponents of family resource programs and principles to determine how best to bring their experience and knowledge to these legislative deliberations. With the exception of Head Start, the program areas listed here are not closely linked to family resource and support concepts. Significant groundwork — information sharing, education, and so forth — will be necessary if family resource ideas are to be accepted as necessary components of these legislative strategies. Considering how these tasks can be accomplished raises the final issue to be considered in this chapter: What needs to occur within the family resource field if this substantial federal policy agenda is to be sustained?

Making the Case for Strong Federal Policy

The fact that federal policy interest in family resource initiatives has been piqued does not mean that it will be sustained. Continued progress will depend on how well the family resource field—including all those who govern, participate in, provide, fund, and *care* about these programs—generates the substantive knowledge and advocacy that strong policy requires.

Substantively, several steps are important. The field needs wider agreement on what constitutes family resource and support principles and programs. The lack of a clear, concise definition, generally accepted by the field, continues to create confusion that, while tolerable in small-scale legislative initiatives, will be a barrier to broader policy mandates.

For the same reasons, the field must soon generate more detailed knowledge about (and greater ability to communicate) the essential ingredients of effective family resource programs and community initiatives. This is difficult because of the wide variety in program forms, and because of the fact that staff-parent relationships (at the heart of all effective programs) are ultimately intangible. Nevertheless, the ability to help new communities develop effective family resource initiatives is critical to their large-scale promotion through federal policy.

Family resource initiatives must be designed and implemented with a stronger outcomes orientation. The balance to be struck here involves conceiving programs as part of communitywide strategies to achieve clear goals (whether the goals are to improve educational achievement, obtain better maternal and infant health, or increase family safety and stability) while retaining programs' flexibility and responsiveness to individual needs. Several exemplary initiatives (such as the Caring Communities Program in St. Louis) have managed to do both, and the field must follow their example.

As program elements are more clearly defined, and as outcomes are set more precisely, the family resource field will be able to generate more substantial practice-based research and self-assessment of impacts. The field needs an improved research paradigm, one that will look more closely at innovative, community-oriented, nonbureaucratic program forms, and one that provides programs with ongoing feedback and encourages program evolution.

Strategically, too, the family resource field must broaden its scope if these directions in federal policy are to evolve. Advocacy will have to be carried out in partnership with people and organizations in the health, education, community development, and other arenas if this agenda is to be pursued. Forming these partnerships will depend on how clearly family resource advocates can communicate what their initiatives can contribute toward accomplishing clearly defined goals.

The evolution of public policy in the family resource field seems to be following a natural and appropriate course. Local activism has led to state action, and that in turn is prompting incremental federal activity. The movement toward broader mandates, however, will require a strategic continuity and an as yet unrealized coherence on the part of all who care about these issues.

The rewards of pushing for more family-supportive public policies are not in doubt. For all those people who have observed the pivotal differences that local and state family resource initiatives can make in parents' and children's lives, the task of creating new ways to make these initiatives the norm, rather than the exception, is worth the effort.

▢ Part Five ▢

CHALLENGES FOR THE FAMILY SUPPORT MOVEMENT

$$\square \ \mathbf{17} \ \square$$

Defining and Achieving Quality in Family Support

Sharon L. Kagan

As the chapters in this volume consistently suggest, family support is no longer a fledgling, underrecognized construct; to the contrary. If anything, family support has burgeoned, theoretically and practically, with initiatives manifest at the federal, state, and local levels in the form of vigorous legislation, inventive programs, and new commitments to family support principles by normative service delivery systems. No longer the purview of a limited number of people, family support is national — if not international — in concept, acceptance, and spread. Indeed, it has come of age.

The sequelae of "coming of age" rapidly pose critical but exciting challenges for the field: communicating the missions of family support in ways that are comprehensible to those less familiar with them; training sufficient practitioners; procuring funding for programs; infusing family support principles into mainstream and mainline agencies; and affirming the veracity of evaluation approaches, to mention a few. While each of these challenges demands different skills and approaches, they all share

The author wishes to acknowledge the research and editorial work of Eliza Pritchard and the helpful comments of Peter Neville.

a common and perhaps primary need—that of adding precision to the definition of quality in family support. If we are not certain what constitutes both the definition and standards of quality in family support, how can we construct appropriate training programs for prospective workers in the field? How can we encourage and guide the development of new programs? How can we frame policy to safeguard quality? And how can we evaluate the actual quality of programs?

Past Efforts at Defining Quality in Family Support

In principle and in practice, quality in family support is not a new issue: practitioners have long been concerned about it. The issue of quality has come up informally at conferences, in discussions with evaluators, and in planning legislation with policy makers. Indeed, among practitioners, there has been a certain unspoken agreement about what constitutes program quality, often manifested in statements such as "We know it when we see it" or "It reflects the family support principles."

Good for starters, such oblique and comparatively imprecise statements reflect the limited attention actually paid to defining or quantifying quality in family support. A review of past Family Resource Coalition conference programs (Family Resource Coalition, 1986, 1988, 1990, 1992) indicates that while the conferences were richly filled with sessions designed to strengthen families, build communities, and share information about innovative programs, efforts to actually define what was meant by quality—the key ingredient undergirding virtually all the topics—were noticeably absent. Key periodicals appearing regularly over the decade have addressed a cluster of issues related to family support (family support and the handicapped, business's role in family support, the minority family and family support), but few if any have devoted serious attention to defining quality. Similarly, the editors' previous volume, coedited with Douglas Powell and Edward Zigler, does not list quality in the index (Kagan, Powell, Weissbourd, & Zigler, 1987). The few references to quality in this volume focus on how to achieve it, without ever attempting to define it.

Limited attention to defining quality in family support should not surprise us, for several reasons. First, for the past decade, the family support movement has been concerned with defining its basic principles and communicating them to policy makers and service providers at large. Second, the energies of practitioners were appropriately vested in planning, mounting, funding, and sustaining their programs. Interest in practical survival took precedence over an academic task of defining quality. Third, while networking mechanisms within the field grew, they too remained small and fragile, providing limited opportunities for convening the substantive discussions necessary to define quality in family support. Fourth, and perhaps most important, the field itself was not ready to define quality; it was still working through what family support meant, how it could take shape, and the forms of support that seemed to work best under various conditions. In short, as in any other field, the first decade was an era devoted to stabilization and de facto experimentation. Understandably, defining quality was not high on the agenda.

Despite these realities, there were several important and tangential efforts to examine elements of effective services for children and families generally. While not explicitly designed to cover family support programs, these efforts not only reflected general family support principles but also advanced the thinking of those in the family support movement, beckoning them to consider how such elements interacted with those of their agenda. Perhaps most notable among the efforts was that of Schorr and Schorr (1988), wherein characteristics of effective programs were delineated on the basis of extensive research and observation. A source of optimism, the characteristics included flexible program structures; provision of a broad spectrum of coherent, continuous, user-friendly services; trustworthy professionals who care for and respect service recipients; consideration of the child in the context of the family and the family in the context of society; and regular crossing of professional and bureaucratic boundaries. Building on the Schorrs' inventive work, other efforts to define quality in broad-based service delivery ensued. For example, United Way, in its Mobilization for

America's Children (1993), offers ten standards for effective family programs, including the need for rooting services in the community, respecting diversity, maintaining an undivided focus on the needs of children and families, taking a long-term view of program work, employing persistent outreach efforts, attracting and retaining highly committed and competent staff, specifying long-term and short-term outcomes, and securing adequate and stable financial support.

As promising as these efforts are, they open rather than close the case for adding precision to the definition of quality in family support. What is most helpful in each effort is that generic program conditions are presented; rarely, however, are the actual substance (content) or performance criteria specified. At the brink of national interest and of institutional reform in multiple sectors, ripe with a body of practical experience, family support has the capacity and responsibility to consider how it will define quality. Having captured the interest of new scholars, fresh practitioners, foundations, civic leaders, policy makers, and bureaucrats, family support stands at the threshold of a new era that will demand careful refinement of its principles into quality standards that can guide practice.

Guidelines for Defining Quality in Family Support

Given the diversity of opinion on what constitutes quality, any attempt by a single individual to define quality in family support is both dangerous and premature. Quality specification in family support, as in any other field, must be an evolutionary, consensual process developed over time. Moreover, it must engage large numbers of individuals representing diverse experiences and backgrounds, so that the richest possible definitions of quality can be extracted from experience and knowledge.

Despite these realities, there are important issues to be considered as the field embarks on the process of defining quality. Guidelines for the process should be contemplated, as should implementation strategies that will enable any definition of quality to become useful for the field. To that end, this section offers a number of guidelines for the field to ponder as it defines quality.

The section following this discussion focuses on potential quality-implementation strategies.

1. *Any definition of quality in family support must be firmly grounded in the principles developed by the field and must be sufficiently flexible to accommodate changes in them.* Defining quality in family support does not begin with a clean slate; principles that have guided the evolution of family support programs and the family support movement have been extracted from experience and provide the fundamental premises for considerations of quality. These include the following:

- *A focus on prevention and a recognition of the importance of the early years.* Family support programs move beyond treating problems to preventing them and promoting optimal development of children and families.
- *An ecological approach to service delivery.* Programs develop not just child-centered but also child/family/community–focused services.
- *A developmental view of parents.* Programs recognize the importance of parental nurturing and seek to enhance parents' capacity for growth and development.
- *The universal value of support.* Programs understand that support can strengthen family coping capacities and strive to foster independence and empowerment (Weissbourd & Kagan, 1989).

Not merely statements of philosophy, these principles have tangible manifestations for the ways in which families and staff interact, for the nature of the power relationships among them, for the content of the programs, and for the lens through which family support activities are conducted. As such, these principles, while modifiable over time, represent the terra firma on which definitions of quality must be built.

2. *The definition of quality in family support will resemble and build on definitions from other fields but will of necessity be unique to*

family support. As the preceding principles suggest, the field of family support bears some resemblance to other fields that provide care and support for children and adults. Indeed, because of this similarity, some of the quality definitions may be transferable across fields. Family support programs, however, by their very nature, are designed to be different from conventional service delivery efforts in their relationships with families, in the way they conceptualize services, and in the perspectives they espouse, making wholesale transferability of quality definitions impossible. Therefore, the development of quality standards constitutes a fresh and challenging task that may have transcendent benefits. For example, working definitions of quality in family support, once crafted, may serve as beacons of reform, not simply for mainstream family support programs but also for normative institutions (schools and welfare agencies) that may not routinely conceptualize human interactions in a holistic manner. In short, the extent to which definitions of quality in family support will have wholesale value is directly proportional to the degree to which such definitions build on lessons from other fields while still honoring the fundamental integrity of the basic family support principles.

3. *The definition of quality in family support must clearly discern its domain(s) of focus: content standards, performance/outcome standards, and/or delivery/input standards.* While defining quality in family support sounds like a promising idea, the task recalls the elephant who, when touched by blind men in different areas, appeared at once to be a fan, a tree trunk, and a fountain. To avoid such ambiguity, the intentions of any quality-definition endeavor must be clear, because quality definition, like the elephant, may be viewed from different perspectives. One approach to quality definition would be to concentrate on delineating content standards. Content standards describe the knowledge, skills, and understanding that guide family support practices aimed at improving outcomes for families. A second approach to quality definition would be to define performance or outcome standards for family support. Performance or outcome standards specify the performance or threshold levels that constitute com-

petence in the knowledge, skills, and understanding set out in the content standards. Performance standards specify the outcomes expected as a result of family support efforts. Complicating matters in family support, there are at least six different domains of performance or outcome standards that could be considered: outcome standards for children, for families, for family support programs, for communities, for normative institutions adopting family support practices, and for the family support system as a whole. Finally, a quality-definition initiative could focus on a third type of standard, different from content and performance or outcome standards: delivery or input standards. The term *delivery standards* refers to the inputs or resources that programs, agencies, or systems provide to enable them to meet their specified performance or outcome standards. Delivery standards, for example, might involve the number of staff members per family, or a program's per-family expenditures.

Family support currently lacks clear content, performance, and delivery standards, forcing a decision regarding which of the three types of standards to develop, and in what order. Sadly, there are few clear lessons to be gleaned from other fields. Making eminent sense, many in the educational field began their work by defining content standards, premised on the assumption that before one could set performance levels for content, or even define outcome, one had to be clear about the content and its intent (National Council on Education Standards and Testing, 1992). Conversely, others have assumed that in order to achieve maximum productivity, outcomes must be clearly specified first. The destination must be defined before the tracks are laid and the timetables are drawn. However logical, beginning with outcomes presents considerable challenges for family support, because unlike the train aiming for a singular destination, family support, as already noted, has multiple outcome domains (children, families, programs, communities, normative institutions, and/or the family support system). The issue of whether the quality-definition effort should begin with content, performance, or input standards deserves consideration.

Moreover, and in keeping with the first two guidelines, wherever the quality definition initially focuses, the standards themselves must be sufficiently prescriptive to enable the setting of threshold levels of quality yet sufficiently broad to embrace the variety of extant (and yet to be born) family support approaches. Given the diversity of family support efforts, quality definitions will need to balance specificity and generality, a commitment to precision with the need for flexibility.

4. *The definition of quality in family support must be rooted in the field, reflecting its best practices; and, simultaneously, it must be ahead of the field, anticipating next-stage vistas and possibilities for family support.* To date, the family support movement has emerged in many ways: first, and most popularly, as independent programs; second, and growing in popularity, as programs working within normative institutions; and, third, as a set of principles being used to recontour normative public agencies and service delivery systems. In each of these forms, exemplary approaches exist and have been well chronicled elsewhere (Goetz, 1992). The challenge for those seeking to define quality in family support is to decide whether these efforts are the best we *do* have or the best we *could* have. In other words, should our models of today set the quality threshold — in effect, creating a floor of quality — or should the proposed definitions of quality be more bold and audacious, setting higher standards for future achievement? We need to consider whether definitions of quality — via content, performance, and/or delivery standards — should be reflectors of what is or anticipators of what could be.

5. *The definition of quality in family support must be conceptualized to be theoretically (but not necessarily empirically) grounded, as well as sufficiently practical to guide field-based quality-enhancement efforts.* Family support is not represented by any single academic discipline from which it can extract "scientific truths" in the form of empirical data. This, however, is not to say that family support does not have roots in theory and allied disciplines. From psychology, we glean lessons about adult and family development. From learning theory, we gain understanding of adult learning processes. From sociology, we learn of community de-

velopment and community action literature. From organizational theory, we learn about change strategies. All of these are fundamental components of family support. The definition of quality in family support must be extracted from these disciplines but not delimited by them.

It is the unique integration of theories from different disciplines, coupled with lessons from the field, that makes the process of defining quality in family support akin to defining a new, hybrid discipline—one that of necessity must be field-driven. As in medicine, architecture, and law, laboratory theories (however heuristically interesting) that fail to meet the reality test soon become extinct. The ultimate template against which definitions of quality in family support must be gauged is whether they have sufficient muscle and thought to guide field-based quality-enhancement efforts.

The preceding five guidelines suggest that the task of defining quality in family support will not be an easy or quick undertaking. To the contrary, it has been suggested that it is a Herculean task embracing nothing less than the following:

- Building a reform strategy for human services
- Defining the parameters of a new field of scientific and practical endeavor
- Establishing a mode of practice that incorporates knowledge of and respect for the diversity of human development
- Redefining what constitutes a just and equitable scope of family support services between government and its citizens

Such tasks, embraced in the defining of quality within family support, can be regarded as primarily conceptual and ideological. At the same time, as I have attempted to suggest in the preceding guidelines, defining quality involves far more than that. It is a profoundly political undertaking, one that must be handled carefully, timed sensitively, and supported by real-world strategies.

Real-World Strategies: Implementing the Definition

Defining quality, while absolutely necessary, will never be sufficient to foster real-world quality enhancement for the field.
Something more than paper definitions is necessary if the specification of quality in family support is actually to take root.
Therefore, it seems essential to accompany any discussion of
definitional guidelines with considerations of well-articulated action strategies used in diverse fields to propel quality agendas
forward. Indeed, it is the assumption of this chapter that, simultaneous with discerning quality criteria for family support,
a parallel effort to examine implementation mechanisms should
be launched, so that considerations of the two quality efforts —
definition and implementation — can be synergistic rather than
sequential. The following discussion provides a preliminary overview of quality-enhancement strategies that could be evaluated
for their applicability to achieving field-based quality in family
support programs, systems, and normative institutions.

Fortunately for family support, numerous other fields and
professions have grappled with diverse strategies to enhance the
implementation of quality. While various fields approach quality implementation quite differently, and while there is no single best approach yet discerned, five quality-enhancement strategies are commonly used. In some cases, fields use a combination
of approaches; in other cases, they rely more heavily on one
approach than on others. The family support movement will
need to discern which approaches fit best with its history and
its belief system, and which seem to be the most efficacious, given
the unique nature of the field.

Five frequently discussed strategies for quality enhancement are mandated regulation, voluntary accreditation, monetary
and/or nonmonetary incentives, a focus on delivery (or input)
standards, and a focus on performance (or outcome) standards.
Each constitutes a separate domain of inquiry, replete with scholarly volumes and journals, and — in some cases — specially established research institutions or organizations. Therefore, the
following review is not intended to be exhaustive but rather sug-
gestive of the concerns that the family support movement will

need to consider as it plans to enhance and sustain the implementation of quality in the field.

Mandated Regulation

Often regarded as a partial panacea to protect the rights of the citizenry, regulation has been touted widely as a potent vehicle for maintaining a modicum of quality in the production of goods and services. Ideological support for regulation stems from the conviction that a market economy will do its best to maximize profit at the expense of the consumer. Regulations therefore provide one socially sanctioned vehicle for preventing harm to citizens while protecting the moral rights of individuals. Moreover, the existence of regulations adds clarity to and makes explicit the intent of legislation, which is often the product of political ambiguity.

In recent years, attitudes toward the viability of regulation as a quality safeguard have shifted considerably. First, and consistent with the general loss of confidence in government, there is a growing feeling that regulations rarely serve to raise quality, providing only minimal protection rather than encouraging more extensive efforts (Gormley, 1990). Second, increasing skepticism about the value of regulations stems from concerns about the temporal and economic costs of regulatory implementation; regulations simply do not seem to be a cost-effective or socially efficient way to ensure that obligations are being met. Third, with resistance to regulation growing, it is not uncommon for regulations to provide exemptions. This propensity to exempt some providers or producers creates an uneven floor, where fair competition is eliminated and acrimony festers. Notable examples of uneven regulation exist in child care, where church, school, and part-day programs are often exempt (Morgan, in press). Fourth, with state and federal deficits mounting, there is concern that resource constraints will prevent the effective monitoring and enforcement of regulations, thus seriously delimiting regulatory efficacy. Although integral to their viability, the enforcement of regulations is so complicated that it is often regarded as the most controversial and least implemented part of the regulatory process (Edelman, 1992). Fifth, there is a growing sense that regulatory mechanisms are often unnecessary because they target systems already self-regulated by the marketplace.

These considerations notwithstanding, the dilemma is considerably more complex for those concerned about instituting regulations related to strengthening services for families. Historically, the nation has been averse to intervening in the privacy and hegemony of the family (Kagan, 1991), with this aversion manifested in a reluctance to remove children from their families and in the courts' hesitation to intervene in cases of battered children and women. Moreover, the thought of formally regulating family support programs is repugnant on ideological grounds in that the arbitrary and strict nature of regulations directly contradicts the evolutionary and flexible approach that has been the cornerstone of family support success.

If large increases in federal funds flowed into the family support movement, however, the question of federal regulation would be sure to surface. Such regulation would not be automatic. First, from the perspective of government, there would need to be a clear rationale for regulatory intervention, articulated through the legislation (Jacobs, 1989; Silber, 1983). Second, in cases where safety standards are being considered, government intervention has typically been predicated on the existence of a catastrophic event, such as the exploding Pinto, fires from gas heaters, and so on (Cheit, 1990). Third, it must appear that expert knowledge and intervention could have prevented the catastrophe. In the case of family support, these conditions are not yet evident, and so concern about the influence of regulation from the government's perspective may be somewhat premature.

Conversely, ignoring the possibility of regulatory safeguards seems naïve on two counts. First, they may emerge; and, second, the family support movement may be able to use regulation to its advantage. The field needs to consider what (if any) kinds of regulations might hasten the implementation of quality in family support. Could minimum regulations differ for programs and mainstream state institutions (welfare departments and the like), so that they could be tailored to foster quality? And where would the regulatory span end? Would regulations apply to those receiving federal and/or state support? Would programs in the private sector be required to meet such regulations? Jurisdictional issues would arise because family support programs emanate from different governmental agencies, each no doubt wanting to formulate its own set of regulations.

In short, using regulations, at either the federal or the state level, as a means of enhancing and perhaps standardizing quality in family support can neither be relied on as a quality accelerator nor simply be disregarded as out of the question. Regulation is, however, the most complex of the quality-enhancement strategies, given fiscal, ideological, and practical constraints. Other fields—following but not fully buying into a comprehensive or federal regulatory approach—have considered developing national guidelines that would provide direction to program workers and policy makers without imposing the punitive nature and extensive costs of developing and implementing full-scale regulations. (This has been true of the child-care field, for example.) At this critical juncture, the field of family support needs to carefully examine the pros and cons of safeguards, discerning if and where their utilization, either in regulatory or in guideline form, could be most helpful. The preceding discussion suggests that, although regulations as we know them may not be a preferred strategy for family support, with inventive thinking family support could commandeer new ideas from the regulatory process and contour conventional approaches to regulation that fit the family support agenda.

Voluntary Accreditation

Turning from a mandated strategy for infusing quality, we now focus on the voluntary strategy of accreditation. Originating from efforts to standardize professional education programs in the early 1900s (Nelson, 1987), accreditation systems now focus on accrediting a wide variety of institutions. For example, the American Psychological Association's Council on Postsecondary Accreditation certifies educational institutions and programs that prepare individuals for professional careers in psychology (American Psychological Association Committee on Accreditation and Accreditation Office, 1986). The Joint Commission on the Accreditation of Healthcare Organizations accredits health care facilities (Wells & Brook, 1988). The National Association for the Education of Young Children (NAEYC) accreditation system accredits programs in child care and early education (National Association for the Education of Young Children, 1984). Accreditation under all these systems differs from regulation in that it is a voluntary mechanism for quality enhancement and is not intended to be universally applicable. Neither regulation nor accreditation is now universal, but in some fields the implementation of accreditation has become so important that it achieves nearly universal status. Referred to as the "conscience" of an institution or a program (Nelson, 1987), accreditation requires both self-motivation and dedication to quality enhancement on the part of the accredited agency. As such, accreditation typically moves beyond establishing a floor of quality, with most systems certifying high levels of quality.

Although it is used in diverse fields, accreditation is based on a fairly common three-step process: first, a program self-study; second, on-site peer evaluation; and, third, a review and decision by the accreditation committee (American Psychological Association Committee on Accreditation and Accreditation Office, 1986; Bredekamp, 1989; Council on Accreditation of Services for Families and Children, 1993; Nelson, 1987). Different accreditation programs have their own guidelines for the first step, self-study; most, however, involve the indispensable activities of articulating program goals, assessing progress toward those goals, and evaluating management, personnel, outcomes, use of resources, and assessment procedures. After a program has completed its self-study, a group of professionals from the field observes the agency for several days and compiles a report on its conformity to accreditation standards. The committee then comes to an accreditation decision, which is based on both the organization's application and the peer review.

Most research on the impact of accreditation has been limited to accreditation outcomes within particular fields. For example, reviewing surveys completed over a four-year period by the Accreditation Council on Services for People with Developmental Disabilities (ACDD), Hemp and Braddock (1988) found that accreditation rates had improved for all surveyed agencies, by comparison with the low rate of ACDD accreditation recorded in 1973–1974. McGurrin and Hadley (1991) examined two years of data (1984–1986) from 216 state psychiatric hospitals to determine the motivational value of accreditation. Finding that 94.9 percent of the previously accredited hospitals had maintained accreditation, and that 13.9 percent of the nonaccredited hospitals had achieved accreditation by 1986, the authors suggest that accreditation may motivate hospitals to maintain or improve the quality of their services.

Bredekamp (1993), illustrating accreditation's impact on quality, cites the National Child Care Staffing Study, which reported in 1988 that NAEYC-accredited centers had lower staff turnover rates, more developmentally appropriate activities, and more formally trained and educated staff than nonaccredited centers. Four years later, the same accredited centers were found to have higher wages and still lower turnover rates, leading the researchers to conclude that accreditation does enhance quality.

Preliminary research on specific accreditation systems does seem promising, but some researchers express doubt regarding the reliability of accreditation as a quality-enhancement mechanism generally. For example, McGurrin and Hadley (1991) indicate that accreditation may be too subjective a method for quality assurance. In the same vein, Hemp and Braddock (1988) caution that accreditation is based too heavily on "paper goals," as opposed to outcomes, and they criticize the accreditation survey process, which allows agencies to prepare in advance for site visits and, later on, to revert to inadequate service delivery.

Perhaps the most constructive criticism of accreditation has been generated by the Joint Commission on Accreditation of Healthcare Organizations (JCAHO). Beginning in 1986, JCAHO launched its Agenda for Change, which identified key problems with the standards, survey process, and monitoring mechanisms of its accreditation system. Despite the breadth of its concerns, JCAHO has proffered viable solutions: revised standards based on continual improvement of client outcomes; increased presurvey analysis and surveyor education; and an outcome-based monitoring system involving a process of data collection and feedback to help organizations continually improve (Roberts, Schyve, Prevost, Ente, & Carr, 1990).

In short, while accreditation seems to be a promising strategy, it includes inherent procedural challenges that render it insufficient as the sole accelerator of quality. Nevertheless, given lessons from other fields, accreditation is a strategy that warrants serious consideration by family support advocates. Developing a family support accreditation system forces the specification of quality standards and simultaneously makes them public. Given the ambiguity that has surrounded family support — its confusion with welfare reform and with family preservation are but two examples — an accreditation effort might clearly and definitively put family support, as conceived by its practitioners and theoreticians, on the American landscape. Those concerned about accreditation in family support should carefully examine the work on accreditation in allied fields, especially that being undertaken by the Council on Accreditation of Services for Families and Children, Inc. (1993). Such work provides an appropriate portal through which to regard accreditation in family support.

Monetary and/or Nonmonetary Incentives

In recognition of the limitations of regulatory and accreditation systems alike, there has been keen interest in how incentives might enhance quality. For example, Roe (1989) notes that "rather than trying to seal up the holes and cracks in the traditional regulation[s] one by one, [we] sought instead to recast structural incentives in the system itself" (p. 180). Indeed, interest in using incentive systems has permeated the human services, in part because of expanded experimentation in the business sector.

Monetary incentives are perhaps best known in business. Responding to the combined pressures of inflation, economic insecurity, and globalization of the economy (Committee for Economic Development, 1992), businesses have begun to adopt new forms of employee compensation — namely, incentives or performance-based pay plans. These plans are designed to enhance workers' productivity — and, as a result, companies' profits — by linking pay directly to performance. Different types of monetary incentives have developed, including profit sharing, stock options, gainsharing, individual incentives, merit bonuses, organizationwide bonuses, and small-group incentives.

Small group incentives (SGIs) perhaps come the closest to capturing the spirit of family support. Designed to systematically measure and reward group efforts, SGIs engage small, relatively autonomous groups of employees in reaching predetermined goals. The success of SGIs in enhancing workers' performance is based on an organizational culture's receptivity to trust and open communication, on its provision of sufficient training for any new skills that participants might need, and on its system for evaluating group progress toward a stated goal (Berson-Besthoff & Peck, 1992). The effects of such employee involvement strategies have been found to include increased satisfaction among workers, improved quality of work life, and enhanced service, productivity, and profitability (Lawler, Mohrman, & Ledford, 1992).

Certain types of monetary incentives may be applicable to human services, but broad implementation of such incentives in the nonprofit sector has not been sufficiently examined. Some experimentation with monetary incentives in this sector has occurred in education, with the use of merit and "combat" pay. There is still a need for more research in this area, but the studies to date are less than promising. For example, Cellio and Jacobi (1987) have discerned a number of problems with salary incentives in education, among them ineffectiveness in improving education in all classrooms for all students, heightened competition and reduced professionalism among teachers, replacement of intrinsic motivation with material goals, and, on the practical side, inadequate evaluation instruments and higher implementation costs. "Combat pay," or the practice of

providing teachers with extra stipends for working in dangerous settings, has been tried with equivocal results.

Although the problems with monetary incentives in the
nonprofit/human service sector appear to be considerable, non-
monetary incentives have been used widely, with notable developments in nursing and education. Recently, the nursing field
has attempted decentralized quality-assurance models, which
place responsibility for quality at the level of the nursing unit.
Under these models, all nurses are held accountable for nursing practice and are given increased control over the procedures
they perform. In the best of the decentralization efforts, this
process is enhanced by providing nurses with education, guidance, and extra compensation for their participation in quality-
assurance activities. As a result, many nurses have gained a
heightened sense of professional responsibility and a renewed
commitment to improving the quality of care (Schroeder, 1991).
Similar efforts are gaining currency in educational reform, under
the guises of site-based management and power decentralization (William T. Grant Foundation Commission on Work, Family and Citizenship, 1991).

As family support explores alternate incentives for enhancing quality, it must consider the unique culture of family support programs, many of which already embrace the commitment to teamwork and power decentralization. Ironically, these
"new" incentives are the very warp and woof of family support,
which makes their inclusion a somewhat artificial addition to
routine operations. Family support needs to consider incentives
as a means of enhancing the quality of services but must at the
same time respect the inherent principles and practices that have
characterized the movement historically.

Focus on Delivery (Input) Standards

Yet another approach to quality enhancement being widely discussed today is the specification of delivery standards. Delivery
standards involve the inputs that programs, agencies, or systems need to provide in order to meet their stated performance
of outcome standards. In family support, delivery or input stan-

dards would specify the nature and level of services that those espousing the movement's principles would need to provide.

Although considered "inventive" in today's parlance, delivery standards (not always called by that name) have been in existence for decades. For example, the American Medical Association has worked for over fifty years to facilitate the development of practice parameters designed to help practitioners make clinical decisions and foster high-quality management of patients (Kelly & Toepp, 1992). Since 1920, the Child Welfare League of America has set standards of excellence to stimulate the improvement of services for children and their families (Child Welfare League of America, 1992). Head Start developed program performance standards in 1975 to remedy the highly uneven quality of the early Head Start programs, and the standards, although revised, remain in effect today (Zigler & Muenchow, 1992).

Recent initiatives have called for the development of delivery standards as a means of fostering quality and equality. The National Council on Education Standards and Testing (1992) has urged states to establish school delivery standards to ensure the instructional conditions necessary for all children to succeed. The council lists a number of important elements to be addressed by such standards, including improved instructional materials, teachers' enhanced knowledge of subject matter and understanding of pedagogy, in-service professional development, and training in educational technology. Along similar lines, the Clinton administration seeks to certify voluntary national opportunity-to-learn standards, which will define the conditions necessary for all students to have equal opportunity for meeting national content and performance standards.

There is still only minimal research linking delivery standards to quality, but much discussion has been generated regarding the elements that help make such standards successful. Among agencies that have developed delivery standards, it is generally accepted that the standards should be precise but not excessively prescriptive, and that they should demand high levels of quality while still allowing for local or individual variation (Child Welfare League of America, 1992; Kelly & Toepp, 1992).

Most also assert that delivery standards should be developed in conjunction with field experts and should be based on the most advanced thinking in the field. Furthermore, new delivery standards should be subjected to extensive peer review and should continue to be evaluated and revised on a regular basis.

Delivery standards for family support seem to be a critical next step in the evolution of the family support movement. Such indicators of program and institutional need will provide a basis for the functioning of family support programs and will establish a baseline for quality in a nonpunitive way. Delivery standards will also clarify the program elements and resources necessary for successful family support endeavors.

Focus on Performance (Outcome) Standards

States and public institutions in America, having learned from the business experience, have taken an interest in specifying performance or outcome standards as a means of quality enhancement (Harvard Project on Effective Services, Center for the Study of Social Policy, & National Center for Education and the Economy, 1993; Oregon Progress Board, 1991). Different from delivery standards, which focus on inputs, performance standards specify the precise outcomes that a state, a service, or an intervention should produce.

It is widely acknowledged that setting performance standards is a challenging and controversial task. Standards must be set at a realistic level—not so high that they are impossible to meet, and not so low that quality will not be enhanced (Chynoweth & Dyer, 1991). Determining the middle ground is a particularly difficult process in human services, where experience with outcome evaluation is minimal, and where models for realistic standards are rare (see Brizius and Campbell [1991], who suggest that setting realistic standards is a long-term process, involving the development of initial outcome statements, comparisons between statements and actual performance, and revision of performance standards upward or downward).

Beyond the complex task of setting performance standards, it is necessary to measure their effects, a process that inevitably makes performance standards part of a larger account-ability system. Even if clear performance standards can be delineated, the tools to measure outputs often do not exist. We know, for example, that parent and community empowerment are desirable outcomes of family support, but how do we say precisely what constitutes community empowerment? Moreover, how do we measure it, and at what threshold? The responses to such questions can become a basis for program funding or for commendations of meritorious accomplishment. Arguing that realistic performance standards are difficult to develop, and that local variations affect the performance of agencies attempting to comply with state norms, many programs complain that too much hinges on their ability to meet outcome standards. Hence they resist their development and implementation.

Helpful safeguards for minimizing such negative conse-quences have been established. For example, those judging per-formance, as well as those held accountable for outcomes, should be involved in setting standards. Performance standards should not be linked to budget decisions unless there is sufficient evi-dence that the established standards are realistic. Separate stan-dards should be set for subgroups of the target population. Out-come measures should be consistent but flexible (Brizius & Campbell, 1991). Nevertheless, the possibility of misusing per-formance or outcome standards persists, particularly in family support, where outcome variation is pervasive by design.

Beyond accountability, there are further issues to be con-sidered in using performance standards. Many caution that per-formance or outcome standards should not be separated from delivery or input standards, because when outcomes become independent goals, perverse or inadequate processes can be used for the sake of meeting the goal expediently (Chynoweth & Dyer, 1991). Teachers may teach to the test, nurses may artificially hasten recovery processes, and family support workers may sac-rifice their focus on relationship building for the sake of out-come accomplishment.

However fraught with challenges, the specification of out-come and performance standards is essential to enhancing qual-ity in family support. The field must be clear on its goals, must offer the goals for honest evaluation, and must understand that, without accountability, family support will fail despite its good intentions. Should a decision be made to focus on defining performance standards, the field will need to decide where such efforts should be directed — at children, families, family support programs, communities, normative institutions adopting family support practices, or the family support system as a whole. Another challenge lies in creating performance standards that do not violate the intent and integrity of family support principles. This is not a quick process, and family support will need to face up to the challenge over time if the movement is to be durable, sustained, and permanently legitimated. Nothing less than the future of families and family support is at stake.

Toward Excellence in Family Support

Throughout this nation, thousands of high-quality family support programs open their doors each Monday, and many of them never close all week. Family support workers, by whatever title, work collaboratively with families to provide resources, strength, and support. The point is that good things happen without the specification of a quality definition, and without a neatly mapped-out strategy to implement quality. The purpose of this discussion has not been to negate the extraordinary dedication of the field, or to suggest that quality is a scarce commodity. The sense of urgency that propels quality definition and quality implementation comes not from a groundswell to redo or to alter what has come before, or from a secret concern that all is not well in family support. To the contrary, the desire for specificity emanates from the knowledge that good practice exists, and that the next stage for the field is to capitalize on and coalesce what we know, making it more accessible as family support expands beyond its pioneer stage. As more attention is focused on family support, the need for an infrastructure that delineates standards of excellence becomes more acute. Indeed, because family support has expanded to and flourished in so many domains, multiple standards of excellence may need to be considered.

Promising efforts to grapple with this challenge are under way in some states and communities, as noted elsewhere in this volume. We fully endorse these efforts and look to them for new knowledge and insights. In addition, the Family Resource Coalition, under its Best Practices Project, is striving to delineate quality standards of best practices in community-based family support programs. The standards will be developed and supported by a national constituency of practitioners, academicians, and leaders in the field. Launched in 1992, this effort will explore the field and academic knowledge bases, commission papers, conduct focus groups, and synthesize information into a usable format, so that a clear picture emerges of excellence in family support practice.

Critically important, the Best Practices Project is a landmark first step for the field, but it alone will not solve the quality challenges raised in this chapter. Working side by side and in conjunction with that effort, the family support movement needs to be concerned with how best practices are infused into normative institutions, and how integrated systems of family support can and should be developed. Moreover, as this chapter has suggested, attention must be paid simultaneously to the implementation of quality and to the development of quality definitions.

It has been noted that there is nothing so challenging as the pursuit of excellence. As the family support movement enters its second decade, it stands at the threshold of excellence. The field is at once challenged to codify and implement its standards of quality, to press for the metamorphosis of normative institutions toward those standards, and to create a family support system characterized by quality throughout. None of this will happen until brave people clearly understand the construct of family support, and nothing will hasten that so much as crisp specification of quality standards for the field.

References

American Psychological Association Committee on Accreditation and Accreditation Office. (1986). *Accreditation handbook.* Washington, DC: Author.

Berson-Besthoff, P., & Peck, C. (1992). *Small group incentives: Goal-based pay.* New York: The Conference Board, Inc.

Bredekamp, S. (1989, March). *Regulating child care quality: Evidence from NAEYC's accreditation system.* Paper presented at the annual meeting of the American Educational Research Association, San Francisco.

Bredekamp, S. (1993, April). *Lessons on quality from national accreditation.* Paper presented at the annual meeting of the American Educational Research Association, Atlanta.

Brizius, J. A., & Campbell, M. D. (1991). *Getting results: A guide for government accountability.* Washington, DC: Council of Governors' Policy Advisors.

Cellio, J. J., & Jacobi, C. L. (1987). Non-monetary incentives. In J. R. Gress (Ed.), *Incentives for excellence: Agendas and arenas* (pp. 71–76). Toledo, OH: Toledo University.

Cheit, R. E. (1990). *Setting safety standards: Regulation in the public and private sectors.* Berkeley: University of California Press.

Child Welfare League of America. (1992). *Child Welfare League of America standards of excellence for child day care services.* Washington, DC: Author.

Chynoweth, J. K., & Dyer, B. R. (1991). *Strengthening families: A guide for state policymaking.* Washington, DC: Council of Governors' Policy Advisors.

Committee for Economic Development. (1992). *The United States in the new global economy: A rallier of nations.* New York: Author.

Council on Accreditation of Services for Families and Children. (1993). *Standards for agency management and service delivery.* New York: Author.

Edelman, T. (1992, December). *Enforcement of the nursing home reform law: We're not there yet.* Washington, DC: National Citizens' Coalition for Nursing Home Reform.

Family Resource Coalition. (1986). *Changing families, changing responses.* Conference program. Chicago: Author.

Family Resource Coalition. (1988). *Families: A national resource, a national priority.* Conference program. Chicago: Author.

Family Resource Coalition. (1990). *Building community.* Conference program. Chicago: Author.

Family Resource Coalition. (1992). *Family support: Framework for the future.* Conference program. Chicago: Author.

Goetz, K. (Ed.). (1992). *Programs to strengthen families: A resource guide.* Chicago: Family Resource Coalition.

Gormley, W. T. (1990). Regulating Mister Rogers' neighborhood: The dilemmas of day care regulation. *Brookings Review, 8*(4), 21–28.

Harvard Project on Effective Services, Center for the Study of Social Policy, & National Center for Education and the Economy. (1993). *Community services and supports to improve outcomes for children.* Unpublished manuscript.

Hemp, R., & Braddock, D. (1988). Accreditation of developmental disabilities programs. *Mental Retardation, 26*(5), 257–267.

Jacobs, J. B. (1989). *Drunk driving: An American dilemma.* Chicago: University of Chicago Press.

Kagan, S. L. (1991). *United we stand: Collaboration for child care and early education services.* New York: Teachers College Press.

Kagan, S. L., Powell, D. R., Weissbourd, B., & Zigler, E. F. (Eds.). (1987). *America's family support movement: Perspectives and prospects.* New Haven, CT: Yale University Press.

Kelly, J. T., & Toepp, M. C. (1992). Development, evaluation, and implementation of medical practice parameters. *The Medical Staff Counselor, 6*(4), 45–49.

Lawler, E. E., Mohrman, S. A., & Ledford, G. E. (1992). *Employee involvement and total quality management: Practices and results in Fortune 1000 companies.* San Francisco: Jossey-Bass.

McGurrin, M. C., & Hadley, T. R. (1991). Quality care and accreditation status of state psychiatric hospitals. *Hospital and Community Psychology, 42*(10), 1060–1061.

Mobilization for America's Children. (1993). *Standards for success: Building community supports for America's children.* Alexandria, VA: United Way of America.

Morgan, G. (in press). Does this system work? In G. Morgan, (Ed.), *The national state of child care regulation: 1989.* Washington, DC: National Association for the Education of Young Children.

National Association for the Education of Young Children. (1984). *Accreditation criteria and procedures of the National Academy of Early Childhood Programs.* Washington, DC: Author.

National Council on Education Standards and Testing. (1992). *Raising standards for American education: A report to Congress, the*

Secretary of Education, the National Education Goals Panel, and the American people. Washington, DC: Author.

Nelson, P. D. (1987). Accreditation of training programs. In G. C. Stone et al. (Eds.), *Health psychology: A discipline and a profession* (pp. 413–424). Chicago: University of Chicago Press.

Oregon Progress Board. (1991). *Oregon benchmarks: Setting measurable standards for progress.* Report to the 1991 Oregon state legislature. Salem, OR: Author.

Roberts, J. S., Schyve, P. M., Prevost, J. A., Ente, B. H., & Carr, M. P. (1990). The agenda for change: Future directions of the Joint Commission on Accreditation of Healthcare Organizations. In N. O. Graham (Ed.), *Quality assurance in hospitals: Strategies for assessment and implementation* (pp. 44–65). Rockville, MD: Aspen.

Roe, D. (1989). An incentive-conscious approach to toxic chemical controls. *Economic Development Quarterly, 3*(3), 179–187.

Schorr, L. B., & Schorr, D. (1988). *Within our reach: Breaking the cycle of disadvantage.* New York: Doubleday.

Schroeder, P. (1991). Nursing quality assurance programs: Unit-based nursing quality assurance models. In P. Schroeder (Ed.), *Issues and strategies for nursing care quality* (pp. 43–48). Rockville, MD: Aspen.

Silber, N. I. (1983). *Test and protest: The influence of Consumer's Union.* New York: Holmes and Meier.

Weissbourd, B., & Kagan, S. L. (1989). Family support programs: Catalysts for change. *American Journal of Orthopsychiatry, 59*(1), 20–31.

Wells, K. B., & Brook, R. H. (1988). Historical trends in quality assurance for mental health services. In G. Stricker & A. Rodriguez (Eds.), *Handbook of quality assurance in mental health* (pp. 39–63). New York: Plenum Press.

William T. Grant Foundation Commission on Work, Family and Citizenship. (1991). *Voices from the field: 30 expert opinions on America 2000.* Washington, DC: Author.

Zigler, E., & Muenchow, S. (1992). *Head Start: The inside story of America's most successful experiment.* New York: Basic Books.

☐ 18 ☐

Education for Professionals in Family Support

Dolores G. Norton

One of the major challenges facing family support today is the task of educating effective staff to work in the programs in direct service, in program development, and in creating appropriate policy initiatives. Melding basic knowledge, specialized knowledge, and practice skills needed from the different disciplines with the goals, values, principles, and attitudes of family support may be in conflict with some professional training. Education for family support also requires at least two levels of training: preservice preparation, and meaningful high-quality in-service training. Education for family support is a "lifelong proposition," as new research and new intervention approaches are implemented and evaluated (Fenichel & Eggbeer, 1990). The core content of training and education for family support is continuously evolving as different groups of service providers, educators, policy makers, and researchers explore and evaluate what knowledge and practice skills are needed and begin to translate them into a comprehensive curriculum (Carter, 1992; Delany-Cole, 1992b; Dunst, 1990; Family Resource Coalition, 1992; Fenichel & Eggbeer, 1990; Klein & Campbell, 1990; McCollum, 1992; Powell, 1988, 1991; Weissbourd & Kagan, 1989).

This chapter attempts to advance this content by using family support principles guiding effective, "best" practice to specify what content and skills are needed to implement the principles. The work is based on an examination of the growing literature on the best practices of family support programs; conferences on family support and early intervention; participation in training sessions; examination of the work of states as they develop criteria for the credentialing and certification of family support personnel, particularly the work of the Illinois State Board of Education's Early Intervention Personnel Development Committee; and the pioneering work of such groups as Minnesota's Early Childhood and Family Education program, the Training Approaches for Skills and Knowledge Project of Zero to Three of the National Center for Clinical Infant Programs, and the Best Practices Project and *Resource Guide* of the Family Resource Coalition. The chapter presents the common goals of all family support programs and the principles that have evolved from these goals. The major portion of the chapter uses these family support principles to tease out and specify the basic knowledge, specialized knowledge, and practice skills needed to educate personnel for family support, moving toward the development of a conceptual framework for family support education. The last section of the chapter prioritizes the content areas of the conceptual framework and examines its implications for preservice and in-service education.

Challenges for Education for Family Support

With recognition of the importance of the earliest years to optimal child development and emphasis on preventive services to families of young children, the demand for more trained personnel for family support programs has increased. Family support service teams must be interdisciplinary, with their specific disciplines and professions depending on the needs of the targeted families and children, and parents must be vital elements of the team partnership. Currently, interdisciplinary teams might include persons from special education, child development, psychiatry, psychology, social work, occupational therapy, audiology, speech pathology, physical therapy, nursing, and pediatrics (Fenichel & Eggbeer, 1990). The challenge is to develop preservice and in-service educational programs that will integrate this range of interdisciplinary expertise with common family support principles (Delany-Cole, 1992b, p. 5). This requires specification of the requisite content and pedagogical practices needed to educate practitioners and policy makers from different disciplines and levels of practice to work smoothly and coherently in family support programs.

Providing the preservice education to build a cadre of well-trained, interdisciplinary, qualified, and capable staff for effective family support is a challenge. Few of the needed professions offer a synthesis of the content, processes, and skills needed for early family support. In preservice education, the professional programs are hampered by concerns about space in their already overcrowded curricula and by the lack of faculty knowledgeable enough to teach in these areas (Delany-Cole, 1992a; Dunst, 1990; Family Resource Coalition, 1992; Fenichel & Eggbeer, 1990; McCollum, 1992; Powell, 1991; Weissbourd & Kagan, 1989). Regional faculty development institutes are springing up to assist multidisciplinary faculty to integrate this knowledge. Some, like the Midwestern Consortium for Faculty Development, include all the states in their region in an annual training institute, with the specific goal of enhancing each state's capacity to train early intervention providers and to develop individualized state training plans (Midwestern Consortium for Faculty Development, 1993). Parents are included in these institutes, not only for their contribution to the interdisciplinary skills but also for their own development as advocates for their children and community resources.

In-service education also presents some hurdles. The various levels of expertise encountered in family support programs render it difficult to arrange training that meets the needs of the entire staff. Much of the in-service training is delivered in one-shot or daylong sessions, with little sequential building on concepts over time and few follow-up sessions. Daily activities of the program make in-service training difficult to schedule. Often the content and skill areas presented are not the most pressing areas where help is needed, according to the staff. Guidelines for in-service education should include the following elements:

- Ensuring that the selected in-service topics relate to the staff's perceived needs by soliciting staff, administrative, and parental opinion about areas in which help is needed
- Securing program administrative support in obtaining free time for staff to attend the training sessions
- Integrating in-service topics and training over time, as opposed to one-shot, independent topics and sessions that are not linked to other in-service education being received
- Using a variety of teaching techniques in the in-service sessions, which provides for different styles of learning and hands-on involvement (lecture, small-group discussion, role playing, video, observation of actual practice)
- Appropriate and timely follow-up of in-service training sessions to help staff use, practice, and evaluate the new learning

Goals of the in-service education should be clearly expressed, including the overall level of learning expectations for the training (for example, is the in-service education aiming for only awareness of the area, or toward actual change in staff behavior?).

All of these challenges must be considered if effective education to fulfill the goals of family support is to occur. In attempting to derive the content and skill areas needed for such education, this chapter first examines the goals of family support programs and then asks what principles are necessary to guide the activities of those trying to meet those goals.

Goals of Family Support Programs

As illustrated many times in this volume, family support programs are very disparate in "whom they serve, their focus, their staff, funding sources, and the auspices under which they emerge" (Weissbourd & Kagan, 1989, p. 21). Programs targeting children who are developmentally disabled, environmentally at risk, chronically ill, whether designated as programs in child mental health, infant and maternal health, or child welfare, can all be considered family support programs. Despite the program differences, they have common goals to facilitate optimal development in children and their families. Weissbourd and Kagan (1989) and Weissbourd (1991) summarize the overall common goals of family support programs as (1) focusing on enhancing the capacity of parents in their child-rearing roles, (2) creating settings in which parents are empowered to act on their own behalf and become advocates for change, and (3) providing a community resource for parents. The operative word here is *parents,* which appears in all three goals. The assumption is that children are embedded in and dependent on families for their survival, nurturance, and socialization. Their parents become their first teachers about what the world is like, what and when one eats, how one feels and adapts, how one actually thinks, and how one even views the world. Rogoff (1990) refers to this process of socialization as the children's "apprenticeship," occurring through guided parental participation. In this guided collaborative process, children develop understanding and skills to participate in the activities of their communities.

This conceptualization of the child, as embedded in the context of social relationships and sociocultural values, activities, and tools within the family, necessitates a family-centered approach to early intervention. Young children can be served effectively only within the context of their families, within a partnership with parents and other appropriate family members (Hanft, 1989). Therefore, the family must be the unit with which to work. Given our diverse, pluralistic society, the family must be defined not merely in terms of traditional norms but also according to the culture and definitions of the family being served. This diversity must consider not only individual family structure, attitudes, and values but also the racial, ethnic, socioeconomic, cultural diversity, and world view of the family. Respecting each family, with its own structure, strengths, values, and beliefs, and building on those characteristics on behalf of the child are the assumptions underlying these family support goals. The family can best care for its children if its strengths to meet its own needs, as well as the children's needs, are developed and enabled in mutually respecting and involved partnerships.

Systems theory, with its emphasis on the interdependent, connected relationships of all elements of a system influencing each other, teaches us that the family system is in turn a part of the larger system of its own neighborhood and community. Thus a major approach to families reaches beyond traditional boundaries of practice and establishes partnerships with a range of community resources and services for comprehensive family support.

A Conceptual Framework

The success of family support programs depends on whether they attain the preceding goals, as well as any specific goals set by the particular program. Program staff, parents, collaborating community resources, program coalitions, and involved educators and researchers around the country gradually have begun to enunciate a set of principles to guide their activities in moving toward these goals. Certain commonalities in principles for practice have become evident, regardless of the specific form of the program. Thus the common goals of family support programs have led to a set of principles for guiding activities to meet the particular needs of the population being served. Based on these common principles of practice, family support can be broadly conceptualized as an approach or a synthesis of processes and methods, which is generic to all work with families and young children. These processes and the principles guiding them can be infused throughout social services and child welfare programs and systems in work with young children and their families (Family Resource Coalition, 1992).

This chapter assumes that these principles are not belief systems, but that they rest on interdisciplinary theory and research. In their article describing the growth of family support programs, Weissbourd and Kagan (1989) examine many programs, explore literature describing family support program principles, and summarize a group of crucial principles that most family support programs hold in common to guide their activities. Their work is echoed throughout the literature on effective early intervention with families on behalf of children. The assumption underlying all the principles is that the cornerstone of a healthy society is the well-being of its children and families (Weissbourd, 1990).

A synthesis of family support principles, which would cross all services and provide guidelines to develop culturally appropriate, family-centered, preventive goals, includes the following:

I. An ecological approach to understanding children and families in service delivery. The ecological approach assumes that the child and family interaction, development, and functioning are embedded within the broader aspects of the environment, which includes a community with cultural, ethnic, racial, and socioeconomic characteristics, which in turn must be understood in service development and delivery, policy, and research. This ecological context includes the following:
   a. Biological/physical factors
   b. Sociocultural, racial, ethnic, socioeconomic factors in the family's community, including community resources, worldview, values, and life-styles
   c. Personality, psychological/emotional factors
   d. Cognitive/intellectual factors
II. A focus on primary prevention and promoting the optimal development of children and families
III. Recognition of the importance of the early years
IV. A developmental view of parents and inclusion of parents as partners in the planning and implementation of services
V. An understanding of the universal value of support

The major portion of this chapter examines these principles of family support and uses them as a conceptual framework through which to evolve the knowledge and skills content necessary to train and educate family support personnel. The content evolved from each principle will be divided into three areas: basic knowledge, specialized knowledge, and practice skills. *Basic knowledge* includes the multidisciplinary, theoretical, and research-based information that supplies the foundation of systematic knowledge for family support staff. Basic knowledge permits us to understand and assess the family situation and has implications for the appropriate actions to be taken (Schön, 1988). It is the core knowledge that underlies professional practice. *Specialized knowledge* is the specific knowledge needed to serve the particular family, community, or cultural group targeted by the program. Specialized knowledge augments basic knowledge. *Practice skills* embody the application of basic knowledge, specialized knowledge, and use of self in competent practice to achieve the goals of the program. Schön (1988) refers to practice skills as a "kind of knowing," "an artistry" that is the hallmark of the competent practitioner (p. 13).

Education for family support is basically training for competence by teaching people how to integrate the three areas just defined. Fenichel and Eggbeer (1990) define competence as the ability "to do the right thing at the right time for the right reasons" (p. 8). They see competence as involving the skill and capacity to use basic and specialized knowledge to assess a situation, consider and evaluate alternative approaches to handling the situation, and select and skillfully apply the most appropriate practice skill that will improve the situation. The process leading to competence is most difficult to teach. It cannot be done only in the classroom or in training sessions, in the laboratory, or in observation; it is basically learned through the experience of applying basic and specialized knowledge to real-life situations, mediated through the self. This usually requires a supervised internship or fieldwork with some combination of classroom-based, sequential, systematic learning.

Prioritizing Knowledge and Skills

There is danger in attempting to build a unified approach to family support services, as this chapter does. No specific human behavior can be limited to a category because of the fluidity and multiple influences involved in any behavior. There is obvious overlap across the knowledge and skills connected with each principle described. Content described under one principle is often relevant to other principles. In an approach based on systems theory, where all principles are interconnected and interacting, overlap is impossible to eliminate, since by definition all the knowledge is interrelated. Educators and trainers need to stress the *interactive qualities* of these domains constantly. Each domain influences all others. Any change in one reverberates throughout the whole person-environment system, causing change throughout. A sick child, marital tension, or a low-birthweight baby will affect the entire family, including the children's school behavior, parental efficiency at work, the extended family, and even the local agency resources for service. The domains in this chapter are separated for conceptual teaching purposes and clarity.

What priorities can be set about which specified content areas should be given precedence in training? This chapter attempts to chart and set these priorities, based upon a scheme developed by the Illinois Early Intervention Personnel Development Committee (1993) to rate competence and skill areas. This committee rated competence, content, and skill areas for family support and early intervention specialists by placing numbers after each area, indicating at which level the area should be learned. The higher numbers indicate that the area should be learned at a level at which it can be applied independently by the learner. This chapter uses the Illinois scale with some modifications, placing ratings after each knowledge and skill domain to indicate the level at which students should be prepared:

1 = awareness level (exposed to ideas and concepts)
2 = knowledge level (knows main ideas and concepts and how they relate to the practitioner's discipline and practice)
3 = application level (prepared to apply concepts in everyday practice independently) (Illinois Early Intervention Personnel Development Committee, 1993)
4 = application level (specific to families served)

Use of this scheme will require further group consensus as we advance education for family support.

The next section attempts to tease out from each principle those domains of knowledge and skill considered necessary for professional and paraprofessional family support practice. Additions and integration must be made by each discipline, with its own goals, training, and curriculum. The basic knowledge, specialized knowledge, and practice skills that follow, using the family support principles as a conceptual framework, can be used to prepare family support staff to work effectively in a variety of programs.

Evolving Knowledge and Skills for Training and Education from the Family Support Principles

I: An Ecological Approach to Service Delivery

The family support principle advocating an ecological approach to services is presented first because it is so comprehensive and encompasses a major body of knowledge and skills. This principle stipulates that family support staff need to employ a systems-ecological framework, which forces them to consider the child in the total family environment and all interrelationships within it. In considering the children and family in their total ecological context in a heterogeneous society such as that of the United States, the diversity of parents must be understood, including their individual, family, racial, sociocultural, ethnic, and socioeconomic characteristics. One set of interrelationships cannot be separated from another, since all are elements of the parent or child's social system. Any change in any part of the system reverberates throughout the whole system (Bertalanffy, 1968; Parsons, 1964; Sameroff, 1986; Sameroff & Fiese, 1990; Bronfenbrenner, 1979, 1986), including the extended family, the neighborhood, and the racial and ethnic community.

Using the science of ecology, a branch of science concerned with the interrelationships of organisms and their environment (Gibson, 1979), Bronfenbrenner (1979) combines the ecological view with a systems perspective, emphasizing the interconnectedness and interdependence of individuals with their total ecological environment. Concerned about research in which children from different cultural milieus were studied and compared without consideration of the variations in their environmental contexts, he searched for a model that would force researchers and clinicians to include the entire network of social systems in which a child's life was embedded. His ecological approach assumes that the child and the environment are inseparable, and that both must be considered in all aspects in any assessment of functioning (Garbarino, 1982). The interaction is reciprocal in that each shapes the other.

Using the ecological approach, one of set categories that ensures integration of all relevant areas of the parent/child's interrelationships and environment includes biological/physical factors; sociocultural, economic, and structural factors; psychological/emotional factors; and cognitive/intellectual factors. The interactions of these categories or domains of content have been called the sources of human behavior (that is, all human behavior flows from the interaction of the content of these domains; see Berger & Federico, 1982). Problems in living arise from the complex interrelationships between and within domains. The knowledge and skill areas needed under each of these domains are discussed and prioritized in Table 18.1 and illustrated in Table 18.10.

I.a: Biological/Physical Domain. The biological/physical domain of the child and family includes all those factors of biological/genetic endowment and the physical environment. This domain does not stand alone but is affected by others. For example, how other family members deal with disability or illness of a member is certainly influenced by their own and the family's cultural attitudes and beliefs about illness. In keeping with the interconnectedness of the system's perspective, one's sociocultural and socioeconomic status clearly affects not only how one handles disabilities but also one's opportunity for and access to remedies.

I.b: Sociocultural/Socioeconomic/Structural Factors. The second domain of content of the ecological approach involves the cultural and socioeconomic context of the child and family in society. Children enter the world embedded in the interpersonal cultural system of their families, social institutions, and

Table 18.1. Ecological Content: Biological/Physical Domain.

A. *Basic Knowledge*   *Rating*
    (1) Normal biological and physical development milestones includ-
         ing post- and prenatal development, maternal and child health,
         and biological needs of expectant mothers   3
    (2) Endowment, maturation and individual differences of the de-
         veloping child, including temperament   3
    (3) Infant, toddler, early childhood biological development, includ-
         ing sensory, perceptual, and motor development   3
    (4) Atypical development and medical issues   4
         Developmental disabilities, prenatal problems (such as fetal
         alcohol syndrome, substance abuse, AIDS, HIV)
         Biological factors placing child at risk for abnormalities, in-
         cluding prematurity, low birthweight, prenatal maternal sub-
         stance abuse, and birth trauma
         Developmental disabilities, organic disabilities placing child
         at risk for developmental disabilities
         Other disabilities and biological factors placing child at risk
    (5) Normal health care needs (see Parmelee, 1993)   3
         Nutrition and feeding
         Communicable diseases
         Safety (adaptations, equipment, physical habitat, and envi-
         ronmental conditions)
    (6) Physical environmental factors affecting child and family   3
         Neighborhood traditions, routines, and activities, including
         not only cultural traditions but also such restrictions as street-
         gang territoriality
    (7) Theoretical and research findings on vulnerability, coping, and
         adaptation in early childhood   3
B. *Specialized Knowledge*
    (1) Knowledge of issues and procedures in current medical and
         health management of specific health problems of families
         served, including etiologies and characteristics of such condi-
         tions as cerebral palsy, Down's syndrome, and hearing, speech,
         and visual impairment   4
    (2) Societal attitudes toward disabilities in families served   4
    (3) Individual family's cultural response to illness or disability,
         understanding how variations in the perception of illness may
         affect the use of and compliance with health procedures (see
         Grossman, 1976)   4
    (4) Knowledge of community resources for evaluation, such as spe-
         cial clinics, physicians, speech therapists   3
C. *Practice Skills*
    (1) Ability to evaluate and assess normal development   3
    (2) Ability to recognize and refer atypical conditions, including
         evaluation and identification of children at risk biologically,
         socially, and environmentally   4

Table 18.1. Ecological Content: Biological/Physical Domain, Cont'd.

		Rating
(3)	Capacity to engage in effective team processes with health professionals serving the family (this includes case management, if appropriate)	3
(4)	Skill in establishing collaborative relationships with health care and other professionals, to facilitate referrals without unnecessary waiting and red tape	3
(5)	Ability to help parents and other professionals form partnerships with other needed resources for service planning and delivery	3

technologies (Rogoff, 1990). The family is located in society primarily according to its race, ethnic and religious background, and educational and occupational status. These factors influence where family members live, their access to resources and opportunities, their attitudes and aspirations, their values, and their preferred life-styles. They learn preferred family and community functioning through socialization within the family and acquire the knowledge, attitudes, behavioral patterns, and role expectations that will enable them to function adequately in their own community as adults (Fantini & Cardenas, 1980). Thus the culture of the group is passed on.

Culture can be defined as the way of life of a people, and it provides a framework for what is considered effective behavior in a specific society, ranging from toolmaking to parenting and child-rearing styles (LeVine, 1990). In a diverse society such as the United States, emphasis on certain elements of parenting can differ between different cultural groups (Norton, 1990, 1993). Family support staff need awareness of these differences, must respect them, and should work within the framework of the family's cultural beliefs. Some practices in the parenting of some cultural groups do not always match "best practices" of parenting in the United States developed through research, theory, and practice. How do family support staff handle this and remain culturally sensitive to difference and supportive of the family? The worker must not succumb to deficit thinking, assuming that the parents lack some essential skill to promote success in their children. The first step is to ask questions, in order to uncover the meaning of the practice to the parent. For example, efforts to educate a teenage mother to be responsive to her crying baby will hardly be successful if the adults in her environment tell her that she is spoiling the baby by doing so (Freel, 1987). We need to know how seemingly undesirable features have developed, and their meaning and function to the parents. If we attempt to introduce new behavior or remove existing behavior without understanding the meaning of the practice to the parent, our efforts will probably fail or provoke undesirable consequences.

Lieberman (1990), in her work with Latina mothers, found that new behavior must be worked out with families in accordance with their needs and beliefs. She presents an example of a young mother who gave birth to several children in such quick succession that her infants had low birthweight and failed to thrive, yet her religion forbade any consideration of birth control. Only after the mother's own fears for the health of her children and her fears for her own religious beliefs were understood fully and balanced and a spiritual leader got involved could a partial solution be found. Auerbach's research (1989) supports Lieberman's work. She also found that new practices must acknowledge a family's social reality, relate to the daily experience of their lives, and be seen as something that will improve their lives enough for them to move toward changes that may not always be supported by immediate friends and family members.

The core knowledge we need for understanding families within the content domain of sociocultural, socioeconomic, racial, and ethnic differences, as part of the ecological context, is shown in Table 18.2. Course materials in this area should reflect theories and research on multicultural, racial, and ethnic perspectives. There must be constant efforts to evaluate and revise the material in the courses on these dimensions, based on newer research, theories, and practice. This multicultural perspective is not always included in many of the courses of undergraduate and professional schools or in-service training. Therefore, seminars for family support students must include a model

Table 18.2. Ecological Content:
Cultural, Socioeconomic, Racial/Ethnic Domain.

			Rating
A.	*Basic Knowledge*		
	(1)	Theories and models to understand family systems, family processes, family functions, and family development	3
	(2)	Theories, models, and methods to understand and support diversity in families; understanding variations in traditions, values, and family roles and functioning across cultural groups in American society	4
	(3)	Structural factors of race, socioeconomic status, and gender that can strengthen or inhibit optimal child development	4
	(4)	Effects of such variations on interrelationships between child, family, school; understanding such variations and differential behavior, and building on strengths found in families	4
	(5)	Knowledge of economic, political, and social policies and attitudes that affect various family groups differentially	2
B.	*Specialized Knowledge*		
	(1)	Specific knowledge of the variations of racial, ethnic, economic, sociocultural characteristics, history, values, beliefs, and other particular issues of the families being served	4
	(2)	Issues of societal discrimination and prejudice about any demographic characteristics (including health and disabilities) of the children and families served	4
	(3)	Knowledge of legal and policy issues regarding the group served (for example, immigration policies regarding families of Hispanic origin; legal basis of early intervention at federal and state levels)	4
	(4)	Knowledge of environmental hazards and dynamics (for example, gang turf limitations)	4
	(5)	Specialized services for varying cultural groups (courses such as English as a Second Language)	4
C.	*Practice Skills*		
	(1)	Ability to be sensitive to and empathetic with the sociocultural variations of behavior and attitude of the children and family being served (ability to engage in culturally and ethnically sensitive competent practice and culturally relevant programming)	4
	(2)	Ability to build on the strengths of the family	3
	(3)	Ability to ask questions in a manner that does not put families off but elicits their traditions, the origins and function of their values, and the meaning of behavior to them	3

for including and using this domain of the ecological principle of family support and for ensuring a multicultural perspective.

I.c: Psychological/Emotional Domain. The third domain of the ecological framework considers psychological/emotional factors. In the early social interactive processes with parental figures and family, the child begins to learn about self and the world around himself or herself, and about how to participate in human interactions. Stern (1977) writes of this interactive "choreography" between the child and the family as the raw material out of which the child begins to construct knowledge of all things human. The child is not passive in this process but brings individual temperament and personality to the interaction, as does the parent. Attachment, bonding, knowledge of reality, and beginning identity all grow out of the interactive processes with a primary parent or caretaker within the family, group, or community (Ainsworth, 1969; Bowlby, 1951; Fenichel & Eggbeer, 1990; Greenspan, 1988; Shonkoff & Meisels, 1990; Rogoff, 1990; Stern, 1977; Zigler, 1990). Psychosocial theories, behavioral theories, and social learning and cognitive theories, all with very different assumptions, explain the child's psychological, emotional, and behavioral development. The individual characteristrics of the child and those of the parent, integrated with all other ecological circumstances of the family, influence the quality of the early child-parent interaction (Barnard & Kelly, 1990). Successful, reciprocal parent-child interaction produces a goodness of fit that is mutually satisfying. The psychological domain of knowledge needed to understand, assess, and foster parental skills for engendering positive and healthy relationships is shown in Table 18.3.

I.d: Cognitive/Intellectual Content. The final domain under the ecological approach involves cognitive/intellectual content. Cognition is the process of perception and thinking through which we process all the other domains (Piaget, 1926, 1952). One perceives new information, assimilates it, accommodates old information to the new information, makes some decision, and perhaps takes some action. From earliest infancy, children seek to share meaning with caretakers and others. Through Rogoff's concept (1990) of "guided participation" by parents, children come to understand what they perceive, and they think about the world from the perspective of those around them. Therefore, it is essential to view children's cognitive activities within the cultural ecological context of family adults.

Language is an important part of cognition. Although

**Table 18.3. Ecological Content:
Psychological/Emotional Domain.**

			Rating
A.	*Basic Knowledge*		
	(1)	Major theories of child and human development (psychodynamic, behavioral, social learning, cognitive); understanding implications for intervention of the various theories	3
	(2)	Normal emotional development in transactions between the infant and the environment; some understanding of synchrony and repair (see Tronick, 1986)	3
	(3)	Development of attachment, socioemotional development, bonding, and coping styles	3
	(4)	Play and its role in development (both social and object play)	2
	(5)	Risk, coping, adaptation, and mastery	3
	(6)	Abnormal psychological development	4
	(7)	Understanding emotional responses to changes in family's life course	3
	(8)	Understanding interrelationships in psychological development across all domains of the ecological system (biological/physical, sociocultural, and cognitive)	3
B.	*Specialized Knowledge*		
	(1)	Impact of specific disabilities or risk factors on parent-child interactions, attachment, and other socioemotional development	4
	(2)	Knowledge of appropriate referral sources for assessed problem areas	3
	(3)	Knowledge of the interplay between sociocultural issues and psychological health	3
	(4)	Knowledge of importance of touching, positioning, and handling young children, especially those with disabilities (see Williamson, 1988; Zeitlin & Williamson, 1988)	2
	(5)	Understanding the dynamics of abuse and neglect and identifying indicators	3
	(6)	Knowledge of the state and local child welfare system in regard to disability, child neglect, and abuse	2
	(7)	Understanding the clinical and collaborative processes for reporting such conditions as neglect, abuse, and AIDS	3
C.	*Practice Skills*		
	(1)	Ability to assess quality of attunement and synchrony in parent-child interaction	2
	(2)	Ability to evaluate the child's overall socioemotional development, using appropriate theoretical approach	3
	(3)	Approaches to observing parent-child interactions and child-environment interactions in home, in daily routines, in play environments, and in any setting where behavior is reasonably naturalistic	1
	(4)	Assessment of overall family functioning, including all domains (and, if appropriate, decision making, marital relationship, employment, health, intergenerational issues, child-rearing styles, and gender roles)	3

Table 18.3. Ecological Content:
Psychological/Emotional Domain, Cont'd.

		Rating
(5)	Planning with team and family intervention goals and objectives for parent-child pairs with attachment problems or other psychological/emotional issues	3
(6)	Methods to provide interventive help to strengthen families through a variety of appropriate formats, including play, role modeling, environmental behavioral routines, parent-mediated activities, counseling, and crisis intervention	3

research findings are still unclear on the exact process through which children learn language, most studies indicate that its development certainly occurs within the family's sociocultural system. The major goal for language is a functional one: achieving understanding of expressed, shared thinking between the child and the caregiver (Halliday, 1986; Rogoff, 1990). Research shows a relationship between quantity and synchrony of parent-child interaction and language development in children (Rogoff, 1990; Snow, 1982; Moerk, 1985). The more frequent and responsive the mother's interaction to the infant or toddler, the greater the child's competence to communicate its wants and needs, even if not in sentences. Children are more active in getting their own messages across if parents have been sensitive to their utterances and have contingently reinforced their verbal explorations (Moerk, 1985; Snow, 1982). Some researchers also believe it is highly correlated with literacy when reading and writing become other ways of sharing meaning (McLane & McNamee, 1991).

Again, the interrelationship of the domain of cognitive and linguistic development with the biological/physical, sociocultural, and psychological/emotional domains must be stressed. The knowledge and skills required of family support staff by this last domain of the ecological principle are shown in Table 18.4.

II: Focus on Promoting Primary Prevention and Optimalism

A second major principle cited as common to family support programs is the emphasis on primary prevention and optimalism

Table 18.4. Ecological Content: Cognitive/Intellectual Domain.

			Rating
A.	*Basic Knowledge*		
	(1)	Theories and research on early cognitive development	1
	(2)	Early sensory, perceptual, and motor development	3
	(3)	Cognitive, communication, and language development	2
	(4)	Individual differences in language development	2
	(5)	Age-appropriate learning styles	3
	(6)	Age-appropriate enrichment activities (vocalization and word play, fantasy)	2
B.	*Specialized Knowledge*		
	(1)	Knowledge of relationship of family's cultural background to theories and research on early cognitive development (any programs must fit with family's cultural concerns and interests)	4
	(2)	Referral network of appropriate programs, planned with family (family literacy programs, Even Start)	3
	(3)	Adult literacy programs (basic literacy, GED, English as a Second Language, A.A. and college-level courses)	2
	(4)	Appropriate materials to foster parent/child interaction, cognitive development (games, toys, books)	1
C.	*Practice Skills*		
	(1)	Techniques to encourage parents to interact with their children in cognitively stimulating ways	1
	(2)	Influencing families to use print materials as part of daily-life activities, to strengthen their own knowledge and use of resources for the family (providing newspapers or appropriate books to keep, whenever possible)	2
	(3)	Facilitating parental involvement with the school	3
	(4)	Effective teamwork with appropriate professionals (child development specialists, speech pathologists)	3

(Weissbourd & Kagan, 1989). Primary prevention implies that services are provided before the need develops and a problem occurs. The assumption is that enabling parents in their childrearing capacities prevents problems before they develop and helps children evolve toward their optimal development. Helping families in ways that may prevent problems is more efficient in physical, social, emotional, and financial ways and provides for a smoother development over the life course.

Primary prevention is considered far less costly than secondary prevention (providing health services once a health condition is identified) or tertiary prevention (treatment and management of a disease once it has occurred) (Upshur, 1990). However, primary prevention is often the most difficult of the three to provide because it requires knowledge of causal influences. The worker must know that there is a high risk that the condition will occur if the current situation does not change. Family support programs that have a comprehensive focus on services in all domains of the systems ecological approach, give parents support before they have a problem, and serve the parents as early in the child's life as possible will come closer to reaching primary prevention than other service programs.

Weissbourd and Kagan (1989) go a step farther than primary prevention and urge that family support programs also be moving toward what they call "optimalism." They define optimalism as *promoting* optimal development of children and families, rather than merely *preventing* a problem, as in primary prevention; it means "maximizing children's healthy growth and development" (1989, p. 22). They argue that since we cannot know (even though we target high-risk groups) what children may experience problems, preventive services must be available to all children and their families. We use this principle of primary prevention and optimalism to further specify the content of basic knowledge, specialized knowledge, and practice skills needed by family support staff, as shown in Table 18.5.

III: Recognition of the Importance of the Early Years

The third family support principle stresses the importance of the early years for optimal development. Although there is unparalleled growth in all domains of development in the first three years of life, it is also accepted that all periods of a child's life are "important and magical" (Zigler, 1990) and that each period of development is influenced by and builds on the preceding periods. Therefore, the first periods of life clearly have an especially important influence on the course of a child's development. Embedded in families, children obtain their first perceptions and attitudes about the world from their families, and the parents automatically become their children's first teachers, for better or for worse. The crucial importance of relationships in the first three years of life to the rest of the developmental process has been supported consistently in the literature, theoretically and empirically, during the past forty years (Ainsworth, 1969; Bowlby,

Table 18.5. Content on Prevention.

			Rating
A.	*Basic Knowledge*		
	(1)	Knowledge of theories and research on prevention (primary, secondary, and tertiary prevention; benefits of prevention)	1
	(2)	Knowledge of research on factors most highly correlated with developmental delay or disabling conditions	1
	(3)	Knowledge of signs predictive of common risk or disabling conditions	3
	(4)	Legal basis of early intervention, including federal, state, and local initiatives	2
	(5)	Ethical and policy issues related to working with young children and their families	3
B.	*Specialized Knowledge*		
	(1)	Federal, state, and local funding sources for child and family services	1
	(2)	Typical prevention and intervention methods as they apply to children at risk or with disabilities in the families being served	4
	(3)	Extensive preventive resource information for families (child-care preschool programs)	3
	(4)	Outreach strategies; understanding that one cannot wait until families come with a problem, or it may be too late for primary prevention	3
C.	*Practice Skills*		
	(1)	Creative and comprehensive outreach skills (particularly necessary if the ultimate goal of prevention/optimal service is to reach children before problems occur)	3
	(2)	Ability to speak informally and formally (workshops, PTA) to families about the importance of early development (outreach)	3
	(3)	Interviewing skills that elicit information from and involve families who may not have a defined problem	3
	(4)	Ability to build partnerships with agencies who are natural gatekeepers with families (physicians, well-baby clinics, self-help groups, day care)	3

1951; Brazelton, 1988; Greenspan & Greenspan, 1985; Kaye, 1977; Shanok, 1990; Stern, 1977; Sroufe, 1983; Tronick, 1986). If family support programs are to focus on promoting optimal development of children and families, as discussed earlier, then the earlier the support, the more likely one can prevent a problem before it occurs, and the more opportunity to support the optimal development of the child. Knowledge needed on the importance of the early years includes what is shown in Table 18.6.

Table 18.6. Content on Importance of Early Years.

			Rating
A.	*Basic Knowledge*		
	(1)	Endowment, and major milestones of the first three years	3
	(2)	Links of certain aspects of parent-child interaction to socio-cultural and socioeconomic values of parent	3
	(3)	Approaches to supporting and facilitating parent-child interaction as the primary context for learning and development	3
B.	*Specialized Knowledge*		
	(1)	Family social and cultural attitudes about appropriate parent-child interaction	4
	(2)	Assessment of parent-child interaction in age-appropriate domains	3
	(3)	Models of early intervention services, including federal, state, and local initiatives (see Goetz, 1992)	3
C.	*Practice Skills*		
	(1)	Techniques to assess early development of the child	3
	(2)	Techniques to assess parent-child interaction	3
	(3)	Techniques for supporting child-family interaction in positive ways (strategies of involving parents in joyful management of their young children)	3
	(4)	Assisting parents to recognize and respond contingently to infants' signals	3

IV: Taking a Developmental View of Parenthood and Inclusion of Parents as Partners

This principle stresses that parenthood is another phase of the human life course, and that parents can use the experience of parenthood for their own growth and development. This capacity for growth and development is not limited to their role as nurturers and advocates for their children. It includes their own personal growth and advancement and their knowledge of the child. Parents who are nurtured, and whose own needs are met, will be better prepared to nurture and meet the needs of their children (Weissbourd & Kagan, 1989). Parenthood is viewed as a developmental process, and family support programs should focus on the child and the parents and family simultaneously (Meisels, 1992). Parents should be involved in a partnership with staff on behalf of their mutual goals for the child and themselves. Facilitating parental effectiveness in parenting roles not only will meet the goals of protecting and advocating for the child but also will improve the plan for service as a result of parents' input. In terms of parental development, the team partnership can teach parents new roles and aid them in furthering their own self-confidence, leading to their own effectiveness and overall development (Cochran, 1985).

This view of the family, as capable of growth and development in each stage of its existence, is supported by family therapy and family process literature (Carter & McGoldrick, 1988) and prevents a view of the family as having a "deficit." The worker not only needs to be able to assess the normal tasks of the family life cycle but also must be knowledgeable about the life-course needs of the individual parents. The family life cycle consists of developmental phases, ranging from family formation and birth of young children through the launching of those children much later to dealing with the preparation for old age (Carter & McGoldrick, 1988; Walsh, 1982). There can be conflict between accomplishing the family life-phase tasks and the individual parental life-course tasks if the parent's life course is out of sync with family needs (as with an adolescent parent, for example). The normal tasks of adolescence — to find one's identity and continue with one's education — come easily into conflict with the selfless, consistent tasks needed to mother and nurture an infant. The worker must understand this potential conflict and engage in a partnership with the parent to find a balance between the sometimes conflicting needs (see Table 18.7).

V: The Universal Value of Support

The final family support principle cited by Weissbourd and Kagan (1989) is promotion of the universal value of support. In their review of family support programs, they found that most make use of the ability of families to develop supportive friendships and join with groups as sources for support, information, and advice. The role of social support in human well-being is much documented as being vital in the sociological, psychological, social work, and child development research. This interdisciplinary research over the past decade has shown that social

Table 18.7. Content on Parenthood and Parents as Partners.

			Rating
A.	*Basic Knowledge*		
	(1)	Theories of family life cycle and family processes	3
	(2)	Theories and models of family systems	3
	(3)	Issues of adult stress, coping, and adaptation	3
	(4)	Theories of self-esteem	2
	(5)	Role of family in contemporary society, as affected by family's sociocultural and socioeconomic background	4
	(6)	Knowledge of family structure, family dynamics, and roles	3
	(7)	Adult life-cycle knowledge	3
B.	*Specialized Knowledge*		
	(1)	Fatherhood services (availability of resources to enhance role of the father, such as parenting information, social support, positive social outlets)	3
	(2)	Issues faced by all members of a family with special-needs children	4
	(3)	How the appropriate tasks of parenthood are influenced by sociocultural, ethnic, and racial factors and by socioeconomic status and age of the specific families being served	4
C.	*Practice Skills*		
	(1)	Empowering parents in collaboration with other resources	3
	(2)	Sharing case management skills with parents	3
	(3)	Systematic assessment and ability to evaluate needs of total family	3
	(4)	Ability to work nonjudgmentally with the family	3
	(5)	Facilitation of coequal parental participation in setting individual family service plan goals	3
	(6)	Role modeling with parents in parent-child interaction	3
	(7)	Ability to include parents in assessing family organization and functioning	3
	(8)	Ability to help parents assess age-appropriate life-developmental tasks for their lives	3
	(9)	Ability to help parents assess family life-phase tasks	3

support is related to better coping across a variety of population groups, settings, and life problems (Belsky, 1984; Uehara, 1990; Weissbourd, 1981). Parents and children are embedded in family, neighborhood, and community, all of which become potential resources for support. From an ecological perspective, social support seems to have a beneficial effect on all domains of the parent-child interaction — physically, socially, psychologically, and cognitively — including effective parental functioning (Belsky, 1984).

These findings have implications for family support staff

who are trying to develop positive social supports for families. As in all other helping relationships, the family support worker must have enough knowledge and skills to enable, not disable. For example, in referrals to and use of other agency resources, the worker must develop a process that supports rather than supplants the natural, informal caregiving role of families and friends (Norton, Morales, & Andrews, 1980). Uehara's research (1990) cautions us that social support is not just a simple, positive concept; by relating social support and social exchange, her research demonstrates that social support is not a one-way provision of caring and assistance but can involve costs as well as benefits. She argues that the social support process is better characterized as a social exchange process: in the long term, there may be the expectation of some return (for example, the grandmother who babysits exacts full compliance from the mother). Before linkages are made, workers and parents must work in a partnership to anticipate what the costs are in certain familial relationships. Staff need important knowledge and skills in working with families and children to develop positive, effective social support systems, as shown in Table 18.8.

Table 18.8. Content on Social Support.

			Rating
A.	*Basic Knowledge*		
	(1)	Knowledge of group and informal supports and natural helping networks	3
	(2)	Understanding the potential conflicts and negatives that occur sometimes in social support	3
B.	*Specialized Knowledge*		
	(1)	Models to build partnerships with families of children with specific disabilities, to maximize active involvement in intervention services	3
	(2)	Understanding the role of social support through the sociocultural lens of the families being served	4
C.	*Practice Skills*		
	(1)	Procedures to facilitate parents as coequals in early supportive relationships	3
	(2)	Skill in helping parents mobilize available support systems	3
	(3)	Equal skill in helping parents think through the ramifications of certain social supports in the context of their specific lives	3
	(4)	Group dynamic skills (enabling peer support groups)	3
	(5)	Collaboration with other agencies in resource development	4

VI: Generalized Knowledge and Skills
Applicable to All Principles and Domains

It cannot be overstressed that in a social systems/ecological approach to family support, all domains and categories of knowledge and skills overlap and are interdependent. This chapter categorizes these areas conceptually under the principles of family support and attempts to place the most needed knowledge and skills under each principle, for the purpose of clarity and understanding. This section lists the knowledge and skills needed to implement all the principles successfully (see Table 18.9).

Implications of the Conceptual Framework for Educational Issues

Table 18.10 summarizes the domains of content of the conceptual framework and lists the priorities for each knowledge and skill. Using Table 18.10, this section discusses some of the implications of the conceptual framework for family support education. It should be noted that the content rated as number 3

Table 18.9. Professional Content Needed in All Domains.

		Rating
A.	*Basic Knowledge*	
	(1) Conflict-resolution theories and practices	3
	(2) Human dynamics of interaction	3
B.	*Specialized Knowledge*	
	(1) Confidentiality issues and procedures	3
	(2) Requirements for reporting and record keeping	3
C.	*Practice Skills*	
	(1) Professional work habits of time management, independence, appropriate responsibility	3
	(2) Interviewing skills (active listening, knowledge of idiomatic language and preferences of expression of particular group being served	3
	(3) Monitoring and evaluation of child-family outcomes, as set by the individual family service plan	3
	(4) Ability to engage in professional self-reflection, individually or with supervision (see Schön, 1988)	3
	(5) Critical reading and application of family support and appropriate interdisciplinary literature	3

and as number 4 is probably the most important content necessary for effective family support practice.

Preservice Education and Training

Many states are working now to specify the educational content and skills needed for family support programs and to develop certification requirements for a variety of professionals who work in such programs. The professionals involved include audiologists, nurses, nutritionists, occupational therapists, physicians, psychologists, social workers, special educators, and speech and language pathologists. Early credentialing seems to be moving to a collaboration between states and universities. Many states are devising criteria to license workers and approve educational programs. This means that each professional discipline needs to articulate specific competence criteria for its practitioners, which can become the basis for appropriate approval and licensing standards (Fenichel & Eggbeer, 1990).

In many states, there is a push to stimulate the development of university programs directed toward providing personnel who meet requirements for the new occupational categories needed at professional levels, including that of family support specialist. We have already pointed out that tight curricula and lack of prepared faculty are two of the challenges faced by professional schools interested in educating for family support and early intervention. Examination of Table 18.10 further supports the complexity of these challenges. The required content designated as 3 occurs far more frequently. By definition, this content is at the application level and is necessary to learn in depth. It would be difficult to add all the number 3's to the already crowded professional curricula. In addition, the number 3 content is also very broad and eclectic in nature, requiring a wide range of faculty knowledge to teach it. Some professions seeking to handle these challenges have examined their curricula and found that some of the specific knowledge and practice skills are already included (Delany-Cole, 1992b; Fenichel & Eggbeer, 1990). They have found that, with fine-tuning and modification, the content can be put in place. Courses in other departments are

Table 18.10. Knowledge and Skills Related to Family Support Principles: Conceptual Framework of Education for Family Support.

I. An Ecological Approach

I.1	*Biological/Physical Factors*	*Rating**
A.	Basic Knowledge	
	(1) Developmental milestones	3
	(2) Maturational & individual differences between children	3
	(3) Sensory, perceptual, & motor development	3
	(4) Atypical development & medical issues	4
	(a) prenatal problems	
	(b) biological factors placing child at risk	
	(c) developmental disabilities	
	(5) Normal health care needs	3
	(6) Physical/environmental factors affecting child	3
	(7) Theoretical findings on vulnerability, coping, and adaptation	3
B.	Specialized Knowledge	
	(1) Current medical management of specific health problems	4
	(2) Societal attitudes toward disabilities in families served	4
	(3) Family's cultural response to illness/disability	4
	(4) Knowledge of community resource for evaluation	3
C.	Practice Skills	
	(1) Ability to evaluate and assess normal development	3
	(2) Ability to recognize and refer typical conditions	4
	(3) Capacity to engage in team processes with health professionals	3
	(4) Skill in working collaboratively with health care professionals to facilitate referrals	3
	(5) Ability to help parents and professionals form partnerships with service resources	3
I.2	*Sociocultural/Socioeconomic/Structural Factors*	
A.	Basic Knowledge	
	(1) Theories of family systems, functions, processes, and development	3
	(2) Theories/models to understand and support diversity of families	4
	(3) Effects of structural factors of race, socioeconomic status, and gender on development	4
	(4) Effects of such variations on interrelationships between child, family, and school	4
	(5) Knowledge of economic, political, and social policies that affect family groups differentially	2
B.	Specialized Knowledge	
	(1) Variations of racial, ethnic, economic, sociocultural characteristics, values, benefits, and particular issues of families served	4

*Each competency has been rated according to the following scale: 1 = awareness level (exposed to ideas and concepts), 2 = knowledge level (knows main ideas and concepts and how they relate to practice), 3 = application level (prepared to apply concepts in everyday practice), 4 = application level (specific to families served)

Table 18.10. Knowledge and Skills Related to Family Support Principles: Conceptual Framework of Education for Family Support, Cont'd.

		Rating
(2)	Societal discrimination and prejudice about demographic characteristics of families served	4
(3)	Legal and policy issues regarding families served	4
(4)	Knowledge of environmental hazards and dynamics	4
(5)	Specialized services based on cultures of families served	4
C.	Practice Skills	
(1)	Ability to be sensitive/empathetic to sociocultural variations of behavior/attitudes of families served	4
(2)	Ability to build upon the strengths of family	3
(3)	Ability to ask questions in a manner that does not "put off" families but elicits traditions, origins, and functions of their values, and meaning of the behaviors to them	3
I.3	*Psychological/Emotional Domains*	
A.	Basic Knowledge	
(1)	Major theories of human development, and implications for implementation	3
(2)	Normal emotional development in transaction between infant and environment (i.e., synchrony and repair)	3
(3)	Development of attachment, socioemotional development, bonding, and coping styles	3
(4)	Play and its role in development	2
(5)	Risk, coping, adaptation, and mastery	3
(6)	Abnormal psychological development	4
(7)	Understanding emotional responses to changes in family life course	3
(8)	Understanding interrelationships in development across all domains of the ecological system	3
B.	Specialized Knowledge	
(1)	Impact of disabilities on parent/child interactions	4
(2)	Knowledge of appropriate referral sources	3
(3)	Knowledge of interplay between sociocultural issues and psychological health	3
(4)	Knowledge of importance of touching and handling young child, especially those with disabilities	2
(5)	Understanding dynamics of abuse/neglect and identifying indicators	3
(6)	Knowledge of state/local child welfare system regarding disabilities, neglect, and abuse	2
(7)	Understanding the clinical/collaborative process of reporting conditions such as abuse, neglect, AIDS	3
C.	Practice Skills	
(1)	Ability to assess quality of attunement/synchrony in parent-child interactions	2
(2)	Ability to evaluate child's socioemotional development using theoretical approaches	3

Table 18.10. Knowledge and Skills Related to Family Support Principles: Conceptual Framework of Education for Family Support, Cont'd.

		Rating
(3)	Approaches to observing parent-child interactions & child-environment interactions in home	1
(4)	Assessment of overall family functions	3
(5)	Planning intervention goals and objectives with team and family	3
(6)	Methods to provide interventive help to strengthen family through a variety of appropriate formats	3

I.4 Cognitive Intellectual Domains

A. Basic Knowledge

(1)	Theories/research on early cognitive development	1
(2)	Early sensory, perceptual, and motor development	3
(3)	Cognitive, communication, and language development	2
(4)	Individual differences in language development	2
(5)	Age-appropriate learning styles	3
(6)	Age-appropriate enrichment activities	2

B. Specialized Knowledge

(1)	Knowledge of relationship of family's cultural background to theories and research on early cognitive development	4
(2)	Referral network of appropriate programs, planned with family	3
(3)	Adult literacy programs	2
(4)	Appropriate materials to foster parent-child interaction, cognitive development	1

C. Practice Skills

(1)	Techniques to encourage parents to interact with their children in cognitively stimulating ways	1
(2)	Influence families to use print materials as part of daily life activities to strengthen their own knowledge and use of resources for their family (e.g., provide newspapers or appropriate books to keep whenever possible)	2
(3)	Facilitate parental involvement with the school	3
(4)	Effective teamwork with appropriate discipline (e.g. child development specialist)	3

II. Primary Prevention and Optimalism

A. Basic Knowledge

(1)	Theories and research on prevention	1
(2)	Research on factors most highly correlated with developmental delay or disabling conditions	1
(3)	Signs predictive of common risk or disabling condition	3
(4)	Legal basis of early intervention	2
(5)	Ethical and policy issues related to young children and their families	3

B. Specialized Knowledge

(1)	Federal, state, and local funding sources for child and family services	1

Table 18.10. Knowledge and Skills Related to Family Support Principles: Conceptual Framework of Education for Family Support, Cont'd.

		Rating
(2)	Typical prevention and intervention methods as applied to children at risk or with disabilities	4
(3)	Extensive prevention resource information for families	3
(4)	Outreach strategies cannot wait until families come with a problem or it may be too late for primary prevention	3
C.	Practice Skills	
(1)	Creative, comprehensive outreach skills	3
(2)	Ability to speak informally and formally	3
(3)	Interviewing skills that elicit information from and involve family who may not have a defined problem	3
(4)	Ability to build partnerships with agencies who are natural gatekeepers with families	3

III. Recognition of the Importance of the Early Years

A.	Basic Knowledge	
(1)	Endowment and major milestones of the first three years	3
(2)	Links of certain aspects of parent-child interaction to sociocultural and socioeconomic values of parent	3
(3)	Approaches to support and facilitate parent-child interactions as the primary contexts for learning and development	3
B.	Specialized Knowledge	
(1)	Family social and cultural attitudes about appropriate parent-child interaction	4
(2)	Assessment of parent-child interaction in appropriate domains and age	3
(3)	Models of early intervention services	3
C.	Practice Skills	
(1)	Techniques to assess early development of the chld	3
(2)	Techniques to assess parent-child interaction	3
(3)	Techniques for supporting child-family interaction in positive ways	3
(4)	Assisting parents to recognize and respond contingently to infant signals	3

IV. Taking a Developmental View of Parenthood,
Inclusion of Parents as Partners

A.	Basic Knowledge	
(1)	Theories of family life cycle and family process	3
(2)	Theories and models of family systems	3
(3)	Issues of adult stress, coping, and adaptation	3
(4)	Theories of self-esteem	2
(5)	Role of family in contemporary society as affected by family's sociocultural, socioeconomic background	4
(6)	Knowledge of family structure, dynamics, and roles	3
(7)	Adult life cycle knowledge	3

Table 18.10. Knowledge and Skills Related to Family Support Principles: Conceptual Framework of Education for Family Support, Cont'd.

Rating

B. Specialized Knowledge
   (1) Fatherhood services: availability of resources to enhance parental role of the father   3
   (2) Issues faced by all members of family with special needs children   4
   (3) How the appropriate tasks of parenthood are influenced by sociocultural, ethnic, racial, socioeconomic status, and age of the specific families being served   4

C. Practice Skills
   (1) Collaboration with other resources   3
   (2) Case-management skills   3
   (3) Systematic assessment and ability to evaluate needs of total family   3
   (4) Ability to work nonjudgmentally with the family   3
   (5) Facilitation of coequal parental participation in setting individual family service plan (IFSP) goals   3
   (6) Role modeling with parents in parent-child interaction   3
   (7) Ability to assess family organization and functioning   3
   (8) Ability to assess age-appropriate life developmental tasks   3
   (9) Ability to assess family life phase tasks   3

V. The Universal Value of Support

A. Basic Knowledge
   (1) Knowledge of group and informal supports and natural helping networks   3
   (2) Understanding potential conflicts and negatives that may occur in the social support   4

B. Specialized Knowledge
   (1) Models to build partnerships with families of children with specific disabilities to maximize active involvement in intervention services   3
   (2) Understanding role of social support from the sociocultural lens of the families being served   4

C. Practice Skills
   (1) Procedures to facilitate parents as coequals in early supportive relationships   3
   (2) Skill in helping parents mobilize available support systems   3
   (3) Equal skill in helping parents think through the ramifications of certain social supports in the context of their lives   3
   (4) Group dynamic skills   3
   (5) Collaborative work with other agencies in resource development   4

VI. Generalized Knowledge and Skills Applicable to All Principles and Domains

A. Basic Knowledge
   (1) Conflict-resolution theories and practices   3
   (2) Human dynamics of interaction   3

Table 18.10. Knowledge and Skills Related to Family Support Principles: Conceptual Framework of Education for Family Support, Cont'd.

	Rating
B. Specialized Knowledge	
(1) Confidentiality issues and procedures	3
(2) Requirements of reporting and record keeping	3
C. Practice Skills	
(1) Professional work habits of time management, independence-appropriate responsibilitiy	3
(2) Interviewing skills	3
(3) Monitoring and evaluation of child/family outcomes as set by the IFSP	3
(4) Ability to engage in professional self-reflection individually or with supervision	3
(5) Critical reading and application of family support and appropriate interdisciplinary literature	3

another source from which to obtain some of this content, especially that under basic knowledge in Table 18.10).

Content rated as number 4 is also highly crucial and is usually augmented through internships or field placements, which are already part of training in many of the professions involved in family support. It has been mentioned that developing competencies in family support practice occurs through applying basic and specialized knowledge to real-life situations, and this requires some form of supervised internship or fieldwork. Finding appropriate mentors or supervisors, and practice settings where the professional goals and practices of the discipline can be melded with those of the family support program, may be difficult. Several programs are writing grants to have field placements and internships by their own faculty-based field instructors.

Sequencing and providing the content in Table 18.10 requires a committed faculty and interdisciplinary faculty group. Faculty usually work in relatively separate departments, and there is little interdisciplinary work. Much work still needs to be done in bridging disciplines and in bridging the gap between those engaged in family support policy and those engaged in direct service. In terms of content itself, mention should be made of another challenge inherent in the conceptual framework. This is the approach to parents and families as "partners," in which parents are included in academic planning. In some universities, parents and professors coteach certain courses. Most faculty will find this unusual, and some university administrators will frown on such partnerships as not being academic enough, seeing parental contributions as merely anecdotal or illustrative. Factoring in this principle with the profession's goals and academic expectations will take creativity in different forms. A number of innovative strategies are being planned by several states; for example, Colorado, Minnesota, and Illinois have planned to provide training to faculty across disciplines, including parents (McCollum & Bailey, 1991).

In-Service Education and Training

We have already discussed the many challenges of in-service education. It should be mentioned that in-service education can be very helpful in providing content rated as number 4. The content can focus directly and in depth on the specific types of families with certain problems being served. It requires creative and judicial planning across disciplines and involving the community and parents as consultants and partners. It also requires developing training programs that can meet different levels of need.

Many family support services are performed by paraprofessionals, and much of in-service is targeted toward them. Paraprofessionals serving under various names, such as community advocates, indigenous workers, and family advocates, have been key workers in community-based programs since Head Start began. At that time, it was a strategic political move to hire them, because advocates of the program could argue for program support in Congress on the basis that jobs would be created in the community. Community workers have been used in community-based parent-children programs ever since. Often they are vital, valid, and effective components of the program (for example, as "mentors" to adolescent mothers). In other circumstances, they are less valid, as when their presence permits professional staff to remain in their offices to plan and develop programs while the paraprofessionals go into the community and make contact because they "understand" the community. They become the bridge to the community programs. Professional staff members who cannot go into the community and become partners with those served, and who must use paraprofessional go-betweens, should not be in the community. Paraprofessionals should not be used merely because they "understand the culture" (unless they are hired as paid consultants to the staff). Otherwise, they become middlepersons. Professional staff should have the ability to go into the community, learn about it, and form partnerships that validate what they are trying to do. Since many programs are staffed heavily by paraprofessionals, they must be involved to foster effective in-service training.

This chapter has attempted to unify a large quantity of knowledge and skills related to the goals and principles of family support that are crucial to the development of effective personnel. Education of enough personnel for effective family support will take time, money, enormous creativity, and commitment. Yet we can do no less. We have the responsibility to plan for the high standards we wish to see in the future in regard to best practices and competencies. Children are our most important national resource in determining the future and quality of life for our entire society. We cannot afford to trust them to those who cannot serve them well.

References

Ainsworth, M.D.S. (1969). Object relations dependency and attachment: A theoretical review of the mother-infant relationship. *Child Development, 40,* 969–1025.

Auerbach, E. R. (1989). Toward a social contextual approach to family literacy. *Harvard Educational Review, 59,* 165–181.

Barnard, K. E., & Kelly, J. F. (1990). Assessment of parent-child interaction. In S. J. Meisels & J. P. Shonkoff (Eds.), *Handbook of early childhood intervention* (pp. 278–302). New York: Cambridge University Press.

Belsky, J. (1984). The determinants of parenting: A process model. *Child Development, 55,* 83–96.

Berger, R., & Federico, C. (1982). *Human behavior: A social work perspective.* New York: Longman.

Bertalanffy, L. V. (1968). *General system theory.* New York: George Braziller.

Bowlby, J. (1951). *Maternal care and mental health.* Geneva, Switzerland: World Health Organization.

Brazelton, T. B. (1988). Importance of early intervention. In E. Hibbs (Ed.), *Children and families: Studies in prevention and intervention* (pp. 107–120). Madison, CT: International Universities Press.

Bronfenbrenner, U. (1979). *The ecology of human development: Experiments by nature and design.* Cambridge, MA: Harvard University Press.

Bronfenbrenner, U. (1986). Ecology of the family as a context for human development. *Developmental Psychology, 22*(6), 723–742.

Carter, B., & McGoldrick, M. (1988). *Family life cycle: A framework for family therapy.* New York: Gardner Press.

Carter, J. L. (1992). Better than welfare: Teach families success skills. *Wingspread Journal, 14,* 1–10.

Cochran, M. (1985). The parental empowerment process: Building upon family strengths. *Equity and Choice, 4,* 3–7.

Delany-Cole, H. (1992a). *Data gathering for family support specialization planning.* Report to faculty planning committee. Chicago: University of Chicago School of Social Service Administration.

Delany-Cole, H. (1992b.) *Development of a children and family services specialization.* Report to faculty planning committee. Chicago: University of Chicago School of Social Service Administration.

Dunst, C. J. (1990). New directions for family resources and support programs. In D. G. Unger & D. R. Powell (Eds.), *Families as nurturing systems: Support across the life span* (pp. 23–24). New York: Haworth Press.

Family Resource Coalition. (1992). *Best Practices Project: Summary report of the planning committee.* Chicago: Author.

Fantini, M. D., & Cardenas, R. (1980). *Parenting in a multicultural society.* New York: Longman.

Fenichel, E. S., & Eggbeer, L. (1990). *Preparing practitioners to work with infants, toddlers and their families: Issues and recommendations for the professions.* Arlington, VA: National Center for Clinical Infant Programs.

Freel, K. (1987, December). *Toward an understanding of inner-city patterns of parent-infant interactions.* Paper presented at the National Center for Clinical Infant Programs Fifth Biennial National Training Institute, Washington, DC.

Garbarino, J. (1982). *Children and families in the social environment.* Hawthorne, NY: Aldine.

Gibson, J. J. (1979). *The ecological approach to visual perception.* Boston: Houghton Mifflin.

Goetz, K. (Ed.). (1992). *Programs to strengthen families: A resource guide.* Chicago: Family Resource Coalition.

Greenspan, S. I. (1988). Fostering emotional and social development in infants with disabilities. *Zero to Three, 9,* 8–18.

Greenspan, S. I., & Greenspan, N. T. (1985). *First feelings: Milestones in the emotional development of your baby and child from birth to age 4.* New York: Viking.

Grossman, L. (1976). Ethnicity and health delivery systems. In P. Cafferty & L. Chestang (Eds.), *The diverse society: Implications for social policy* (pp. 129–148). Washington, DC: National Association of Social Workers.

Halliday, M.A.K. (1986). *Learning how to mean: Explorations in the development of language.* London: Edward Arnold.

Hanft, B. E. (Ed.). (1989). *Family-centered care: An early intervention resource manual.* Rockville, MD: American Occupational Therapy Association, Inc.

Illinois Early Intervention Personnel Development Committee. (1993). *Recommended criteria for developing an approved university program to prepare personnel for the role of family support specialist.* Springfield: Illinois State Board of Education.

Kaye, K. (1977). Toward the origin of dialogue. In H. R. Schaffer (Ed.), *Studies in mother-infant interaction* (pp. 89–117). San Diego, CA: Academic Press.

Klein, N. K., & Campbell, P. (1990). Preparing personnel to serve at-risk and disabled infants, toddlers and preschoolers. In S. J. Meisels & J. P. Shonkoff (Eds.), *Handbook of early childhood intervention* (pp. 679–699). New York: Cambridge University Press.

LeVine, R. A. (1990). Infant environments in psychoanalysis: A cross-cultural view. In J. W. Stigler, R. A. Schweder, & G. Herdt (Eds.), *Cultural psychology: Essays on comparative human development* (pp. 454–474). New York: Cambridge University press.

Lieberman, A. (1990). Infant-parent intervention with recent immigrants: Reflections on a study with Latino families. *Zero to Three, 10,* 8–11.

McCollum, J. A. (1992). *Family support specialist: Program approval criteria.* Working paper, Early Intervention Personnel Development Committee. Springfield: Illinois State Board of Education.

McCollum, J. A., & Bailey, D. B. (1991). Developing comprehensive personnel systems: Issues and alternatives. *Journal of Early Intervention, 15,* 60.

McLane, J. B., & McNamee, G. D. (1991). The beginnings of literacy. *Zero to Three, 12,* 1–8.

Meisels, S. J. (1992). Early intervention: A matter of context. *Zero to Three, 12,* 1–6.

Midwestern Consortium for Faculty Development. (1993). *Early childhood research programs.* Minneapolis: University of Minnesota, Institute on Community Integration, College of Education.

Moerk, E. L. (1985). A differential interactive analysis of language teaching and learning. *Discourses Processes, 8,* 113–142.

Norton, D. G. (1990). Culturally and ecologically relevant research as a guide to support families. *Zero to Three, 10,* 1–8.

Norton, D. G. (1993). Diversity, early socialization and temporal development. *Social Work, 38,* 82–90.

Norton, D. G., Morales, J., & Andrews, E. (1980). *The Neighborhood Self-Help Project.* Occasional paper No. 9, School of Social Service Administration. Chicago: University of Chicago.

Parmelee, A. H. (1993). Children's illnesses and normal behavioral development: The role of caregivers. *Zero to Three, 13,* 1–9.

Parsons, T. (1964). *The social system.* New York: Free Press.

Piaget, J. (1926). *The language and thought of the child.* Orlando, FL: Harcourt Brace Jovanovich.

Piaget, J. (1952). *The origins of intelligence in children.* New York: Norton.

Powell, D. R. (1988). *Parent education as early childhood intervention.* Norwood, NJ: Ablex.

Powell, D. R. (1991). Staff development in family resource programs. *Family Resource Coalition Report, 10,* 14–15.

Rogoff, B. (1990). *Apprenticeship in thinking: Cognitive development in social context.* New York: Oxford University Press.

Sameroff, A. J. (1986). Environmental context of child development. *Journal of Pediatrics, 109,* 192–200.

Sameroff, A. J., & Fiese, B. H. (1990). Transactional regulation and early intervention. In S. J. Meisels & J. P. Shonkoff (Eds.), *Handbook of early childhood intervention* (pp. 119–149). New York: Cambridge University Press.

Schön, D. A. (1988). *Educating the reflective practitioner.* San Francisco: Jossey-Bass.

Shanok, R. S. (1990). Parenthood: A process marking identity and intimacy capacities. *Zero to Three, 11,* 1–9.

Shonkoff, J. P., & Meisels, S. J. (1990). Early childhood intervention: The evolution of a concept. In S. J. Meisels & J. P. Shonkoff (Eds.), *Handbook of early childhood intervention* (pp. 3–31). New York: Cambridge University Press.

Snow, C. E. (1982). Are parents language teachers? In K. Borman (Ed.), *Social life of children in a changing society* (pp. 81–95). Hillsdale, NJ: Erlbaum.

Sroufe, L. A. (1983). Infant-caregiver attachment and patterns of adaptation in preschool: The roots of maladaptation and competence. In M. Perlmutter (Ed.), *The Minnesota Symposia on Child Psychology* (pp. 16, 41–84). Hillsdale, NJ: Erlbaum.

Stern, D. (1977). *The first relationship: Mother and infant.* Cambridge, MA: Harvard University Press.

Tronick, E. Z. (1986). Interactive mismatch and repair: Challenges to the coping infant. *Zero to Three, 6,* 1–6.

Uehara, E. (1990). Dual exchange theory, social networks, and informal social support. *American Journal of Sociology, 96,* 521–557.

Upshur, C. C. (1990). Early intervention in preventive intervention. In S. J. Meisels & J. P. Shonkoff (Eds.), *Handbook of early childhood intervention* (pp. 633–650). New York: Cambridge University Press.

Walsh, F. (1982). *Normal family processes.* New York: Guilford Press.

Weissbourd, B. (1981). Supporting parents as people. In B. Weissbourd & J. Musick, (Eds.), *Infants: Their social environments* (pp. 169–183). Washington, DC: National Association for the Education of Young Children.

Weissbourd, B. (1990). Family resource and support programs: Changes and challenges in human services. In D. G. Unger & D. R. Powell (Eds.), *Families as nurturing systems: Support across the life span* (pp. 69–89). New York: Haworth Press.

Weissbourd, B., & Kagan, S. L. (1989). Family support programs: Catalysts for change. *American Journal of Orthopsychiatry, 59*(1), 20–31.

Williamson, G. G. (1988). Motor control as a resource for adaptive coping. *Zero to Three, 9,* 1–8.

Zeitlin, S., & Williamson, G. G. (1988). *Early coping inventory.* Bensenville, IL: Scholastic Testing Service.

Zigler, E. F. (1990). Foreword. In S. J. Meisels & J. P. Shonkoff (Eds.), *Handbook of early childhood intervention* (pp. ix–xiv). New York: Cambridge University Press.

□ 19 □

Evaluating
Family Support Programs

Are We Making Progress?

Douglas R. Powell

The development and expansion of family support programs have far outpaced the availability of research information on program implementation and effectiveness. This is not a field where science has played a major role in informing practice. The complexity of family support programs poses major evaluation challenges, and severe limits on government-sponsored research for most of the 1980s seriously restricted opportunities to address the methodological hurdles inherent in evaluating comprehensive programs for families.

Given this context, it is surprising that progress is being made on the evaluation front. It is not progress that can be measured in major leaps. The advances appear minor when considered individually, but collectively they provide evidence of solid movement toward a stronger set of approaches to evaluation and a firmer base of useful research knowledge.

This chapter reviews recent developments in the evaluation of family support programs. The first section briefly summarizes current thinking and practice in the evaluation of family support programs. The primary intent is to provide an overview of existing and emerging directions in the questions asked and methodologies employed in investigations of programs designed to support families. The second section reviews some recent major studies and literature reviews on the implementation and effects of family support programs. The final section discusses conclusions drawn from the evaluation literature.

Approaches to Evaluation

Evaluations of family support programs increasingly are asking a more complicated set of questions than had been explored in the past. However, the prevalence of quasi-experimental research designs and the limited range of available measures have changed little. Interest in cost-benefit analyses and in the process by which evaluations are conducted is growing. Each development is discussed here.

Questions Asked

In recent years, there has been a refinement of the questions examined in evaluations of family support programs. In outcome studies, the question "Are family support programs effective?" has given way to interest in a more differentiated set of questions about what types of programs or strategies work with whom, how, where, and why (Weiss, 1988). This change reflects growing awareness of the importance of *context* in individual, family, and program functioning, and the concomitant need for sensitivity to population differences in policy and program decisions (Laosa, 1990). As a result, there is increased understanding that programs found to work with one type of population (for example, middle-class families) or setting (for example, rural) may not be effective in other contexts.

There also has been a refinement of evaluation work beyond a focus on program outcomes. Data collected prior to program design and implementation are of increasing importance to a field interested in tailoring programs to their contexts. For instance, differences in the program preferences of Mexican immigrant versus Mexican American mothers have major implications for the design of a culturally responsive family support program aimed at Mexican-origin women (Powell, Zambrana,

& Silva-Palacios, 1990). Jacobs (1988) has identified preimplementation information of this type as the first level of a five-tiered approach to evaluating family support programs. The other levels focus on accountability, clarification regarding program services and intents, progress toward meeting program objectives, and program impacts.

Evaluation Designs

Random assignment has been the exception rather than the norm in evaluations of family support programs. Randomly assigning families to different conditions—a core element of experimental designs—is the best way to determine whether a program is effective. Alternative designs leave unanswered the nagging question of whether preexisting characteristics in the program and comparison groups contributed to evaluation results. This is especially problematic in evaluations of voluntary programs, such as family support programs, because factors that facilitate an individual's joining and participating in a program (personal resourcefulness, or community connections) may be difficult to secure in a nonrandom comparison group.

Nonetheless, the stark realities of providing community-based family support programs conflict with the ideals of experimental design. Often there are ethical, political, and/or logistical problems of withholding services or assigning families to particular services through random assignment procedures (Powell, 1987). Consequently, most evaluations employ some sort of quasi-experimental design.

The evaluation designs of seven programs represented in the Child Survival/Fair Start for Children initiative are illustrative. Five programs used comparison groups, sometimes without the benefit of preprogram data from the comparison group; one program had no comparison or contrast group, and one program attempted to employ an experimental design. This latter effort provides an instructive reminder that random assignment is not a problem-free design. In the Haitian Perinatal Intervention Project serving Florida's Broward County, a "clean" control group was constructed initially through random assignment, but many control mothers were neighbors of program mothers who proudly shared program toys and information, including demonstrations of what the interventionist had done during the home visit. One program mother even set up classes for other mothers in the courtyard of her apartment house (Widmayer, Peterson, Calderon, Carnahan, & Wingerd, 1992). This experience is a contemporary example of the "horizontal diffusion" of a home-visiting intervention identified more than two decades ago by Klaus and Gray (1968).

Random assignment of families to two or more different versions of an intervention continues to hold significant potential in evaluating family support programs (Seitz, 1987). A recent example of an evaluation employing this design — technically known as treatment partitioning — is Project CARE, which randomly assigned families to one of three conditions: two interventions differing in intensity, and a control group (Wasik, Ramey, Bryant, & Sparling, 1990; see subsequent discussion in this chapter). Treatment partitioning is an especially appropriate design for evaluating the contributions of various components of comprehensive interventions. As interest increases in programs that provide a range of services (for example, two-generation programs), efficient use of limited resources for programs will require information about the effects of different intervention components (Smith, Blank, & Collins, 1992).

In striking contrast to the conventional scientific paradigm, recent evaluation literature on family support programs points to some interest in participatory evaluations that emphasize the process through which an investigation is carried out; see the September 1991 issue of *Networking Bulletin,* devoted to evaluation and empowerment (Cornell Empowerment Project, 1991). This approach recognizes research as a political process and is concerned about power relationships among the various "stakeholders," or individuals tied to the program or topic under investigation. Participatory evaluation models stem from an empowerment perspective and focus on the role of knowledge creation in helping those with less power gain some control over their lives. Hence, in participatory evaluations, it is expected that program participants themselves will play major roles in defining research questions or problems, gathering data, determining the meaning of the data through collective analysis, and presenting the data to a larger audience for action (Whitmore, 1991). For example, in a recent participatory evaluation conducted by the Maternal Infant Health Outreach Worker project, study questions were formulated through extensive use of focus or small-discussion groups involving program staff and participants in rural, low-income Appalachian communities served by the program. Subsequently, individual interviews and additional focus groups were used to gather data, yielding some four hundred pages of transcribed material that served as the basis of a report on parenting in disadvantaged communities (Clinton, 1990).

Measures

The availability of sufficiently valid and reliable measures has been a superordinate problem in the evaluation of family support programs. Leaders in the field question whether evaluations will tap what really matters in programs serving families (Schorr & Schorr, 1988), a position shared by program administrators as well (Ellwood, 1988). Concerns about measures of child outcomes are an extension of long-standing problems in the early childhood program field regarding appropriate measures of child functioning (Zigler & Trickett, 1978; Hauser-Cram & Shonkoff, 1988).

Evaluations of family support programs have the additional burden of adequately capturing effects at the level of parent, family, and community. Program staff typically are convinced that their programs have impacts not represented in the assessment batteries of most evaluations (Larner, 1992). To be sure, there is limited or no systematic attention to program effects on such usual program targets as family functioning (Walker & Crocker, 1988) and stress and coping (Krauss, 1988). Instrument development has not been a high priority among research funders, and there are major technical and conceptual obstacles to overcome in any child and family measurement work.

The evaluation literature on family support programs contains few descriptions of efforts to generate new measures. A notable effort in this direction is the work of Carl Dunst and his colleagues (Dunst & Trivette, 1988) to develop measures of family support, resources, and parental expectations of the child. Also, Popp (1992) is developing a portfolio assessment system to describe qualitative changes in parent-child interactions as a function of participation in a family literacy program. The portfolio is designed to document changes in knowledge and beliefs about parent-child relationships, as well as changes in parenting practices. The portfolio assessment is a collaboration between teachers and families and involves at least monthly contributions to a collection of representations of parent-child activities (drawings, stories, photographs, audiotapes). Parent and child are encouraged to prepare a written description of the entry, thereby prompting reflection on the activity. Portfolio guidelines include suggestions for teachers to develop a systematic content analysis of portfolio contents.

In addition to limitations in the general availability of measures appropriate for assessing family support program outcomes, high-risk populations served by many programs pose special problems in the selection and administration of outcome measures. These include barriers in self-administered forms for populations with low levels of reading ability and the content-appropriateness of measure items typically generated for middle-class samples (Miller, 1992).

Cost-Benefit Analysis

The results of cost-benefit analyses of early intervention programs have contributed significantly to policy-level interest in early childhood education programs (Haskins, 1989), even though many economic evaluations have methodological flaws (Barnett, 1986). The cost-benefit analysis of the Perry Preschool Program stands out as particularly strong in demonstrating the financial benefits of investing dollars in early childhood programs for children from lower-income families (Barnett, 1985).

There is growing interest in cost-benefit analyses of family support programs, but there are also some major barriers to overcome in achieving a credible economic evaluation (see White, 1988). It is difficult to place a monetary value on some of the outcome areas often targeted by family support programs (parents' self-esteem, or participation in community political processes). There also can be problems in identifying actual program costs: facilities may be donated; in-kind contributions may be made by the sponsoring agency and other community organizations; parents and high school or college students may provide volunteer hours; administrative overhead expenses may be a hidden cost absorbed by the host agency.

Economic assessments of family support programs are in an early stage of development (see Barnett, 1993), but information from existing cost-benefit analyses provides a useful foundation for designing future work. Available economic analyses include but are not limited to estimates of the costs of welfare and school services for control families not involved in an intensive family support intervention (Seitz, Rosenbaum, & Apfel, 1985); calculations of savings from a home-visiting program following early discharge of low-birthweight newborns (Brooten et al., 1986); and cost estimates of averted government services (for example, food stamps) for the first four years of a child's life due to maternal participation in a nurse-conducted home-visiting program (Olds et al., 1993).

While it is not a cost-benefit analysis, attention to costs in the Child Survival/Fair Start initiative is illuminating (Harkavy & Bond, 1992). Analysts found, for instance, that the cost differential of using paraprofessionals versus professionals may not be as large as often assumed. Time-use analyses indicate that the programs expended considerable time in providing ongoing training and supervision for paraprofessional workers. The cost analysis also pointed to a tremendous range in the actual expense of a one-hour planned home visit across programs (from $34 to $106, in 1987–1988 dollars). This pattern has been found in examinations of other home-visiting programs (see Olds & Kitzman, 1993) and is partly a function of local differences in wage structures and the intensity of training and supervision (Barnett, 1993).

Evaluations in Context

A particularly helpful addition to the recent evaluation literature on family support programs are the in-depth, analytical
descriptions of evaluation processes. A volume edited by Weiss
and Jacobs (1988) includes ten case studies of major program
evaluations, and many recent evaluation reports include sections or insightful discussions of the evaluation process (Johnson & Walker, 1991; Larner, Halpern, & Harkavy, 1992).

Reflective reports of evaluation processes help to demystify
the task of evaluating a program and often challenge the view
of evaluations as distant enterprises by describing interactions
between evaluations and their contexts. For example, local programs evaluated in the Child and Family Resource Program
exerted considerable influence on the evaluation design when
interim results showed no child development outcomes. Criti-
cisms of the evaluation's emphasis on child outcomes and perceived inability to measure effects on families led to an ethnographic study focused on participant experiences in the programs
(Nauta & Hewett, 1988).

Descriptions of evaluation-program interactions in family support programs indicate that the act of evaluating a program has an influence on the program prior to the release of
any findings. The presence of outside evaluators in one family
support program, for instance, led staff to question the quality
of the child-care component, eventually resulting in the shift
from a custodial to an educational focus (Johnson & Walker,
1991).

Summary

The literature on evaluations of family support programs points
to refinements in evaluation questions, with a greater concern
for context (What type of program or strategy works with what
kinds of populations, under what circumstances?) and descriptive data that can be used to fine-tune program design and implementation. Quasi-experimental designs dominate investigations of program outcomes, and the availability of valid and

reliable measures continues to be a serious problem. Cost-benefit analyses of family support programs are at an early stage of development. Case studies of evaluation efforts are a useful addition to the recent literature on evaluating family support programs.

Recent Contributions to the Knowledge Base

This section provides highlights of recent additions to the research literature on family support programs. It is divided into two major areas: evaluations focused on determining program effects, and research on program processes. This overview is not inclusive of all available studies and is therefore not an exhaustive review of the research literature. The intent is to offer a selective summary of recent major studies and literature reviews regarding family support programs, all published since 1989.

Effectiveness of Family Support Programs

Reviews of the research literature on family support programs conducted through 1988 provide a mixed picture of program effectiveness (Powell, 1989; Weiss, 1988). Some evaluations found short-term program effects on children's intellectual functioning, while other evaluations did not. Long-term program effects on standardized tests of children's intellectual abilities generally were not found. Evidence of short-term program effects on at least one aspect of parents' child-rearing attitudes, knowledge, and/or behavior was secured in some evaluations, and a few studies identified improvements in family functioning. Typically, a narrow range of child-related outcome variables was assessed, and an even narrower set of parental outcomes was considered.

Experimental Designs

Avance. An evaluation of Avance, a parent-child education and family support program serving low-income Mexican

American families in San Antonio, is one of the few recent studies to employ random assignment to examine effects (Johnson & Walker, 1991). Random assignment was used at one of the two study sites; at the other site, a matched group design was employed. Two annual cohorts of families participated in the evaluation. Analyses were done separately for the two sites and for each cohort. In the first year of the Avance program, mothers attend classes one morning per week for three hours for nine months, and their newborn to two-year-old children participate in a child-care program. There also are monthly home visits conducted by trained educators. In the second year, mothers may choose to participate in classes to develop their educational and vocational skills.

At the end of the first program year in both sites, there were strong program effects on mothers' provision of an educationally stimulating and emotionally encouraging environment for their children, knowledge of community resources for families, attitudes about child rearing (less strict), and attitudes toward their role as teachers of their young children (more positive). At the end of the second program year, mothers at both sites, more often than control-group mothers, were enrolled in or had completed courses for the General Equivalency Diploma (GED) or English as a Second Language (ESL). With regard to children, there were no significant differences between program and control-group children in performance on intelligence tests and mothers' reports of children's behavior problems.

Avance evaluators note that most of the program goals given highest priority by Avance staff were attained. A notable exception were children's cognitive competence and verbal skills, ranked as high-priority goals by the staff. Johnson and Walker (1991) indicate that the absence of group differences on the child measures is not surprising because the program was "directed at the mother to a greater extent than it was directed at the child" (p. 73). Avance was designed primarily to assist mothers of young children to develop their own skills in child rearing and homemaking and continue their formal education. While acknowledging the program expectation that improved adult competencies would enable mothers to assist their children over the years, the Avance evaluation report recommends additional attention to improving the quality of the child-care program and providing more specific training about cognitive and language stimulation.

Home-Visiting Programs. Random assignment has been employed in a number of evaluations of home-visiting programs. Olds and Kitzman (1993) recently reviewed randomized trials of home-visiting programs for pregnant women and parents of young children. Some of the findings are disappointing. For studies of prenatal programs designed to reduce rates of preterm delivery and low birthweight, there is no evidence to indicate that home-visiting programs reduced overall rates of preterm delivery or low birthweight, although one intervention yielded a significant reduction in the rates of preterm delivery among Caucasian women who smoked cigarettes and an increase in birthweight among the infants of very young Caucasian adolescents (Olds, Henderson, Tatelbaum, & Chamberlain, 1986). More positive results are found for home-visiting programs directed at parents of preterm and low-birthweight babies. Here, there is evidence of positive effects on children's intellectual test performance and on the quality of maternal caregiving.

The Olds and Kitzman review (1993) points to inconsistent results from home-visiting programs targeted at low-income families. Six of fifteen studies found positive effects on children's intellectual functioning, and a similar mixed pattern was found for program effects on parental caregiving. Three programs that included major attention to maternal life-course development produced positive effects on such outcomes as mothers' educational achievement, labor-force participation, and family planning.

Among home-visiting programs for families at risk for child maltreatment, Olds and Kitzman (1993) found no evidence to indicate that the programs produced overall reductions in rates of child abuse and neglect, as determined from state child protective service records. However, Olds and Kitzman note that these records tend to underestimate the frequency with which child maltreatment occurs and are prone to detection biases. Evaluations of programs targeted at families at risk for child maltreatment have found positive effects on aspects of children's behavior, but few studies have employed standardized measures to assess children's behavioral functioning. Few home-visiting programs for parents of developmentally disabled and chronically ill children have been subjected to evaluations employing random assignment, but the results of available randomized trials led Olds and Kitzman (1993) to conclude that home-visiting programs can help parents and children effectively manage disabilities, especially chronic illnesses.

Parents as Interveners. In a review of research on early intervention programs designed with a major focus on parents as interveners with their children, White and his colleagues concluded that there is no convincing evidence for programs' being more effective when parents are involved as interveners (White, Taylor, & Moss, 1992). The early intervention programs were for children who were handicapped, disadvantaged, or at risk; 80 percent of the 172 intervention studies examined in the review involved parents as interveners, either as the sole focus or as the major focus of a parental involvement program that features several other components. This pattern was consistent across the three populations of children (handicapped, disadvantaged, at risk). Parent-as-intervener activities included the parent's teaching the child such developmental skills as motor, language, and self-help. Thus the White, Taylor, & Moss conclusion cannot be generalized to other forms of parent involvement, such as providing emotional support and other resources to parents.

The review also points to the paucity of studies that experimentally manipulate the degree of parental involvement (that is, children in an early intervention program with parental involvement, and children in an early intervention group without parental involvement). White and his colleagues identify only sixteen studies that provided direct comparisons of degree of parental involvement (eight with handicapped children and eight with disadvantaged populations). Many other studies provide indirect comparisons of degree of parental involvement by confounding the parental involvement level with other variables (for example, parental involvement levels also vary by center-versus home-based delivery systems). Moreover, of the sixteen direct-comparison studies, nine were judged to be of low internal validity, given the absence of analyses of intervention and control-group comparability, participant attrition, fidelity of the intervention program, and other threats to internal validity.

Quasi-experimental Designs

Child Survival/Fair Start. Evaluation results from six programs in the Child Survival/Fair Start for Children initiative, funded by the Ford Foundation, represent an important contribution to the recent research literature on family support programs (Halpern & Larner, 1988; Larner, Halpern, & Harkavy, 1992). As noted earlier, five of the six programs employed quasi-experimental designs. The initiative was launched in the early 1980s to improve chances for the survival and healthy development of infants and young children in disadvantaged low-income families. The programs adhered to a preventive focus on pregnancy and infancy, provided multidisciplinary content and services, and worked extensively through paraprofessional outreach workers who were members of the community being served by the program. Among the six projects with evaluation components, populations included barrio families in Texas, young African American mothers in rural Alabama, isolated families in Appalachia, migrant Mexican American farmworkers in south Florida, recent Haitian immigrants, and adolescent parents in several cities.

Were the programs effective? The answer is a "mixed, conditional one," as noted by Larner (1992, p. 242) in her summary of evaluation results across the projects. Most programs effected one or more important outcomes, but none demonstrated overwhelming success.

For the five programs that worked with participants during pregnancy, evaluation results indicate that three had positive effects on prenatal care utilization, but none of the projects had an impact on the physical status of the newborns. One project had an impact on the health habits of the pregnant women. Two of these three projects realized the desired goal of having mothers breastfeed their infants, at least briefly. Data indicate that four of the six projects contributed to increased use of such preventive services as well-child checkups and immunizations.

The findings regarding program effects on parenting and child development offer a different picture. In one project, program participants received higher total scores on the HOME scale than comparison families. (The HOME scale assesses the quality and quantity of stimulation and support for social, emotional, and cognitive development available to a young child in the home.) In a second program, evaluators found some differences on several HOME subscales. In a third project, program mothers talked and played more with their infants than comparison mothers did during a structured, videotaped play session, but there were no program–comparison group differences on the HOME scale. Four projects assessed infants' cognitive performance at twelve, eighteen, or twenty-four months of age. In two of the four, the program infants scored better than the comparison infants. In a fifth project, there was evidence of positive program effects on infants through use of a shortened form of the Denver Developmental Screening Test.

In sum, five of the six programs in the Child Survival/Fair Start initiative had significant effects on at least three major outcomes, some in the prenatal period and others following birth. Nonetheless, the evaluation results emphasize the difficulty of changing patterns of parenting (Larner, 1992). Child rearing is a complex, value-laden set of behaviors and beliefs deeply embedded in cultural and family traditions. Larner speculates that many program families "were not motivated to substantially change their childrearing styles, and the program messages and services were too weak to persuade them to change" (p. 238). In the program serving Haitian mothers, for instance, the recent-immigrant mothers did not believe that their babies could learn during their first year, and they preferred quiet, passive children.

Statewide Initiatives. Two nationally prominent statewide family support programs released evaluation reports in the early 1990s. Neither study involved a comparison group.

Missouri's Parents as Teachers program examined the question "What types of program services are most effective for different types of families for various outcome measures?" (Pfannenstiel, Lambson, & Yarnell, 1991). An earlier study considered program effects through the use of a comparison group (Pfannenstiel & Selzer, 1989). In the more recent study, 400 program families from thirty-seven diverse school districts were selected randomly from a larger pool of participants stratified by demographic characteristics. Data were collected from program staff, parents, and external observers and testers. There also was an observational study of a subsample of 142 families in two major metropolitan areas, focused on the quality of the home environment.

The Missouri Parents as Teachers evaluation found, among other results, that families with developmentally delayed children participated in significantly more home visits; nonminority mothers lacking a high school education demonstrated the largest gains in parent knowledge during their three years of program participation; parent knowledge of child development increased significantly for all types of families after three years of program participation; and, for one-third of the families at risk, observed risks were resolved by the completion of the program. A major component of the Parents as Teachers program is a home visit (on average, seven were completed a year by participant families) (Pfannenstiel, Lambson, & Yarnell, 1991).

Minnesota's Early Childhood and Family Education Program secured interview data from 183 program participants prior to their first program session and again at the end of the school year. Responses indicated that participants believed the program had increased their feelings of support from others, sense of confidence and self-esteem as parents, and knowledge, awareness, and understanding of children, child development, and the parental role. There also were self-reports of changed perceptions and expectations of themselves as parents and for their children, and of changes in parenting behavior. The Minnesota program offers a number of components. Typically, a family attends a two-hour session each week, which includes parent-child interaction time and additional learning opportunities for infants, toddlers, and preschoolers while parents are involved in a discussion group (Cooke, 1992).

Program and Population Characteristics

Family support programs are not constructed by simply putting together a series of service components without careful attention to population and program characteristics. Findings from a study of Project CARE are illustrative in this regard (Wasik, Ramey, Bryant, & Sparling, 1990). Project CARE was an outgrowth of the Carolina Abecedarian Project, an educational day-care program serving children from early infancy through school entrance, which yielded improvements in the intelletual functioning of children from eighteen months on (Ramey, Yates, & Short, 1984). Abecedarian Project designers were impressed by prevailing judgments in the early intervention field about the essential role of family involvement in early intervention, and by the positive results of other home-based early interventions. It was thought that the addition of a family education component to the Abecedarian day-care program would lead to modifications in the home environment, thereby yielding effects much larger than possible with a child-focused program in a center setting.

In a study of Project CARE, families were randomly assigned to one of three experimental conditions: (1) child development center (full-day, educational day care) plus family education (home visits plus parent group meetings); (2) family education only; and (3) a control group. The sample consisted of families whose infants were judged to be at risk for delayed development due to disadvantaged educational or social circumstances of the parent.

The family education component (home visiting) did not affect the home environment as measured by the HOME scale. There also were no effects on parents' attitudes, children's behavior, or parents' behavior. The children in the educational day-care program with a family education component performed significantly better on measures of cognitive performance than did children in the other two groups.

Thus, in Project CARE, more services did not lead to stronger outcomes. Because home visiting has been found to be effective in some other studies, it would be inappropriate to quickly dismiss the potential of home visiting to have positive impacts on child and parent outcomes. The search for better program designs may best be carried out with an interest in the finer details of family charactertistics, frequency of program contact, and quality of the family's program experiences.

For example, the investigators of Project CARE (Wasik, Ramey, Bryant, & Sparling, 1990) speculate that the home-visiting component did not contribute to child and parent outcomes because the actual number of visits was less than weekly (an average of 2.5 per month for families in the first condition and 2.7 per month in the second condition). Effects also may have been achieved if the program began prenatally. Interventions that begin during pregnancy may be more effective than programs that begin at a later stage of parenthood (Larson, 1980). Contact with pregnant women may lay the groundwork for a trusting relationship that enables subsequent discussions of infant care and child rearing (Larner, 1992). In addition, more intensive training and supervision of home visitors, and a stronger focus on health issues, may have strengthened the effects of home visiting (Wasik, Ramey, Bryant, & Sparling, 1990).

While speculative, these ideas of how to strengthen the impact of home visiting for particular types of families are indicative of a necessary direction in research on family support programs. What program and population characteristics are associated with the magnitude of program effects? Olds and Kitzman (1993) have made a concerted effort in this direction in their aforementioned review of randomized trials of home-visiting programs. Mostly, they were unable to discern patterns of program effects in relation to program attributes or types of families, although there are some indications that low-income, unmarried adolescent parents seem particularly responsive to home-visiting programs. There also were indications that, for programs serving low-income families, comprehensive interventions were more effective than programs circumscribed by a narrow content domain.

Parents' Perceptions of Children's Vulnerability. An intriguing albeit tentative guideline emerges from the Olds and Kitzman review (1993): a major factor affecting a program's

success is the parents' belief that their children are vulnerable
or that the family needs help. Recall that studies of home-visiting
programs for parents of preterm and low-birthweight newborns,
and for parents of children with disabilities or chronic illnesses,
pointed to a more consistent pattern of positive effect than did
home-visiting programs for low-income families and families
at risk for child maltreatment. Olds and Kitzman suspect that the
parents' sense of children's vulnerability may be greater in these
populations, thereby heightening interest in and receptivity to
home visitors. As noted earlier, it appears that some parents
in the Child Survival/Fair Start programs also saw little reason
to deviate from the practices of their own parents: "That's how
my mama did me, and I turned out fine" (Larner, 1992, p. 239).

Quality of Relationship with Program Staff. The quality
of the relationship between families and program staff surfaces
as a key contributor to program success in the recent research
literature on family support programs. For example, in the Child
Survival/Fair Start initiative, "it became clear that the heart and
soul of services are caring relationships, not information, instruction, or procedures" (Larner, Halpern, & Harkavy, 1992,
p. 248).

While the level of trust and affect in the staff-parent relationship may be difficult to quantify in policies affecting program practices, a reasonable interpretation of available evidence
points to the frequency of program contact with families as a
critical enabling factor. In one of the few studies to experimentally alter the frequency of home visits, it was found that as the
frequency of visiting increased from none to monthly, and bi-
weekly to weekly, the benefits to children's development increased
in magnitude and in the number of different areas of development affected. The researchers concluded that for the population in their study (urban, low-income families in Jamaica),
weekly home visits were necessary in order to realize a significant influence on children's development (Powell & Grantham-
McGregory, 1989). Also, an analysis of twenty early intervention
programs targeted at family functioning led to the conclusion
that more pervasive and sustained effects are likely to be realized
when the intervention includes eleven or more contacts over at

least a three-month period (Heinicke, Beckwith, & Thompson, 1988). The investigators suggest that a certain duration of contact is needed in order to permit the development of a trusting relationship between family and program staff.

Whether the primary program worker should be a professional or a paraprofessional is a long-standing question with cost-sensitive implications for policies affecting the provision of family support programs. To date, there is no definitive research answer to this question. Across-program comparisons of the effectiveness of paraprofessional versus professional staff typically are confounded by other variables. For example, among randomized trials of home-visiting programs aimed at low-income families, there is a tendency for professionally delivered programs to yield positive outcomes for children and for programs with paraprofessionals as home visitors to be ineffective in improving children's intellectual functioning. However, in the random trials, the programs with paraprofessional home visitors also tend to have a narrower focus than the more comprehensive programs staffed by professionals (Olds & Kitzman, 1993). Thus it is far from clear whether program scope or staff is associated with improved outcomes for children in these across-program comparisons.

Parental Dialogues. Studies of two markedly different programs serving dissimilar populations suggest that an important program element may be the opportunity for parents to talk about themselves and their child-rearing experiences. The Listening Partners Project used dialogue in audiotaped recordings and group discussion to encourage socially isolated, low-income mothers living in rural Vermont to "gain a voice" and become more actively engaged in conceptualizing and interacting with their children in ways that would promote cognitive development and a sense of self-competence (Bond, Belenky, & Weinstock, 1992). The intervention was based on women's five "ways of knowing," as set forth by Belenky and colleagues (Belenky, Clinchy, Goldberger, & Tarule, 1986).

A study of the program, which employed a quasi-experimental design involving a comparison group of mothers who resided in a county different from that of the program participants, suggests that the program increased participants' perceived social support and the complexity of their understandings of knowledge and its development. There also was evidence to suggest that the program participants were more likely not to smoke and to secure (or be in the process of securing) a driver's license.

A longitudinal study of the effects of the MELD program also provides evidence regarding the role of parental discussion in long-term programs (Powell, 1994). The MELD model is a modified peer self-help group with laypersons as facilitators of twice-monthly discussions stemming partly from MELD curriculum materials dealing with child and parent development. The study gathered data from middle-class couples (all first-time parents) involved in fifteen groups and from a matched comparison group over a two-year period. Total sample size was 212 couples. Within the comparison group, couples were assigned randomly to one of two conditions: (1) receipt by mail, twice monthly, of written materials on child and parental development, content identical to the MELD curriculum materials (but with all references to MELD deleted), and (2) no receipt of written materials. Thus the evaluation design considered three conditions: (1) MELD discussion groups and written MELD materials, (2) written MELD materials but no MELD discussion group, and (3) no MELD group or written MELD materials. Results at the end of two years indicated that mothers and fathers involved in the MELD groups with written materials had more democratic child-rearing beliefs and practices than mothers and fathers who received written materials only, or who had access neither to groups nor to materials. The experimental design that compared parents receiving written materials by mail to parents not receiving written materials by mail indicated no differences between the two groups. Thus it was in the sample of parents who participated in twice-monthly peer-group discussions that changes in child-rearing beliefs and practices were found.

Summary

Recent outcome studies of family support programs continue to provide a mixed picture of program effects. Improvements in child outcomes are not easily secured through programs that maintain a strong focus on parents and family functioning. Impacts on parenting can be realized, but not without considerable program effort. There are tentative but promising findings regarding the characteristics of programs and populations that seem to contribute to program effectiveness.

Studies of Program Design and Implementation

By design, community-based family support programs are to maintain adaptive relationships with their local contexts. This critical program attribute has prompted evaluators to examine a host of questions about program processes. The growing research interest in how family support programs are designed and implemented stems from the need to (1) identify specific program strategies that are well suited to particular types of populations; (2) depict stages of program design and implementation as a guide for other initiatives; and (3) describe program variables that contribute to outcomes.

Most of the recent literature on program processes approaches family support programs as dynamic entities that change and grow as a function of interactions with participants and the program's environment. This is in contrast with a mechanistic view of programs as static interventions that provide a uniform treatment on a passive set of subjects. Compared to an earlier generation of research on the implementation of social programs (Williams & Elmore, 1976), there is now less interest in determining the integrity of a predetermined program design at the implementation stage. Instead of asking whether participants are involved in an intervention in the ways intended by program designers, an increasingly common research goal is to describe different patterns of program participation and their correlates (Eisenstadt & Powell, 1987). Program elements that heretofore were viewed as insignificant — for instance, the informal "kitchen talk" that occurs among participants during a center-based program's break time (Powell & Eisenstadt, 1988) — are now under scrutiny as evaluators attempt to understand the kaleidoscopic nature of family support programs.

Examinations of the internal workings of family support programs have come in the form of in-depth ethnographic studies (Travers, Irwin, & Nauta, 1981), telephone interviews and brief site visits (Goodson, Swartz, & Millsap, 1991), and quantitative data secured through observational methods and structured interviews (Powell & Eisenstadt, 1988; Powell, 1993). A major issue regarding process studies of family support programs is the generalizability of the findings. While some recent work has identified general patterns across sets of programs (Goodson, Swartz, & Millsap, 1991; Halpern, 1992), the process literature in general is uneven in content and method, thereby limiting the understanding of whether a specific finding is generalizable to similar programs and populations or unique to a program and its context. Nonetheless, themes emerge from the existing work.

The program implementation literature indicates that new family support programs require enormous amounts of time to reach a stable level of operation (Powell, 1993), generally from one to three years (Halpern, 1992). Comprehensive programs are exceedingly difficult to launch in high-risk communities. Major challenges include recruiting and sustaining the participation of families (Goodson, Swartz, & Millsap, 1991), finding a suitable program role within the host agency (Halpern, 1992; Powell, 1993), and, in some situations, negotiating a relatively safe physical space for program operations in increasingly violent surroundings (Ounce of Prevention Fund, 1992). Studies of participant recruitment procedures point to the importance of person-to-person contact (Goodson, Swartz, & Millsap, 1991), local images of the program (Powell, 1988), and the benefits of embedding the program within the interpersonal networks of individuals in the target population (Powell, 1993).

A related theme in program implementation studies is the complexity of program policy development and implementation at the local level. A recent national survey of family support programs for persons with developmental disabilities found that a host of political, economic, and human factors, especially belief systems, influenced how practitioners rendered services to families. Program elements at one level (for example, the case manager's helping style) typically were mediated or influenced by program elements at another level (for example, agency adherence to family support principles as a guiding belief) (Dunst, Trivette, Starnes, Hamby, & Gordon, 1993).

Attention to staff recruitment, selection, and roles is prominent in the program implementation literature. The power of staff orientations to working with families (for example, didactic methods) is described (Halpern & Larner, 1988; Halpern, 1992; Powell, 1993), as well as issues surrounding the use of paraprofessional staff (Halpern, 1992; Musick & Stott, 1990). There also are descriptions of the individualization of program services at the participant level (Alexander et al., 1988; Travers, Irwin, & Nauta, 1981) and of the struggles of staff carving out a role in triangular relationships involving parent and child (Mindick, 1986).

Tensions in program focus, on child development and parenting content versus famly functioning, are given extensive treatment in the process literature on family support programs (Nauta & Hewett, 1988; Powell, 1993). One of the typical steps in the implementation of a comprehensive program is to narrow the range of program messages to a manageable number (Halpern, 1992).

All in all the research literature on how family support programs take shape and provide services to communities is in an early stage of development. Taken together, the studies of program processes point to critical issues and provide a rich description of program life. Studies of program implementation hold strong potential for identifying key program elements and contributing to explanations of program outcomes and lack of outcomes. Questions about the generalizability of findings from process studies are likely to diminish as additional research enables scholars to identify patterns of results across programs and populations.

Conclusions

The following conclusions can be drawn from the evaluation literature on family support programs published since 1989.

First, *there is growing interest in context.* Outcome evaluation questions have been refined to examine the conditions under which programs are effective. Studies of program implementation increasingly consider the influence of host agencies and other site characteristics on program services. Interactions between evaluations and their program and political contexts have become the subject of descriptive reports of evaluation processes.

Second, *there have been limited advances in evaluation methodologies.* There is prevalent use of quasi-experimental designs that yield equivocal outcome results, and there have been few efforts to improve the definitiveness and amount of evaluation information through adaptation of experimental designs and development of new valid and reliable measures. There is some interest in participatory evaluations, where all stakeholders, including program participants and staff, play major roles in knowledge generation. Cost-benefit assessments of family support programs are in an early stage of development.

Third, *outcome studies provide a mixed picture of program effects.* Evaluations suggest that family support programs can be modestly but not overwhelmingly successful. Improvements in child functioning are the least likely to be demonstrated, and there are inconsistent results across programs regarding impacts on parental and family variables.

Fourth, *there are promising evaluation directions aimed at describing program implementation and identifying the contributions of program and population characteristics to program outcomes.* Recent attempts to describe how programs maintain adaptive relationships with their communities, and to determine the relation of program and population attributes to program effects, suggest the importance of interpersonal relationships within programs, the time-consuming complexities of launching comprehensive programs in high-risk circumstances, and the need for intense, long-term programs for supporting populations living in disadvantaged conditions.

References

Alexander, N., et al. (1988). *Study of the home-based option in Head Start, final report. Vol. II: Case studies.* Report to the Administration for Children, Youth, and Families, U.S. Department of Health and Human Services. Contract No. 105-86-1602. Portsmouth, NH: RMC Research Corp.

Barnett, W. S. (1985). *The Perry Preschool Program and its long-term effects: A benefit-cost analysis.* Ypsilanti, MI: High/Scope Press.

Barnett, W. S. (1986). Methodological issues in economic evaluation of early intervention programs. *Early Childhood Research Quarterly, 1,* 249–268.

Barnett, W. S. (1993). Economic evaluation of home visiting programs. *Future of Children, 3*(3), 93–112.

Belenky, M. F., Clinchy, B. M., Goldberger, N. R., & Tarule, J. M. (1986). *Women's ways of knowing: The development of self, voice, and mind.* New York: Basic Books.

Bond, L. A., Belenky, M. F., & Weinstock, J. S. (1992). Listening partners: Helping rural mothers find a voice. *Family Resource Coalition Report, 11,* 18–19.

Brooten, D., et al. (1986). A randomized clinical trial of early hospital discharge and home follow-up of very low-birthweight infants. *New England Journal of Medicine, 315,* 934–939.

Clinton, B. (1990). *Against the odds: Parenting in disadvantaged communities.* Report to the Bernard van Leer Foundation. Nashville, TN: Center for Health Services, Vanderbilt University.

Cooke, B. (1992). *Changing times, changing families: Minnesota Early Childhood and Family Education parent outcome interview study.* St. Paul: Minnesota Department of Education.

Cornell Empowerment Project. (1991, September). *Networking Bulletin: Empowerment and Family Support.* Special issue on evaluation and empowerment. Ithaca, NY: Cornell University.

Dunst, C. J., & Trivette, C. M. (1988). A family systems model of early intervention with handicapped and developmentally at-risk children. In D. R. Powell (Ed.), *Parent education as early childhood intervention* (pp. 131–179). Norwood, NJ: Ablex.

Dunst, C. J., Trivette, C. M., Starnes, A. L., Hamby, D. W., & Gordon, N. J. (1993). *Building and evaluating family support initiatives: A national study of programs for persons with developmental disabilities.* Baltimore, MD: Paul H. Brookes.

Eisenstadt, J. W., & Powell, D. R. (1987). Processes of participation in a mother-infant program as modified by stress and impulse control. *Journal of Applied Developmental Psychology, 8,* 17–37.

Ellwood, A. (1988). Prove to me that MELD makes a difference. In H. B. Weiss & F. H. Jacobs (Eds.), *Evaluating family programs* (pp. 303–313). Hawthorne, NY: Aldine.

Goodson, B. D., Swartz, J. P., & Millsap, M. A. (1991). *Working with families: Promising programs to help parents support young children's learning.* Final report for the U.S. Department of Education. Contract No. LC 8808901. Cambridge, MA: Abt Associates.

Halpern, R. (1992). Issues of program design and implementation. In M. Larner, R. Halpern, & O. Harkavy (Eds.), *Fair start for children* (pp. 179–197). New Haven, CT: Yale University Press.

Halpern, R., & Larner, M. (1988). The design of family support programs in high-risk communities: Lessons from the Child Survival/Fair Start initiative. In D. R. Powell (Ed.), *Parent education as early childhood intervention* (pp. 181–207). Norwood, NJ: Ablex.

Harkavy, O., & Bond, J. T. (1992). Program operations: Time allocation and cost analysis. In M. Larner, R. Halpern, & O. Harkavy (Eds.), *Fair start for children* (pp. 179–197). New Haven, CT: Yale University Press.

Haskins, R. (1989). Beyond metaphor: The efficacy of early childhood education. *American Psychologist, 44,* 274–282.

Hauser-Cram, P., & Shonkoff, J. P. (1988). Rethinking the assessment of child-focused outcomes. In H. B. Weiss & F. H. Jacobs (Eds.), *Evaluating family programs* (pp. 73–94). Hawthorne, NY: Aldine.

Heinicke, C. M., Beckwith, L., & Thompson, A. (1988). Early intervention in the family system: A framework and review. *Infant Mental Health Journal, 9,* 111–141.

Jacobs, F. H. (1988). The five-tiered approach to evaluation: Context and implementation. In H. B. Weiss & F. H. Jacobs (Eds.), *Evaluating family programs* (pp. 37–68). Hawthorne, NY: Aldine.

Johnson, D. L., & Walker, T. B. (1991). *Final report of an evaluation of the Avance Parent Education and Family Support Program.*

Report submitted to the Carnegie Corporation. San Antonio, TX: Avance.

Klaus, R. A., & Gray, S. W. (1968). The Early Training Project for Disadvantaged Children: A report after five years. *Monographs of the Society for Research in Child Development, 33* (4, Serial No. 120).

Krauss, M. W. (1988). Measures of stress and coping in families. In H. B. Weiss & F. H. Jacobs (Eds.), *Evaluating family programs* (pp. 177–194). Hawthorne, NY: Aldine.

Laosa, L. (1990). Population generalizability, cultural sensitivity, and ethical dilemmas. In C. B. Fisher & W. W. Tyron (Eds.), *Ethics in applied developmental psychology* (pp. 227–251). Norwood, NJ: Ablex.

Larner, M. (1992). Realistic expectations: Review of evaluation findings. In M. Larner, R. Halpern, & O. Harkavy (Eds.), *Fair start for children* (pp. 218–245). New Haven, CT: Yale University Press.

Larner, M., Halpern, R., & Harkavy, O. (1992). *Fair start for children.* New Haven, CT: Yale University Press.

Larson, C. (1980). Efficacy of prenatal and postpartum home visits on child health and development. *Pediatrics, 66,* 191–197.

Miller, S. H. (1992). The Adolescent Parents Project: Sharing the transition. In M. Larner, R. Halpern, & O. Harkavy (Eds.), *Fair start for children* (pp. 136–158). New Haven, CT: Yale University Press.

Mindick, B. (1986). *Social engineering in family matters.* New York: Praeger.

Musick, J. S., & Stott, F. (1990). Paraprofessionals, parenting, and child development: Understanding the problems and seeking solutions. In S. J. Meisels & J. P. Shonkoff (Eds.), *Handbook of early childhood intervention* (pp. 651–667). New York: Cambridge University Press.

Nauta, M. J., & Hewett, K. (1988). Studying complexity: The case of the Child and Family Resource Program. In H. B. Weiss & F. H. Jacobs (Eds.), *Evaluating family programs* (pp. 389–405). Hawthorne, NY: Aldine.

Olds, D. L., et al. (1993). Effect of prenatal and infancy nurse home visitation on government spending. *Medical Care, 3,* 1–20.

Olds, D. L., Henderson, C. R., Tatelbaum, R., & Chamberlain, R. (1986). Improving the delivery of prenatal care and outcomes of pregnancy: A randomized trial of nurse home visitation. *Pediatrics, 77,* 16–28.

Olds, D., & Kitzman, H. (1993). Review of research on home visiting for pregnant women and parents of young children. *Future of Children, 3*(3), 53–92.

Ounce of Prevention Fund. (1992). *Beethoven's fifth: The first five years of the Center for Successful Child Development.* Chicago: Author.

Pfannenstiel, J., Lambson, T., & Yarnell, V. (1991). *Second wave study of the Parents as Teachers Program: Final report.* St. Louis, MO: Research and Training Associates.

Pfannenstiel, J., & Seltzer, D. (1989). New parents as teachers: Evaluation of an early parent education program. *Early Childhood Research Quarterly, 4*(1), 1–18.

Popp, R. J. (1992). *Family portfolios: Documenting change in parent-child relationships.* Louisville, KY: National Center for Family Literacy.

Powell, C., & Grantham-McGregory, S. (1989). Home visiting of varying frequency and child development. *Pediatrics, 84,* 157–164.

Powell, D. R. (1987). Methodological and conceptual issues in research. In S. L. Kagan, D. R. Powell, B. Weissbourd, & E. F. Zigler (Eds.), *America's family support programs: Perspectives and prospects* (pp. 311–328). New Haven, CT: Yale University Press.

Powell, D. R. (1988). Client characteristics and the design of community-based intervention programs. In A. Pence (Ed.), *Ecological research on children and families: From concepts to methods* (pp. 122–142). New York: Teachers College Press.

Powell, D. R. (1989). *Families and early childhood programs.* Washington, DC: National Association for the Education of Young Children.

Powell, D. R. (1993). *Implementing a model parent education and support program for low-income Latino families: A process study.* Final technical report. West Lafayette, IN: Purdue University.

Powell, D. R. (1994). *Effects of information and social support dur-*

ing the early years of parenthood: A longitudinal study of MELD. Final technical report to the Bush Foundation. West Lafayette, IN: Purdue University.

Powell, D. R., & Eisenstadt, J. W. (1988). Informal and formal conversations in parent education groups: An observational study. *Family Relations, 37,* 166–170.

Powell, D. R., Zambrana, R., & Silva-Palacios, V. (1990). Designing culturally responsive parent education: A comparison of low-income Mexican and Mexican-American mothers' preferences. *Family Relations, 39,* 298–304.

Ramey, C. T., Yates, K. O., & Short, E. J. (1984). The plasticity of intellectual development: Insights from preventive intervention. *Child Development, 55,* 1913–1925.

Schorr, L. B., & Schorr, D. (1988). *Within our reach: Breaking the cycle of disadvantage.* New York: Doubleday.

Seitz, V. (1987). Outcome evaluation of family support programs: Research design alternatives to true experiments. In S. L. Kagan, D. R. Powell, B. Weissbourd, & E. F. Zigler (Eds.), *America's family support programs: Perspectives and prospects* (pp. 329–344). New Haven, CT: Yale University Press.

Seitz, V., Rosenbaum, L. K., & Apfel, N. (1985). Effects of family support intervention: A ten-year follow-up. *Child Development, 56,* 376–391.

Smith, S., Blank, S., & Collins, R. (1992). *Pathways to self-sufficiency for two generations.* New York: Foundation for Child Development.

Travers, J., Irwin, N., & Nauta, M. (1981). *The culture of a social program: An ethnographic study of the Child and Family Resource Program.* Report prepared for the Administration for Children, Youth and Families. Cambridge, MA: Abt Associates.

Walker, D. K., & Crocker, R. W. (1988). Measuring family systems outcomes. In H. B. Weiss & F. H. Jacobs (Eds.), *Evaluating family programs* (pp. 153–176). Hawthorne, NY: Aldine.

Wasik, B. H., Ramey, C. T., Bryant, D. M., & Sparling, J. J. (1990). A longitudinal study of two early intervention strategies: Project CARE. *Child Development, 61,* 1682–1696.

Weiss, H. B. (1988). Family support and education programs:

Working through ecological theories of human development. In H. B. Weiss & F. H. Jacobs (Eds.), *Evaluating family programs* (pp. 3–36). Hawthorne, NY: Aldine.

Weiss, H. B., & Jacobs, F. H. (Eds.). (1988). *Evaluating family programs*. Hawthorne, NY: Aldine.

White, K. R. (1988). Cost analyses in family support programs. In H. B. Weiss & F. H. Jacobs (Eds.), *Evaluating family programs* (pp. 429–443). Hawthorne, NY: Aldine.

White, K. R., Taylor, M. J., & Moss, V. D. (1992). Does research support claims about the benefits of involving parents in early intervention programs? *Review of Educational Research, 62,* 91–125.

Whitmore, E. (1991). Evaluation and empowerment: It's the process that counts. *Networking Bulletin: Empowerment and Family Support, 2,* 1–7.

Widmayer, S., Peterson, L., Calderon, A., Carnahan, S., & Wingerd, J. L. (1992). The Haitian Perinatal Intervention Project: Bridge to a new culture. In M. Larner, R. Halpern, & O. Harkavy (Eds.), *Fair start for children* (pp. 115–135). New Haven, CT: Yale University Press.

Williams, W., & Elmore, R. F. (1976). *Social program implementation*. San Diego, CA: Academic Press.

Zigler, E., & Trickett, P. K. (1978). IQ, social competence, and evaluation of early childhood intervention. *American Psychologist, 33,* 789–798.

□ Part Six □

CONCLUSION

□ 20 □

Toward a New Normative System of Family Support

Sharon L. Kagan
Bernice Weissbourd

Recently at a family support meeting, a participant noted that members of the family support movement resembled Ralph Nader, vociferously advocating for the consumer while espousing a cause with impeccable information and unparalleled gusto. Although rarely likening family support to a consumer revolution per se, many engaged in this pioneering movement do have the sense that they are on the cusp of something special, something that may well indeed be at the heart of a new social revolution (Weissbourd, 1992).

As one reads this volume, there is an inescapable sense that family support in 1994 is not about business as usual. Indeed, an underlying premise of the chapters has been that family support is at a new and pivotal evolutionary stage—the match ready to be ignited, the firecracker ready to burst gloriously in the sky. Anticipating such changes, there is a sense of suspense and vulnerability. Are we ready for the new incarnation of family support? How precarious is the leap? What will such changes mean?

In this concluding chapter, we assume that the family support movement is on the verge of a metamorphosis—that it stands poised, although perhaps not fully prepared, for its tran-

473

sition to a normative approach to human service provision. We, like many of the other authors in this volume, recognize that as the conditions of families and society have changed over the years, so has family support. Indeed, family support has never been a constant, staid phenomenon; rather, it has passed through phases. Specifically, we suggest that it has already gone through two phases, rests currently in a third, and is on the brink of moving to a fourth. After describing the phases and delineating their legacies, we will focus on the challenges that the last stage — the new normative system of family support — presents.

The Phases of Family Support

Contemporary family support began as a grass-roots, field-based movement, with hundreds of providers steadily coalescing around twin assumptions: first, that they were not alone in their philosophy and efforts; and, second, that there was the potential to learn from each other. No one predicted the emergence of a movement; it grew from the voices of practitioners who wanted to give and share support with one another.

Phase One: The Program Era

During these early years, family support grew in visibility. Several national conferences were held, growing numbers of articles stressing families' needs for support were published, and periodicals emerged. Perhaps most important, a set of structures was put in place. Principles that gave expression to the work of the field were extruded from experience, refined, and redefined. A coalition was established to act as a resource for information (Family Resource Coalition, 1981). A compendium of programs and a classification schema to represent their different types was developed (Weiss, 1983; Yale University Bush Center & the Family Resource Coalition, 1983). And struggling to sustain themselves, programs realized the importance of assessment and sought to establish mechanisms by which program evaluation could take place.

Ideologically, the era was framed by uncertainty, balanced

by dogged determination. There was a powerful sense that family support, still imprecisely defined, was badly needed. Family conditions, even among the well-to-do, were worsening, as was competition for increasingly scarce resources. Commandeering support for programs — financial and otherwise — preoccupied the workers of the era.

Practically, during this stage, family support was thought of primarily in terms of programs — generally free-standing entities, with staff and services providing family support either as their sole or their primary goal. Programs varied greatly in type, style, setting, and sector auspices, with the programs, although many were launched by the private sector, divided fairly evenly between the private and the public sectors. However diverse the programs, they remained at the core of how family support envisioned itself. In fact, when one thought about expansion of family support, it was tacitly understood that expansion meant the proliferation of programs. "A family support program on every corner" was the goal. In retrospect, and given what was to come, it was a fairly uncomplicated phase.

Phase Two: The Approaches Era

Appealing as it was, family support began to catch on. In addition to free-standing programs, other kinds of programs and services began to adopt a family-supportive approach. The principles of family support were found to be compatible with other movements — decentralized decision making, as in business and education; according power to the consumer, as in the choice and consumer-protection movements; and preventing problems before they began, as in the preventive health and mental health movements. In short, family support principles had salience that transcended the programs originally designed to contain them. The family support approach was spilling over its original boundaries, infiltrating numerous separate organizations — schools, child-care centers, and health-maintenance organizations, to mention a few.

With the spread of the family support approach came new resources and new demands. Once the prized jewel of a limited number of advocates, family support was gaining currency more broadly. As a result, it needed to be explained in concrete ways to a second generation of implementers, and to power brokers and agency heads who might be willing to alter their programs or orientations to accommodate family support. It was an era framed by a recurrent need to get the word out. Summing up the sentiment of the time, Moroney (1983) noted that program advocates simply needed to learn to tell their story better.

Phase two, then, devoted much of its energy to propagating the meaning of family support to broader constituencies and to determining ways that the family support agenda could be linked with other movements and mainstream institutions. No longer programmatically self-contained, family support broadened its emphasis to include a focus on developing family-supportive approaches that were malleable and suitable for large numbers of settings and institutions. To accommodate family support, the individual institutions that made commitments to family support often needed to alter their ways of doing things, leading family support efforts to become agents for institutional change. It should be noted that, during this phase, family support reform efforts were concerned with change as a means of making individual settings — a school, a health center — receptive to and supportive of family support. Change was regarded as instrumental to implementing a family support approach and was usually idiosyncratic to individual settings. Typically, family support efforts of this era were not systemic in orientation. They did not typically attempt to reform entire school systems; rather, they focused on individual schools. Similarly, they did not think about, nor did they attempt to link, entire systems (the health system, the education system). However, their focus on a broadened approach and on institutional change predicted and set the stage for the systems era that was to follow.

Phase Three: The Systems Era

As family support continued to expand into new domains, proponents worried that its understandings were becoming watered down and misunderstood. Did new converts to the family support approach really understand the movement's inherent commitment to honoring family diversity or to sharing power in relationships? Would the institutional bureaucracies in which family support now found itself be genuinely hospitable to what, until recently, had been fairly foreign constructs? Moreover, advocates were concerned that, under the rhetoric of family support, ideologically diverse and occasionally discordant groups waved the family support banner with quite different goals and intents. Less disconcerting but equally problematic was the fact that the welfare reform legislation of 1988 became known to the public under the rubric of family support, lending yet another interpretation to the term.

As both the movement and the term *family support* grew in popularity, diverse programs, approaches, and ideologies proliferated. It became clear that limited capacity and cohesion existed. The concepts of capacity building, infrastructure, and systems infiltrated the nomenclature of family support. To be sure, there was a growing concern about capacity. Where would funding come from? How would family support programs be staffed? What were the qualities, skills, and knowledge bases required of workers? Where was the infrastructure? Who should train staff? How would quality be monitored and safeguarded? What would be an appropriate role for government in family support? How would family support be "bully-pulpited"? In short, the questions boiled down to concerns about systems: How should systemic shortfalls be addressed to maximize the social utility of family support? How should family support interact with larger mainstream institutions individually, as in the health *or* social services system? How should it interact to foster integrated or linked systems? How should family support be taken to scale, and what did we actually mean by *scale* in family support?

As thoughts of altering the existing systems surged forward, others were daring to think more boldly. They were not asking questions about simply recontouring existing systems or infusing them with a quick, one-time, and perhaps faddish inoculation of family support. They were asking the phase-four question of how to create an entirely new normative system of family support: What will it take to abandon the tinkering-at-the-edges approach and mount a broad-scale, top-down/bottom-up, comprehensive approach to the way the nation approaches families? What will it take to make America a family-supportive nation?

Considering and Creating the New Normative System

We suggest that the American family support movement is hovering somewhere between phases three and four; or, perhaps more precisely, we contend that, intellectually, the American family support movement is pondering phase four while, strategically, the field remains legitimately concerned with addressing phase-three issues. Many of the chapters contained in this volume have done just that: they have addressed systemic shortfalls, positing inventive ways of establishing family-supportive systems while suggesting that such systems be framed by a more pervasive ethos conducive to family well-being. To that end, we turn our attention to what we believe are the prescient issues surrounding phase four, the new normative system.

Considering the New Normative Family Support System

Sometimes considering the new and the unknown is made easier by contrasting it with the old and the known. The new normative family support system is not a cacophony of unconnected programs or services, mounted willy-nilly on top of one another, precarious in political stability or funding. It is not a set of scattershot policies that perpetuate categorical, top-down programs. It is not a set of principles begging to be adopted, in whatever form, by recalcitrant institutions. It is not the espousal of unity and diversity — institutional, ethnic, gender, religious — simultaneous to the toleration of de jure or de facto fragmentation and segregation. Finally, it does not allow the richest nation on earth to deny real support to families while rhetorically espousing their cause with vigor.

The new normative family support system is built on an appended set of principles that accord with those enunciated by the family support movement earlier in its history. But the new principles are different from them in scope and intentionality. The new normative family support system, by definition, does not resemble the old patchwork system. It represents a standard that should be followed. It is not haphazard, special, or unique, but constitutes what prevails and what is considered normal. Gerry (1993) discusses the construct within the domain of the social philosophy of normalization — making normal or routine that which has been exceptional. Indeed, the philosophy of normalization seeks to eliminate the atypical. Whereas the original family support principles are *implicit* in their commitment to universality, the new normative system is *explicit* in its commitment to universality, typicality, and regularity. Via the process of normalization, or of creating a new normative system, the spirit and practice of family support will be as normative as traffic lights in cities, grains of wheat on American farms, and the seasons of the year — predictable, durable, ubiquitous, and embedded in the social fabric of the nation.

Inherent in the definition is the word *system,* a word not new to family support but one that has had varied meanings ascribed to it in the family support lexicon over time. In phase two, when the word *system* was used, it generally referred to human services institutions (welfare, education, social services), differentiating the locus of family support in small, voluntary programs from the locus of larger and more institutionalized organizations. *System,* as used in this context, did not conjure images of entities that were integrated, that functioned well, or that achieved stated outcomes. By contrast, *system* as conceptualized in phase three, and as used in the new normative system, suggests an arrangement of things so connected as to function as a unity or a whole. It suggests a logical order and arrangement in the way components of the system are linked, an established manner of functioning that is predictable and orderly.

Beyond strict definitional boundaries, the words *new normative system* imply that there is a durable structure and a supportive ethos for family support, and that such characteristics are compatible with the principles that have framed the movement. First, the new normative system must be extruded from a fierce and penetrating commitment by the society to its families. There must be a public mandate to make family support accessible and available, on a voluntary basis, to all. Second, such a mandate must be augmented by durable, consistent fiscal support from the public. Third, such a mandate must honor the diversity of families and communities in this nation and must not fashion policies that create paper-doll practices, all identical and cut from the same template. Honoring diversity means according flexibility and autonomy to communities. It means abolishing the word *client* and requiring that services focus on including the community in planning, implementation, and evaluation. Fourth, the new normative family support system needs to be outcome-based, so that expectations for achievement are clear, accomplishments are recognized, and dependence is minimized. Targeted outcomes should be collaboratively developed through a comprehensive process that relies on sustained input from neighborhood residents, community organizations, businesses, and the public sector, including local, state, and federal government. The new normative system must also build in collective responsibility for meeting specified outcomes and offer incentives that will encourage reform. Finally, the new normative system must be so enmeshed in the social fabric of this nation that family support will not be regarded as a treatment or as an intervention but, as Garbarino and Kostelny suggest, a condition of life (see Chapter Thirteen).

In short, the normative system for children and families does not resemble anything that currently exists. That is not to say that components of the system are not already in place; indeed they are. Throughout America, programs and communities are working on realigning relationships between the empowered and the unempowered (Himmelman, 1990), and state and community planning efforts are burgeoning (California Tomorrow and the Children and Youth Policy Project, 1991; Missouri Child Care Advisory Committee, 1992; Mitchell & The Early Education/Child Care Work Group, 1992; New Mexico's Children's Agenda, 1993).

However impressive, these efforts do not—and, more important, will not—add up to a normative system unless we conceptualize what it will take to put such a system in place. Indeed, if we continue to concentrate on isolated inventions, we will be forced to follow up with concerted efforts at going to scale, few of which have been successful. Alternatively, we suggest that a normative system be envisioned, with specified incremental strategies toward its accomplishment.

Creating the New Normative Family Support System

There is a vast literature on social change, replete with numerous theories and strategies. Richmond and Kotelchuck (1984), for example, have suggested that in order for significant social change to occur, three conditions are necessary: a strong public will for social change, an informed knowledge base, and a well-planned social strategy. Others have contended that a mobilized constituency is a necessary requisite (Howard, 1993), or that having well-placed sympathetic friends in the halls of power, along with a force of multiple coalesced professional organizations, is helpful (Turnbull & Turnbull, 1993). Each of these approaches has merit; and, no doubt, if each is used in concert with the other, each one can have considerable impact.

For the new normative system of family support, we build on these recommendations, as well as on others suggested in this volume (see Chapters Fifteen, Sixteen, and Thirteen). We suggest that for a new normative system to take hold, three major conditions must be met: family support must become a profession, although in a new sense of that word; family support must amplify its vision of the normative system even more clearly and must define the roles of responsible parties, including government and the private sector, in addressing that vision; and family support must nourish and broaden public knowledge of and support for the new normative system.

Becoming a New Kind of Profession

Great ambiguity now surrounds the issue of the professionalization of family support, with some contending that professionalization — accompanied by likely bureaucratization — will quash the vitality, responsiveness, and inclusiveness of the family support movement as it has evolved. These concerns, not unreasonable, build on decades of skepticism regarding the "disease of professionalization" generally (Sarason, 1987) and the sense that there is an inherent antipathy between professionalization and family support specifically. Therefore, to professionalize family support is to jeopardize its unique potential contributions.

Another school of thought suggests that family support, like an elastic band, has been stretched to its limit. Without the correlates attendant on professionalization — sufficient salaries, benefits, specified entry requirements — the movement's growth will be capped, and it will not mature to its potential. By shying away from professionalization, family support relegates itself permanently to second-class status. Moreover, it precludes its workers from the recognition and autonomy conventionally accorded professionals.

In many ways, both positions are accurate, making the professionalization of family support not only contentious but complex. The real question seems to revolve around how one defines *professionalization* and around how a field goes about gaining "professional" recognition. While much has been written about professionalization (Bowman, 1989; Katz, 1985; Spodek, 1987), three characteristics conventionally hallmark the literature: a profession has a body of scientific knowledge derived from theories and empirical evidence; this knowledge is conveyed through those who have specific training (often accompanied by an apprenticeship) over time; and individuals meet professionally developed and recognized standards, often represented by a credential or certificate.

Where does family support stand on these hallmarks? Family support already has its own unique knowledge base, some of it theoretical and a growing body of it empirical (see Chapter Eighteen), yet the current knowledge base is not robust. For example, there is general understanding of the skills and attributes associated with being a family support "worker," but these have not been systematically and consensually delineated by the field. Moreover, there is a serious question as to whether these skills and attributes should constitute a new field, should be fashioned as part of existing fields, or should be encompassed by both approaches. As for other dimensions of the knowledge base, there is not yet a sufficient data base on family support outcomes (see Chapter Nineteen), although the knowledge on program inputs is growing. In short, the family support knowledge base, much like the field itself, is maturing and becoming coalesced. Tough issues are being addressed, and there is promise, as more scholars and practitioners become engaged in family support work, that the knowledge base will become richer.

The second criterion—that of specialized training related to the knowledge base—poses challenges for family support. Without the codified knowledge base, it is difficult to prescribe the content of training with precision, even though we know it must be different from that which is already in place in most training institutions and must include far greater emphasis on collaboration, community engagement and empowerment, human and family development, and family systems. Whether to render this as preservice training, in-service training, or both is in question. Moreover, if such training is to be handled on both a preservice basis and an in-service basis, the field needs to address the appropriate balance of such training. It must assess the institutional auspices (colleges, private training programs) under which such training should be conducted, as well as the qualifications of trainers. Family support is considering these issues, but they remain unresolved.

The third criterion—professionally developed and recognized standards—is equally problematic. Family support currently has its own brand of practitioners, who practice their craft in ways that require special knowledge, skills, and attributes. Some are professionals, according to the foregoing definitions, and some are not; indeed, we would contend that the very strength of family support resides in blending professionals with other levels of staff who have this unique knowledge base. Yet the field has not defined the degree to which the profession must be flanked by professionals, as conventionally defined, versus the degree to which the field can and should be staffed by other levels of personnel, who may bring special and requisite knowledge of local communities. The questions to be addressed, then, include the following: What are appropriate differential roles for professionals and paraprofessionals? How do we effectively create staffing patterns for family support that blend various levels of staff? How should staff be trained and credentialed for various roles? How can a profession enrich itself by the inclusion of multiple levels and types of personnel?

A related issue concerns not the level of training and credentialing but its domain. Currently, there are individuals in family support who qualify as professionals, although they derive their status from allied professions (social work, education). A critical question to be faced is whether family support should aim to be a distinct profession, meeting the preceding criteria; whether it is sufficient for family support to remain an amalgam of disciplines without a unique knowledge base, entry standards, and certifications; or whether it is advisable and feasible for family support to be both.

If adhering to conventional definitions of the term *professionalization* means that family support currently falls short of the criteria of *being* a profession, that still does not mean that it necessarily falls short of *becoming* a profession. Indeed, efforts to address many of the issues discussed here are under way. We recommend that such efforts continue, along with corollary endeavors to define content, performance, and delivery standards.

As the efforts develop, however, they need to safeguard the uniqueness of family support, preventing it from becoming another "precious" profession overtaken by burdensome requirements and inequitable access provisions. Rooted in the principles that have successfully steered the family support movement to date, such efforts must focus on the processes of inclusion and evolution. Moreover, endeavors to professionalize the field must retain fidelity to fostering diversity in many domains (for example, race and role). To do so means tackling the hard issues raised by Stott and Musick (Chapter Nine), Garcia (Chapter Eleven), and Norton (Chapter Eighteen): discerning between group and individual conceptions of culture, delineating genuine and appropriate roles for professionals and others, and reconciling the differentials between high professional standards and low professional salaries.

In part, then, professionalizing family support embraces

the elements associated with converting any field to a profession — defining the body of knowledge, discerning the content of training, and determining standards for credentialing. But professionalizing family support means something quite different as well. It demands that we go beyond the conventional criteria and think inventively about what it means to be a profession. Should family support become a new kind of profession that infuses its principles into mainstream professions? Should its body of knowledge be integrated with existing training modalities and curricula, or should it create its own body of knowledge and curricula, or should it do both? Thinking about professionalizing family support requires us to feel free to challenge basic assumptions regarding what it means to be both a profession and a professional. It means that family support must bear the burden and responsibility of creating a new kind of profession.

Defining and Strategizing the New Normative Family Support System

Many of the chapters in this volume have demonstrated just how far family support has advanced and how its span has been broadened to include new domains of services (Chapters Five and Eight) and new types of support (Chapters Ten and Thirteen). In addition, strong recommendations have been made to expand even further the purview of family support to states (Chapter Fifteen) and to the federal government (Chapter Sixteen). We applaud these accomplishments and support these recommendations, underscoring their symbolic and strategic importance in the development of family support. As noted, however, we suspect that such advancements, while necessary, will be insufficient to achieve large-scale implementation of family support. Incremental and important, they need to be nested within the larger goal of creating a normative system of family support.

The hallmarks, already discussed, of such a normative system are still rudimentary and reflective of preliminary thinking. To become workable, the hallmarks must be more carefully and consensually articulated, crafted in language that is clear, and understood as a vision that embraces current family support premises, principles, and programs. In short, the field must move from a generalized understanding of what is meant by a normative system to a definition that is laced with precision.

In creating a more refined definition of a normative system, strategic issues must be addressed. The field must discern whether such a system will find optimal expression in a variety of extant settings and institutions, or whether the new normative (and, by definition, comprehensive) system demands a different kind of social infrastructure. What precedents are there for a nation's mounting a truly normative system without creating specialized institutions to meet the intended goals? Can the nation have any kind of a normative system (education, health, or family support) without separate facilities (schools, hospitals) where its functions are carried out? Alternatively, if a new normative system is created with the intention of redefining individual and institutional relationships, will the establishment of a system of new structures for family support sidestep the goal of altering the current modus operandi of human services? What form should the new normative system take?

Reality demands that any consideration of a new normative system address federalist, governance, and fiscal issues. Who will own such a system — local, state, federal, or a combination of governments? Given that we know effective family support happens as a result of strong and durable community input, how will the system provide for such input? How do other normative systems (education, health) ensure consumer ownership? Do they? Or is there an inherent contradiction between a normative system and local control? The role of governments in the normative system must be clarified.

Moreover, any serious discussion of creating a normative system, even over decades, must consider the resource assumptions that undergird the effort. Is the existence of a normative system fully contingent on public support? Can a normative system emerge in the private sector? Can mixed-sector financing work over time? We must also go beyond examining the sector of funding and consider the amount, as well as whether such funding will emerge from generation of new sources or from reallocation of current funds. Will the new normative system be supported by a reallocation of $500 billion, the investment of $50 billion of new money, or both?

Given the nature of these challenges, creating a new normative system may be too much of a stretch for a movement that is, comparatively speaking, in its infancy. Parents with high hopes for their child would take care to plan, nourish, and guide their infant's development so as to meet ambitious goals. Similarly, if a new normative system is the goal of family support, then strategizing to that end now is appropriate, if not necessary.

Broadening Awareness and Community and Public Support

The Herculean task of creating a new normative system of family support will not come to fruition unless the need for such a system is recognized throughout the population. Family support must be viewed as fundamental and requisite, as no less important to human well-being than health, education, libraries, or parks. To gain public backing, it must also be regarded as something that will significantly improve the quality of life in a democracy. It must have supporters among the power elite, and it must have advocates.

Family support, always strong at the community level, has gained currency in the last five years at the state level and, to a lesser degree, at the federal level in the last two years. Such federal and state gains, impressive as they are, must be understood within the context of community. Indeed, it may be said that while states and the federal government can be family-supportive, the community is the heart of family support.

As important as the community has been in engendering family support and carrying the movement forward, community commitment is not ubiquitous. Much work remains to be done to foster community action in creating a more normative system. To date, many efforts to build family support in communities have been launched through family support itself, rather than through the allied fields of community development, housing, community action, and community empowerment. If family support is to become a normative system, the approach to engaging communities must be broadened and must capitalize on existing efforts in multiple domains. Further, greater effort should be fostered to build networks among communities, so that they can share lessons and support one another. Family support needs to be nested firmly within community empowerment and needs to be nourished through the systematic exchange of information and strategies.

The creation of a normative system cannot rely on communities solely or primarily. Public support must also be nurtured and commandeered. More systematic use of the broadcast and print media needs to be considered, to elucidate the definition and the necessity of family support. By publicizing effective family support efforts, the media could help negate the sense of hopelessness that exists. Family support, with its emphasis on prevention, needs to be marketed and sold as a cost-effective antidote to many social problems. Beyond publicizing the accomplishments of specific family or community support efforts, the media need to create an opinion climate in which families are regarded as central to individual well-being. To carry out this task, the media need to commit greater print space and broadcast time to family support coverage, review existing coverage and programming to ascertain how families and family-life issues are being presented, and give priority to hiring professionals versed in the issues of family support.

Finally, if a normative system of family support is to take root, it must be supported by a sustained advocacy capacity, consisting of an organized advocacy plan and a strategy to train and support advocates. To date, despite strong efforts by individuals, no such capacity exists; where advocates have been successful, it has been by dint of sheer personal will. Today's advocates for family support are most likely to include those whose primary interest is the field itself. But there is an entire network, however loosely organized, that is dedicated to advancing America's commitment to families. The challenge is to coalesce individual efforts and make them effective and synergistic. A related challenge is to engage parents more effectively in voicing concern for family well-being.

Family support is an evolving, dynamic movement at the cusp of significant change. Given the state of American families, the emerging data, and the growing recognition of the importance of family support, there is little doubt that family support will expand. Throughout this volume, we have seen stunning examples of various approaches to broadening the movement, both conceptually and practically. The question on the table has shifted, from whether family support will survive to how it can best thrive. In this context, to consider family support as a new normative system seems both prudent and prescient.

References

Bowman, B. (1989). Self-reflection as an element of professionalism. *Teachers College Record, 90*(3), 444–451.

California Tomorrow and the Children and Youth Policy Project. (1991). *Fighting fragmentation: Collaborative efforts to serve California's children and families in California's counties.* San Francisco, CA: Author.

Family Resource Coalition. (1981). *Statement of philosophy, goals, and structure.* Chicago: Author.

Gerry, M. (1993). *A joint enterprise with America's families to ensure student success.* Washington, DC: Council of Chief State School Officers.

Himmelman, A. T. (1990). *Communities working collaboratively for change.* Minneapolis: Hubert H. Humphrey Institute of Public Affairs.

Howard, C. (1993, July). *Transforming access into influence: The alchemy of citizen participation in U.S. politics.* Paper presented at the Quality 2000 Essential Functions Task Force Meeting, Elkridge, MD.

Katz, L. G. (1985, September). *The nature of professions: Where is early childhood?* Paper presented at the Early Childhood Organisation Conference, Bristol, England.

Missouri Child Care Advisory Committee. (1992). *Missouri's child care infrastructure: Building for the future.* Columbia, MO: Office of Social and Economic Data Analysis.

Mitchell, A., & The Early Education/Child Care Work Group.

(1992). *Toward a unified system of child development and family sup-port services in Vermont.* Waterbury and Montpelier: Depart-ment of Social and Rehabilitative Services and Vermont Department of Education.

Moroney, R. (1983). Summary remarks, presented at confer-ence on Family Support Programs: The State of the Art. New Haven, CT: Yale University Bush Center in Child Devel-opment and Social Policy.

New Mexico's Children's Agenda. (1993). *A framework for New Mexico's services for children, youth, and families.* Santa Fe, NM: Office of the Governor.

Richmond, J. B., & Kotelchuck, M. (1984). Commentary on changed lives. In J. Berrueta-Clement, L. Schweinhart, W. Barnett, A. Epstein, & D. Weikart (Eds.), *Changed lives: The effects of the Perry Preschool Program on youths through age 19.* Mono-graphs of the High/Scope Educational Research Foundation, No. 8. Ypsilanti, MI: High/Scope Press.

Sarason, S. (1987). Policy, implementation and the problem of change. In S. L. Kagan & E. Zigler (Eds.), *Early schooling: The national debate* (pp. 116–126). New Haven, CT: Yale University Press.

Spodek, B. (1987). Early childhood teacher training: Linking theory and practice. In S. L. Kagan (Ed.), *The care and educa-tion of America's young children: Obstacles and opportunities* (pp. 118–139). Chicago: University of Chicago Press.

Turnbull, H. R., & Turnbull, A. P. (1993, June). *The Individ-uals with Disabilities Education Act: The synchrony of stakeholders in the law reform process.* Paper presented at the Quality 2000 Essential Functions Task Force meeting, Elkridge, MD.

Weiss, H. B. (1983). *Strengthening families and rebuilding the social infrastructure: A review of family support and education programs.* Washington, DC: Urban Institute.

Weissbourd, B. (May 1992). *Family support: Moving an agenda.* Keynote presentation, Family Resource Coalition Confer-ence, Chicago.

Yale University Bush Center & The Family Resource Coalition. (1983). *Programs to strengthen families.* New Haven, CT: Author.

☐ Name Index ☐

☐ **Subject Index** ☐

A

A. L. Mailman Family Foundation, 37

Abuse and neglect: and community development, 306, 308–309, 310, 311–312, 315–316; extent of, 33; funding preventive programs for, 279; of unwanted children, 78

Academic achievement, and family support, 54–58

Accreditation, for quality, 387–390

Accreditation Council on Services for People with Developmental Disabilities (ACDD), 389

Acculturation, and diversity, 259–260

Addictions, and child health, 79–80, 81–82, 85

Administrators, roles and functions of, 197–198

Advocacy, in evolution of family support, 29, 38–39, 45, 488

African American children: challenge of, 245, 251–252, 261, 268; self-esteem of, 55; and school performance, 56, 58, 63

African American families: and Black churches, 137–160; challenges for, 137; and child care, 118; evaluation of programs for, 453–454; of incarcerated men, 167; tantrums in, 84

African Baptist Church, 139

African Methodist Episcopal Church, 141

Aid to Families with Dependent Children (AFDC), 75, 106, 366

Alabama, evaluation in, 453

Alaskan Native students, challenge of, 268

Alcohol abuse, and child health, 79, 81–82

Alcoholics Anonymous, 29

American Association for Retarded Children, 29

American Association of Retired Persons, 217, 218, 237

American Correctional Association, 166, 182

American Medical Association, 393

American Psychological Association, 387–388, 397

American Public Welfare Association, 106, 111, 341, 356

Americanization, and diversity, 260–263

Ann Arbor, Michigan, policies in, 329

Annie E. Casey Foundation, 100–101, 344, 354–355

Apostolic churches, 145

Arkansas, policies in, 339

Asian families, support by, 56

Asian students, challenge of, 244, 268

Assimilation, and diversity, 261–262

Atlanta: child care study in, 116, 117–118; Project Spirit in, 142

Australia, family context in, 9, 248

Austria, family context in, 20

Avance, 277, 449–451

B

Baptist churches, 141, 145

Bedford Hills Correctional Facility, Nursery at, 173–174

501